D0961461

NIGHTMARE SCENARIO

NIGHTMARE SCENARIO

INSIDE THE TRUMP ADMINISTRATION'S RESPONSE TO THE PANDEMIC THAT CHANGED HISTORY

YASMEEN ABUTALEB AND DAMIAN PALETTA

HARPER

An Imprint of HarperCollinsPublishers

NIGHTMARE SCENARIO. Copyright © 2021 by Yasmeen Abutaleb and Damian Paletta. All rights reserved. Printed in the United States of America. No part of this book may be used or reproduced in any manner whatsoever without written permission except in the case of brief quotations embodied in critical articles and reviews. For information, address HarperCollins Publishers, 195 Broadway, New York, NY 10007.

HarperCollins books may be purchased for educational, business, or sales promotional use. For information, please email the Special Markets Department at SPsales@harpercollins.com.

FIRST EDITION

Library of Congress Cataloging-in-Publication Data has been applied for.

ISBN 978-0-06-306605-2

21 22 23 24 25   LSC   10 9 8 7 6 5 4 3 2 1

To Ibrahim, Mom, Dad, Ehab, and Maryam

To Colleen, Connor, and Megan

CONTENTS

AUTHORS' NOTE

Nightmare Scenario aims to provide the first, complete narrative of what really happened inside the Trump administration between January 2020 and January 2021, when more than 400,000 Americans died of a terrifying illness known as COVID-19.

In collecting our account, we interviewed more than 180 people, reviewed text messages, internal documents, and thousands of pages of emails. We spoke to top White House officials, US lawmakers, government health leaders, outside advisers, and public health and infectious diseases experts (and one professional baseball player). We interviewed members of the White House Coronavirus Task Force. Many of them told us stories they had not shared before. And we found that not a single one defended their collective response. It was a failure. No one held their work up as a model for the future. Many of them offered explanations for their own actions and tried to point blame at a colleague (they often pointed to the *same* colleague, but more on that later). Others humbly admitted mistakes but said they were lost in the fog of war.

In January, February, and March 2021, we sought to arrange an interview with President Trump to hear his account of events. We were invited to meet with him at 5 p.m. on Friday, March 5, for a one-hour interview in the lobby of his Mar-a-Lago estate. We booked our travel and provided Trump's aides with our personal information for Secret Service clearance. Two days before the interview was scheduled to occur, Trump's team canceled the interview and it was not rescheduled. We regret that.

In order to allow certain interview subjects to speak freely, many of them confided in us on the condition they not be quoted. They helped us refine our reporting so that we could strike closer to the truth. Conversations in this book were presented to us by people with first-hand knowledge and confirmed by others.

There were times when sources offered us conflicting accounts of the same event. As journalists, this posed a challenge, but it was understandable. People have different memories and vantage points. Still, some people, we believe, were not fully forthcoming with us. This was either out of embarrassment or, quite frankly, because they worked in a White House environment where deception was a norm.

We did everything we could to reconcile conflicting accounts and ascertain the truth. In cases where anecdotes did not line up, we sorted through all of our reporting and evidence to present readers with what we believe is the most accurate picture. Scenes re-created in this book are based on firsthand knowledge of multiple people who participated. Dialogue was also recreated by those with firsthand knowledge and often corroborated by others.

Many people we spoke with for this book felt a responsibility to help us understand the unvarnished truth. They wanted the current administration and future generations to learn from their mistakes as a way to ensure something like this never happens again.

NIGHTMARE
SCENARIO

PROLOGUE

COVERED IN DEATH

August 27, 2020
CONFIRMED US COVID-19 CASES: **5,800,000**
CONFIRMED US COVID-19 DEATHS: **180,000**

Anthony Stephen Fauci slid the blade of a bronze letter opener under the flap of a white legal-sized envelope and slit it across the top. Inside was a single sheet of paper, folded into thirds. When he pulled it out and opened it, a cloud of white powder wafted into the air. It settled downward, coating his chin, his tie, his suit, and his desk.

Fauci froze in his black leather chair, quickly assessing his predicament. He could be covered in nothing. Or he could be covered in death.

There are three possibilities here, he thought. *This could be anthrax. There's an antibiotic I can take for a month and a half, and I'll probably be fine. This could be a hoax, someone trying to scare me. I'll be fine. But if it's ricin, that's bad. There is no antidote. A* dose of purified ricin equivalent to a few grains of salt is enough to kill someone. *If it's ricin, I'm screwed. I'm a dead duck.*

Fauci cautiously walked to his office door and yelled for his assistant, Kimberly Barasch, to summon his security detail. Moments later, a security official came barreling down the hallway to find Fauci standing in the doorway, covered in powder.

"Don't go any farther!" he barked at Fauci. "Stay in the room!" He didn't want Fauci to contaminate anything or anyone else.

Several other officials clad in hazardous material suits arrived soon after Barasch and one other person nearby had to evacuate, a cautionary step to ensure that no one else got hurt. The team covered Fauci in a chemical spray to decontaminate his clothing and prevent the mysterious substance from drifting farther into the air. Then they led him into another office, where they had set up a portable shower.

It was August 2020. The seventy-nine-year-old doctor, one of the most famous people in the United States at the time, stripped to his underwear and was doused with chemicals in an effort to save his life. He was then instructed to take off his underwear and finish cleaning the remainder of his body by himself.

This was shaping up to be one of the deadliest years in US history. And each day, thousands of letters addressed to Fauci arrived at the National Institute of Allergy and Infectious Diseases, where he was the director. The vast majority of these letters praised him, while a small number called him some version of Satan and wished him dead.

And then there were the letters sent to his house in suburban Washington, D.C., presumably by internet sleuths who had found his address online. He carried those envelopes to the NIH office each day, placing them in a pile on his desk until he had a brief moment to relax and look at them. This letter had been sitting in that stack, with his home address typed in a strange font.

These were extraordinary times, and Fauci was omnipresent in public six months into the novel coronavirus pandemic. Bespectacled and bookish, for months he had been explaining to Americans that yes, this virus was very much something to worry about, even as President Trump and his top aides had insisted it would all go away and everything would be fine. Fauci had never been more loved. Or more hated. He had become America's doctor but also a foil to the mercurial and tempestuous president who was waging a war against science, a war that the United States was losing badly. The virus had killed more than 180,000 Americans as of that day, and close to 6 million others had become sick.

Fauci's public and private pleas for the American people—and the White House—to take the virus more seriously had made him an acutely polarizing figure. It was a far cry from the dark days of the AIDS epidemic in the 1980s, when Fauci had become the target of activists' ire. Back then, protesters outside his office window had shouted, "Fire Fauci! Fire Fauci!," but those same protesters had believed deeply in science.

This was something entirely different. Now he was receiving death threats. His wife and daughters were receiving various forms of harassment, including obscene texts and letters. So there he stood in something that looked like a swimming pool for toddlers, naked and stunned, unsure as to how it would all end.

Fauci had no idea that another envelope with white powder had arrived in the mailbox of Robert Redfield, the director of the Centers for Disease Control and Prevention. And between ten and twenty letters were arriving each week at the home mailbox of Deborah Birx, the White House's Coronavirus Task Force coordinator. Some of them instructed her to hang herself. The existence of these letters, however, was kept confidential.

How had it come to this? What had happened to the country?

After Fauci finished the decontamination process, he was given a hazmat suit to wear. He is five feet, seven inches tall, but the suit had been designed for someone 7 inches taller. As he made his way down the hallway to the elevator and into the basement to go to the NIH showers to further rinse off the decontaminant he had been sprayed down with in his office, the legs of the suit dragged on the floor behind him.

After a twenty-five-minute shower, Fauci put on surgical scrubs and a coat. He called Dr. Christine Grady, his wife, best friend, and confidante. "Please don't get upset," he told her, explaining the situation. "Don't panic."

A scientist and medical expert herself, Grady knew, just as Fauci did, that there were only three options: anthrax, ricin, or a hoax. Her husband could either be completely fine or soon fall fatally ill.

Fauci's security detail drove him back home, where he waited with Grady for the toxicology results.

A few hours later, his phone rang and he was given the all clear. No proteins had been detected in the powder. That meant it wasn't anthrax or ricin or anything else poisonous. It appeared to be a hoax, some sort of cosmetic or makeup powder.

Fauci took a deep breath and exhaled. His office was being decontaminated. So he continued his work from home.

Ever since Trump had heard about the coronavirus in January, he had been determined to will it away, as he had—often successfully—willed away so many other problems in his presidency. There were brief flashes of humility, when he and his top aides would tell people to brace for a hard few weeks and promise that the country would come out stronger afterward. But these moments were few and far between, drowned out by the drumbeat of misinformation and dangerous proclamations that the virus was no big deal and people should go about living their lives.

Instead of emphatically recommending that people wear masks to protect themselves and others—a simple act that studies predicted could have saved tens of thousands of lives—Trump eschewed them, viewing face coverings as a sign of weakness and some kind of political symbol. Instead of heeding the advice of top scientists and public health officials, he and his aides took their willingness to change recommendations as they learned more about the never-before-seen virus as an opportunity to discredit and ignore them. And instead of uniting the country to fight a common enemy—a microscopic assassin threatening to destroy the country's health, economy, and well-being—he used it as a wedge to further divide an already deeply fractured nation.

Trump did not act alone. He was enabled by a cadre of advisers, cabinet members, friends, and family who shared his view about the virus and in some cases harbored an even greater disdain for the government's scientific and public health experts than the president himself did. Even those who knew the right thing to do lost sight of the bigger mission—protecting the country against the virus—and instead became consumed with trying to keep their jobs and win the November presidential election, no matter the cost.

By the time this book was published, more than 550,000 Americans had died from the coronavirus—far more than the number of Americans who died in World War II and nearly 200 times more than died on 9/11. Another 30 million became infected, some with health complications that will stay with them for the rest of their lives. More than 20 million people lost their jobs, forcing many out of their homes and rendering them unable to put food on the table. Many of those jobs will never come back.

The government was supposed to be prepared for something like this. There were playbooks, strategy sessions, and briefing papers. None of them took account of the scale of the devastation the coronavirus would cause. The United States has some of the top minds in the world on pandemic preparedness. Beyond Trump, there were systemic issues that plagued the response from the outset: chronic underinvestment in public health, a depleted Strategic National Stockpile of emergency medical equipment, a decentralized health care system with little flexibility, understaffed and underresourced hospitals and communities, and an economy without the safeguards needed to protect against a massive shutdown.

But there were unforced errors, petty rivalries, and dangerous attitudes toward the virus that devastated the government's response. Perhaps most dangerous was the administration's assault on science and those who defended it.

By pushing back on the president's misstatements and obfuscations about miracle cures and how quickly a vaccine would become available, Fauci had drawn the ire of Trump, his aides, and his legions of followers. Fauci and others on the task force were not always perfect, and they sometimes misspoke. Some of their statements and assumptions about the virus were later disproven, often because the novel coronavirus upended scientists' understanding of how these viruses behaved.

And some health advisers contorted themselves to avoid rebuking Trump in public, either cowed by the president or because they had convinced themselves that the only way to remain influential was to bite their tongues. They wanted to serve as a check against the misinformation that often began in the White House and then took on a life of its own. But for many Americans, refusing to speak up more vociferously and refusing to correct and challenge the president at every turn was an unforgivable act of cowardice and an act of betrayal to the United States.

The puff of powder that floated into the air that August day in front of Fauci's face was the physical manifestation of this year from hell. Trump had had enough of Fauci, and so had his followers. The nation was so divided that people could no longer agree on a basic set of facts. Either you were with Trump and trusted that the coronavirus could be ignored, or you listened to the experts and thought that Trump was an archvillain.

As the nation's leader, Trump played a key role in the disastrous response. But the failures extended far beyond him. There were imperfect government officials, trying their best against a dysfunctional federal bureaucracy to lead the country out of the morass and save lives. There were also officials who cast themselves in Trump's image, adopting his bullying and self-preservation tactics to survive the year. And there were still more who were well intentioned but simply weren't the right leaders for this moment.

We have tried to document it all here: the government leaders who played critical roles and the decisions, meetings, and moments that shaped one of the worst years in US history. We have tried to give readers a full account of how the response unfolded and the myriad decisions and missteps along the way that led us to this point. Eighteen months after the US government received its first official warning about the virus, the country still has not returned to normal. The death and infection tolls have shattered the early forecasts. Hundreds of thousands of family members are dead. Millions of families will never be the same. And the long-term ramifications of this disease are still unknown. Will it haunt its survivors for another year? Another decade? Forever?

Scientists and historians will debate for decades what caused this particular coronavirus, in this particular year, to kill with such reckless abandon. The impact was uneven across the world. Numerous countries in Europe, for example, suffered greatly even though their leaders lacked Trump's autocratic bent and, in many cases, followed the science and urged residents to wear masks and social distance. South Korea, meanwhile, deftly dodged the brunt of the virus's terror.

But there was something much different about the way the tragedy unfolded in the United States. Political leaders not only failed, but they managed to turn the country against itself with disastrous consequences. People weren't just sick or scared. They were angry and hostile. They didn't know who to trust. The virus fed off of this. There were many other reasons the US was ill-equipped to protect its citizens against the coronavirus. This book focuses on the political leadership and decisions that exacerbated an already enormous challenge.

The outcome speaks for itself. The country that was supposed to be the world's leader in public health and science was brought to its knees and ripped apart by a virus, enduring the worst casualties of any developed nation. Instead of being a model, the United States became a nightmare scenario, a cautionary tale, an example of exactly what not to do in the face of a pandemic.

PART 1

CHAPTER 1

THE INVISIBLE ENEMY

January 24, 2020

CONFIRMED US COVID-19 CASES: **2**

CONFIRMED US COVID-19 DEATHS: **0**

Alex Azar quietly backed out of the Oval Office and then sprinted across the West Wing, trying to outrun President Trump's tweet. The fifty-two-year-old health and human services secretary burst into national security advisor Robert O'Brien's White House workroom. "Robert, you've got to stop this," Azar told him. "You can't let him tweet praising President Xi. It's premature. It's not accurate. We can't do this."

Just minutes earlier, Azar had sat across the Resolute Desk from Trump, hoping to finally convince him that the new virus in China was a major problem. "Mr. President, this is really bad," he had said. "This is getting really bad in China, and this is coming to us."

Azar stressed that the Department of Health and Human Services and the White House National Security Council were doing everything they could to prevent the virus from spreading in the United States. He ticked off what the Centers for Disease Control and Prevention and other agencies had already done: they were screening travelers, working to bring home Americans from China. But the virus was presenting an enormous challenge.

Trump paused. "Well, how's China being?" he had asked Azar. "Are they cooperating?"

The answer was more complicated than what Trump wanted to hear. Yes, Azar explained, China was cooperating somewhat. It was doing more than it had done during the SARS outbreak in 2003, when it had concealed virtually all information about the outbreak for months. But that was a low bar. The Chinese still wouldn't let the CDC enter Wuhan to understand the outbreak. They weren't sharing samples of the virus with the United States that would allow scientists to study it and accelerate the development of diagnostics and treatments. Without the CDC on the ground, the US government had little visibility into what was actually happening and what the risks were. They couldn't understand how it was spreading and how aggressive it was. All they had were half-truths from the Chinese government, which was already silencing Chinese doctors and citizens who were trying to speak out.

Trump thought out loud, "I'm going to put out a tweet praising Xi."

"For the love of God, don't do that," Azar responded immediately.

The United States needed to squeeze China for more cooperation. If President Xi Jinping thought Trump was happy with the way things were going, China would clam up, feeling it had fulfilled its obligations with the tiny bits of information it had put out. The proposed tweet would be a huge gift that Xi didn't deserve and that would only further empower the Chinese president.

But Trump wanted to butter Xi up. The two countries had signed a trade deal just nine days earlier, and Trump saw the economic pact as critical to his reelection. He thought China was going to purchase tens of billions of dollars' worth of soybeans and corn, which would help him lock up political support in midwestern states.

Brushing aside Azar's protests, Trump summoned his social media guru, Dan Scavino, to begin drafting the tweet. When Scavino entered the Oval Office, Azar took the opportunity to duck out. And run.

When O'Brien heard what was happening, he dropped what he was doing and rushed into the Oval Office. Azar stopped for a moment. Who else could he get to intervene? Mike Pompeo!

Secretary of State Pompeo was also in the West Wing that day, and Azar rushed to find him to deliver the same message. But by the time he made it back to the Oval Office, it was too late; the tweet had been sent.

"China has been working very hard to contain the Coronavirus," Trump wrote. "The United States greatly appreciates their efforts and transparency. It will all work out well. In particular, on behalf of the American people, I want to thank President Xi."

Twenty-one days earlier, on January 3, Azar had first heard about the virus when CDC director Robert Redfield had recounted a disturbing phone call he had just had with his Chinese counterpart, the director-general of the Chinese Center for Disease Control and Prevention, George Gao.

Redfield and other top CDC leaders had known that something was amiss on December 31, when they had read a report in a medical journal about twenty-seven cases of an unidentified pneumonia outbreak linked to a wet market in Wuhan, China. The CDC had a team on the ground in Beijing, and Redfield was trying to send twenty or thirty more people into the country to investigate what was going on. Shortly after reading the report, he had spoken with Gao, whom he knew well. Both men were virologists, and they held each other in high regard.

During the January 3 call, Gao assured Redfield that the Chinese had the outbreak under control. Chinese health officials didn't believe that there had been any human-to-human transmission. The virus, they believed, would burn itself out. When Redfield asked who was officially being classified as sick from the virus, Gao replied that the government was looking for people with unidentified pneumonia who had visited the wet market. Redfield pressed him:

What about people with unidentified pneumonia who hadn't visited the market? Gao had said he would look into it.

When the two spoke a couple days later, Gao's story changed slightly; he told Redfield that there were clusters of infection within families. Redfield pushed Gao again; he simply didn't believe that there had been no human-to-human transmission. What was the likelihood of an entire family visiting the same food market and all of its members catching the same virus from animals? It didn't make sense. They had to be spreading it to one another. Gao would have to expand the case definition, Redfield urged, and look for people with unspecified pneumonia, people who hadn't visited the wet market.

A few days later, when the two spoke again, a distraught Gao broke down on the phone. "We're in trouble," he told Redfield, his voice cracking. He had initially been confident that there had been no transmission in the hospital and that the disease would not be very contagious. But he now knew that was wrong; the virus was on the move.

Redfield needed to get a CDC team on the ground to assess the situation and provide assistance. He wrote a formal letter on January 6, after one of his earlier conversations with Gao, expecting an invitation. But even as China was dealing with the virus, it was reluctant to allow entry to foreigners. Beijing ignored the CDC request, as well as subsequent requests from both the United States and the World Health Organization. The Chinese government did not have a reputation for transparency or collaboration when it came to infectious disease outbreaks that originated there, and this was no exception.

Instead, as the outbreak grew, US officials received only spotty and selective information out of China. There were reports of the country quickly building giant hospitals and workers on airplanes in full hazmat suits screening passengers, even as the government insisted that human-to-human transmission was not happening.

Back in Washington, a small group began working on how to address the outbreak. Azar had instructed his chief of staff, Brian

Harrison, to inform the National Security Council after the January 3 call between Redfield and Gao. There was little recourse possible for the limited information the administration was getting out of China. The United States couldn't exactly invade the country. So Azar and Matt Pottinger, the deputy national security advisor, began convening daily meetings with their teams to share what little they knew and to discuss steps to prevent the virus from spreading in the United States.

At first Azar felt that the small group was handling the situation well. On January 17, the CDC activated its emergency response center and began screening travelers from Wuhan. It activated the entire agency on January 19. During past crises, such initial steps might have proven sufficient.

Perhaps no one in the Trump administration had more enemies than Alex Azar. He had served in the George W. Bush administration as general counsel, and then deputy secretary, of Health and Human Services, and his past experience dealing with health outbreaks gave him some authority in this moment. But his personality (his few allies would call it confidence and competence; his many critics called it unchecked arrogance) was a major problem. And during those days in January, he was clinging to political life support. The president was still livid that Azar had convinced him to propose banning most flavored e-cigarettes a few months earlier, an idea that Trump's conservative base had revolted against. Ever since that blowup, Azar had done his best to claw back into Trump's good graces, trying to wrap both arms around whatever the White House was working on. But by the time the coronavirus hit, Azar, who seemed to be perpetually on the brink of being fired, had a major credibility deficit within the administration.

In addition to the e-cigarette fiasco, Azar's bitter rivalries consumed an inordinate amount of time and energy. His ongoing feud with Centers for Medicare & Medicaid Services administrator

Seema Verma, one of his subordinates, was proving a particular headache for the White House. Someone had leaked damaging reports to the media about Verma's alleged use of taxpayer money to pay outside contractors with the purpose of boosting CMS and its work. White House officials were convinced that the leaks had come from Azar's team, and Verma's own staffers had concluded that only HHS possessed some of the emails leaked to reporters. Having that petty stuff come out in the media was embarrassing. Azar had been especially angry at Verma for opposing one of his signature drug pricing policies in 2019. The White House had hoped to present a unified health care plan to voters but instead had a health policy team whose members were constantly at one another's throats.

In November 2019, Verma told Trump that she and her staff felt bullied by Azar and that his behavior was interfering with the president's health agenda. Things got to the point that President Trump, Vice President Mike Pence, and acting Chief of Staff Mick Mulvaney all had to intervene. In an attempt to broker some sort of truce, Pence told the two, "we all just have to make it for eleven months together."

Being HHS secretary was Azar's dream job, and he fought like hell to keep it. Some associates observed that he was enamored with the perks that came with being a cabinet official: the White House events, the security detail and limousine service, the regular access to the president. He knew that his survival in the job depended on his relationship with Trump, and he was willing to go to extensive lengths to butter the president up and keep him happy, even when his demands were unreasonable—which they often were. Still, Azar frequently served as a punching bag for Trump, being yelled at over bad health care polling numbers and Trump's perception that the health agencies weren't moving fast enough to implement various policies. Azar took it and his subordinates in turn often felt bullied by him in his desperate attempts to deliver for the president.

With Trump not taking him seriously, Azar felt compelled to play the game and used his Twitter account to promote Trump-related propaganda. On January 13, Azar's account posted a flattering article about the president's daughter Ivanka. Three days later, he posted a picture of himself on Twitter smiling alongside a Fox News host touting "Religious Freedom Day." Azar still hadn't spoken publicly about the virus. He might have been panicking about the virus in internal meetings, but he was shilling for Trump on Twitter. And people were noticing.

On January 18, Scott Gottlieb, a former FDA commissioner under Trump, texted Joe Grogan, the director of the White House Domestic Policy Council. Grogan was another of Azar's bitter rivals. Grogan's portfolio covered all domestic policy, but his background was in health policy and he had known Redfield for years. Grogan and Azar had been having ugly knock-down, drag-out fights for months over drug-pricing policy and Grogan knew how to trigger Azar's temper and make him look foolish inside the White House. Some officials thought he was secretly gunning for Azar's job.

Gottlieb had left the administration almost ten months earlier, but he was one of the few former officials who had left on their own terms and maintained the respect of the president and most of the top advisers.

Alarmed at the spread of the novel coronavirus, Gottlieb texted Grogan that dreary, freezing, snowy January day. The CDC, FDA, National Institutes of Health, and Centers for Medicare & Medicaid Services all fell under HHS's control. Grogan might want to make sure that Azar was coordinating a response across the entire agency, Gottlieb said.

"Between us, while Azar is spending time buffing his image on Twitter, you might check in and make sure he's coordinating his response to Wuhan," Gottlieb texted.

"You mean the Chinese virus deal?" Grogan wrote back.

"Yes. Redfield I'm sure is focused but you want to make sure Azar is coordinating across HHS. . . . Redfield is smart and good but not an aggressive leader. I'm not saying it will spiral worse but it could," Gottlieb texted. "I can't talk to HHS so I talk to you. Airport screening is of questionable value. More in the vein of seeming like something that stops importation spread."

"Constantly astounded by how little Azar knows about what's going on in HHS," Grogan responded. "That's a good flag, thanks."

"Reason to believe it's a limited outbreak related to a zoonotic source," Gottlieb texted. "Not trying to be alarmist, but if we're wrong, the downside is bad." He added that Grogan should ask HHS for a briefing, which Grogan did later that day.

At that point, Azar was working primarily with the White House National Security Council on the White House's response, but now Grogan was poking around. That meant trouble for the HHS secretary. The following week, there were three different sets of meetings one day on the coronavirus. Everyone just kept bouncing from meeting to meeting without doing much of anything concrete. And with Grogan now in the picture, there was a good chance that Azar would be elbowed out. He needed to assert his authority and demonstrate he had matters under control. That meant briefing the president, who happened to be in an extremely foul mood.

The House of Representatives had impeached Trump the previous month for trying to coerce Ukraine into digging up dirt on Joe Biden's family. The Republican-controlled Senate was preparing to conduct its trial, which everyone anticipated would result in an acquittal. But becoming just the third president in US history to be impeached was still a slap in the face. Aides knew that the best way to cheer up Trump was to get him out of Washington and send him to one of his private clubs, where he would be surrounded by his most fawning admirers. And that was where he was, at his Palm Beach resort, Mar-a-Lago, when Azar tracked him down that mid-January afternoon by calling through the White House switchboard.

The HHS secretary could barely get a word in before Trump started shouting. He was still angry at Azar about the e-cigarette debacle and said it would cost him his reelection. Then Trump asked where the health care plan was to replace Obamacare when the Supreme Court struck it down. Azar, a lawyer by training, had long said that Trump's legal strategy didn't stand a chance. He told Trump, as he had on several occasions, that he would lose the Supreme Court case 9-0, so there wouldn't be an opportunity for a replacement plan.

Trump then tried to end the conversation, but Azar cut in. "Mr. President, I've got to tell you something," he said. "There's this new virus out of China that could be extremely dangerous. It could be the kind of thing we have been preparing for and worried about." He told Trump that the CDC had begun screening travelers coming into the United States from China, but it might need to do more.

"Yeah, okay," Trump said. And he abruptly ended the call.

Azar left the call feeling defeated. He just didn't know how to break through to the president and massage his ego the way other more skilled aides and confidants did.

A few days later, Trump flew to Davos, Switzerland, for the World Economic Forum, an annual gathering of foreign leaders and financial elites, where he liked to brag about the US economy's dominance. He went with O'Brien, his national security advisor, acting chief of staff Mulvaney, and a cadre of other aides. The US stock market was near an all-time high, and Trump had just signed the Chinese trade deal. He was up for reelection in ten months and wanted to schmooze, to show that he wasn't sweating the impeachment nonsense. During the conference, Grogan frantically called Mulvaney from Washington. We have a US case of the coronavirus, Grogan said. It's here.

Toward the end of the summit, Trump sat down for an interview with CNBC. He was asked about the new coronavirus and whether he was concerned about it. "We have it totally under control. It's one person coming in from China, and we have it under control," he told the interviewer. ". . . It's going to be just fine."

Back in the United States, Azar was crestfallen when he heard the comments. He tried to phone O'Brien but was unsuccessful. By the time O'Brien called back, the HHS secretary was in a shop in the Van Ness neighborhood of Washington, D.C., buying piano sheet music. Azar stepped outside on the street to take the call.

"Robert, this is really bad," he said. "This is going to explode. The president isn't paying attention to this. He can't say it's under control." He also warned O'Brien that Grogan was trying to take the issue over inside the West Wing. O'Brien needed to get his team in line and reassert the NSC's authority over the response. This was turning into a clusterfuck.

Shortly after leaving the George W. Bush administration, Azar had joined the US division of Eli Lilly, eventually becoming its president. During his time there, the pharmaceutical giant had doubled the price of its best-selling insulin medication. He had made a career—and a lot of money—through the industry-to-government-to-industry-to-government revolving door. When he spoke at industry conferences or gave speeches at HHS, he tried to present himself as a caring, technocratic bureaucrat. But at his core, he was a political animal who had learned early on that politics is a blood sport. A lawyer by training, he had worked for Kenneth Starr on the Whitewater investigation into the Clintons in the 1990s, apprenticing under one of the United States' fiercest political assassins. He remained close to Laura Ingraham, the Fox News star he had first met when they had both been students at Dartmouth College in the 1980s.

Azar could be vindictive and immensely controlling of subordinates, according to more than a dozen people who worked with him, and he hated feeling upstaged or disobeyed. He wasn't really a "Trumper," but he craved power, and few jobs appealed to him more than the job of HHS secretary, a role with immense influence over the sprawling $3.6 trillion US health care system.

Trump's first HHS secretary, Tom Price, had resigned in disgrace in 2017 after it had been revealed that he had used taxpayer money to pay for private jets. Vice President Pence knew Azar from their time together in Indiana, when Pence had been governor and Azar had been a top health care industry executive based in Indianapolis. Pence had spent most of his political career fighting to outlaw abortion, and Azar would soon publicly adopt more of the religious Right's rhetoric about the sanctity of life. Pence saw Azar as an ally and had recommended him to Trump for the HHS job, as had Laura Ingraham, whose opinion and instincts Trump trusted.

The administration needed Congress to enact major health care changes, delivering on Trump's campaign promise to repeal and replace the Affordable Care Act with a vaguely defined "great" new plan. That wasn't happening. So under Azar's watch and at Trump's insistence, HHS unilaterally pushed its regulatory authority to the brink. The department also exerted all the authority it could to restrict access to abortion and roll back the Obama administration's protections for gay and transgender patients.

But Azar quickly learned that his decades of experience weren't necessarily welcome in the White House, where Trump had promised to crush pharmaceutical companies that the president had accused of "getting away with murder," the same kind of rhetoric that many Democrats had long used in seeking to lower drug prices. Azar had spent his career fighting such proposals and even after assuming the HHS secretaryship had dismissed one of Trump's favored ideas as a "gimmick." But by his second year as the nation's top health official, he was under immense pressure to fall in line. He pivoted hard and tried to lower drug prices through some of Trump's proposed policies, only to see federal courts intervene to stop him. And he had spent a year and a half on what Trump in 2018 had touted as the administration's signature drug-pricing policy, only for his rivals in the White House to convince Trump to ax the entire thing at the last minute. (Azar would find redemption in November 2020, months after those same rivals had left the administration, by resurrecting the rule.)

Other proposals had never made it out the door because Azar had viciously fought with White House aides for months about how best to advance them, leaving them unresolved. To make clear where his new loyalties resided, he lavished praise on Trump at every turn, a type of public sycophancy that was mandated for survival in Trump's cabinet. He credited Trump's "bold vision" for health care and the "significant action" that the president was taking to help Americans better afford health care, even though Trump showed little interest in the details that were necessary to push any of the ideas into force.

Azar's opportunism drew attention in a White House full of backstabbers. He made enemies who conspired to take him down. Whenever he realized he was being outmaneuvered, he fumed with jealousy. He wasn't one to back down, though; he knew how to destroy people, even if it could mean destroying himself.

CHAPTER 2

LIKE WATER THROUGH A NET

January 27, 2020
CONFIRMED US COVID-19 CASES: 5
CONFIRMED US COVID-19 DEATHS: 0

As two dozen government officials filed into the Situation Room, it immediately became clear that something was wrong. There were no handouts, no agendas. Many were unsure what exactly they were doing there. What were they supposed to discuss? Here, behind soundproof walls that spies can't penetrate, is where the most sensitive conversations happen. Military attacks are discussed around the rectangular table. Meetings in the Situation Room were often scripted the day before. But this one had been hastily arranged just a few hours earlier.

Where should I sit? one attendee asked a National Security Council official. Wherever you want, the official said.

As people took their seats, they sensed an awkward tension at one end of the room. Matt Pottinger, the deputy national security advisor, sat at the head of the table in front of the large presidential seal. To his left was Alex Azar.

Then acting White House chief of staff Mick Mulvaney entered the "Sit Room," and Pottinger immediately moved one chair over, ceding him the main seat.

People kept filing in. Soon there was nowhere left to sit, so attendees began standing against the wall, as though they were wait-ing for their order at the deli. Counselor to the President Kellyanne Conway arrived. Then came Deputy Chief of Staff for Communications Dan Scavino. They were just a few feet from Robert Redfield, the CDC director.

On a large television screen on the far wall, several other senior health officials were beamed in through a secure video conference.

"I want to have an open discussion," Mulvaney finally began. "I don't have an agenda. I want to have an open discussion about these issues. Over to you, Alex."

"These issues" were the strange, pneumonia-like virus that was spreading rapidly through China.

Azar said that it was a very serious matter but the health agencies were taking action. They knew what to do. He exuded confidence; too much confidence. But Azar felt his career had prepared him for something like this. He had been a top official at HHS when the Bush administration had dealt with anthrax and monkeypox. He had been part of efforts to create the federal government's emer-gency preparedness infrastructure more than fifteen years before. He was the most qualified HHS secretary in history, as he liked to tell people. And the CDC, under HHS's leadership, was the gold standard for dealing with infectious diseases.

Around the conference table, sitting against the wall and standing throughout the room, the other government officials listened in rapt attention as Azar peppered through his fifteen-minute monologue. But the self-assured, confident mood he projected didn't last long. When Azar was done, it was Pottinger's turn.

Few people in the room knew it, but Pottinger had actually called the meeting. The Chinese weren't providing the US govern-ment much information about the virus, and Pottinger didn't trust what they were disclosing anyway. He had spent two weeks scour-ing Chinese social media feeds and had uncovered dramatic reports of the new infectious disease suggesting that it was much worse than the Chinese government had revealed. He had also seen reports that the virus might have escaped from a lab in Wuhan, China. There were too many unanswered questions. He told everyone in the Sit Room that they needed to consider enacting a travel ban immediately: ban all travel from China; shut it down.

Pottinger had an extraordinary—and unusual—background dealing with the Chinese government and infectious diseases. As a reporter for the *Wall Street Journal* in the early 2000s based in China and Hong Kong, he had covered the SARS outbreak and the Communist government's efforts to conceal the scope of the health crisis. SARS had infected roughly 8,000 people and killed 774 worldwide, and the Chinese government had tried to keep all information about the virus under wraps. In 2003, Pottinger had written an article about a Chinese surgeon whistleblower who had challenged Beijing's lies about the pandemic, cementing his reputation as a pugnacious, fearless reporter willing to challenge a Communist regime. He had left journalism in 2005 to join the marines, recounting in his farewell column the time he had been arrested in China, punched in the face in a Beijing Starbucks by a government agent, and forced to flush his notes down a toilet to protect his sources from Chinese officials. He had witnessed Chinese deception up close.

Pottinger, who was now forty-six, felt that the same type of cover-up could be occurring again. He had spent several days calling some of his old contacts in China, doctors who would tell him the truth. And they had told him that things were bad—and only going to get worse.

Pottinger's discourse was measured but he conveyed the gravity of the threat. He said that the virus was spreading fast. He said that dramatic actions would need to be taken, which was why the government should consider banning travel from China to the United States until it had a better understanding of what was going on. As he continued, people sat up in their chairs. This was not the "we've got everything handled" message that Azar had conveyed just minutes earlier. How could the government ban travel from China? A top State Department official chimed in to say that the State Department was currently at a Travel Advisory Level 2 but could go to Level 3, which advises Americans to reconsider travel. The next step, the most extreme, would be to launch Level 4. People nodded nervously.

Someone whispered, "What the hell is Level Three? What the hell is Level Four?"

"Nobody wanted to ask the question because they didn't want to look dumb," one attendee recalled.

Level 4, the State Department official said, is "De facto, as close to a travel ban as you can do."

The abrupt change in tone from Azar to Pottinger signaled to those in the room that the White House wasn't coordinating its strategy. People seemed to be acting independently of one another. Who was in charge?

Mulvaney finally piped up: If the State Department is currently at Level 2, and the CDC recently went to Level 3, and now the State Department is preparing for Level 4, what on earth is happening? Why is nobody coordinating?

"Everybody was deer in headlights," the attendee said. "I'm looking at this thinking, 'Holy shit. This is our government. . . . This is how it is working.'"

As Azar watched the room become more tense and confused, he became rattled. He had helped quietly lead the government's response to the virus for weeks, but now it was becoming a convoluted mess. And it was all unraveling in the Situation Room, with everyone jostling for power.

Other health officials tried to weigh in, but Azar kept interrupting them. The stoic sense of control he had tried to exude at the beginning of the meeting was gone. Now he was jumping in, erratically. While most of the people in the Situation Room were distracted by the back-and-forth, an aide walked into the room and whispered into Mulvaney's ear. A few minutes later, Vice President Mike Pence entered, and Mulvaney gave him his chair at the head of the table.

"The president is concerned," Pence said matter-of-factly, adding that he had talked to Donald Trump about the coronavirus several times that day. He didn't deliver any specific marching orders, though his being in the room did convey the urgency of the situation. But when Pence left and Mulvaney took over again, things went downhill fast.

At one point, a short, diminutive woman quietly entered and joined the group standing along the side wall. Secretary of Transportation Elaine Chao, a veteran of both the George H. W. Bush administration and the George W. Bush administration, watched the back-and-forth silently. She had been in the White House for another meeting and had come down to the Situation Room when she'd heard what was going on.

She was used to order and structure and didn't suffer fools or free-for-alls. When it became clear that the State Department was preparing to restrict travel to and from China, she recognized that it could be a fiasco in the making. "I want to go back to my staff because there's a lot of cargo that goes back and forth to China," she said. "I'm concerned if the commercial traffic isn't flying, there's a lot of cargo under those planes, and I wouldn't want to disrupt that."

Attempting to reassert order, Mulvaney tried to reel everyone in. He told the State Department officials present not to do anything before he had a chance to brief Trump. They would all meet again tomorrow to discuss next steps.

But not everyone was ready to leave. Ken Cuccinelli, the acting deputy secretary of homeland security—he had been blocked from filling the job permanently by Chao's husband, Senate majority leader Mitch McConnell—was stewing. Some people believed "The Cooch," as he was known inside the West Wing, was particularly good at causing trouble and rooting out weakness. He made clear that Azar's leadership wasn't working. "I disagree with how the secretary of HHS portrayed the situation," he said.

He then went off for several minutes about everything that HHS was doing wrong. The messaging was all twisted. Americans were confused over what was happening and federal agencies weren't explaining things clearly. Operationally, Cuccinelli told a colleague,

HHS looked completely unprepared and inexperienced for this moment—aside from Robert Kadlec, the agency's assistant secretary for preparedness and response. There are thousands of people entering the United States from China each day, he noted. Why doesn't DHS know what HHS knows? "All of our messages are different," he protested. "I don't understand. We aren't speaking with one voice publicly on this."

Cuccinelli and Azar sat just two chairs apart at the conference room's large rectangular table, but they didn't make eye contact. Azar stared straight ahead. That winter he had grown a beard that was mostly brown but for two snowy patches on his chin. As Cuccinelli spoke, a red hue built in Azar's cheeks. Azar had developed a reputation in the White House for his short temper, and his intensely flushed face always betrayed his emotion. Many aides referred to the phenomenon as "Purple Rage."

"This is the first I'm hearing of this," Azar said before going on to dispute nearly everything Cuccinelli had said.

Mulvaney intervened to wrap things up. He could tell that Pottinger and a few others were calling for a dramatic change, one that was an anathema to his libertarian instincts. He was pretty skeptical of Pottinger's "sources" in China, too. They weren't going to be setting US policy based on what someone had heard from their "friend" thousands of miles away. Mulvaney reiterated that they would reconvene the next day to discuss matters again before anything was settled. He warned attendees not to leak any details of the meeting to the media.

Azar couldn't exit the Situation Room fast enough. For three weeks, he had tried to sound the alarms inside the White House about the mysterious virus, but he had repeatedly been ignored. Now everyone wanted to be involved. Now seemingly every person in the Trump administration had an opinion about the virus they knew nothing about.

The Cooch was given a wide berth and made a beeline to White House press secretary Stephanie Grisham's office to complain about the lack of coordination among the various agencies and the White House.

As the other government officials filed out of the room, there was a feeling that things had changed. The virus, the coronavirus, whatever it was, was exposing the deep rifts in Trump's White House. Who was in control? No one, really. But the virus was already here. Could they be sure that there were only these five people infected in the United States? There had already been more than 1,300 flights from China to the United States that month, carrying 381,000 passengers. How many of those people might be sick?

There were no newspapers in the Situation Room that day. But upstairs, in the press section of the West Wing, there was a neatly folded copy of *USA Today*. A headline splashed across the front page that reflected much of the consensus of many government officials at the time: "Coronavirus Not a Global Crisis, WHO Says." But in the back of the newspaper was an opinion column written by former vice president Joe Biden, who was vying for the Democratic presidential nomination. It struck a much different tone. "Trump's demonstrated failures of judgment and his repeated rejection of science make him the worst possible person to lead our country through a global health challenge," he wrote. "The outbreak of a new coronavirus, which has already infected more than 2,700 people and killed over 80 in China, will get worse before it gets better. Cases have been confirmed in a dozen countries, with at least five in the United States. There will likely be more."

That was the beginning of year four of the Trump administration. Many of the senior staff and cabinet members who had joined him in January 2017 had already left. More than twenty had been pushed out or fired. Others had resigned in disgust. At least one appeared to be headed to jail.

Who was left? A mix of family members, twentysomethings, hangers-on, fourth-stringers, former lobbyists, sycophants, and a scattering of competent, well-meaning aides such as Pottinger, who mostly kept their heads down.

In 2017, Trump had boasted about assembling a team that represented "by far the highest IQ of any cabinet ever assembled." That was false, but no matter. What he really prized in his aides was loyalty—not to their country but to him. His first batch of advisers had run the gamut. Some had proved to be too loyal to the United States, smarty-pants advisers who had sighed behind his back and rejected his impulsive actions and decisions. So Trump had forced them out. Others had tripped over themselves to praise him, so he had let them stick around. By the beginning of 2020, the White House was packed with the latter type: people who were constantly worried about their job security; people Trump could fire at a moment's notice; people who had to grovel to keep their jobs.

Much has been written about Trump's temperament, paranoia, nonexistent attention span, disaffection, susceptibility to conspiracy theories, and disregard for facts. It was all true. He didn't read briefing materials. While in office, President George W. Bush—whose intellect was often mocked by the pundits and comedians—had read John M. Barry's *The Great Influenza: The Story of the Deadliest Pandemic in History* about the 1918 Spanish flu. He held twelve briefings, demanding to know what his team was going to do to avoid another pandemic outbreak. (Trump would later refer to the Spanish flu repeatedly as "the 1917 flu.") Trump wouldn't even read his briefing materials. He read the *New York Post*. He scrolled through the dark side of Twitter. He couldn't be swayed by a packet of intelligence from his national security advisors. But he could be swayed by a single piece of paper with a picture on it or a chart.

Still, that wasn't how you got Trump's attention. He was obsessed with abstract numbers or photographs that he viewed as reflections of him personally. If the stock market went up, that was because of him. When he filled an arena for a rally, that was a reflection of him. When a company announced that it was going to hire more workers, it was a reflection of him. Everything was about him: the media cycle; the economy; poll numbers. Making everything about himself was a major part of his popularity. He constantly controlled the conversation and the narrative, playing by his own rules and making up his own facts. The US government was a big, lumbering battleship that was no match for his spastic energy. His political foes constantly underestimated him—and lost.

There was, of course, a downside to all that. And the consequences of his personality became devastatingly apparent when he disregarded or downplayed more than a dozen warnings from US intelligence agencies about the coronavirus in those early days.

Trump had weathered so many scandals that had threatened to bring down his presidency. He had survived a two-year investigation into his campaign's ties with Russia, a series of incendiary racist comments, congressional investigations, and advisers who had been convicted of crimes and gone to jail. None of it had stuck. He was as popular as ever among his base. He could seemingly will everything and everyone into submission.

What does all this have to do with the coronavirus? Ultimately, everything. He pitted his aides against one another like roosters at a cockfight, gladiator matches for his amusement. He didn't want to deal with the coronavirus and believed he could make it go away by willing it to do so, as he had done with so much else in his presidency.

That created tremendous pressure on the government officials who remained in their positions in 2020. Many of them were totally unprepared for what was coming. Many of them were so focused on their own survival that it never occurred to them to focus on anyone else's.

On January 28, Pottinger found himself in the Oval Office with the president. He had already tried to shock Trump's cabinet and top advisers; now he had an opening with the president himself. Trump would be hearing a more dire warning, this time directly from his national security team.

"This will be the largest national security crisis of your presidency," Robert O'Brien warned the president. Pottinger, seated nearby, went a step further. He said it could be the deadliest pandemic since the 1918 flu pandemic.

Trump appeared to absorb the information.

A few hours later, Pottinger and other government officials filed back into the Situation Room. Pottinger knew he was going to be outnumbered. Mulvaney and his allies didn't want to allow the NSC to do anything that might be too disruptive. Blocking travel from China would be an unprecedented intervention. And over what? Five cases of the sniffles in the United States? President Trump had just launched his reelection bid and signed a trade agreement with Beijing. He wouldn't rock the boat by approving something so drastic. But Pottinger came to the meeting prepared.

Earlier that day, he had connected with another former source in China from his journalism days, a doctor. That person had told him that roughly half of the people who had tested positive for COVID-19 in China had showed no symptoms of being sick. They were called "asymptomatic." That meant that a seemingly healthy person could actually be sick and transmit the virus to someone else. The implications were explosive, Pottinger knew. (The Chinese minister in charge of the National Health Commission, Ma Xiaowei, had also recently announced that there was evidence of asymptomatic transmission but hadn't provided data to back up the assertion.)

Even though China had initially downplayed the severity of the virus, photographs and videos had been circulating of large parts of China completely shutting down, a massive government response. On January 23, China announced that it was locking down Wuhan, a city of 11 million people. The shutdown was extended to several more cities in the coming days, with travel prohibited inside much of the country. Tens of millions of people were effectively locked in their homes. The Chinese were rapidly building an entire hospital in Wuhan that was completed within days. Everyone in the country was wearing a mask. People in hazmat suits took passengers' temperatures before anyone was allowed into the subway. China had gone from reluctantly admitting that there had been a few cases of person-to-person spread to shutting down the world's second largest economy. If the virus had brought the world's most populous country to a standstill, some top US officials, especially Pottinger, knew they should be doing more.

But as deputy national security advisor, Pottinger was in an awkward position. He was supposed to be chairing the meeting, which meant that his job was to solicit input from others in the room and avoid arguing forcefully for any particular outcome. That fact tied his hands. He needed someone else to make the more pointed parts of his argument for him. Someone who would stand up to everyone else in the room unflinchingly.

He knew just the person: a reviled troublemaker named Peter Navarro, the director of the White House National Trade Council.

As people began taking their seats in the Situation Room, Navarro walked in purposefully and slid into a chair halfway down the table. Decades of exercise had preserved his tight, wiry frame. Most people in the room didn't recognize him, but Mulvaney knew all about Navarro. About his penchant for slamming China. About the times he used an anagram of his last name and inserted someone named Ron Vara in his books to make disparaging comments about China. Some White House officials believed he had no credibility. At first, Navarro didn't move or speak but sat upright and coiled, like a cobra waiting for its moment to strike.

Azar and Redfield began the briefing by again reassuring everyone gathered that the situation was very serious but the health agencies were taking the proper steps to respond. This kind of outbreak was what they were designed to deal with.

That quickly uncorked Navarro. "You don't know what you are

dealing with!" he shouted across the room. One participant recalled that it was as if Navarro was "foaming at the mouth."

China lies, Navarro went on. It spawns these viruses and covers everything up and then it's too late. Americans are going to die. A lot of Americans. We can't trust the information we are getting from China. The US government will have to ban travel from China immediately. Few at the table knew it, but Navarro had coauthored a book nine years earlier entitled *Death by China: Confronting the Dragon—a Global Call to Action*. He believed that the Chinese had no qualms about killing large numbers of Americans. He believed it in his bones.

Pottinger's plan to use Navarro as his mouthpiece seemed to work initially, but then Navarro kept going. And going. He went around the room, lighting into the other experts present. The health team, what did they know? Nothing. What did any of them know? Nothing. They needed to ban travel, and they needed to do it now.

Pottinger had been waiting for an opening. He told his colleagues that he had come across some alarming information: Chinese officials were no longer able to contact trace the virus. In other words, it was so widespread that they couldn't determine where people had contracted it. And he relayed the Chinese suspicions about asymptomatic spread: people who seemed perfectly healthy were transmitting the virus, not just in China but potentially everywhere, including in the United States.

Azar cut in. The CDC is the gold standard for this kind of thing, he said. No one is better prepared to deal with the situation than officials at the Department of Health and Human Services and their colleagues at the CDC. They know how to do contact tracing, so they can track down every single person that an infected person has interacted with and lock them all down. That could stop the virus from spreading further or causing an outbreak.

Most in the room were leery of a travel ban, but they worried that imposing harsh restrictions could make the Chinese cut off all information. Then the United States would be flying blind.

The World Health Organization, which still had not declared the coronavirus a public health emergency of international concern, had explicitly advised against travel restrictions. The administration's medical experts, including NIAID director Anthony Fauci and CDC director Robert Redfield, argued that travelers from China might be importing cases of the virus into the United States—but so were people coming in from other countries. Travel restrictions might buy time, but they couldn't stop a virus. What they might stop, the health officials worried, was any cooperation from the Chinese.

What about travel from China to other countries? another participant asked. Someone could travel from China to France, then to the United States. Or to England and then to the United States. Was the United States supposed to shut down travel from everywhere? What about the thousands of Americans all over the world who were flying home from abroad every day? What if they were sick? The virus could seep through US borders and into communities like water through a net.

Mulvaney couldn't believe what he was witnessing. Pottinger and Navarro had nearly pulled off a policy ambush.

"Look," Mulvaney told someone at the meeting, "I've got Pottinger with a friend of his in Hong Kong as a source. I've got Navarro, who makes up his sources, and then on the other side of the equation I've got Kadlec and Fauci and Redfield, three experts, who say not to shut down flights just yet." (Mulvaney was mistaken on how exactly the doctors felt about a ban at the time.)

Trump's new trade deal with China, not even two weeks old, complicated matters. China was one of the United States' top trading partners, and Trump was counting on the country to help him win reelection by buying up US goods. Would blocking Chinese citizens from entering the United States destroy the trade deal that Trump considered to be one of his biggest accomplishments?

The meeting wrapped up, and Mulvaney looked at the room and said, "We have a consensus. No flight ban."

Pottinger threw up his hands in exasperation, and Navarro quickly interjected, "We don't have a consensus on anything."

As people filed out, Mulvaney turned to an aide and said that Navarro was to be banned from the meetings for the foreseeable future. Azar, stunned, asked someone, "Who *was* that guy?"

One of the government health experts pulled Pottinger aside. The stat Pottinger had cited, the one about half of all people with the virus being asymptomatic, there's just no way that can be true, the person said. No one has ever heard of a coronavirus similar to SARS or MERS whose spread can be driven in part by asymptomatic carriers. That would be a game changer.

Trump would soon tell the journalist Bob Woodward that a terrible, "deadly" virus had arrived, one that was much more severe than the flu.

He would often boast that the things he dealt with, whether they were hurricanes or tornadoes or investigations, were the biggest ever, the biggest of all time, the most challenging thing any president had ever faced. But in the moment, he usually delegated responsibility to others and then blamed them for their mistakes if their solutions didn't work. This virus was different, though; he didn't know how to deal with it.

So he opted to do what he always did in such situations: will it away.

The key to willing it away was to ensure that his public remarks conveyed no concern, no apprehension. His life, in public and private, was built on a stack of fakes and lies, an amoral brazenness that gave him a decided advantage over his adversaries, whether they were women, real estate counterparts, or political leaders and heads of state. He would use the same tactic on this virus, this microbe, this tiny thing no one could see.

And so, like a magician winking at his audience, he promised Americans that the coronavirus would just disappear. "We have very little problem in this country at this moment," he said in Michigan two days later, referring to the now five reported cases. ". . . And those people are all recuperating successfully. But we're working very closely with China and other countries, and we think it's going to have a very good ending for it, so that I can assure you."

But it was clear to many in the White House that even with only five cases, the outbreak was starting to pose a logistical nightmare. The State Department had so far chartered one flight back from Wuhan with about two hundred Americans on board. There were thousands more who still wanted to come home. Were any of them sick? The lockdowns in China were extending almost every day, far beyond Wuhan. And the people the State Department brought home would have to be quarantined somewhere for two weeks until it was relatively certain that they couldn't spread the virus to their families or communities.

There were now too many people involved in the discussions. Mulvaney and Chris Liddell, the White House deputy chief of staff for policy, decided to formalize the working group that had been meeting for the last several days, naming it the Coronavirus Task Force. Navarro was barred from participating, and Azar asked Mulvaney and other White House officials to exclude Joe Grogan, but they refused. Azar would lead the group, though. He would have the control he craved.

The task force began as about a dozen people, swelling to more than twenty as the outbreak raged on. At first it consisted of mostly health and national security experts, but it grew to include economic advisers and even people with backgrounds in agricultural and housing policy. Cabinet secretaries usually attended with one or two of their top staffers.

The group's initial mandate was almost entirely the repatriation and quarantining of Americans returning from abroad. To some of Trump's aides, just naming the group a "task force" made the White House look as though it was doing something.

They typically met in the White House Situation Room, a secure, windowless chamber near the White House mess hall. Attendees had to ring a doorbell before they were allowed to enter, and they were prohibited from bringing phones into the meetings. Unable to track real-time news developments while locked in multihour meetings, when the group took short breaks, there was often a stampede of officials running to their phones for updates.

Trump joined the new task force for a meeting the next day and posted a photograph of the group on Twitter. White House officials didn't anticipate the backlash when it became clear that the task force was all men and almost all white. It looked like an echo chamber. Were they really the best experts on preventing an outbreak, or were they just the best that Trump could muster?

The members realized that they would have to come up with some sort of plan quickly. The next day, the World Health Organization declared COVID-19 a public health emergency, and researchers at the *New England Journal of Medicine* published a paper that confirmed what Pottinger had told others in the Situation Room: people with no symptoms could spread the disease, a nightmare scenario.

The news finally convinced the principal health officials, including Fauci and Redfield, that a travel ban was necessary, because there was no way to identify all infected travelers at the airport through screening. The morning of January 30, the CDC recommended to Azar that the US ban travel from China. Azar agreed, and presented the recommendation at the task force meeting that afternoon in the Situation Room. Pottinger and others who had supported the travel ban idea for more than a week were frustrated that it had taken so long but happy that there was finally a consensus. But how on earth could the United States ban travelers from the world's biggest country?

The task force members huddled to try to map out a strategy. Because of the dramatic spike in cases of the novel coronavirus in China, they would start by banning most travelers from China from entering the United States. Then, if the virus began to explode in other countries—Italy, for example, was starting to look worrying— they could consider more restrictions.

Later that evening, Trump was on Air Force One with a group of aides, on his way to hold a rally in Iowa. Trump had planned the trip as a way to steal attention from the upcoming Democratic primary caucus there and create his own spectacle. As he settled into the president's cabin on the plane, he received a call from a tense-sounding Azar.

The State Department, Azar told him, was ready to raise its China travel advisory to Level 4—the "do not travel" advisory that is the agency's highest level of caution—and Azar was seeking Trump's permission. Trump was opposed to the move. There was more. With the public still in the dark about the severity of the situation, Azar wanted to go on all the Sunday talk shows, such as *Meet the Press* and *Face the Nation*, to talk about it. He tried to stress to Trump how serious the situation was and said he needed to keep the country informed.

The president, who didn't like being outshone, immediately sensed that Azar was being opportunistic by pitching himself for television. Secretary of State Mike Pompeo had just spent weeks serving as the White House's public face as it dealt with Trump's directive to kill the top Iranian general, Qasem Soleimani. Now Azar wanted to be the public face of a health crisis that was making its way from China?

"He wasn't asking him, 'What do you think we should do, sir?' He was saying 'This is a huge problem, but I've got it and this is what we're going to do,'" one White House aide recalled.

Trump grew irritated as Azar continued speaking. "You're panicking," Trump told him. "You can't go out there and bash the Chinese."

Farther back on the plane, Joe Grogan explained to Jared Kushner, the president's son-in-law and a White House senior adviser, that the administration was struggling to get reliable data from the Chinese about the outbreak. Redfield, the CDC director, had raised the issue in a recent meeting. The data were crucial for US health officials to be able to determine when to switch from containment—which meant identifying and isolating every confirmed case in an effort to keep the number of infections as close to zero as possible—to mitigation, when they would have to prepare hospitals and communities to reduce transmission, with the understanding that there would be persistent spread of the disease. Pivoting from containment to mitigation at the right time could have a huge impact on limiting the virus's spread.

Kushner had a sprawling portfolio inside the White House; essentially he focused on whatever he wanted to, while also serving as the de facto head of Trump's reelection effort. At various points he saw himself as playing a lead role in confronting the opioid crisis, brokering Middle East peace, orchestrating US–China relations, serving as chief intermediary with the Mexican government, and inking new trade deals. He had Trump's blessing to insert himself into any issue, at any point. Most recently, he had been consumed with trying to help Trump navigate the impeachment. Before Trump's inauguration in 2017, he had lacked any government experience, but he had supreme confidence in his ability to cut through government red tape. He believed, without hesitation, that he could do things better than bureaucrats could.

Kushner chastised Grogan. You're calling some low-level bureaucrat in China, he said. That low-level bureaucrat is then going to a slightly higher level bureaucrat, and they are both afraid of losing their jobs. Kushner, seemingly unaware of the fraught history of the Chinese government's suppressing information about public health crises, said that he would just call the Chinese government himself and get all the information necessary.

Despite Trump's annoyance, the State Department announced the elevated travel advisory that night. The next day, the task force members decided that they needed to announce the more formal ban on Chinese travelers as soon as possible. But no one had briefed Trump on it, and Mulvaney and his aides agreed that Azar needed to present the plan to the president. They knew that only the president could sign off on a decision this big.

A handful of aides, including Azar, made the recommendation to Trump in the Oval Office. The president wasn't thrilled about it, but the fact that all of his advisers were unified behind the idea made it hard for him to say no. He authorized the travel ban, but he and his top aides weren't going to stick around to announce it. He wanted political cover in case it went awry, and he did not want to be visibly part of the announcement. He instructed Azar to announce it from the White House podium.

In the hours before the 3:00 p.m. briefing, three US airlines announced that they planned to halt all flights to mainland China. American Airlines, Delta, and United, which had previously said they would curtail flights but not stop them altogether, said the State Department's travel advisory had prompted them to cease flights from China to the United States. Other international carriers also sharply curtailed or stopped flights to and from China, including British Airways, Lufthansa Group, Air France, and Lion Air.

As Azar prepared to take the podium that afternoon, the boundaries of international travel had dramatically shifted. Was the travel ban too late? There was tremendous confusion. So much had changed in the four days since the initial Situation Room meeting. Everything was happening so fast. Azar was going to have to own this decision if it went south, and he worried it could be the next vaping nightmare. The president might well backtrack if the move backfired politically—and direct his ire at the HHS secretary, who had pushed him to agree to it. Azar didn't have Trump by his side in front of the cameras. In fact, Trump was on a plane to Florida.

When he walked onto the White House Briefing Room podium forty minutes behind schedule, Azar was flanked by several of his task force members: Fauci, Redfield, Deputy Secretary of State Stephen Biegun, Department of Homeland Security acting deputy secretary Cuccinelli, and Assistant Secretary of Transportation for Aviation and International Affairs Joel Szabat. Aside from Fauci and

Cuccinelli, none of the other faces was recognizable by most Americans.

Azar began with the least controversial announcement: the United States was declaring the coronavirus a public health emergency, which would give the government more flexibility and resources to respond to the outbreak. Then came the real news: beginning at 5:00 p.m. that Sunday, the United States would bar non–US citizens who had recently visited China, except for those who were immediate family members of citizens and permanent residents, from entering the country. He also announced that any American citizens who had visited China's Hubei province, where the virus had spread well beyond its capital, Wuhan, in the last fourteen days would be subject to a mandatory government quarantine, the first in more than sixty years. He didn't specify how that would work, in part because the administration hadn't figured it out yet. The couple hundred Americans who had so far been repatriated from China were in quarantine, but now the government officials were talking about thousands of people.

Azar was walking a tightrope; he needed to convey why the White House was taking such an extreme step while also trying to tamp down any concerns that Americans could become sick. He leaned hard into the idea that the risk was coming from abroad. He wanted Americans to understand that he was in charge of the effort that would keep the virus outside the United States. He would keep them safe. "I want to stress: The risk of infection for Americans remains low," he said confidently. "And with these and our previous actions, we are working to keep the risk low."

After Azar's remarks, some White House aides and government officials thought they would soon put the coronavirus mess behind them. The travel ban, as they called it, would keep the virus outside the United States, and the government would be able to deal with the few cases that cropped up here or there. Most political aides wanted to shift their attention to the reelection campaign. Trump's impeachment acquittal by the Senate was expected in a few days. The Dow

Jones Industrial Average had fallen 600 points, or 2 percent, on the day the travel restrictions were announced, but the officials felt it would bounce back in no time.

The task force members had spent almost the entire week debating whether to ban some travel from China and then figuring out how to tell the president. But each day that month, more than 10,000 travelers arrived at US airports on direct flights from China.

The virus wasn't about to board a flight from China; it had already landed.

CHAPTER 3

TRAPPED AT SEA

February 1, 2020
CONFIRMED US COVID-19 CASES: **8**
CONFIRMED US COVID-19 DEATHS: **0**

The *Diamond Princess*, a massive eighteen-deck gleaming white cruise ship, had weaved its way through East Asia and was returning north for the completion of its fifteen-day tour. At 952 feet, it was 69 feet longer than the *Titanic*. More than a thousand crew members serviced 2,666 passengers from fifty-five different countries, including 328 Americans. It was a floating city, offering a packed agenda of cultural activities for its passengers, many of them retirees. One night, Western tourists dressed in kimonos. There was a casino and dances. The restaurants were always full.

That particular cruise was designed to be a huge draw, as the passengers would spend Lunar New Year beneath an elaborate fireworks show in Hong Kong. But by the time they arrived in that pulsating city, all the festivities had been canceled. Hong Kong officials didn't want Chinese tourists to come and bring the virus with them. The cruise was supposed to be the trip of a lifetime, but now the *Diamond Princess* was under a pall.

Still, the dejected passengers were allowed to disembark for the day and briefly explore the city. They reboarded the *Diamond Princess* that afternoon in preparation to sail to their next port in

Vietnam, but the ship stayed put. An hour passed, then another. The passengers were confused. Typically the timetables on a cruise were meticulously honored. Crew members appeared to be searching for a passenger who had disembarked but never returned. Eventually the ship left, sailing on to Vietnam, with no formal explanation of the delay.

A few days before it was set to return to its origin port of Yokohama, the ship's officers received a strange report. An eighty-year-old man had in fact quietly disembarked in Hong Kong and never returned. He had tested positive for COVID-19 and pneumonia at a local hospital. The person (the US National Institutes of Health would later call him "Mr. A." but the *South China Morning Post* interviewed him and called him "Mr. Wu") had not visited the medical center on the ship, though his two daughters had remained on board. The crew had no record of his illness or symptoms. He had just walked off the ship and disappeared.

Still, he had been on board for some days, so the *Diamond Princess* was told to return to Yokohama immediately. When it neared the city, it was kept offshore like a "modern-day plague ship," one passenger, Gay Courter, recalled.

Passengers were told that Japanese officials were going to board the ship to test everyone for the virus and they could then disembark in the morning. But when the next morning came, there was another announcement: testing all of the passengers was incredibly time-consuming, and this would take a bit longer than anticipated. The passengers were told that they could mingle and continue to enjoy the plethora of activities on the ship while they waited. Meanwhile, the ship's crew was required to continue working, even though some of them weren't feeling well.

The next morning, a new male voice sounded over the speaker system. Ten people had tested positive for the virus, the man announced. All passengers would have to stay in their cabins for fourteen days. Three meals would be brought to each cabin daily, and everyone was prohibited from leaving their rooms.

Each day that followed, there was an announcement of how many additional people had tested positive. The number grew at an alarming rate. The passengers felt trapped. And greeting them each morning with the sunrise was the sight of more ambulances at the port, some days as many as forty, to take sick passengers away from the ship.

How had the virus spread to so many people so quickly? Researchers would later find that the coronavirus was not only able to spread through close encounters but could also hang in the air in small particles called "aerosols" that are transmitted by breathing. Viruses that are spread by inhaled aerosols are incredibly difficult to contain.

Back in Washington, 6,800 miles away, US officials read the *Diamond Princess* reports in horror. The task force had spent the last week of January struggling to come up with a plan to ban incoming flights in an attempt to keep the virus out of the United States. Now they had to figure out what to do with US citizens who were already sick overseas. Should they bring them home? Should they risk bringing the virus into the United States in order to make sure Americans could return to their families? They had little time to debate what to do. Each day, more Americans became sick on the ship. And the *Diamond Princess* wasn't the only cruise liner turning into a floating petri dish; there were dozens of others carrying thousands of American travelers, many of them older retirees, sailing all over the world.

The US officials closely monitoring the *Diamond Princess* were relying on the Japanese health ministry for information. The CDC advised that it keep the 328 Americans on board the ship for fourteen days, so they could serve their quarantine away from others. The task force agreed; the Americans would just have to hunker down and wait it out.

What was making people so sick?

A new virus, roughly 100 nanometers in diameter—10,000 of

them can fit on the head of a pin—had emerged out of China and swept around the globe, transported by unsuspecting carriers, traveling like a speck of lint on a winter coat.

A coronavirus is named for the protein spikes that cover its outer surface, giving it a crownlike shape. The spikes enable it to bind to parts of human cells called ACE2 receptors. These are present on cells throughout the respiratory tract, which is why the virus can cause severe lung infections. (ACE2 receptors are on the surface of many other cells throughout the body, which may explain why COVID-19 can impact so many different organ systems beyond just the respiratory system.) From there, each virus can break through the protective outer membrane of a cell, burrow its way in, and lodge itself. Viruses are strange pathogens, neither living nor dead. They cannot reproduce on their own and have to find a human or animal cell to invade. They then take over the cell's machinery, where they can replicate themselves millions of times. That's exactly what the new coronavirus was doing with its victims: it grabbed on to cells in the nose or throat, injected its genetic material into them, then replicated itself throughout the body, mounting a full attack, like a stick of dynamite stuffed inside a suitcase. And it would find its next victim—and therefore, ensure its survival—once the sick person shed the virus through coughing, sneezing, or even just breathing. Then the vicious cycle would begin anew. The virus was named SARS-CoV-2, but the disease it caused would be called coronavirus disease 2019, or COVID-19.

When Chinese researchers released the virus's genetic code on January 10, 2020, on an open-access repository for genetic information, scientists jumped at the opportunity to see what they were dealing with. The National Institutes of Health director, Francis Collins, and Anthony Fauci convened global experts on viral genome evolution to scrutinize the sequence and try to determine whether it was a human-engineered virus or a naturally occurring one. Initially, there were fears that someone might have deliberately engineered a virus to harm the United States and other countries, a scenario that several administrations had spent considerable time contemplating and preparing for.

What the experts found stunned them—and left them almost certain that there was no way a human could have designed the virus. "It violated what we thought we knew about what would make a coronavirus dangerous," Collins said. "It had features that were really surprising and unheard of that nobody could have imagined would actually work, but there it was."

Scientists still cannot completely rule out the possibility that the virus was engineered. But the novel coronavirus has a so-called cleavage site, where the spike protein splits into two parts and is better able to attack human cells. (The protein does not spontaneously split, but is cut by a host protein called a protease, which is an enzyme that acts like molecular scissors and cuts at that specific site.) The novel coronavirus's cleavage site was unusual and unique, and other coronaviruses that have been found in bats have similar sites, suggesting this was a feature that could evolve naturally. And the virus's spike proteins are made up of a string of amino acids that initially didn't make sense to scientists but turned out to be one of the reasons it was able to spread so ruthlessly. The spike proteins give the virus considerable "stickiness" when it bonds with an ACE2 receptor, meaning that it's more likely to invade the cell successfully and replicate itself. Even though the virus has several unique features, the experts determined that it was most closely related to a 2014 coronavirus that had come from a bat in a cave in China. These two viruses were more like distant cousins, rather than siblings; experts still haven't found the "parent" of the novel coronavirus.

There have always been coronaviruses—virtually everyone has had a coronavirus-caused disease in his or her lifetime because some common colds are caused by coronaviruses—but this one was new. The dominant theory was that it had originated in an animal somewhere in China and then made its way into an animal market, where it had spread to humans. China had been criticized for not shutting down so-called wet markets, where unsanitized wild animals were sold, for exactly that reason. Obscure viruses can find their way from the recesses of a cave or wild animal habitat to humans; that's all it takes to change human history. (There is also a theory that the virus may have escaped from a lab in Wuhan. In March 2021, Redfield revealed he believed this was the "most likely" cause of the novel coronavirus's spread.)

Coronaviruses are a large family of viruses that have been around for ages. Many of them exist only in animals and never make their way to people. There are seven known coronaviruses that can infect humans, some relatively harmless, while others can be deadly. Over time, humans build up immunity to these viruses so they don't cause too much sickness, or scientific advances produce drugs and vaccines to treat them. But a new or "novel" coronavirus that could jump from human to human was a particular challenge. When confronted by a new disease, humans don't have any antibodies, or virus-specific proteins from prior exposures or infections, that can fight off a specific pathogen and provide protection in their immune systems. There is no vaccine and no effective treatment. That was the state of affairs in 2020. There were breakthrough scientific treatments for some of the most complicated infections and diseases, as well as centuries' worth of immunity built up to fight all manner of infections. But the world was completely unprepared to deal with COVID-19.

And, scientists and doctors were only just discovering that the novel coronavirus had an ability to spread undetected in a way that the previous coronaviruses SARS and MERS did not. People could be infected with the virus but show no symptoms. Worse, they could infect others even when there was no clear sign that they were sick, something known as asymptomatic transmission. That made the virus almost impossible to stop, because there was no simple way to isolate the sick from the healthy. It raised the possibility that the virus had been spreading undetected in numerous countries. No previous coronavirus like SARS or MERS had been driven by asymptomatic transmission. The novel coronavirus would turn that precedent on

its head. (Some data would later show that presymptomatic transmission, or spreading the virus before a person showed any symptoms, was a large driver of spread.)

Within two days of becoming infected, a person can begin shed-
ding the virus and infecting others. By the time someone knows she
is sick, if she does ever know, she may have infected a dozen other
people, perhaps days earlier and miles away. Then that dozen infects
hundreds, those hundreds infect thousands, and so on.

So the virus is always on the move in two directions, like a seed:
part of it goes down into a person's respiratory system (the roots),
and part of it goes up and sheds out through the nose and mouth (the
branches and leaves). It can take one person to the brink of death
while simultaneously beginning a hunt for new targets. One microscopic killer launches millions of arrows, again and again.

Further confounding experts, the virus did not make a uniform
assault on the more than 140 million human hosts it eventually infected. It would glide through some like a ghost, leaving no trace.
But in others, it would launch a murderous stranglehold, causing serious lung damage by either filling them with fluid—almost drown-
ing them—or preventing them from working properly. In others, it
would cause severe heart damage and inflammation.

And although some infected people recovered from the virus just
fine, in many older patients and those with chronic health conditions, the body mounted a chaotic immune response in an effort to
kill the invading virus, overwhelming the lungs and several other
organs. Ironically, the body's immune response to the virus, not the
virus itself, causes the most severe complications or eventual death.
Some people suffered intense coughing fits as the virus burrowed its
way farther into their lungs. And there were stories about people effectively suffocating. Though older people were the most susceptible
to the virus, it claimed victims from nearly every demographic. The
sick and the healthy. The old and the young. The rich and the poor.
For many victims, it could not be outrun.

It is much easier to quickly identify and isolate infected people when an infectious disease produces intense, easily distinguishable symptoms. That was why Ebola, though far more deadly and violent in people who became infected, never spread out of control in a developed country. (Ebola also is not transmitted by aerosols and doesn't spread through breathing.) For many people, the new virus's symptoms resembled little more than the common cold. Until it was too late.

A small group of the nation's top infectious disease doctors and medical experts, both in government and in prestigious academic institutions, were growing increasingly alarmed. They exchanged ideas, questions, and emerging information about the virus in an email group they dubbed "Red Dawn," a reference to the 1984 Cold War film about a character played by Patrick Swayze and a group of teenagers who stop Russians, Nicaraguans, and Cubans from overthrowing the United States through hardscrabble battles (most of the heroes in the film, though, end up dead). The members of the "Red Dawn" email group were far more worried than most senior White House officials were.

But there was at least one member of the task force who was also on the Red Dawn chain: Assistant Secretary for Preparedness and Response at HHS Robert Kadlec. Kadlec was an air force veteran who wore rimless glasses and had a wave of sandy brown hair. He was also a Washington veteran in every sense of the word: former congressional staffer, former Pentagon official, former biodefense contractor. But his air force record—he had been named US Air Force Flight Surgeon of the Year in 1986—served as a sort of compass. He had several assignments supporting air force and joint special operations, including hostage rescues. He believed that no one was to be left behind on the battlefield. He had also worked on things such as anthrax radiological threats and was well acquainted with the nasty side of medicine. His participation both in the task force and in the

Red Dawn email chain gave him a foot inside in the Situation Room but also a look into the field of scientists, many of whom he had worked with in the George W. Bush administration, who thought the situation could get ugly.

For many in the Red Dawn email chain, the *Diamond Princess* was a looming disaster. A basic understanding of the virus's lethality had emerged. And one thing was crystal clear: the elderly were among those most vulnerable to serious complications or death from the virus. And most of the passengers on the *Diamond Princess* fell into that risk group.

The experts watched helplessly as the ship's outbreak expanded from 10 people to 61 to 136 on February 10. They also quickly recognized that the *Diamond Princess* was giving them their best opportunity to get data to understand how the coronavirus attacked and spread. Nothing they saw was comforting. One of the most alarmed officials in the Red Dawn email chain was Carter Mecher, the senior medical adviser at the Department of Veterans Affairs. "Over the span of 21 days (from Jan 20–Feb 10), this outbreak has expanded to 136 confirmed cases. That is a prevalence of 3.7% over the span of 3 weeks. That is unbelievable," he wrote in an email on February 10. "But go back and compare the dynamics of the nCov outbreak to the spring wave of H1N1, this outbreak is even faster," he added, referring to the 2009 flu outbreak that had infected more than 60 million Americans and killed nearly 13,000.

Two days later, Anne Schuchat, the principal deputy director of the CDC, Kadlec, Fauci, a representative from the Department of Homeland Security, and a State Department official briefed members of the House of Representatives about the *Diamond Princess*. They assured House members that they were closely monitoring the outbreak. It was best for the Americans to stay on the ship, Schuchat argued, so they could serve out their fourteen-day quarantines and then be repatriated to the United States.

Representative Phil Roe, a Tennessee Republican, grew more

agitated the longer Schuchat spoke. Finally he broke in. "You guys don't know anything about what's going on there!" he bellowed, going on to berate her for much of the meeting.

Afterward, Kadlec pulled Roe aside. What had that all been about? Roe, also a doctor, explained that Arnold Hopland, an emergency room doctor and former colleague in Tennessee, was trapped on the *Diamond Princess* with his wife, Jeanie. Hopland and Roe had been calling and texting each other, giving Roe an unfiltered view into the horror movie that the *Diamond Princess* had become. Roe was convinced that the US officials didn't know how bad things were. Otherwise, they would never think it was a good idea to leave Americans on the ship.

Kadlec quickly arranged a call with Hopland and a group of physicians from HHS, CDC, HHS's Office of the Assistant Secretary for Preparedness and Response, and the DHS. Hopland's update was a sobering one for the government physicians. The ship crew that was responsible for implementing the isolation and quarantine measures didn't know what they were doing because they did not have any experience doing so. The situation was far beyond their expertise and skill set, and although the crew were doing their best to follow the instructions of the Japanese government, the massive ship simply had not been designed for a quarantine on this scale. Thousands of people were packed tightly together in a confined space. Unsurprisingly, the crew itself was being ravaged by the virus, and now they were infecting the passengers. The ship had become the site of an uncontrollable outbreak. The officials needed to get the Americans off the ship, Hopland said.

Kadlec believed that the government could repatriate the Americans on the *Diamond Princess* and get them home safely. In fact, the US government had been working closely with the Japanese government for a year and a half, preparing for a possible infectious disease outbreak at the planned 2020 Summer Olympics in Tokyo. ASPR and their Japanese counterparts planned to conduct an exercise in March 2020 practicing repatriating American tourists who were infected with a highly infectious disease. The *Diamond Princess* was a far more complicated operation than that exercise, but Kadlec was confident that they could do it. If the quarantine wasn't being implemented effectively, and the ship wasn't safe, they had to bring the Americans home, he argued. Officials at the CDC disagreed. Schuchat and others believed that flying them back was too risky, especially if someone became infected on the journey home. The plane was a small space, and flying sick passengers with healthy ones automatically put other elderly passengers at high risk for severe cases of coronavirus in danger.

But two days later, on Friday, February 14, the US officials came to a decision: they would try to repatriate as many Americans as they could. ASPR and State Department officials acknowledged the CDC concerns but countered that it was a reality they had to be prepared for, and set up a chartered State Department aircraft to try to minimize the risk. The flight and medical crews would sit in the front of the plane; passengers who tested negative or had no symptoms of the disease would sit in the middle; and the back of the plane would be separated from the front with a plastic sheet, so that those who began showing symptoms during the flight could sit there, physically isolated from the rest of the passengers, and be evaluated.

When the government decided it was going to evacuate as many passengers as it could, the CDC wrote to each American on the ship detailing the plan, promising them they would not be put into a position where they were on a bus or plane with someone who tested positive. They would test those who wanted to be evacuated once they disembarked the *Diamond Princess* and before loading them onto buses for the ninety-minute drive to Tokyo's Haneda Airport. Those who had symptoms or tested positive would be transferred to Japanese hospitals. No one who tested positive would be allowed to board the plane. No one would be put in danger, the CDC assured the passengers.

As rain pattered on the pavement outside, the 328 passengers sat on the buses, clad in surgical masks and gloves. Most were elderly, in their seventies and eighties, and they were exhausted. They had risen early to begin the long journey to Haneda and were now, at 10:00 p.m., still idling on the tarmac. Many were uncomfortable after having worn masks and other protective gear for hours. As they waited, officials back in Washington received troubling news.

A batch of test results had just come in, and at least fourteen of the disembarked American passengers had tested positive for COVID-19, but they weren't showing symptoms. The officials hadn't been prepared for that. Of all the scenarios they had planned for, none of them had included test results coming back after the passengers had already been loaded onto buses and been taken to the airport, expecting to board the plane any minute. Making matters worse, the asymptomatic infected passengers were now crowded onto buses with everyone else.

The US officials hastily convened a conference call to decide what to do. Schuchat was adamant that they had to leave the Americans who had tested positive behind.

"Anne," Kadlec began tersely, "unless somebody makes contact with someone from the Japanese government and we can do a transfer and ensure they're taken care of, we don't have a plan B to do that. But we do have a plan B to put people on the back of the plane because we had planned for if anybody became sick with suspected COVID."

Schuchat was becoming increasingly irritated. This was supposed to be the CDC's call, and they had a game plan that everyone had agreed to. The flimsy plastic sheet separating healthy passengers from infected ones was hardly adequate protection. Almost all of the passengers were in a high-risk age group for developing serious complications from the disease. "We gave these people a letter," she shot back. If they knowingly put passengers with the coronavirus on the flight, the CDC would be breaking their promise to hundreds of Americans that they would not put them in danger.

Fauci was equivocal, but ultimately indicated that they should bring back the fourteen infected passengers. Neither Schuchat nor

Kadlec would back down. Schuchat reiterated that those who tested positive could not board the plane, given the risk to the otherwise healthy passengers. Kadlec was incredulous. Where the hell were they going to put all those people? Were they just going to leave them in Japan without a clear plan? CDC officials believed there were other obvious options. Put the passengers back on the boat and spread them out until they recovered from the virus. Or perhaps bring the infected passengers back on a separate State Department aircraft. Those options, however, weren't discussed.

The State Department officials quickly made their decision: the infected passengers would be flown home over the CDC's objections. The nation's premier public health agency wasn't supposed to be overruled on decisions like that, and days later the *Washington Post* published an in-depth article about the internal debate. The article highlighted the fact that the CDC had been overruled and that Kadlec had pushed to bring the sick passengers home.

Because officials had been forced to scramble to make the decision, they had not had time to loop in the president before he saw the dispute reported in the press. Besides, such issues weren't supposed to rise to his level, and Kadlec's efforts to quickly consult with top National Security Council officials had been rebuffed.

Trump, who was obsessed with keeping the US case count as low as possible, was furious. The returning infected passengers would double the US case count from fourteen to twenty-eight people. For the last three weeks, ever since the decision to ban travel from China, political aides had assured him that they could contain the virus in the United States. Trump saw the US case count almost like a golf score; he wanted to keep it low. It was an arbitrary number to him, like a school grade, like the stock market. Now the number of infected Americans was going up!

Trump called Azar on February 20, the same day the *Washington Post* article was published. He was audibly angry, demanding to know who had made the decision to allow the sick passengers on the flight back to the United States. Whenever Trump called, Azar, seemingly relying on his law training, would wave for his closest aides to come into the room and listen so that someone else would be a witness to the call. His chief of staff and general counsel joined him in his office shortly after Trump began to raise his voice.

Azar told Trump that he was frustrated with the decision and that nobody had bothered to call him to weigh in on the dispute. Trump had made clear to his aides that he didn't want any sick Americans coming back to the United States. But, Azar added, these are tough calls that people have to make on the ground. We have to back up the people who make these calls on the battlefield.

"You need to fire whoever made that decision," Trump replied.

Azar tried to explain that a State Department official in Tokyo had technically made the final decision, and that person was under Mike Pompeo. "Fire him anyway," Trump said.

Azar couldn't fire State Department employees. But Trump was furious and wanted someone to take action, so he told Mulvaney to find a way to fire the person, who happened to be a seasoned diplomat. (Trump was always telling Mulvaney to fire people, but this time he appeared to mean it.) Mulvaney told Biegun, a senior State Department official, to fire the diplomat, but Biegun refused. Eventually, Trump and Mulvaney gave up. Many State Department officials would later believe that the diplomat's decision to send the sick Americans home (there was no later flight for them to catch) likely saved lives.

Trump was most angry about what the sick passengers meant for him. Now that the State Department had brought back fourteen sick passengers, there were twenty-eight official US cases. "That doubles my numbers overnight," he complained to Azar. He wanted the confirmed COVID-19 cases of repatriated Americans to be reported differently so that the numbers would not reflect poorly on him.

Azar agreed to report the numbers differently, but he wanted to make something clear to Trump. "What are you going to do when you have hundreds or thousands of cases in the United States? That can happen," he explained, his tone growing combative.

"Really?" Trump asked.

"Yes," Azar said. "We're going to have more cases in the country. You're not going to have numbers in the five or ten." Trump took in what he said, then ended the call.

When Trump read about Kadlec's role in the matter, he told Mulvaney more than once to "fire his ass." Kadlec was tipped off to that. A few days later, along with Azar, Fauci, and Redfield, he was summoned to see the president.

When the four officials walked into the Oval Office, the setting was ominous, with four chairs positioned directly in front of the English oak Resolute Desk. Kadlec was sure that Trump would dispense with him at that meeting. *I don't like the looks of this*, he thought when he saw the four chairs. *At least I have a chair*, he reassured himself.

The president began the meeting. "Anthony, did we do the right thing by bringing those people back from Japan?" he asked Fauci. Trump called him Anthony, even though no one else addressed Fauci by his full first name; everybody else called him Tony.

"Mr. President," Fauci responded, "it was exactly the right thing to do."

Trump nodded his head. "Anthony, you're exactly right. It was the right thing to do."

Trump never looked at Kadlec or addressed him, but the meeting ended and no one had lost his job.

The *Diamond Princess* was just the beginning. Trump made it clear going forward that he didn't want anyone suffering from COVID-19 to enter the United States. He didn't care if they were Americans. He wanted them kept off US soil. And he had dramatic ideas about how to achieve it.

"We import so many things," he told aides during one Situation Room meeting in February. "We import goods. We are not going to import a virus. No, why don't we send it somewhere. Don't we have an island that we own?"

The room was silent. Where was Trump going with this?

He continued, "What about Guantánamo?"

Everyone froze.

He was suggesting sending all of the sick passengers, most of whom were elderly, to Guantánamo Bay, Cuba, where there was a US naval base.

The military compound, colloquially known as Gitmo, was not known for rolling out the red carpet for senior citizen cruise passengers. It was known instead for its military prison, where terror suspects had been held indefinitely since shortly after the September 11, 2001, terror attacks (forty were still detained there, many without ever having faced criminal charges, during the coronavirus outbreak). Trump's musing raised the prospect of sending sick grandmothers and grandfathers to a base where they would be near US terror suspects.

This idea showed the lengths Trump would go to in a vain effort to try to prevent infected people from setting foot in the continental United States. He simply wanted to keep the "numbers" down as much as possible. If they were in Gitmo, the reasoning went, they wouldn't count.

The aides couldn't tell if Trump was kidding, but several knew instantly that if news leaked out that they were considering such a move, there would be a huge public relations crisis. Azar told Trump that they would look into several options and report back. But Trump wasn't kidding, and he raised the idea again during a subsequent Oval Office meeting. His aides conferred and agreed again to scuttle the idea. They knew it was completely unacceptable. Eventually Trump stopped bringing it up.

It sent chills through his team, though, causing fresh panic whenever a cruise ship appeared to be close to disembarking passengers. At one point, when a ship with infected passengers started allowing passengers to exit in Long Beach, California, Mulvaney rushed into the Situation Room and shouted, "Stop the disembarkation!" Officials scrambled to see if they could demand that the local sheriff's office force people back onto the ship, but they ultimately gave up.

The fixation on cruise ships had serious repercussions. The task force spent weeks strategizing how to deal with infected passengers on those ships, an effort that took the focus away from the thousands of people entering the United States each day from other countries on planes or through Mexico and Canada. The White House also wasn't noticing the growing number of people in the United States who suddenly felt ill even though they had never left the country.

"In hindsight, we were focusing all of the task force on getting a kitty cat off the third floor, while the whole building was on fire and there were a thousand people in it," a member of the task force would later confide.

CHAPTER 4

TESTING, TESTING

The task force members' agonizing over cruise ships continued until one Saturday conference call when Stephen Biegun, a top State Department official, said they needed to end the debate. The average age of travelers on these cruise ships was eighty years old. It was just too risky. "We are done with cruise ships," he told the others. "This is enough. We need to do a no sail order."

The CDC was the agency that had the authority to mandate such an order and had been pushing for it. But for some on the call, it was as though a light bulb had gone off: Just stop any more people from getting onto ships. Of course that was the answer. ("I was like 'Why the fuck didn't I think of that?'" one person on the call said.) The cruise ship industry, a powerful political force, had been furiously lobbying the White House to allow it to continue operating, and the administration was reluctant to crack down. But the current state of affairs was clearly unsustainable. The task force was spending all its time trying to figure out what to do with Americans trapped on cruise ships around the world instead of responding to the growing global outbreak.

During the initial task force meetings, so often dominated by the cruise ship dilemma, Domestic Policy Council director Joe Grogan would briefly ask the health experts how the coronavirus diagnostic test was coming along. Testing is the most critical part of the response. The only way health officials would be able to keep the virus from spreading out of control was to identify and quarantine those who tested positive until they recovered and trace all their contacts to ensure that it didn't spread further into the community. Test, trace, and isolate, CDC director Robert Redfield had told the group, describing it as "blocking and tackling."

The CDC was developing the test, as it had in every other health emergency. The FDA was responsible for authorizing the final diagnostic test from the CDC. The Biomedical Advanced Research and Development Authority (BARDA) was tasked with working with private industry to spur development of treatments, vaccines, and diagnostics against health threats. The Centers for Medicare & Medicaid Services regulated all laboratory testing. As HHS is the parent agency of all four agencies, Alex Azar therefore had a critical role to play in ensuring that the country's testing needs were met. Few others on the task force, though, had significant health experience and knew much about the test or how the process was supposed to work.

Within days of the CDC distributing the initial tests to state public health labs on February 6, problems emerged. The labs were getting false-positive results on control samples. Robert Redfield relayed the problem to Azar, confident that the issue could be quickly resolved. But it soon became clear that it was more than a small hiccup and a fix would take much longer than they hoped. Days turned into weeks. Azar and Redfield kept the problem under wraps in the hope that things would turn around quickly. Others on the task force were mostly in the dark about what was going on.

But there were outside scientists and experts who knew that the CDC test had serious problems, and Joe Grogan began hearing rumblings. That was why he kept peppering Redfield and Azar for updates on testing; he knew the test was a mess, though he didn't reveal that knowledge to them. Every day the United States' testing capacity seemed to fall further and further behind that of other countries. But US health officials, several of whom did not understand why

Grogan of all people was hounding them about the subject, brushed him off again and again.

The situation with the tests is fine, Redfield kept assuring Grogan and the rest of the task force. There are some slight bumps, but a fix will be coming in no time. Everything is taken care of, Azar similarly assured the group. The CDC is remedying the situation. The tests are almost ready.

But, Azar and Redfield would soon learn, they weren't almost ready. Not even close.

In 2018, Donald Trump's first pick for CDC director abruptly resigned after *Politico* revealed that she had purchased stock in tobacco companies. As one of the CDC's key initiatives was smoking prevention, that was a big no-no. So the White House needed to find a replacement, and fast.

It had kicked the tires on Robert Redfield the year before. A plump, grandfatherly scientist, Redfield was well liked by the religious Right because he was a devout Catholic and a Republican and had championed abstinence as a central way to combat HIV during the 1990s. He had argued at the time that traditional Christian family values were the solution to many of America's ills. He wasn't well connected to Trump's inner circle, though, and had been passed over in 2017.

A year later, when the government needed someone, they turned to Redfield. The sharp knives and big egos within the Trump administration's health team were already proving problematic. A go-along-to-get-along scientist like Redfield might help calm things down.

Though Redfield was sixty-seven years old when he took over at the CDC, his childhood experiences continued to shape him. He was born in Bethesda, Maryland, and his father was a scientist at the National Institutes of Health. Redfield's earliest memory is of being a five-year-old in 1956 and finding his father's dead body in their home. He wouldn't learn until sixty-two years later, when he finally saw the death certificate, that his father had died by suicide. Young Bob was raised by his mother and had his first job at age seven, waking up at 4:30 a.m. each day to deliver copies of the *Washington Post*.

His mother would also take a job at the NIH, where Bob would go to after school to study in the library. He loved being surrounded by the country's top scientists. In 1966, the teenage Redfield was in the hallway of Building 10, when word spread through the NIH that one of its scientists, Marshall Nirenberg, had deciphered the genetic code. He would become the first federally employed scientist to win the Nobel Prize. The NIH was the place of rock stars. It was the place of magic. It was the place where Redfield wanted to be.

He graduated from Georgetown University Medical School and then did his residency at Walter Reed Army Medical Center. He worked in virology, or the study of viruses, and immunology, conducting clinical research along the way. His mother wanted him to be a lab researcher, but he wanted to interact with patients, so he thought he had found a happy middle ground.

At the time, in the late 1980s, virology and immunology were dominated by one perplexing and deadly disease: HIV/AIDS. The mysterious virus was spreading rapidly through the United States, particularly among young gay men. And where was there a notable concentration of young men? In the US military.

Redfield helped design the army's program for HIV testing, and it initially amounted to a crude, privacy-invasive practice. In October 1985, the Defense Department required mandatory testing of all troops. If someone tested positive, his commanding officers were notified. Then the soldier was interviewed—some would say interrogated—about his sexual partners. Openly gay men were not accepted into the military at the time, so troops who tested positive often faced humiliating treatment. HIV-positive men could remain in the military until they were too sick to work, but at that point many of them would lose their health insurance and have to battle the disease without access to quality medical care.

Up to that time, Redfield had believed in a sort of celestial scientific force: if you create more good in your life, you will go to Heaven; if you leave the world in worse shape than you found it, you will go to Hell. He wanted to create more good. He was hung up on how much Americans spent each year on popcorn at movie theaters and how that amount dwarfed what was spent on AIDS research. Couldn't they help more people if they just invested more in research? Shouldn't they try harder? He attempted to engage the religious community and appealed to Catholic leaders in New York. So in 1989, he was invited to an AIDS conference at the Vatican entitled "To Live: Why?" It was a three-day summit to talk about the role of faith and the Catholic Church in tackling these big scientific questions. Redfield was selected to give a presentation to Pope John Paul II, and at the conclusion of the gathering he was granted another meeting with the religious leader. It was a transformational moment for him, and suddenly his whole outlook changed. He felt a spiritual connection with the pope that would guide him and his work. He came away from it believing strongly in the power of prayer.

Redfield rose to the rank of lieutenant colonel and immersed himself in the military's efforts to find a vaccine for HIV. He quickly became enthusiastic about a vaccine developed by MicroGeneSys, a small upstart Connecticut company, that was promoted aggressively by Shepherd Smith, an evangelical activist who ran Americans for a Sound AIDS/HIV Policy, or ASAP. Redfield was on ASAP's advisory board, and Smith would visit him at Walter Reed. A number of government scientists found Redfield's coziness with ASAP disconcerting.

In 1990, Redfield wrote the introduction to Smith's book, *Christians in the Age of AIDS*, in which Smith claimed that AIDS was "God's judgment" against gay people. "It is time to reject the temptation of denial of the AIDS/HIV crisis; to reject false prophets who preach the quick-fix strategies of condoms and free needles; to reject those who preach prejudice; and to reject those who try to replace God as judge. The time has come for the Christian community—members and leaders alike—to confront the epidemic," he wrote. In testimony before Congress, he also argued that single-parent households created more opportunities for numerous sexual partners and that abstaining from sex until marriage was the most effective way—though not the only way—to prevent infection.

Redfield made international headlines in 1992 when he attended a conference in Amsterdam and told an audience of researchers that the MicroGeneSys vaccine was showing promise. That alarmed other vaccine researchers at Walter Reed, who said there was no such evidence and panned Redfield's interpretation of the data. Redfield's apparent promotion of MicroGeneSys' vaccine led to a huge scandal within the army, triggering an investigation. Redfield was eventually cleared of wrongdoing, with investigators saying that his comments had been misinterpreted (the vaccine did not show promise, however).

The experience scarred Redfield. He felt the sting of jealous backbiting, believing that his words had been twisted and misconstrued. His leadership at Walter Reed had not always been gracious. He could be stern and mean and had developed some enemies. Even though the investigation didn't take him down, he was transferred out of Walter Reed two years later "by mutual agreement with his superiors," and in 1996 he retired from the military with the rank of colonel. His friends, though, say he isn't easily deterred. He can be slow and meandering, a doctor who stops to talk to everyone he sees and enjoys three-hour lunches. But at heart he is a scientist who is endlessly fascinated by viruses and the intricate ways in which they attack. It's what keeps him going. So he kept going.

He continued to devote his life to virology and AIDS research. After leaving the military, he joined the internationally acclaimed biomedical researcher Robert Gallo and cofounded the Institute of Human Virology at the University of Maryland School of Medicine.

He put his career back on track, fostering a reputation as a caring and compassionate doctor who treated people in marginalized and low-income communities. It was clear how genuinely he cared for his patients.

But even in his cushy perch at the University of Maryland, Redfield still longed to follow in his parents' footsteps and work at one of the government's preeminent health agencies. He had been passed over multiple times. In 2018, when the Trump White House called upon Joe Grogan's recommendation, Redfield finally had his chance.

When Redfield's appointment was announced, many of the top CDC scientists were skeptical. The agency, based in Atlanta, is made up mostly of career scientists and has few political appointees apart from its director. One year into his presidency, Donald Trump looked to be one of the most antiscience presidents in modern history. (He had long flirted with the debunked theory that vaccines cause autism, for example.) Many of Redfield's new employees knew all about his support for the MicroGeneSys vaccine and his papers calling for abstinence as the best prevention for HIV. They were serious scientists, many of whom had been at the agency twenty or thirty years and could have made a lot more money working outside of government but had chosen to dedicate their careers to public service. Redfield had no public health experience, nor had he ever overseen an organization anywhere near the size of the CDC.

On his first day there in March 2018, Redfield summoned top CDC officials into a huge auditorium on the second floor of the CDC's Tom Harkin Global Communications Center. Hundreds of people filled the chairs, and CDC officials beamed the event into its satellite offices around the world. Thousands of people were watching.

"I'm standing here in front of the world's premier public health scientists, and I have an opportunity to be part of the team," Redfield told the attendees, his eyes welling with tears. He paused for a moment to collect himself. You could hear a pin drop.

That made an immediate impression on the CDC staff. Some of them were still wary, but they appreciated the humility and grace he was displaying. He wanted to be one of them. He had immense respect for what they did. The job meant the world to him, and he wanted to earn their trust.

In his speech, he also said it was an honor to lead the best "science-based, data-driven agency in the world. I've dreamed of doing this for a long time."

Some agency scientists also agreed with some of Redfield's initial priorities. In his first year at the CDC, he focused intently on helping control an emerging Ebola outbreak in the eastern Democratic Republic of the Congo. He had a vision for global health security that many rallied behind. He helped craft the plan to end HIV in ten years that Trump announced in his 2019 State of the Union address. The fight to end the opioid epidemic was personal to him because his son had almost died of an overdose of cocaine mixed with fentanyl.

There was a brief period where some agency scientists and Redfield were united behind common goals. Then it all came crashing down.

Redfield was a large man with a bald head and white chinstrap beard. He rented an apartment across the street from the agency's headquarters. At one point, he hosted government health officials visiting the agency from Washington. He was enormously proud of his top-floor apartment overlooking the CDC's sprawling campus. "Look at my kingdom," he told them.

He liked to wander around the agency. If he passed twelve security guards on his way to the office each morning, he stopped and talked to each one of them, asking about their families. If his first meeting was at 9:00 a.m., he would show up to the office just two minutes prior. It got to the point where aides would put phantom events onto his morning schedule to get him to arrive earlier. Often he had to be walked from meeting to meeting; otherwise he would drift off somewhere or get lost in a conversation.

It wasn't a sign of laziness or lack of commitment to the agency, his supporters stress. Rather, it was the behavior of a sometimes absent-minded scientist who had finally reached the pinnacle of his career. He wanted to soak in this moment. He wanted every meeting to take longer than it needed to. He wanted to talk about the science in excruciating detail. He wasn't a boot-stomping leader; he was more of a gentle giant. And that left him wholly unprepared for Trump's team of vipers.

Redfield's relationship with Azar got off to a rocky start. He was initially offered a salary of $375,000, among the highest government salaries and higher than those of the HHS secretary, FDA commissioner, and NIH director, all of whom made less than $200,000. Senator Patty Murray, a Democrat from Washington state, wrote to Azar expressing concern about Redfield's pay.

Three or four days after Redfield filled out his paperwork, he was called into Azar's office. HHS was getting media inquiries about Redfield's salary, and Azar told him it wouldn't look good if he was paid so much more than other government employees.

Redfield told Azar that he hadn't taken the job for the money—it was already a massive pay cut from his previous job at the University of Maryland School of Medicine—but because it was his dream job and he believed in the agency's mission. "It's about the mission, not the money," he told Azar. Redfield told Azar he could readjust his salary as he saw fit.

When Redfield received his first paycheck, he found that his salary had been cut—substantially. In fact, Redfield's salary was nearly halved. Redfield thought someone was trying to teach him a lesson about who was in charge.

A diagnostic test, at its core, aims to answer a basic question: Is a person sick? Yes or no. But developing a test to detect a new virus is never a simple endeavor. That process is especially complicated when labs don't have real-life samples of the virus to develop and confirm that their tests work (a process called "validating" a diagnostic test).

When a man who arrived in Seattle from Wuhan on January 15 became the first person in the United States to test positive for the virus, the CDC finally had an actual sample to use. The lack of live virus samples from the Chinese government still significantly delayed the development of diagnostic tests. (At one point in January, the US was prepared to send 500,000 masks and other PPE to China if they shared viral samples. China refused and they were never sent.)

The CDC had successfully developed a diagnostic test for new pathogens for nearly every health crisis in recent memory: the H1N1 flu outbreak in 2009, Ebola in 2014, Zika in 2016. Every time, the test had worked and things had (mostly) gone according to plan. In their pandemic planning exercises, health and government officials had prepared for various scenarios, including numerous ways things could go wrong. None of the scenarios had ever contemplated what to do if the CDC diagnostic test didn't work. The idea was simply unfathomable.

Several other countries were relying on a German test that was distributed by the World Health Organization (the countries began using this test before a review of scientific validation data by the WHO). South Korea, which had seen its first cases around the same time as the United States, had immediately launched an aggressive testing strategy. The country, which had contended with a severe MERS outbreak in 2015, had learned from that experience. The government had invested in testing supplies and technology in advance of the coronavirus outbreak, and its representatives met with about twenty commercial manufacturers in late January to encourage them to make tests. In the early days of the outbreak, South Korea successfully worked with that group of private companies to rapidly develop tests and then embarked on testing thousands of people each day at drive-through sites.

There was no such strategy under way in the United States. Amid all the uncertainty, the government fell back on what it knew: the CDC test. The agency had successfully deployed a test several times before and was confident it would do it again. Redfield and other government officials also expected a number of commercial manufacturers, as well as hospital and academic labs, to eventually produce their own tests, and they thought that would be enough to meet the country's testing needs. In hindsight, it was a brazen move of institutional arrogance.

A CDC microbiologist named Stephen Lindstrom took the lead on developing the test along with his colleague Julie Villanueva. The two had worked together during the 2009 H1N1 flu epidemic, when Lindstrom had led a team that had created the H1N1 test at a breakneck pace, shipping it globally within two weeks. The agency's leaders expected him to replicate that success for the coronavirus test, and at first it seemed as though Lindstrom and Villanueva had yet another successful partnership. Lindstrom's team designed and developed the test in just seven days. The agency publicly touted the rapid development of the test as evidence of the swift government response.

The FDA allowed the CDC to send its test to a handful of designated public health labs before it was authorized for use, believing that the public health emergency outweighed any potential risks. On February 6, the CDC sent two hundred test kits across the country with each kit capable of testing about seven hundred to eight hundred patient samples; that meant roughly 150,000 samples in total.

The CDC test had three key components; two of them looked for specific genetic sequences in the novel coronavirus. If a patient's sample matched either of those sequences, it meant the person had the virus. The third component included a different sequence that would detect the virus if it mutated.

To validate the tests, a lab used both a sample that contained the virus, which should produce a positive result, and a negative control, such as distilled water, which should produce a negative one. On Sunday, February 9, lab technicians in New York City's Department of Health ran the test on samples that contained the virus and saw on their computer screens a curve sloping upward logarithmically, an indication of a positive result. But they got the same result when they ran the test using the negative samples. Something was wrong, and more labs soon began reporting similar false positives.

The problem was with the test's third component, the one that had been designed to detect the coronavirus even if the virus mutated. The CDC was going to have to create an entirely new third component, a process that would take at least a few days. Top CDC officials briefed Redfield on the issue; he took their word about the timing of the design of the new component, and the agency alerted the public to the issues in a telebriefing that week.

"Clearly a success is the CDC rapid development of a diagnostic and rapid deployment to the states, which was clearly important to try to bring the testing closer to patients to avoid delays that have been inherent in sending samples to CDC," Nancy Messonnier, the director of the CDC's National Center for Immunization and Respiratory Diseases, said in a February 12 media briefing. ". . . Speed is important, but equally or more important in this situation is making sure that the laboratory results are correct."

There was a more urgent issue that several officials were beginning to realize: even with the testing problems fixed, the CDC could not supply enough tests for the entire country. Its job was mainly to supply the network of public health labs. To get tests into hospitals, doctors' offices, and other health care settings that were accessible to the broader public, Azar would need to instruct the Biomedical Advanced Research and Development Authority (BARDA, which also falls under HHS) to engage with commercial manufacturers, such as Abbott Laboratories, Roche Diagnostics, and Thermo Fisher. Those were the companies that knew how to mass-produce tests, but they couldn't do it overnight; they needed to start now. Many of the companies, however, did not have the materials they needed to validate their tests.

What's more, the government was not putting up the millions or billions of dollars needed to compel these companies to mass-produce tests. Diagnostics manufacturers had been burned in 2003 during the SARS epidemic, when they had jumped into action to develop tests. When SARS did not end up being as bad as feared in the United States, there was no market for the products the manufacturers had invested in heavily. That was why BARDA needed to get more involved, with enough money to offer purchase agreements— to assure the wary private-sector companies that they wouldn't get burned again.

Azar, however, believed a fix to the CDC test was imminent and did not gather all of the agencies under him together for most of February to make sure the country had enough tests, and coordinate outreach to outside companies to help manufacture more, and different, tests. (He did ask FDA officials about their communications with manufacturers about tests and diagnostics.) He was focused on the CDC test, and his leadership style was not inclusive. When some task force officials floated whether they should be exploring other options to get tests out across the country, Redfield assured them the CDC test would be fixed in no time. (Some government officials argued that it was important to first figure out what was wrong with the CDC test to ensure that other labs and companies did not repeat the same mistakes.) The government was used to relying on the CDC test, and officials were slow to recognize the coronavirus required an entirely different, and more aggressive, approach by bringing in commercial manufacturers early in the outbreak.

Joe Grogan, already skeptical of the health agencies, was growing increasingly distrustful of the assurances Azar and Redfield kept
relaying to the task force. Not only were outside experts informing
him about the extent of the testing problems, but some were telling him that asymptomatic carriers were causing significant spread,
the same warning Matt Pottinger had relayed weeks earlier. At one
meeting, Grogan asked if the reason the United States had so few
cases compared to other countries was that it was testing far fewer
people. Should it be trying to test more people?

"What's the epidemiological basis of that question?" Fauci asked
in response. In other words: What public health reason was there for
testing more people? What data did the government have indicating
that cases weren't being counted? States, cities, and the CDC had
surveillance systems in place to detect whether there was an uptick
in emergency room visits from people with flulike symptoms. But so
far, none of the systems had detected any such activity, giving health
officials a false sense of security that the virus was still at bay in the
United States.

Grogan wasn't sure how to respond. "I'm asking you," he said to
Fauci. "I'm asking you why are you so sure there's no asymptomatic
spread?"

The CDC's systems, so far, were not finding evidence of asymptomatic transmission. But the lack of a working test made it impossible to know for sure. And in reality, thousands of people in densely
populated US cities including New York, Seattle, Boston, San Francisco, and Chicago had already contracted the virus and were silently spreading it.

Azar, who had tried to block Grogan from being on the task force
in the first place and did not understand why he was questioning a
scientist like Fauci, tried to end the debate. He also felt Grogan was
taking an exceedingly condescending tone with the doctors. "You
have to talk to the experts," he said dismissively.

———

The coronavirus was the "big one"—the long-feared pandemic that the US government had spent decades, across multiple administrations, trying to prepare for. Presidents Bill Clinton, George W. Bush, and Barack Obama had all known that a pandemic was inevitable—a matter of when, not if, they'd all said. Yet no administration had ever given the possibility the attention or money that such a public health crisis would warrant. Federal agencies had written playbooks, held planning meetings, and published white papers about how to manage the public health side of a pandemic. Plenty of people appreciated the devastation it could cause and the theoretical amounts of money that would be needed to combat it. But few of those plans or papers had captured the scale to which the 2020 coronavirus would upend everyday life for millions of Americans.

The threat of a pandemic was so well recognized that in the last days of the Barack Obama administration and during the Trump transition, top Obama cabinet officials met with senior Trump administration cabinet nominees in the Eisenhower Executive Office Building as part of a "tabletop" exercise to walk through how to respond to three potential crisis scenarios. They discussed how to respond to a terrorist attack on a soft target like a stadium or mall and what to do in the event of a hurricane or other natural disaster. But Lisa Monaco, who at the time was serving as Obama's top homeland security adviser, said they needed to also work through the scenario of how to respond to a health pandemic. The Obama team had grappled with scares caused by Zika and Ebola—which they learned they were not prepared to deal with—and wanted to make sure Trump's team knew how to respond.

The scenario Monaco and her colleagues presented Trump's team focused on "a new strain of flu" that an existing vaccine could not protect against. A respiratory illness "that will quickly become a global challenge because of the ease of global travel and commerce," she recalled in an interview.

The Obama team walked Trump's incoming advisers through the

need for personal protective equipment, travel restrictions, and possible school closures. And they stressed the need for "regular and fact-based communication."

A key plank of any pandemic plan involved the CDC as a lead agency. Combatting a pandemic would take a lot of money. To combat the virus so far, the White House had been relying on about $105 million left over in a fund that Congress had passed years before to fight the 2014 Ebola outbreak. That money was nearly gone. The government needed to purchase protective equipment such as masks and gloves for health care workers before the global supply ran out. It also needed money to scale up testing. But White House budget officials were resistant. They had just spent billions of taxpayer dollars in a recent budget deal. And now Azar and Redfield, whom officials were already starting to distrust, wanted even more?

Redfield and the CDC got to work developing a testing plan anyway that Azar approved. They wanted $100 million for the first year of the initiative—a request that was quickly shot down by the task force due to its cost. But the proposed plan illustrated the degree to which the CDC and HHS were underestimating how quickly the virus could spread out of control and overwhelm the existing testing infrastructure. It would have relied heavily on the CDC's surveillance networks for several months, and did not outline a way to ensure diagnostic tests got into the places that they were needed most: hospitals, academic labs, and doctor's offices. The CDC still believed that it was superior to the Chinese CDC and could contain the virus. Yet, as other officials had already begun to realize, even if the CDC's test had been developed and deployed flawlessly, it would have not been enough. The scale of the epidemic meant there were testing needs that far surpassed the capabilities of the agency's network of labs. Even the national testing plan the CDC had drawn up didn't envision engaging commercial lab companies for up to six months, underscoring some officials' overconfidence that the US could contain the virus for that long.

Azar's high-handedness and perceived micromanagement were proving to be a constant theme in the dysfunctional response. To others, it seemed that Azar's number one priority was remaining in charge of the task force. Leading the coronavirus response not only seemed to help his standing with the president, but associates said he was haunted by what he saw as HHS's failure to lead the 2014 Ebola response. Obama had brought in Ron Klain, a high-ranking member of several Democratic administrations, to manage the White House's response. Though some experts said that White House coordination was necessary to mobilize and coordinate a full government response, Azar saw it as a cautionary tale. If he did not appear to be in full control of the response, it could be taken away from him and someone else put in charge. Azar did think the Ron Klain model was successful in managing Ebola—and sought Klain's advice in January—but seemed determined that HHS remain in charge.

"We were supposed to say 'We've got the testing thing under control' when we didn't," one official who worked closely with Azar explained. "There was this idea that we can't admit when something's not going the way we want it to. That was a problem. [Azar] really wanted this to be an HHS-managed event, and that I think was a very high priority for him."

But during one meeting, CDC officials finally betrayed the confidence Azar had been projecting. Once again it was Grogan who ambushed them by asking how the testing was going.

One of the CDC officials conceded, for the first time, that the tests didn't work, that they were "all fucked up," one participant recalled.

"I didn't check on this for a week," Grogan told them, incredulous. "I asked, and you said everything was groovy."

Azar, sitting across the table with his face reddening, didn't say a word. When he left the meeting, he blew his stack at the CDC officials. They should have given him a heads-up before they conveyed such deep problems to the White House. Why would they take him by surprise like this? From then on, CDC officials noticed the grip from HHS tightening.

Mid-February was becoming late February, and there was still no fix to the tests. A growing number of people were sick with fevers and coughing fits, but health officials couldn't easily separate those with COVID-19 from those with the flu or just a bad cold. Meantime, the CDC's lab in Atlanta was the only one able to test patient samples, inevitably leading to a backlog and long wait times for test results. Americans were starting to panic, and every cough, every sneeze, every sore throat could be misdiagnosed. Health officials across the country wondered if the inability to test many people was the real reason that relatively few Americans had confirmed cases. What if the US numbers were much higher? they wondered.

The FDA felt woefully out of the loop. The CDC had been assuring the agency's regulators that the problems with the tests were limited to a handful of labs. So FDA leaders were curious when they read in a February 20 *Politico* article that only three of the more than one hundred public health labs across the country were able to use the CDC test. Redfield did not seem to have a handle on his agency. He could not explain what was taking so long.

FDA leaders grew even more concerned the following day, when CDC officials traveled from Atlanta to visit with FDA leaders at their Silver Spring, Maryland, headquarters. During that meeting, CDC officials told the FDA that they still did not know the root cause of the issues with the agency's test; they were still trying to determine whether it was a manufacturing or design issue. The difference between a manufacturing issue and a design issue was no small one. A manufacturing issue could be more easily resolved; new parts of the test could simply be produced. But a design problem was much more difficult to solve.

In response, the FDA decided to send Timothy Stenzel, its director of the Office of In Vitro Diagnostics and Radiological Health, down to the CDC's lab in Atlanta to figure out what was going so wrong. FDA director Stephen Hahn called Redfield to let him know, and Redfield gave Stenzel access to all relevant CDC facilities related to the test to hopefully get to the bottom of the problem. When Stenzel gained access to three key labs developing the test, he couldn't believe what he saw. In two of the three labs, the agency wasn't following standard operating procedures. And he discovered the CDC had put together the test in the same lab where it was running the test on live virus samples. That was a violation of the most basic manufacturing practices, greatly increasing the chance that the test could become contaminated with pieces of the virus. That could explain why the lab technicians were getting false positives. And no one person was in charge of the process.

The testing problem had grown so far out of hand that health agency leaders recognized they could no longer depend solely on the CDC. During a meeting in Azar's conference room in late February with several top health officials, the CDC again said a fix would be ready in a week to ten days. This was the third week the agency had said a fix was coming in a matter of days. Azar got visibly angry and banged the table with his hand. "What the hell is going on here?" he asked. He instructed his chief of staff, Brian Harrison, to get matters fixed.

On February 27, HHS asked the FDA, CDC, NIH, and other agencies for options to increase the country's testing capacity and availability. The first call that day was less than productive. Everyone was pointing fingers, trying to pin the blame of the testing debacle on any agency other than their own.

Finally, the FDA had enough. "If you were a commercial entity," said Jeffrey Shuren, the FDA's director of the Center for Devices and Radiological Health, to CDC officials, "I would shut you down."

Brian Harrison held a subsequent conference call with Redfield, Kadlec, Fauci, and a handful of others. Redfield blamed the FDA for limiting the number of tests available across the country, arguing that the agency should have let academic labs and hospitals build and use their own tests right away. One official on the call grabbed his cell phone and texted the FDA chief of staff, Keagan Lenihan, to inform her that Redfield was throwing the FDA under the bus. He suggested to Harrison that the FDA be added to the call. Moments later, Commissioner Hahn and a handful of other FDA leaders were patched through.

For more than thirty minutes, Hahn and Redfield argued about the source of the testing problem.

Harrison, exasperated by all the bickering, grabbed the cell phone he was using to listen to the conference call. "I'm going to put this in a closet until you figure this out," he told Hahn and Redfield. The CDC and FDA spent another two or three hours trying to hash out how to move forward while Harrison's phone sat in the closet. For three weeks, the CDC—and Azar—had been focused on fixing the test, hoping it wouldn't take long, so the country could rely on it, as the CDC had done in every other public health crisis. But by the end of the phone call, they agreed that the country needed other options. They proposed that the FDA put out a guidance that would allow labs to use their own tests developed in-house after the labs ensured that the tests worked and while they waited for an FDA emergency-use authorization. A small group of FDA and CDC officials developed the proposal, which they sent to Azar for approval the following day. On February 29, the White House cleared the new guidance. But they had wasted nearly an entire month.

Researchers would later find that through mid-February, the United States had a critical window where it could have prevented a catastrophic outbreak of COVID-19 from taking hold. But that precious time had been squandered trying to figure out how to fix a CDC test that was never going to be the solution to a rapidly spreading virus. Even if the development and deployment of the test had gone perfectly, the United States would still have fallen behind. The CDC and its network of labs never had enough capacity to keep up with the virus's rapid spread.

The United States lacked a national testing strategy, one that agency leaders could implement and execute in early February. That strategy wasn't rocket science, but it did require focus and money, two things the US pandemic response was sorely lacking. Like South Korea, senior US administration officials would have had to reach out to a handful of diagnostic manufacturers—the companies that created such tests day in and day out—and focus on mass-producing the tests, either through government funding or guaranteed purchasing and reimbursement, to get them to as many labs, hospitals, and clinics across the country as possible. Hahn, the FDA commissioner, had in fact wanted to reach out to those companies in late January and early February, but FDA leaders had been split on whether it would be bad optics for Hahn to be personally calling the companies he regulated. Hahn eventually got the green light to reach out to these executives in mid-February, after a direct conversation with Azar. But that meant no one high up in the government and health leadership had engaged with the commercial companies for the first few weeks of the outbreak in one of many missed opportunities. (Under the Trump administration, no national COVID-19 testing strategy was ever developed, despite the persistent and pressing need for one.)

The CDC test was not the only issue with the United States' pandemic response in February. The government had taken several unprecedented steps, including invoking the first federal quarantine authority in more than sixty years. That meant it had to find housing on military bases and in other facilities across the country for the hundreds of Americans it was repatriating from China and cruise ships and requiring to quarantine for fourteen days. It was an enormously time-consuming, politically complicated task—and a logistical nightmare.

More broadly, the task force and US government had spent all of February focused on the problem of the day, the problem right in front of them. They had squabbled over cruise ships and faulty tests. They spent a lot of time chasing headlines. There had been no serious efforts to prepare for what was to come, no effort to think two or three steps ahead to what the country needed to deal with the way an outbreak could unfold. For example, even though the flawed CDC tests were finally fixed, there was still no way to test large numbers of Americans and receive the results in a timely fashion. The virus would spread much faster than the limited testing capabilities could track.

A troubling pattern had emerged in the Trump administration's response: it was constantly four weeks, or more, behind the virus. The cost of that became abundantly clear on February 26, when the CDC announced the news that health officials had been dreading: a woman in Vacaville, California, had tested positive for the virus. There had already been some US cases, but she was the first person who hadn't traveled to China or come into contact with a person known to have the virus.

That meant the virus had not been contained. It had not been quarantined. It was on the move. And US officials had nowhere near enough tests to track it down.

CHAPTER 5

THE PANIC

February 23, 2020

CONFIRMED US COVID-19 CASES: **30**

CONFIRMED US COVID-19 DEATHS: **0**

In 2016, Donald Trump picked perhaps the best time to run for president on a message of nationalism. Seven years after the global financial crisis, the US economy had shown signs of stalling out. An oversupply of petroleum had caused oil prices to plunge. Oil companies had stopped spending and cut jobs. Farm revenues had also fallen sharply. Slowdowns in the energy, agriculture, and manufacturing sectors had hung an anvil around the economy's neck. In 2016, the economy grew by just 1.6 percent, the worst pace since 2011.

Many US companies were still hiring, but employees' wages didn't rise much. The unemployment rate was low, at 4.7 percent, down from the 2009 peak of 10 percent, but there was a sense that the economy was limping along and the post-2009 recovery had run out of steam. On July 13, 2015, the Dow Jones Industrial Average closed at 18,086. One year later, it closed at 18,517, having gained less than 500 points in a year, or an average of less than 2 points a day. Many voters, particularly white, middle-class voters in midwestern states, soured on the Democrats' promise that prosperity would arrive if they would only be patient. Maybe, they felt, Democrats didn't have all the answers after all.

Enter Donald Trump. His economic message was fairly simple: the American middle class was getting screwed by other countries, both political parties, and the "swamp," a term he coined to refer to lobbyists and special interest groups that bent public policy to their will. He vowed to tear it all down and start from scratch. America first.

The Obama administration had helped lead the United States out of the Great Recession, but the economic platform of Hillary Clinton, Trump's 2016 rival, didn't seem much different from Barack Obama's. Many people envisioned more of the same: a low-wage, sluggish economic future. It wasn't as electrifying as what Trump was promising, even if he was overpromising.

Manufacturing jobs in Michigan, Wisconsin, and Pennsylvania—states long known as the "Blue Wall" because of their long-standing support for Democrats—kept disappearing. Trump's message appealed to those voters. And many union workers, who had supported Democrats for years, liked what they heard from the politically incorrect showman. He won over many steelworkers and autoworkers who were sick of seeing their jobs vanish to China and Mexico. It didn't take much to tip the election. He won those three states by a combined 77,744 votes, enough to make him the forty-fifth president of the United States.

Once he became president in January 2017, Trump's economic stewardship played out in three ways: browbeating, policy changes, and skyrocketing government debt. He publicly berated companies that threatened to move jobs overseas and publicly feted companies that promised to create jobs in the United States. Some companies were so desperate to stay out of his crosshairs that they *reannounced* hiring plans they had already announced during the Obama administration just to try to win his praise. And it often worked.

Trump promised a business-friendly agenda: tax cuts, deregulation, low energy prices. (He had no idea how low they would end up going.) And a new trade agenda that he claimed would create millions of American jobs and lure companies back from overseas.

On December 22, 2017, Trump signed the Tax Cuts and Jobs Act into law. It amounted to a $1.5 trillion tax cut that he claimed would create millions of jobs and boost the US economy. The law was a giant—and permanent—tax cut for businesses and a sizable—but temporary—one for households and families. It was a huge achievement, something Republicans had tried to do since the Reagan administration, but it had been pushed into law so fast that the government had never conducted a serious analysis or review of its potential impact. The cuts weren't, in fact, based on solid economics but rather on a long-held belief among conservatives that cutting taxes would automatically lead to tremendous economic growth, no matter what. They were horribly mistaken.

Still, business groups that had chomped at the bit for the tax cuts lined up to announce their support. Dozens of companies pumped out press releases touting the onetime bonuses they would give employees. Apple pledged to contribute $350 billion in the US economy and create twenty thousand new jobs within five years.

There was a sense that maybe Trump was onto something.

He immediately put Americans' goodwill to the test. On March 1, 2018, less than three months after he signed the tax law, he kicked off an aggressive trade war, threatening to end the United States' free-trade stance. It pitted the United States against all other countries with a pledge to impose tariffs on all steel and aluminum imports into the United States. Trump argued that foreign countries were flooding the United States with cheap processed metal, destroying the US manufacturers of such products. There was some truth to that, but it wasn't that simple. A number of US smelters that made steel and aluminum had indeed closed in recent years because China was pumping the world full of low-cost materials. But much of that cheap metal was being sold at low prices to US manufacturers. So by driving up the prices of those products, he might be helping some US companies, but he would be hurting others. Trump ignored the blowback. "When a country (USA) is losing many billions of dollars on trade with virtually every country it does business with, trade wars are good, and easy to win," he tweeted on March 2.

Trump had pivoted sharply from a 2017 agenda of tax cuts and economic growth to a 2018 agenda of winner-take-all-global-trade-war-hungry-hungry-hippo-incredible-hulk. His strategy was simple: he would use, or perhaps abuse, US trade law to create so much financial pressure through tariffs that other countries would capitulate. If they wanted to sell their products in the United States, they would have to buy more US products, such as wheat, corn, and pork. If they didn't, he would jack up the tariffs on the products they exported to the United States. US farmers and manufacturers were caught in the middle and became collateral damage, but Trump urged patience. The ploy was ruthless and seemed to stretch the law, but it got everyone's attention, which was the point.

Trump felt he was playing with house money. He had given Americans a giant tax cut, and the economy had some tailwind. If he was to launch a trade war, 2018 was the time to do it. During the campaign, he had promised to crack down on China and rip up the North American Free Trade Agreement. A trade war would give him the opportunity to do both.

Tactically, Trump would fight the trade war the same way he had conducted business deals throughout his life: he would create a tremendous amount of leverage over his adversaries (in this case, other countries) to make them cave in to his demands. For that to work, he couldn't simply declare a trade war against another country; he would have to single out the country's leader to apply pressure, make it personal. Trump's trade war had multiple fronts—he was obsessed with Canada's handsome prime minister, Justin Trudeau, for example—but much of his attention was focused on China's president, Xi Jinping.

In April 2017, Xi flew to the United States for his first meeting with Trump at Mar-a-Lago, Trump's home turf. This wasn't about reworking the relationship between China and the United States; it was about reworking Xi's relationship with Trump, and Trump wanted to show off to him. The purpose of the meeting was to launch a discussion about North Korea and the US-China trade relationship.

But as the two leaders dined with their spouses at Mar-a-Lago on that April night, eating Dover sole with champagne sauce and a dry-aged New York strip steak, the White House had a surprise: Trump had quietly authorized air strikes against Syria, which were being conducted while he was sitting at dinner with Xi. The strikes were meant to punish Syrian president Bashar al-Assad for using chemical weapons against his own people, but the timing couldn't have been better for Trump. China had been a defender of Assad, helping him stay in power in the face of international pressure after he had killed thousands of his own citizens. The dinner therefore sent a clear signal to the Chinese: Trump was more than willing to explore the boundaries of his power and to rewrite the United States' relationship with China, even as he was seated across the table from Xi, forking a piece of steak into his mouth.

So by March 2018, when Trump began in earnest to execute his trade war with China, he had already made an impression on Xi. The Chinese government was used to dealing with US presidents, but it hadn't encountered one as unpredictable as Trump in modern times. Trump wanted instant capitulation by Beijing, but that isn't how China works. Still, Trump's trade war posed a big risk to China's fragile economy.

In 2017, the United States exported $130 billion in goods to China, such as aircraft and automobiles. In return, China exported $505 billion in goods to the United States, including furniture, machinery, toys, and sporting equipment. It was one of the largest trading relationships in the world, but Trump felt it was out of whack. Trade policy is inherently complicated, but he saw it as numbers on two sides of a ledger. Why was the United States buying more Chinese products than the other way around? Imposing tariffs was Trump's way to create leverage, to force China to buckle.

If he drove up the tariffs on Chinese imports, they would become less attractive to US consumers, weakening demand and hurting China's giant manufacturing sector. His tactics might be reckless and legally dubious, but they would surely do some damage. What he didn't seem to grasp was that the Chinese wouldn't simply cave in to his demands.

Trump and Xi spent much of 2018 locked in a trade war, firing tariff salvos back and forth. On September 17, Trump imposed tariffs on $200 billion in Chinese imports to the United States, releasing a 194-page list of products that included everything from live eels to refrigerators. China responded by slapping tariffs on imports of soybeans and a range of other products from the United States. American farmers went bananas, but the Chinese weren't backing down. "Our door is open for the resumption of trade consultations and negotiations, but to make the negotiations effective, they should be based on mutual respect and treating each other as equals," China's vice minister of commerce, Wang Shouwen, told reporters in September 2018. "But the US has imposed such large trade restrictions, it is like they are holding a knife to our neck."

Trump seemed to delight in the trade war, but it was wearing on parts of the US economy. Even with the generous new tax cuts, many businesses halted investing, unsure of what his next move would be. The Dow Jones Industrial Average, Trump's favored barometer of success, had climbed to 26,149 by January 31, 2018 (it had been around 19,000 when he had been elected in 2016), but his trade war put investors into sell mode. On November 23, 2018, the Dow closed at just 24,286, having lost nearly 2,000 points since January. China's stock market was faring even worse; it had shed almost 25 percent of its value in 2018, something Trump frequently gloated about, believing he had China in a stranglehold.

On December 1, 2018, Trump and Xi met again, this time in Buenos Aires, Argentina, during the Group of 20 summit with other world leaders. There, they agreed to pause the trade war. Trump halted the looming tariffs, and the White House said that Xi had agreed to formal negotiations over ninety days. It seemed, perhaps, as though Trump's big game of chicken had finally worked.

But the next year proved to be sort of a mess. Trump had over-promised and said a trade deal was imminent. It wasn't. The Chinese had not agreed to anything; it wasn't even clear if they had agreed to talks or not. (The Argentina "announcement" was exposed as half baked almost immediately when Trump's top advisers couldn't explain whether the ninety-day negotiating window had begun on December 1 or January 1. The Chinese, meanwhile, wouldn't even acknowledge that a ninety-day deadline existed.) The deadline came and went. Nothing. Trump fumed. It was embarrassing. On August 1, he said he would impose tariffs on $300 billion in Chinese products, including things such as cell phones, computers, pillows, and toilet seats. China didn't flinch. Trump was running out of cudgels and began to flail more publicly. Two weeks later, he pressured Treasury secretary Steven Mnuchin to label China a "currency manipulator," a rather meaningless label but one that was meant to sting. Once again, Chinese officials didn't blink.

By the end of the month, the Dow was stuck at 26,000. So many business executives had become horrified by Trump's trade war that they had stopped hiring, and the US manufacturing sector had begun contracting. To make matters worse, the Federal Reserve was refusing Trump's demands to slash interest rates.

It was just fifteen months until election day, and there was a sense that Trump had lost his handle. The United States was somehow exporting *less* to China in 2019 than it had in any other year since 2011. Things were going in the wrong direction. Xi had called Trump's bluff.

Searching for victories, even artificial ones, in the lead-up to the November 2020 elections, Trump's team dramatically scaled back their goals in the trade talks with China. In January 2020, they agreed to a slimmed-down pact with Beijing that would do little to rebalance the two countries' trade relationship but did allow Trump to hold an event in the White House East Room, ten months before his reelection, during which he touted the partial agreement as a validation of his hardball strategy. He was never interested in specifics or nuances, and he knew many voters wouldn't be, either. He was more focused on the spectacle. He wanted to put on a show, and it couldn't come at a more opportune moment. The ceremony was held the same day House lawmakers presented Trump's two articles of impeachment to the Senate for a trial. Trump wanted to show that he was moving on, that the impeachment trial wasn't holding him back.

By February, with all that behind him, the Dow Jones Industrial Average hit its highest level ever. For all the chaos and rancor of Trump's first term, many in the administration knew the election would hinge primarily on the country's economic performance. All of a sudden, Trump looked to be in a strong position, maybe even untouchable.

That all changed the week beginning Sunday, February 23, a week that unfolded like a complicated play performed by multiple actors on multiple stages in multiple countries.

Washington, D.C.
Peter Navarro hadn't told anyone at the White House that he was going to appear on television that morning, but so went the special arrangement he had with President Trump. The former economics professor was allowed to go on any show he wanted, say anything he wanted, the more provocative, the better. He had Trump's blessing, and that was all he needed.

So there he was, seated bolt upright in a television studio, his gray-and-white hair straight back, as if he were from a different era. His light blue shirt and navy-and-red-striped tie were crisp on his tight seventy-one-year-old frame, chiseled by decades of intense exercise and abstinence from alcohol. Staring into television cameras was his Zen. He had been doing so for nearly thirty years, going back to when he had hosted *Navarro's News Behind the News* on public access television in San Diego. He had gotten better at concealing the smirk that had gotten him into trouble so many years before; he had replaced it with a Clint Eastwood squint.

Many White House officials reviled Navarro and tried to ignore his appearances on television, so as to not become caught up in what they believed was cringe-inducing, factually dubious babble. But Trump loved having his top trade adviser, who loathed China with his every cell, on television. Trump didn't like nuance; he liked fire-breathers. And Navarro was his dragon.

So that weekend, Navarro—sans approved talking points—had booked himself on Fox News' *Sunday Morning Futures*, a reliably pro-Trump news program. He immediately launched into the type of anti-China screed that had gotten him onto Trump's radar ten years earlier. Navarro's words were aggressive and dark. He said that the Chinese had commandeered a US-controlled mask factory and that other countries would likely try to stiff the United States as well. The virus was very bad, Navarro said, and only Trump could save Americans from its wrath. "For the American people, they need to understand that in crises like this we have no allies," he said.

Crises? No one at the White House was supposed to be calling the coronavirus mess a crisis. Navarro ended the interview by driving home his point: "This, again, is a crisis."

White House aides hadn't caught the program live, but they soon heard about his message of gloom and doom. The country was already on edge about the virus. Workplaces all over the country had begun posting signs imploring people to wash their hands. Stores were selling out of hand sanitizer. Coughing in public was quickly becoming a sin. Navarro was one of the first White House officials to go on television and acknowledge that a storm was coming. What was he doing? Trump had made clear to aides that they weren't supposed to betray any concern about the virus in public. But here was

Navarro talking about the need for masks, vaccines, and other emergency medical supplies. There were still no recorded US deaths and only a few dozen confirmed cases, all of whom had served some sort of quarantine. The White House wanted people to believe it was an Asian problem, irrespective of the poor US souls on the *Diamond Princess*.

Navarro was an expert at working a public game through media appearances and then operating behind the scenes inside the White House to be as provocative as possible. When he unclipped the microphone from his tie and removed his earpiece after the interview, his day had only just begun.

He had recently authored and circulated an unsigned "Memorandum to President." It was quickly shared with the National Security Council, the chief of staff's office, and the entire White House Coronavirus Task Force, though he was careful not to put his name on it. He would later claim sole credit for the memo, but he had in fact consulted with numerous government health officials while drafting it. In mid-February—at the same time the administration was consumed with the *Diamond Princess* debacle—he had asked task force member Robert Kadlec and his deputy assistant secretary and chief of staff, Bryan Shuy, to meet with him in his office in the Eisenhower Executive Office Building. As the leader of the Office of the Assistant Secretary for Preparedness and Response, an agency under HHS that was responsible for the Strategic National Stockpile of emergency medical equipment and supplies, Kadlec was a key source for Navarro in determining what supply chain issues the United States might encounter in the face of a large virus outbreak.

Kadlec and Shuy, a longtime House appropriations staffer, showed up to the Sunday meeting each wearing a suit and a tie. It was their first formal encounter with Navarro, who was clad in gym shorts and a workout shirt. "Guys, you could've been casual," Navarro said. "It's a weekend."

Navarro was a strange character for traditional government

bureaucrats such as Kadlec and Shuy to be teaming up with. But health officials were fully aware that the Strategic National Stockpile of supplies such as masks and gloves was inadequate and were hoping to get the White House to allocate more money for medical supplies before the global supply evaporated. Many of the suppliers were located in China, which had had to shut down several factories after the outbreak, and other countries would be competing to purchase the lifesaving equipment. Navarro wanted to push the White House for more money, and Kadlec and Shuy sensed that he might successfully get the president's attention to advocate for more money. It was worth a shot.

The meeting, initially scheduled for one hour, went on for more than three. Navarro, scribbling on a whiteboard, did the lion's share of the talking, hounding Kadlec and Shuy with questions. "How much does this cost? I'll look on Amazon," he'd say in reference to an N95 mask or other piece of equipment. Kadlec and Shuy would gently explain that that wasn't how they determined prices. "How many do we need?"

The first line of the unsigned Navarro memo was ominous, as it was meant to be: "There is an increasing probability of a full-blown COVID-19 pandemic that could infect as many as 100 million Americans, with a loss of life of as many as 1–2 million souls."

That would mean nearly one out of every three Americans would become sick, making it perhaps the most infectious disease in US history. And Navarro was predicting that more Americans would die of COVID-19 than had died in both world wars and the Vietnam War combined (a prediction that in the end looked to be correct).

The memo called for the White House to ask Congress for $3 billion in emergency aid. It said the United States would likely need 1 billion face masks. (The memo came at the same time that Azar and White House budget hawks were battling over how much money to ask Congress for to address the emerging health crisis. Azar had requested $4.8 billion, an amount White House aides thought was outrageous. The administration ended up sending a $2.5 billion request—Azar was scheduled to testify at several hearings and refused to go to the Hill without an official request—which was pilloried by both Republican and Democratic lawmakers as insufficient.)

The memo quickly made the rounds through an increasingly jittery cadre of White House aides. "The memo, even to me, felt very jarring," said one of the first people inside the West Wing who read it. That person recalled thinking, "If this gets out, the public is going to panic."

Still, the growing number of news reports about the virus made aides nervous. They passed around Navarro's memo on Air Force One as the president was preparing to land in India.

Monday, February 24
Ahmedabad, India
Trump's hulking 250-pound frame leaned awkwardly on a small platform near the floor, smiling as he fumbled with the charkha, a type of wheel that spins cotton. He was in one of the homes of Mahatma Gandhi for part of a thirty-six-hour barnstorm through India. He was there to humor the country's prime minister, Narendra Modi, but draped near the floor with his baggy suit, metallic yellow tie, and orange-tinted facial toner, he looked rather ridiculous. His wife, Melania, stood nearby, her face locked in a giddy smile.

Trump detested foreign travel. A couple of weeks earlier, his aides had been debating whether it was even safe for the team to make the trip, and Trump had immediately jumped at the opportunity to cancel it. Inside the White House, people were growing more worried about the virus getting close to the president. After all, a group of Chinese officials had come to the White House in mid-January to sign the trade deal, just as the virus had been ravaging Wuhan and spreading to the rest of the country.

As much as he hated going overseas, Trump despised even more the idea of being away from the action. And the action on that day

was in the United States. But Modi had promised him a huge celebration with maybe 10 million jubilant guests, and Trump couldn't
say no to that.

The president eventually rose from the ground and was whisked
away to a megarally with Modi and 100,000 spectators. They
chanted, "Namaste Trump" ("Hello, Trump" in Hindi). Trump
looked jubilant. He was obsessed with big crowds and this would be
one of the biggest that had ever gathered for him.

The happy celebration was completely divorced from what was
happening back in the United States. A few hours later, as several
Trump aides gathered for dinner on their final night in India, they
stared at their phones. The Dow Jones Industrial Average had fallen
1,032 points. They knew Trump would have a fit when he found out.
American voters were starting to believe the dire predictions about
the virus and not the hand-wavy dismissals Trump had offered for
more than a month. The president's advisers knew someone had to
tell him, but everyone was afraid to.

The stock market crash must be Navarro's fault, surmised some
of the aides, many of whom resented the fact that he could go on TV
and say whatever he wanted. They also resented his special status.

"Peter, are you getting everything you want?" Trump would ask
Navarro from time to time. "I am now!" Navarro would reply. Now
they were paying the price for his rhetoric.

Once Trump became aware of the precipitous stock market de-
cline, he quickly dashed off a Twitter post to calm things down, but
it was like holding an umbrella in a monsoon. "The Coronavirus is
very much under control in the USA," he wrote. "We are in contact
with everyone and all relevant countries. CDC & World Health have
been working hard and very smart. Stock Market starting to look
very good to me!"

Even though the stock market had fallen sharply on Monday, it
hadn't found its floor. It wasn't even close.

Just after noon in India, before Washingtonians woke up, Trump held a press conference in New Delhi. His tone was slightly different. For the first time publicly, he acknowledged that the virus was starting to move, to spread. "Now you see it's going to South Korea, it's going to Italy, and it's going to other places," he said. "But I spoke to all of them. They're all working very, very hard on it."

It wasn't a threat to the United States, he emphasized, brushing aside the fears that had begun to engulf his advisers. He said that there were only around ten sick people in the United States at that time, and "most of the people are outside of danger right now." (There were actually around forty-five confirmed cases of coronavirus in the United States at the time, but Trump still refused to acknowledge the thirty-five who had been disembarked from cruise ships or repatriated.)

Trump's rosy assurances that the virus would just—*poof!*— disappear were meant to convince Americans and Wall Street, in particular, that there was nothing to fear. (Seven months later, he would tell reporters that even though he had known that the virus was deadly and was going to spread, he wasn't going to "jump up and down in the air and start saying 'People are going to die! People are going to die!' No. No. I'm not going to do that.") He wanted people to think that everything was under control. That was a common Trump tactic: exude confidence even in the face of a crisis, and perhaps you can outlast it. But his words were ringing increasingly hollow.

And no matter how often health officials told him that the virus would inevitably come to the United States, on some fundamental level, Trump refused to believe it. In his three years as president, he had been engulfed by one scandal after another, several threatening to undo his presidency. But so far, he had been able to will everything and everyone into submission. Almost every congressional Republican stood by him through impeachment, through the Mueller Report, even through his incendiary remarks after white supremacists had marched through Charlottesville in 2017. He was convinced that the virus would be no different.

Back in Washington, Trump's health officials knew they had lost the battle to contain the virus. All month long, they had been debating when to switch from containment, the phase in which you isolate and contact trace every single case to prevent the virus from spreading, to mitigation, when the virus is in the community and officials must take steps to slow its spread. A growing chorus of outside health experts had been calling for mitigation steps for weeks, but many CDC officials remained convinced for much of February that it could keep the virus at bay. (The lack of tests masked the disease's true spread.)

The prior Friday, the task force members had convened a two-hour meeting to determine whether it was time to switch from containment to mitigation. They had looked at a big map of the United States showing where the cases were. There was clearly community spread in Santa Clara, California, and the virus seemed to be taking hold in New York City and Seattle. They decided that it was time to move to the next phase in those cities. They would start by limiting or shutting down public transportation, closing schools, and moving everyone they could to remote work.

The health officials and Acting Chief of Staff Mick Mulvaney agreed that they would sit down with Trump when he returned from India to get his sign-off on mitigation measures in those cities. The intervention-style meeting was on Trump's calendar for Wednesday, February 26 at 5:00 p.m., but all hell would break loose well before then.

At 11:30 a.m. on Tuesday, Nancy Messonnier, the director of the CDC's National Center for Immunization and Respiratory Diseases, held a telebriefing with reporters. She had been giving routine briefings like this since January, updating the public on the status of the virus. But her tone that wintry morning was decidedly different. Aware of the determination by health officials that community spread had already begun, she began reading carefully scripted remarks; she was measured but catatonic. She essentially said efforts to keep the virus out of the United States would not work anymore; the virus would not be stopped. "As more and more countries experience community spread, successful containment at our borders becomes harder and harder," she said. "Ultimately, we expect we will see community spread in this country. It's not so much a matter of if this will happen anymore but rather more a question of exactly when this will happen and how many people in this country will have severe illness."

Messonnier was a career government official, a doctor, but she had witnessed the vicious politics of Washington first hand. Her brother, Rod Rosenstein, had been Trump's first deputy attorney general and a constant target of White House attacks for not intervening to stop Robert Mueller's investigation into Trump's ties to Russia. Her comments that morning were both surgical and devastating, the kind of words a doctor delivers to a patient who faces a grim diagnosis but needs to hear the straight truth.

"Disruption to everyday life may be severe. But these are things that people need to start thinking about now."

Severe disruptions? Severe illnesses?

The Dow Jones Industrial Average fell another 879 points, bringing the total drop to almost 2,000 points in two days.

Her remarks might have shocked the public that day, but they reflected the conversations that government officials had been having for nearly three weeks, across all the major agencies—the CDC, HHS, the NSC, the State Department, and the DHS. As much as everyone wanted to believe that the United States could contain the virus and would not become the next China or Italy, all the evidence pointed to the opposite conclusion.

CDC officials had informed senior political leaders at HHS that Messonnier was going to talk about mitigation that day, but her frank assessment of how drastically life would change was, of course, the polar opposite of the message the president was trying to send. Shortly after she wrapped up her briefing, Air Force One was barreling toward the United States, and one ballistic passenger on board called Azar to chew him out. Another relatively aloof White House official, seeing Messonnier's name all over the news, assumed that she was French. (Born Nancy Rosenstein, she had taken the last name of her husband, Mark Messonnier, when they had married.) As most of the other aides on the plane slept, Hogan Gidley, the White House deputy press secretary, began yelling, "The French woman is scaring everyone! The French woman is scaring everyone!" jerking some aides awake.

Messonnier's true but terrifying comments had blown up the plan to brief Trump later that week. Inside the White House, aides watched in horror as the stock market fell sharply amid headlines about Messonnier's warnings.

"People have their televisions on and there were a lot of comments that the stock market is going down the shitter, basically," Olivia Troye, Mike Pence's homeland security, counterterrorism, and coronavirus adviser, who was inside the White House that day, recalled in an interview. "She's just telling the truth. After that, the hammer comes down, and basically it's like, 'We have to get our messaging under control.'"

At this point, there were two crises playing out simultaneously.

First, the virus. Millions of Americans had begun obsessively washing their hands, but they didn't fully understand that the virus was spreading through the air, through breathing, wisping in through noses and windpipes.

Second, fear. A terrifying picture of the virus was emerging, one that was much different from the no-big-deal scenario Trump and his aides were trying to convey. Trump's lies were beginning to catch up with them. Whom could the public trust?

White House officials quickly launched a disorganized, desperate attempt to walk back Messonnier's briefing and downplay the virus once again.

Knowing Trump would be furious at the stock market plunge, Larry Kudlow, a longtime friend of Trump who was serving as director of the National Economic Council, quickly booked himself on CNBC, the cable network that many traders watch, to try to talk the market back up. "We have contained this," he assured viewers about the virus. "I won't say airtight, but pretty close to airtight. We have done a good job in the United States."

Azar, meanwhile, knew he would have to do damage control at an already planned press conference scheduled for that afternoon. He had initially intended to provide a status update and reiterate that the risk to Americans remained low. Anne Schuchat, the CDC's principal deputy director and a highly respected career government scientist, would also attend. "We believe the immediate risk here in the United States remains low, and we're working hard to keep that risk low," she said that afternoon.

But her comments were ignored. Americans could see right through them. Fear had consumed Wall Street and large parts of Washington. Trump had already sown distrust among much of the country by repeatedly waving away the threat of the virus. Now many Americans were becoming increasingly anxious about what was coming.

February 26
Before dawn, Air Force One neared Joint Base Andrews in Maryland, and the long trek back from India was almost over. Trump had stripped his tie off hours earlier, not having slept during the entire flight. (Mulvaney would later say that Trump had stayed awake for thirty-six hours straight, consumed by the brewing crisis.) It was in the early morning hours that Trump was at his most raw. His Twitter posts at the start of each day, while many of his aides were asleep and

he was usually alone, stewing, were often full of misspelled words and vicious attacks. It was when his rage burned brightest.

What had happened while he had been gone on the brief trip to India? The S&P 500 stock market index had hit a record level just *one week* earlier. And now everyone had panicked? Why? He called Azar before the plane landed, furious over Messonnier's briefing and the resulting stock market crash. "We've got to get out there!" he told Azar. "We've got to calm people down!"

Trump felt he needed to make a change. To take control of the message, he needed someone who would be a cheerleader, no matter what. It was clear that Azar couldn't be the head of the task force anymore.

While Azar had labored through three briefings on Capitol Hill that day, White House aides debated who should take over. Trump called Azar during a break in the House Committee on Energy and Commerce hearing. "We have to stem the bleeding," Trump told him. "I've gotta look active. I have to look like we're taking this seriously."

What Trump didn't tell Azar, however, was that they had already made a decision to replace him. During congressional testimony earlier in the day, a lawmaker had asked Azar about reports that the White House might put someone else in charge of the response—a report that Azar denied. But when he arrived at the White House that afternoon for what he thought would be the planned intervention to get Trump to agree to mitigation measures, he was directed to Mulvaney's office, where he was told that Vice President Pence was being made the head of the task force.

Having Pence lead the task force had originally been Trump's idea, and effectively spelled the beginning of the end for Mulvaney. More than a week earlier, Trump told Mulvaney and a group of other aides that they needed to find someone new to lead the task force. Azar wasn't cutting it, Trump told them. What about Scott Gottlieb, the former FDA commissioner? Trump asked the aides. Mulvaney knew

Gottlieb and liked him, but he also knew that bringing Gottlieb in to replace Azar would cause Azar's head to explode. Azar had been Gottlieb's boss when Gottlieb ran the FDA, and now Gottlieb would effectively be Azar's boss. If Trump did that, Azar would quit, Mulvaney told Trump. "Mr. President, we can't have him quit," Mulvaney told Trump in front of the other aides gathered.

"Why not?" Trump responded. "Have him quit."

"Mr. President, we cannot have the head of health and human services quit in what might be the start of a pandemic."

Trump thought about it for a second. "Why not Pence?" he said. Pence it would be.

Before Trump had left for India, Mulvaney had approached Pence's chief of staff, Marc Short, about having the vice president lead the task force. Having Pence run the task force would bring the whole operation inside the White House, giving Mulvaney more visibility. Still, Short thought it would be a recipe for disaster. This was a lose-lose situation. It could set Pence up for all the blame if things went south. And why did the response need to be brought inside the White House? This is what the agencies were for. Don't do this to us, Short begged Mulvaney. He asked Mulvaney to find an alternative, but Trump's embattled chief of staff responded, what other options do we have?

That evening Trump would use the White House podium to try to announce Pence's appointment and take back control of the message. His aides knew that "community spread" was now occurring in multiple parts of the country, but Trump didn't care about that. "When you have 15 people—and the 15 people within a couple of days is going to be down to close to zero—that's a pretty good job we've done," he said.

After the press briefing, Azar's top communications aide spoke to Katie Miller, the vice president's press secretary. Azar's aide mentioned to Miller that the health secretary was booked for *Fox & Friends* the following morning, as well as a handful of other TV spots. Miller said to cancel all media appearances for Azar and other task force members, including Fauci. Pence's team felt the administration's message was all over the place, and they needed to pause and reset. Miller and Short sent clear marching orders: No one was speaking in public unless they were cleared by them first.

Trump announced Pence's new role at a press conference that evening, but by that point the economic and physical health of the United States was cracking. It wasn't just the stock market. Several major companies had begun halting their plans to borrow money, fearful that they wouldn't find investors. If the trend continued, large parts of corporate America could seize up, causing an avalanche of layoffs and bankruptcies. Companies wouldn't have the money to make their payrolls.

At 4:00 p.m. Eastern time on Friday, February 28, the New York Stock Exchange closed for the week. The Dow Jones Industrial Average had fallen 3,583 points over five days, losing 12 percent of its value. It was one of the worst five-day slides in US history.

That was all just money. While Trump and some of his top aides were fixated on the stock market, there would be at least three gatherings that week that would come to be called "superspreader events," events where the virus jumped from one person to dozens or more.

One of the superspreader events was a science conference in Boston. Another was a funeral in Albany, Georgia. In both cases, someone had attended the event sick and many others left infected, taking the virus with them.

But those events paled in comparison to the hypercontagion that occurred that week at Mardi Gras in New Orleans. More than a million people had packed into the city. Some had been partying for more than a week, crowding Bourbon Street, stuffed into bars. The packed spaces filled with people yelling (and therefore emitting even more respiratory droplets into the air) and sweating were the best possible environment for the virus to spread. New Orleans officials had watched reports of the virus but hadn't taken any aggressive measures to squelch the huge annual celebration. So many people would contract the virus over those few days that New Orleans would soon see a bigger spike in new cases and deaths than anywhere else in the world.

Trump's inner circle was buckling down, fervently embracing his insistence that this was all being blown out of proportion intentionally by his enemies. They blamed the media; blamed the Democrats; blamed the Federal Reserve. They needed to divert attention—fast. And there was no better place to do it than the Conservative Political Action Conference, an annual gathering that—conveniently for Trump—was about to take place in nearby Maryland on Saturday, February 29.

CPAC brought together the country's most conservative activists, lawmakers, and White House officials. Apart from Mar-a-Lago, it was Trump's safe space, where he could do no wrong. He was slated to speak on Saturday, but there had already been a parade of his aides at the conference, serving as warm-up acts. Mick Mulvaney was one of the first. "We sit there and watch the markets and there's this huge panic and it's like, why isn't there this huge panic every single year over flu?" he asked the crowd. "Are you going to see some schools shut down? Probably. May you see impacts on public transportation? Sure. But we do this, we know how to handle this."

The next day, CPAC was one of the few places left in the United States that appeared to be in denial about what was happening. One attendee was a New Jersey resident who hadn't been feeling well and mingled with top CPAC officials. Like everyone else, Trump was oblivious to the fact that people who had contracted the virus were among the crowd, and as he walked onstage he was met with a huge standing ovation. The thunderous applause lasted more than two minutes, while the audience screamed and Lee Greenwood's "God Bless the U.S.A." blared from the speakers.

Twin forces were pulling at Trump at that moment: on the one hand, there was a virus that was killing the stock market; on the other, he had finally broken free from the impeachment investigation. He wanted to look forward, but it seemed as though just as he had been shrugging the impeachment away, the virus had come out of nowhere. He mentioned the virus very briefly in the CPAC speech, and his message was clear: the virus might be moving throughout the world, but it wasn't really in the United States. And he wouldn't let it come here. People could trust him. "We are urging Americans to exercise increased caution throughout all of Europe," he said. "We will do everything in our power to keep the virus, and those carrying the infections, from entering our country."

That was all wrong and the exact thing that health officials had tried to get him to stop saying. The virus wasn't only in other countries; it was, in fact, already in the United States.

Shortly after Trump finished speaking, he went back to the White House and held a briefing with Vice President Pence and others about the status of the pandemic efforts. The news was grim. Nearly three thousand miles away, in Kirkland, Washington, several people were clinging to life inside Evergreen Health Hospital. One of them, a man in his fifties, was a peculiar case. He hadn't traveled recently; he had contracted the coronavirus somewhere, somehow, and then died. It was the first known death in the United States. Speaking to reporters later, Trump played it down, but for Anthony Fauci and others, they knew it was just the beginning. Many others in Washington state at a nearby long-term care facility were sick, but local medical officials didn't have the capacity to test them all. The United States now had its first bona fide cluster of cases, and health officials couldn't even keep up with that outbreak. All the scrambling and denials and noise from the White House during the week had done nothing to stop the virus's spread. If anything, it showed how poorly focused the White House was on the crisis.

And as the stock market began a new free fall, Trump was finding that his playbook for surviving crises and coming out on top, a playbook that he had used successfully for five decades, no longer worked. All the other crises that he had survived by using spin and sleight of hand—impeachment, divorces, business scandals—paled in comparison to this one.

CHAPTER 6

THE SHUTDOWN

March 5, 2020

CONFIRMED US COVID-19 CASES: **228**

CONFIRMED US COVID-19 DEATHS: **11**

"I can't believe you're gone!" Donald Trump yelled into the phone at Mick Mulvaney. "How could you leave at a time like this?"

Mulvaney was more than gone; he was in Las Vegas with his brother. It was their annual college basketball getaway weekend, something they had done for more than twenty years.

Mulvaney tried to defend himself. He had informed Trump about the Las Vegas trip for weeks. And he had been kicked off the task force. He wasn't even allowed to go to the meetings. But his protests only made Trump angrier.

The president was in his cabin on Air Force One, heading back to Washington, D.C., after a Fox News town hall meeting in Pennsylvania. The event had been yet another effort to calm down Americans about the virus, but he had failed spectacularly, his usual bag of tricks no longer effective. It seemed as though the whole country was beginning to lose it.

The beginning of the town hall had been normal enough. Trump had been seated onstage in a navy suit, white shirt, and red tie, accompanied by two Fox News hosts, facing a crowd packed in tight. A format like that was usually friendly, but one by one the questioners had gone after him. The first had asked about the confusing federal response to the pandemic. Trump had responded by citing his poll numbers. The second had asked why he kept blaming President Barack Obama for the government's chaotic response so far. "Well, I don't blame anybody," he had replied. "I want to get everybody to understand: they made some decisions which were not good decisions. We inherited the decisions they made, and that's fine."

The event had rattled Trump, and now his acting chief of staff was nowhere to be found. With the president's weekend full of travel and events, Mulvaney had figured that Trump wouldn't even notice he was gone. Mulvaney was no longer coordinating the pandemic response or running daily meetings, and Mike Pence's team had made it clear that they wanted full control. In his absence, Mulvaney had arranged for Principal Deputy Chief of Staff Emma Doyle to travel with Trump. She had accompanied the president to the Pennsylvania town hall and would join Trump on his visit to the CDC the following day. The rest of the weekend would be spent at Mar-a-Lago, where Trump was hosting Brazilian president Jair Bolsonaro.

Marc Short and Katie Miller, from Pence's office, meanwhile, were demanding unilateral control over the pandemic response, despite their limited knowledge of public health. Their focus was on message discipline, even though most of the task force members seemed to recognize that they had a growing disaster on their hands. Short by contrast believed that some of the government health officials had a myopic view of the crisis and were too eager to shut everything down.

The morning after Pence was named the head of the task force, Katie Miller sent a memo to its members and their staff. Nancy Messonnier, Anthony Fauci, and others had been sticking to a version of this message for the last couple of weeks: "While the situation could change rapidly, at this time, Americans don't need to change their day-to-day lives, but should stay informed and practice good hygiene." Miller wanted to alter that, proposing officials take out the phrase "change rapidly" and simply say Americans did not need to change their day-to-day lives. Pence's team was appalled that Messonnier had delivered a message so at odds from the president's, and that wasn't going to happen again under their watch. They knew that the health officials and doctors were used to doing whatever media they wanted. That needed to change, Miller and Short thought, because the message was all over the place.

To some of the health officials, it was beginning to feel like a hostile takeover. Why was Pence's team treating them as though they were the enemy? Also, the revised messaging was all wrong. Community spread was happening, and they needed to talk about mitigation measures: shutting down public transportation in Santa Clara, California, New York City, and Seattle; closing schools; having as many as possible switch to remote work. But Pence and his team made clear that the health officials were not to go on TV without clearing it with them first. (Trump was constantly watching television and would explode at aides if he heard a government official say something he didn't like.)

Sensing that he was being squeezed out, Mulvaney had privately advised Trump that the virus could cost the president his reelection if it was mishandled. "You think you're running on the economy and you're not," he told the president flatly, already regretting his recommendation that Pence take over the task force. Trump ignored the advice. Mulvaney might have had the title "acting chief of staff," but the president didn't think of him in that way, not anymore.

It had been clear for some time that Mulvaney's days as acting chief of staff were numbered. He had seen the way John Kelly, Trump's chief of staff from July 2017 to January 2019, had been humiliated and degraded as Trump had pushed him out, leaving Kelly's team stunned and suddenly unemployed. Mulvaney recognized the same thing was now happening to him, and he instructed his team to begin looking for other jobs.

Jared Kushner was also on the line when Trump called from Air Force One to ream out his acting chief of staff. Later, Kushner spoke with Mulvaney privately, telling him that it was the first time the president had expressed doubts about his leadership. Mulvaney hardly believed that was true. He and his team suspected that Kushner had been maneuvering to have him ousted for some time.

Kushner, not yet forty years old, spry and cocky, had been involved in conversations to jettison Trump's third chief of staff in thirty-eight months. Truth be told, Kushner was the de facto chief of staff, but the other officials had provided him with cannon fodder— and deniability—while he had roamed from issue to issue of his choosing, never staying in one place too long. He still wasn't convinced that the virus was a major problem, but he could see public opinion starting to turn; people were getting worried. It was time for Mulvaney to go.

March 6, 2020

The president's tweet was printed out and sitting on his desk in his Air Force One cabin. Emma Doyle stared at it in disbelief. It announced that Representative Mark Meadows, a congressman from North Carolina who was fiercely loyal to Trump, would be the next chief of staff. The document was like a suspended reality, a piece of paper hovering between what was real now and what was to come.

For now Doyle's boss, Mick Mulvaney, was still acting chief of staff. But once that draft tweet she wasn't supposed to see went out, everything would change. Earlier that day on Marine One, en route to Air Force One, Trump, Kushner, and Doyle sat in the front seats, and Trump announced that he was planning to "make a change" with Mulvaney and "move him to another job." But now Doyle knew—the president had already decided on her boss's replacement and it was all moving much faster than he made it sound on Marine One. No one had told Mulvaney yet. That was the way Trump and Kushner fired people.

They were headed south for a weekend visit to Mar-a-Lago, and Trump could hardly contain his excitement. But first they would stop in Atlanta so Trump could hold a press event at the CDC lab, the one that was producing coronavirus tests. Trump hadn't wanted to go, but some aides advised him to make a show of confidence in the agency. There had been some confusion earlier in the day amid reports that someone at the CDC had tested positive for the virus. Trump was thrilled at the prospect of the trip being canceled, but it had turned out to be a false alarm.

Doyle, numb after seeing the draft tweet on Trump's desk, walked back to the main cabin. There she ran into Kushner. "I'm thinking Meadows," he told her as if the thought had just occurred to him, not aware she had just seen it on paper. She asked Kushner if the president could hold off on the announcement until Monday so Mulvaney and Doyle could prepare their team for the news. Kushner said he had no idea when the president might want to send his tweet. Doyle quickly texted Mulvaney to warn him. A short time later, the plane landed in Atlanta and Trump and his staff headed over to the CDC.

There were two Donald Trumps sauntering through the government lab in Atlanta that afternoon. There was the one exuding confidence and professing to have a brilliant scientific mind, shaking hands with everyone, getting up close to people, and breathing the same air as everyone else. And there was another one, who some sensed was unraveling: the one who looked stressed and bloated, with a red, splotchy face and a tone-deaf red KEEP AMERICA GREAT hat pulled down over his golden helmet of hair.

Trump was, in fact, growing increasingly unsettled. On Air Force One, he had seen on Fox News that there were now 240 confirmed cases of sick Americans, a fivefold increase in only a week. He was still in denial. "It's like a bad flu, that's what they're saying," he protested to aides, even as the evidence increasingly showed otherwise. He had just had an unpleasant conversation with Vice President Pence about the *Grand Princess* cruise ship, which was being held off the California coast. (The *Grand Princess* was run by Princess Cruises, the same entity that owned the *Diamond Princess*.) Trump didn't want to allow the sick passengers—even the Americans—to disembark; as usual, obsessively focused on keeping the number of infected Americans low. He seemed slightly indifferent to whether Americans were actually in danger.

Robert Redfield, Alex Azar, and other senior health officials were by Trump's side in the CDC lab. He was also joined by several Republican politicians who knew nothing about the virus, nothing about the CDC, and nothing about what was happening out in the country. They smiled nervously as the press was brought in to see the entourage.

Redfield immediately praised Trump in front of the cameras for his "decisive leadership." Trump looked pleased. The reporters in the lab pressed the president, Azar, and Redfield about the failed tests. They answered defensively, saying that everything had been sorted out. Azar announced that the government would have access to 4 million tests by the end of the following week. "Anybody that wants a test can get a test. That's what the bottom line is," Trump proclaimed, a false statement that would haunt him for months. There were only 75,000 tests so far for a country of more than 330 million people.

He went on to boast about his innate ability to understand what was happening on the medical side. "I like this stuff," he told reporters. "I really get it. People are surprised that I understand it. Every one of these doctors said, 'How do you know so much about this?' Maybe I have a natural ability."

As Trump departed for his weekend at Mar-a-Lago, his aides continued to spin away the coronavirus crisis with reporters all over the country. "It is being contained," Kellyanne Conway, the counselor to the president, told reporters in the White House that day. "And . . . do you not think it's being contained?"

The chaotic attempt to salvage the response continued into the evening. As Trump's motorcade rolled through southern Florida that evening, the fateful tweet was sent; Mulvaney was fired, and Meadows was now in charge, at least as much as anyone was.

Meadows had already promised to completely shake up the White House's communications team. Trump was convinced that the coronavirus mess was really more of a messaging problem than anything else, an assessment that Pence's team and Meadows shared. Meadows would bring in his own people, and he vowed to stop leaks—a foolish promise in any administration, let alone the Trump administration, which bred resentment and public fights in the media. (Others thought Meadows himself was a prolific leaker.) He also promised to promote Trump's instincts zealously in the eight months leading up to the election.

A smooth communicator who had amassed a huge Rolodex of lawmakers' and reporters' cell phone numbers, Meadows was fluent in the kind of sycophancy Trump required. As the coronavirus's stranglehold on the country tightened every day, panicking even top White House officials, Meadows told Trump exactly what he wanted to hear. At a Mar-a-Lago event that night, Trump boasted about his latest chief of staff. "I think he could be my James Baker," he told one attendee, referencing the iconic Washington insider who had served as Treasury secretary and chief of staff to Ronald Reagan and secretary of state and chief of staff to George H. W. Bush. (Of Mulvaney, Trump had repeatedly dismissed him as "no James Baker.")

Some aides knew that all the happy talk for the president was actually counter-productive. They needed him to focus, not glad-hand, and saw a train wreck coming in slow motion. In Congress, Meadows had helped engineer a government shutdown (though so had Mulvaney). The White House didn't need another loyalist; it needed someone who knew how to handle a crisis, who could tell the president the things he didn't want to hear. Meadows had never handled a crisis before; many believed he had only caused them.

March 7, 2020
"Happy birthday to you!" Trump sang loudly, his face a few feet from a large cake with a giant sparkler for a candle. He was standing

next to his son Don Jr.'s girlfriend, Kimberly Guilfoyle, who was wearing a tight gold sequined dress and basking in all the attention. It was her fifty-first birthday, and they were in the Mar-a-Lago ballroom, where Trump was king. As usual, the president was mixing business with pleasure.

The room was packed; people were shoulder to shoulder, hugging and dancing and sweating and drinking. Trump had invited one of his favorite foreign leaders, Brazilian president Jair Bolsonaro, known as the "Trump of the Tropics," to the party. Bolsonaro had taken office one year earlier. Like Trump, he was a tough-talking, politically incorrect populist. (He would later refer to the virus as a "fantasy" created by the news media.)

Bolsonaro had brought his son Eduardo, and the mood was festive, even celebratory. Eduardo took a photograph with Ivanka Trump, Jared Kushner, and National Security Advisor Robert O'Brien and posted it on Instagram. Trump's longtime friend and lawyer Rudy Giuliani posed for pictures, and Senator Lindsey Graham, the South Carolina Republican, gave a toast. That was how Trump liked to mingle with foreign leaders: at social gatherings he hosted, to show them his power, his popularity, his opulence.

It wouldn't be known until a few days later that twenty-two members of the Brazilian delegation had returned home with the coronavirus. One of them was Fábio Wajngarten, Bolsonaro's press secretary. He had spent the evening working the room full of crowded people, where everyone was eating, drinking, and dancing. It would mark Trump's second known near miss in a week, coming within feet of the stealthy virus, which was penetrating deeper into the country every day, every hour, every minute.

March 9, 2020
Back in the White House Situation Room, the overwhelmed Coronavirus Task Force huddled. More than seventy countries had now reported infections. Boston had just pulled the plug on its St. Patrick's Day parade. Conferences and conventions were being canceled

nationwide. The news kept getting worse and worse, with economic collapse looking all but inevitable. How could the economy work if everything is canceled? If everyone is home? The number of US cases and deaths had doubled in just three days. The White House team wasn't doing much to try to stop the spread. They needed to come up with something. Fast.

Pence was leading the task force meeting, and the discussion turned to cruise ships again. The White House had just allowed the *Grand Princess*, a vessel with 3,500 passengers, to dock in Oakland, California, despite Trump's reservations.

Before Pence had taken over the task force, the CDC wanted to put out a "no sail" order for cruise ships, which the agency had unilateral authority to do. But Pence's team, which insisted on vetting every single action and agenda item, had raised questions about the order. (Shutting down the cruise industry was a move with enormous political considerations, so it was not surprising that the White House would want to weigh in on it.) The CDC scientists were losing their patience. Cruise ships had already spawned multiple outbreaks in the United States and consumed an inordinate amount of government time and resources. More people were going to die if they kept letting cruise ships sail. Azar and Redfield had repeatedly tried to get a discussion about banning cruise ships from having passenger operations onto the task force agenda, but kept running into obstacles.

Jessica Ditto, the White House deputy communications director, sat against the wall, incredulous. She had last been to a task force meeting three weeks earlier, and they had been talking about cruise ships then, too. Why were they still talking about cruise ships?

After Pence's team had taken over the task force in late February, Ditto and others from Trump's communications office had been blocked from attending task force meetings. She had been allowed back only after other White House aides had begun to express concern that Short and Miller were fumbling the coronavirus messaging (Meadows had been chief of staff for just a few days, but he had been forced to quarantine because he had been exposed to someone with the virus). Pence's office had struggled to tighten the leash on Fauci and other doctors who wanted to talk to the media. They were especially miffed after Fauci had said on March 2 that the outbreak was reaching "likely pandemic proportions" without having cleared his use of the word "pandemic" with them first.

To try to clamp down, they had blocked some of Fauci's media appearances and had stymied Azar. (They knew they would never get Fauci to say exactly what they wanted, but would coordinate messaging with him and other top officials each day so they all knew what to expect.) The main Trump official Pence's team had allowed to speak about the virus on the Sunday shows the prior weekend had been Ben Carson, the secretary of housing and urban development, and a neurosurgeon by training. But he wasn't up to speed on anything.

Katie Miller had bounced around rapidly throughout Republican political circles, having worked for the National Republican Senatorial Committee and Montana senator Steve Daines. She had become deputy press secretary at the Department of Homeland Security earlier in the Trump administration and was known for agreeing vigorously with the president's harsh rhetoric on immigration and the treatment of detainees. She had battled frequently with officials at HHS when Trump had enacted a policy to separate migrant children from their parents and images of children in cages had dominated the news media. She had moved over to Pence's office in October 2019.

Miller quickly developed a reputation as a ruthless turf warrior, clashing with other White House aides and mocking anyone who might hesitate to execute a Trump directive. She was not yet thirty but had the confidence and swagger of someone much more seasoned. It was exactly the kind of temperament that excelled in the Trump White House. Dominant personalities tended to thrive; one had to eat or be eaten.

Marc Short was a different type of White House warrior, stealthier but oftentimes devastatingly effective. He had been active in conservative politics since graduating from Washington and Lee University in 1992. He had worked as a congressional aide to then representative Mike Pence of Indiana back in 2009 and had stayed extremely close to the rising GOP star, eventually helping him win election as governor of the midwestern state. After Trump and Pence had won the 2016 election, Short joined them at the White House, working as head of legislative affairs before becoming Pence's chief of staff. Short suspected that liberals and the media were using the virus to create a panic that would lead to more government control over people's lives. He was particularly skeptical over efforts to shut down US businesses to try to curb the pandemic.

The abrasive, dominating force that Miller and Short tried to exert on others in the White House was intimidating by design. Many people, including some on the task force, were afraid to cross them. Miller and Short had strongly held views and rolled their eyes at people they disagreed with. Azar, who had gone from running the show to becoming an almost irrelevant side player, resented their heavy-handed methods. To some White House officials, it felt like the kind of interoffice bullying that would grow worse over time and ultimately be one of the most destructive legacies of the Trump White House.

But it quickly became apparent that their attempts to brush the pandemic off, just like Trump's efforts, weren't working. The public didn't believe their messaging. The stock market kept crashing. Nobody bought their spin. They needed help.

At the March 9 task force meeting, Jessica Ditto told the members that they needed to stop wasting precious time talking about cruise ships. The virus was everywhere. "Guys, the last time I was in here, we were talking about the *Diamond Princess*," she told the group. "That was three weeks ago. We need community mitigation strategies and public buy-in. We need communities to buckle up."

Ditto, who was vocalizing the public and private frustrations of several health officials, didn't understand why the task force wasn't adopting the mitigation recommendations that Nancy Messonnier had called for back in February. Though almost all of the health officials knew that Messonnier was right, many White House aides were determined to project a sense of normalcy for as long as possible. But Ditto believed that if they had specific mitigation policies to advance, she could help craft a communications plan so Americans would understand what they were facing. She had confided to others in the White House that she believed 250,000 Americans could die. They needed to change the way they were handling matters, and fast.

A few minutes later someone motioned for her to meet outside the room. It was Ivanka Trump's chief of staff, Julie Radford. Ivanka had just met with her father and had heard about Ditto's remarks. President Trump was now wanting the White House to change its messaging dramatically, in part because he wanted to call for a huge government bailout of businesses. They needed Ditto to help write the statement. Ditto warned that they would have to call for robust public health measures; they couldn't just say they wanted to do a big business bailout. Fine, but hurry up, was the response.

Ditto didn't have any cell phone service in the White House basement, so she went upstairs to the office of Stephen Miller, the White House director of speechwriting. He had already begun working up some talking points. As it became known that Ditto and Miller were drafting a statement, others began to congregate. Navarro and another top aide began arguing loudly about what Ditto and Miller should include about economic relief.

At 6:30 p.m. someone burst into the room to inform them that the president was headed to the briefing room. He was going to make a statement on his own. They were too late.

Trump walked to the lectern in a dark navy suit, white shirt, and bright gold tie. A parade of senior advisers crowded in behind him. It looked like the largest group of people who had ever been stuffed on the stage in the James S. Brady Press Briefing Room, pressed together shoulder to shoulder, their faces just inches from one another. Trump said he would begin discussing a large economic rescue effort with Republicans the next day. The Dow Jones Industrial Average had fallen 6,000 points in just a few weeks. Businesses, particularly restaurants and tourism-related companies, had begun a massive wave of layoffs. The first change he called for was his favorite: a payroll tax cut. He said that there would be help for small businesses and hotels and their workers. He promised aid was on the way.

Trump made no mention of the community mitigation efforts that many on the task force had wanted to emphasize. According to him, Americans didn't need to change their behavior, they should just prepare for tax cuts and a bailout. Trump then left the room as reporters shouted questions; Pence and the others remained behind. The reporters demanded to know if Trump had been tested for the virus yet, given that he had been in close proximity to several people who were now sick.

"Let me be sure to get you an answer to that," Pence said. "I honestly don't know the answer to that question."

Ditto resigned three weeks later.

March 11, 2020

Jared Kushner and Ivanka Trump sat in the White House's Roosevelt Room, listening as others spoke about the "1 Trillion Trees" initiative, a global conservation effort. Someone in the corner of the room caught Kushner's eye and motioned for him to come to the Oval Office immediately.

Kushner walked in to see all hell breaking loose. Trump's top advisers were at each other's throats debating whether to ban travel from Europe. Half of the advisers wanted to ban travel from Europe immediately, alarmed at the rapid spread of the virus in countries like Italy. Others in the room thought that this was a dramatic overreaction that could pulverize the US economy. Trump squirmed behind the Resolute Desk. He couldn't get a consistent message from any of his aides in that room, and the same thing was happening when he called his friends in New York. Some were telling him that the virus was no big deal, and others were saying it was the biggest crisis in one hundred years. Trump was confused, not knowing whom to trust.

The partial ban that had been put into place to prevent some—not all—travelers arriving from China at the end of January had done little to reduce the number of people entering the United States from overseas. Now National Security Advisor Robert O'Brien and his deputy, Matt Pottinger, Secretary Azar, Navarro, Fauci, and the newly appointed White House coronavirus response coordinator, Deborah Birx, were adamant that the White House needed to block travelers arriving from Europe.

More than 1.8 million people had entered the United States from Europe in February. Italy and several other countries were experiencing big outbreaks, but the US government had no plan for screening arriving passengers and huge planes carrying hundreds of travelers kept landing at airports all over the country. White House officials believed new data was showing that more than thirty of the thirty-seven US states with coronavirus cases had been "seeded" by travelers arriving from Europe, not from China. Several officials had begun discussing a Europe travel ban more than three weeks before, but the conversations had been upended when the president had abruptly changed the leadership of the task force. Birx had been on the task force for only two weeks, and she could already see things getting worse. That was why she was here. That was why she had come back from her work in Africa, to prevent them from underestimating the cataclysmic virus.

Birx, like several other health officials, suspected that the virus was much more widespread in the United States than anyone knew because testing was completely inadequate. She had mined her contacts in European health ministries and obtained their comprehensive data, including the ages, genders, and comorbidities of COVID-19 patients. It showed that the disease was ravaging the continent. The United States had no such records, but surely the virus was rampaging through the United States as well, Birx told them. It must be happening just beneath the surface. She presented the data to make her case that the US government needed to lock down flights immediately, otherwise hospitals in the major US metropolitan areas would soon become overwhelmed with COVID-19 patients.

A number of others in the meeting pushed back. Treasury secretary Steven Mnuchin and National Economic Council director Larry Kudlow predicted that doing so would wreck the economy. "If you shut down air travel from Europe, you will cause a Great Depression," Mnuchin told the group.

Birx, whom most of the people in the room had only just met, challenged Mnuchin immediately. "I present all of my data based on evidence of what I'm seeing globally," she shot back. "Where's your evidence?" She had charts and graphics in hand to show how the virus was spreading. Where were his data about the economic impact? In truth, he had none. He had never needed evidence with Trump. The advisers in the room, who still barely knew Birx, tensed. Nobody talked to Mnuchin, one of Trump's closest aides and confidants, that way. The economic advisers were rattled by Birx's tough stance, but they didn't waver. "They were on the side of 'First, do no harm. Don't fuck up the economy for a bad cold,'" one participant in the meeting recalled.

A Transportation Department official claimed that a shutdown could severely damage the airline industry, to which someone replied, "We don't want to hurt the airline industry either, but who the hell is going to be flying?"

Kushner sensed trouble, seeing how disorganized everything was when the stakes were so high. The debate was heated, with everyone digging in. As the room was evenly split, Kushner told them to retreat to the nearby Cabinet Room so they could come up with concrete options to present the president and then reconvene in the Oval Office in a few hours. Trump looked relieved. They moved rooms but the arguing continued. The health advisers and the national security advisers were relentless. They made a left-hook, right-hook counter-punch insistance that action had to be taken, one of the participants recalled when they took the argument back to Trump a short while later; he broke the tie, agreeing to shut down flights.

Jared Kushner, who was essentially running both Trump's internal policy shop and the reelection campaign, saw the ground shifting beneath their feet. The economy, the country, the election, everything was different now. The president had too many people around him arguing about what to do. Kushner was also wary of Pence and his team leading a task force on which so many people were at odds with one another during what had become a huge US crisis.

The president needed to assert himself and show the public he was taking the pandemic seriously, Kushner thought. He needed to demonstrate that he had decisively made a 180-degree shift from where he had been for weeks. So after the travel ban decision was reached, Kushner immediately started drafting a prime-time Oval Office address, something past presidents had done during the gravest events. It would be Trump's big opportunity to dramatically change the narrative. But his aides needed to do it fast.

Kushner had never written a speech like that before, and he hunkered down in Stephen Miller's office to try to whip something up quickly. Oval Office addresses are supposed to be carefully scripted and used sparingly. They convey the power of the presidency and usually mark a major inflection point, with the world watching. Advisers usually spend days, if not longer, obsessing over every word. That speech was drafted in six hours. Many others weighed in that afternoon, too: Mnuchin, Azar, even Dan Scavino, Trump's social media guru. Everyone was making suggestions, and the ideas were all jumbling together. There were too many hands on the keyboard, one of the people involved in drafting the speech recalled. Mistakes were inserted.

But time was running out. The whole country seemed to be on edge. As Trump's aides wrote and then rewrote the speech, the National Basketball Association announced that it was suspending the remainder of its season until further notice. The National Collegiate Athletic Association announced—for the first time ever—that its annual basketball tournament, scheduled to begin the next week, would allow only limited staff and family members to attend.

The whole country appeared paralyzed, waiting to hear what Trump would say.

At 9:02 p.m., the camera blinked on, and Trump stared straight ahead. He didn't wear his customary red power tie, opting instead for a more muted gray-and-blue-striped tie. A serious tie signaling a serious Trump. But a serious Trump was not the Trump most people knew. It was not the Trump most people felt comfortable with. Trump didn't look very comfortable himself.

Seated behind the Resolute Desk, Trump obviously did not want to be there. His hands were tightly clasped in front of him, but he kept flipping his thumbs up as he spoke. His voice low and muted, he began by reading from the teleprompter so closely that he stumbled over his words. Just forty seconds in, he made his first misstep. "I am confident that by counting," he said, then audibly gasped. He had misread the word "continuing" and said "counting." He decided to keep going. The sentence ended up making no sense, setting up an often incoherent ten-minute speech.

"I am confident that by counting [gasp] and continuing to take these tough measures we will significantly reduce the threat to our citizens and we will ultimately and expeditiously defeat this virus."

Things went downhill from there.

Trump announced he was suspending all travel from Europe to the United States, beginning in forty-eight hours. He added that there would be "exemptions for Americans who have undergone appropriate screenings," a qualifying statement that no one understood.

He kept going: "These prohibitions will not only apply to the tremendous amount of trade and cargo, but various other things as we get approval. Anything coming from Europe to the United States is what we are discussing."

Garbling the words had made his statement misleading. He had meant to say that the shipment of goods from Europe would not be blocked, but instead he said that shipments of goods would be blocked; in other words, that all trade with Europe would end, effective Friday. Stock market futures immediately tanked.

The tone of the speech was apathetic, with little display of empathy or compassion for the Americans who were sick, dying, or scared. Trump congratulated himself on the steps he had taken so far and praised the economy, which he said was "the greatest economy anywhere in the world, by far."

He asked Congress to approve a payroll tax cut, something that virtually no one on Capitol Hill thought would help, and concluded by saying, "Our future remains brighter than anyone can imagine. Acting with compassion and love, we will heal the sick, care for those in need, help our fellow citizens and emerge from this challenge stronger and more unified than ever before."

It wasn't a plan; it was a word salad.

In response, thousands of Americans in Europe began frantically making phone calls to try to arrange immediate flights back to the United States before the Friday ban. No one knew what Trump had meant when he had said that only those who had "undergone appropriate screenings" would be allowed to return home. And not only did no one know, the White House didn't clarify it.

Over the coming days, scared Americans would crowd onto airplanes and into airports, waiting in immigration lines for hours to be let back into the United States. Many healthy passengers were crammed in tight with sick passengers, breathing the same air, through which the virus could spread. And the travelers were bringing it home. (Studies later found that travelers from Europe had begun to seed the coronavirus in New York City in mid-February, meaning that the Europe travel ban was far too late by the time it was implemented.)

Months later, one of Trump's top advisers would provide a different perspective on the Oval Office address. Yes, it had been garbled and had led to confusion. But for the first time, Trump had showed he was taking dramatic action to combat the virus. He was devoting a prime-time Oval Office address to order the unthinkable: a shutdown of flights from Europe. It kicked off a brief but important period when the nation's leaders joined together to try to combat the biggest threat to the United States in decades.

One thing that united Trump's motley crew of advisers—and his millions of adoring fans—was that they followed his lead. And on that day, he led. His devoted supporters would continue to believe his every utterance about the virus. His advisers, though, would not be united much longer.

For the moment, the strange combination of Birx, Fauci, Pottinger, Azar, and Navarro had won the day. Ever since the California woman had been confirmed as the first case of community transmission—meaning cases that were appearing with no known link to one another—they had known that the United States would need to take drastic action to stop the outbreak from spinning out of control.

During all of February, health officials kept hoping they would see some evidence indicating that the coronavirus was less transmissible than they had thought. But as they saw the emerging pattern of outbreaks on cruise ships and in nursing homes, it became clear that the virus was actually even more contagious. The United States was woefully behind the virus and needed to get ahead.

The next morning, Pence pulled Jared Kushner aside and asked for help. He said the crisis was snowballing on them. They seemed to always be playing catch-up because things were moving too fast. A political mess was brewing in New York, as Governor Andrew Cuomo wanted to shut many businesses down but Mayor Bill de Blasio was proving resistant. Everyone was making up the response on the fly.

There was now a discordant reaction to the crisis across the country, with each state acting differently because there were no concrete federal guidelines. Kushner immediately called two of his close friends, Adam Boehler and Nat Turner, and asked them to help put together a set of guidelines over the weekend that could provide some kind of national recommendations. Boehler was a former summer roommate of Kushner's during college and was currently heading a federal institution called the US International Development Finance Corporation. Turner was chief executive of Flatiron Health, a technology and services company that specializes in cancer research.

Boehler and Turner burrowed into a room in the basement of the West Wing and started calling people who grasped both the scale of the crisis but also the politics. Over that weekend, they put together recommendations and then circulated them with Birx and Fauci. The guidelines were refined further before being presented to Trump in the Oval Office. They wanted to recommend shutting down in-person education at schools. Closing indoor dining at restaurants and bars. Canceling travel.

Birx and Fauci saw the guidelines as a crucial pause that would buy them some time to better understand the pandemic. Shutting down flights was not enough, they said; more would have to be done. Fauci told the task force members that the data they were seeing were two weeks old. In other words, the data they saw on any given day reflected what had been happening two weeks earlier, meaning that the real-time situation was likely even worse. Death reports, crucially, lagged a couple of weeks behind reality.

One of Birx's top priorities was to get better data. She didn't know anyone in the White House besides Pottinger, so she was starting from scratch with pretty much everyone else in the West Wing. If she were to convince the president to shut down the entire country, she was going to have to make a compelling case. She spent a weekend assembling all of the data from Europe that she could get her hands on. She then looked at the logarithmic curves of infections and deaths to try to predict when the United States would begin seeing an exponential growth of cases and fatalities. The data revealed how quickly the virus had moved through Italy, and she knew that it wasn't isolated there; the Italians were just more efficient at tracking it. If it was moving like that throughout a major European country, she projected, a similar explosion was about to occur in the United States.

Boehler, Kushner, Birx, Fauci, and other aides presented Trump with the recommendations several days later, anxious over what he might say. Kushner had been preparing Trump for the possibility that they were going to need to take more "draconian" actions. Things were too unsettled. The mess in New York between the governor and the mayor over whether to shut down businesses and schools could play out all over the country. That would be a fiasco.

At the meeting, Birx walked the president through everything that she was seeing in Europe, forecasting what could happen if the US didn't act. Boehler offered the recommendation for fifteen days of restrictions, the kind of government crackdown that was anathema to every one of Trump's instincts.

But when they finished with the presentation, the first two words out of Trump's mouth surprised them. "That's it?" he asked. Trump had thought that they were going to tell him to call in the National Guard and lock people in their homes. He immediately approved their plan. At 3:21 p.m. on March 16, he delivered a speech that he—and many of his advisers—would come to regret.

"This afternoon, we're announcing new guidelines for every American to follow over the next fifteen days as we combat the virus," he said from the James S. Brady Press Briefing Room. ". . . We'd much rather be ahead of the curve than behind it, and that's what we are. Therefore, my administration is recommending that all Americans, including the young and healthy, work to engage in schooling from home when possible. Avoid gathering in groups of more than ten people. Avoid discretionary travel. And avoid eating and drinking at bars, restaurants, and public food courts." He added, "If everyone makes this change or these critical changes and sacrifices now, we will rally together as one nation and we will defeat the virus. And we're going to have a big celebration all together."

Trump was reading from notes. The words had been written for him, but he was reading them nonetheless. He had spent the first three years of his presidency stripping back regulations and restrictions, complaining about the "deep state" and government overreach. He was now putting into place the biggest restrictions on Americans' behavior in the past hundred years.

The government's program was called "15 Days to Slow the Spread." It was a nationwide shutdown until the end of March, an unprecedented action.

Just a few weeks earlier, Trump and his top aides had barely known who Deborah Birx and Anthony Fauci were. Now they were teamed up with Jared Kushner and had played a critical role in convincing Trump to shut much of society down. Others were watching. Someone had to stop them. And fast.

CHAPTER 7

DR. BIRX

March 28, 2020

CONFIRMED US COVID-19 CASES: **112,000**

CONFIRMED US COVID-19 DEATHS: **1,858**

It took only a few days before Donald Trump's economic aides and outside consultants decided that the shutdown was a terrible mistake. They couldn't believe that Deborah Birx and Anthony Fauci—of all people!—had prevailed over them.

Less than a week after the shutdown announcement, one of the outside economic advisers, Stephen Moore, strode into the Oval Office to convince the president to open things up again. Moore, a former writer for the *Wall Street Journal*'s editorial board whom Trump had unsuccessfully sought to install on the Federal Reserve's board of governors, was serving as an emissary for the conservative establishment. There was growing anxiety in the conservative base about whether Fauci and Birx were pushing the president around.

"We said symbolically that opening the economy by Easter would be a smart thing to do because there's a real revolt" among conservatives and business leaders, Moore recalled telling the president that day. "The economic costs of this are mounting and there's not a lot of evidence that lockdowns are working to stop the spread."

Easter, which would fall on April 12, was just a few weeks away. Moore was advising Trump to get the lockdown over with in less than a month. Several of Trump's advisers shared Moore's angst over the lockdown. Mike Pence's chief of staff, Marc Short, told others it was a complete overreaction and a gift to Democratic governors and officials. An Easter re-opening was the polar opposite of what Birx and Fauci were telling him. But Trump liked it. It was what he wanted to hear. "He wanted to protect the businesses and get people back on the job," Moore said.

Shortly after the meeting, it became clear that Moore had struck a nerve. "WE CANNOT LET THE CURE BE WORSE THAN THE PROBLEM ITSELF," Trump wrote on Twitter at 11:50 p.m. on March 22. "AT THE END OF THE 15 DAY PERIOD, WE WILL MAKE A DECISION AS TO WHICH WAY WE WANT TO GO!"

Two days later, on March 24—just eight days into the shutdown—Trump held a "virtual town hall" in the White House Rose Garden. Seated beside him was Pence. Next to Pence was Birx, just eight feet away from the commander in chief.

Birx and Fauci knew that a shutdown would be extraordinarily painful for Americans. But in private briefings and task force meetings in late March, they continued to warn that the worst of the pandemic was yet to come. Even with the shutdown in effect, infections were rising exponentially in major cities across the country. Every day, New York City, New Orleans, and other cities were looking more and more like war zones, with ambulance sirens blaring and hospitals overrun.

Trump had heard all the warnings, but so much had changed in just a week. Companies continued laying off workers. Millions of Americans were out of work as restaurants, shops, movie theaters, live entertainment venues, and small businesses closed. Trump was over it. He wanted the virus just to go away and struck a dismissive tone in the Rose Garden that day. "You are going to lose a number of people to the flu, but you are going to lose more people by putting a country into a massive recession or depression," he said. He kept equating the coronavirus to the flu, despite a death rate that was about ten times worse. "You are going to have suicides by the thousands—you are going to have all sorts of things happen. You are going to have instability. You can't just come in and say let's close up the United States of America, the biggest, the most successful country in the world by far."

Later that day, in a Coronavirus Task Force briefing in the James S. Brady Press Briefing Room, he declared that he wanted to see the country open by Easter.

Why Easter?

"Easter is a very special day for many reasons. For me, for a lot of—a lot of our friends, that's a very special day. And what a great timeline this would be. Easter, as our timeline—what a great timeline that would be," he said. He was hardly a religious person, but his evangelical Christian base hung on his every word and Moore had suggested that an Easter reopening could be seen symbolically as a type of rebirth.

Birx sat in silence, her right leg crossed over her left, staring at the president as the words left his mouth. Her expression betrayed nothing. Her military career had conditioned her to remain impassive while her commanding officer was speaking. But Easter? The idea was a nightmare. She had taken a lead role on the task force just one month earlier, and her influence was already slipping away. She had to try to stop this.

Birx knew that the United States hadn't yet reached the peak of infections, a grim milestone that public health experts didn't anticipate for several more weeks. The number of reported new infections was doubling every few days; it had gone from just more than one thousand cases on March 16, the day the shutdown had gone into effect, to nearly eleven thousand the day of the virtual town hall. The rate wasn't slowing down, and the count was artificially low because the United States was still doing so little testing. The fifteen-day shutdown would hardly be enough to seriously hamper the virus's spread. If Trump reopened the country on Easter, the painful effort would have been for nothing.

When Trump had announced on February 26 that Pence would be taking over the White House Coronavirus Task Force, the science and public health world had tensed. Pence was unfailingly loyal to Trump, and had his own questionable public health track record. As governor of Indiana, Pence had been widely viewed as responsible for more than two hundred people's contracting HIV, in large part because he had been reluctant to set up a needle exchange program even after it had become clear that an outbreak was under way.

So CDC director Robert Redfield and others had been elated one day later when Pence announced that Deborah Birx would serve as the White House coronavirus response coordinator. Birx—whom the press release described as a "scientist, physician, and mom"— would work out of the vice president's office and report directly to Pence. The release misspelled her first name, referring to her as "Debbie." She had always gone by "Debbi." But Birx, ever respectful of the chain of command, never corrected the mistake. She had spent more than thirty years dedicated to HIV/AIDS research and prevention and was revered in some corners of the scientific and public health community.

Redfield was especially hopeful that Birx's ten years at the CDC would help his agency's (and his own) standing within the task force. But some CDC veterans immediately urged caution. "Let's slow your roll here," several CDC officials warned. This might not be the blessing you think it is.

Debbi Birx had been something of an anomaly her whole life: a high achiever but a bit of a puzzle; compassionate and cutthroat at the same time.

Her father, Donald Birx, had been a mathematician and engineer. Her mother, Adele Sparks Birx, had been a nursing professor. Debbi grew up with two brilliant older brothers, one of whom would go on to become a physicist and the other a PhD electrical engineer, and the president of Plymouth State University. (Her brother Danny died in a plane crash in 2000.) Their childhoods were filled with science; young Debbi began working as a hospital candy striper as an adolescent, and she and her brothers conducted science experiments together in a shed behind their Pennsylvania house. Their Christmas presents were Heathkits, home assembly sets of assorted electronics. One holiday she and her brothers built a color television.

But the backyard experiments and Heathkits weren't enough for young Debbi. She entered the local science fair circuit, winning third place in her high school sophomore year at the Lancaster City-County Science Fair. She told a local news outlet at the time, "Third is all right, but I'll be back. I want that first prize." She made good on her word: she won the girls grand champion trophy in her junior year at the Capital Area Science and Engineering Fair, then went on to the Army and Navy's 24th Annual International Science and Engineering Fair in San Diego, which she also won.

She was always pushing herself, graduating from high school at seventeen and then completing her undergraduate degree in chemistry at Houghton College at twenty. She married, received a medical degree from Pennsylvania State University in 1980, and then followed her husband into the army so they could stay close.

Birx was assigned to Walter Reed Army Medical Center. During a fellowship, she trained under a rising star at the NIH, Anthony Fauci. Fauci, fifteen years her senior, was obsessed with a strange new disease that was affecting primarily gay men. In those formative years, Fauci and Birx learned that scientists could be at the leading edge of addressing a public health crisis. But like Redfield, they learned how fraught and political a crisis response could become.

Birx's early awareness of AIDS might have saved her life. When she was giving birth to her first daughter in 1983, she lost a significant amount of blood during the delivery, prompting her obstetrician to order a transfusion. The first CDC report on AIDS had come out only two years earlier, so few people even knew of the disease. Birx did, however, and moments before she passed out from the pain, she screamed, "Do not let them give me blood!" Her husband made sure that Birx did not receive the transfusion, and the hospital later learned that the blood it would have given her was contaminated with HIV.

It was that "gut instinct" that would follow her throughout the winding path of her career. She was the only female doctor at Walter Reed working on clinical immunology and infectious diseases. There were no shoes for her to fill. She had to carve her own path in a male-dominated field during a time when chauvinism often went unchecked. She learned how to cuss like a soldier and fight for herself. She gained an edge, a survival instinct, but also a closely-held moral compass that few people could ever truly read.

Her military training taught her two things: to religiously follow the chain of command; and never to leave someone behind on the battlefield.

Can someone have two North Stars? She did. There were moments when she was pulled in opposite directions and had to weigh what was morally right against the ethos that had been instilled in her in the beginning of her career, often resulting in perilous decisions and no-win situations.

The audacity and brains that had propelled her through the high school science fairs helped vault her ahead in the military. She was also a master networker. And she did everything while deferring religiously to the military's chain of command, impressing her superiors. So she kept advancing. Another thing helped her stand out: she loved taking care of patients.

She treated HIV when it was considered a death sentence, helping HIV-positive active-duty members find ways to keep their medical coverage and still receive an honorable discharge. She worked to ensure that the soldiers could maintain access to their medical insurance by withholding their diagnoses from their superiors.

By the early 1990s, she was a lieutenant colonel working for a top army doctor. His name was Robert Redfield, and he was in a bit of trouble. He was under investigation for promoting the Micro-GeneSys AIDS vaccine. Redfield was accused of cherry-picking data when touting the vaccine's early benefits. Friends at the National Institutes of Health called Birx and told her that Redfield and the vaccine needed to be "collared," she would later tell investigators. In exchange for cutting Redfield loose, she would be given "more freedom to research prevention trials in Thailand," one of her passions.

She was confronted with a classic Washington conundrum, a quid pro quo: to throw her boss under the bus and advance her career or to honor the chain of command and stand by Redfield, even though he had lost the respect of some of their peers. Birx stood by him and told investigators that he had done nothing wrong. The episode underscored the fact that she would always, unfailingly support her superiors, no matter the cost.

Birx's association with Redfield worried some activists and others in the HIV/AIDS world who reviled Redfield. But Birx was undeterred, committed to the balancing act that came with being in the cutthroat world of science—let alone being a woman in science. She continued to blaze her own path and by the early 2000s had "earned her own professional wings," one former associate said.

She made a number of powerful connections along the way. When she became head of the CDC's Division of Global HIV/AIDS, one of her subordinates was a bright virologist named Yen Duong, who developed a widely used HIV test while working at the agency. Duong would eventually marry a *Wall Street Journal* reporter turned marine named Matt Pottinger, a connection that would eventually bring Birx into Trump's orbit.

After working at the CDC from 2005 to 2014, overseeing the

agency's worldwide HIV/AIDS efforts, Birx was picked by President Barack Obama for one of the most coveted jobs in public health: the head of the President's Emergency Plan for AIDS Relief (PEPFAR), the program created in 2003 under President George W. Bush to combat AIDS in low-income and low-resource countries. Birx helped maintain PEPFAR's bipartisan support, beating back proposed budget cuts to the $7-billion-a-year program. In the United States, AIDS was an epidemic, but it paled in comparison to the way the disease was ravaging Africa in the 1990s, when that continent and parts of Asia accounted for 90 percent of global cases. The availability of antiretroviral drugs in the late 1990s meant that HIV was no longer a death sentence; taking pills daily enabled patients to live an otherwise normal, healthy life. But the drugs were available almost exclusively in wealthy Western countries because companies and governments had concluded that it would be too difficult and expensive to send them to impoverished countries around the world. PEPFAR played a critical role in addressing that disparity, and Birx spent the 2000s largely dedicated to HIV/AIDS prevention and treatment in Africa. As the head of PEPFAR, she traveled all over the continent, using a carrot-and-stick approach to pressure African governments to take measures to combat the crisis. The carrot was cash; she controlled it, and if the countries wanted it, they had to follow her instructions and provide her with data to back it up.

African leaders and citizens saw both sides of Birx.

In the early 2000s, she was working in Kericho, Kenya, a rural agricultural town with an exceptionally high rate of HIV prevalence. Matrons at the hospital turned away HIV patients who came to the doors in wheelbarrows. For years, such patients had been rejected by the hospital because local health officials figured they weren't worth the investment; there was no drug to help them and they were going to die anyway, so they might as well do it at home. Birx did not want the town's residents—and millions of others across the continent—to feel that their life was over if they contracted HIV. She asked two HIV-positive American colleagues to accompany her to Africa to show people there that a full life was possible with treatment.

"I got calls from about 150 people who said, 'How dare you take these people to Africa and subject them to such assaults on their immune system which don't exist?'" she would later recall. "But they went with me and they went from community tent to community tent, showing people that you could live successfully with HIV with treatment. People came from all over the hillsides to touch them, to realize that there was hope. That day, the nurses began admitting people to the hospital to receive lifesaving treatment."

She was incredibly compassionate with sick Africans but fierce and unwavering when it came to dealing with African leaders. She took orders from no one. PEPFAR was her program. She was unafraid to link resources and grants to forcing countries to adopt World Health Organization guidelines for treating everyone with lifesaving therapies, as well as removing structural barriers to the treatments. When she saw that a country wasn't moving to save more lives, she would travel there and have very clear private discussions with its leaders, letting them know the consequences of their inaction and the number of lives that were being lost. "She would go to Nigeria and say, 'Look, your child maternal data sucks and you're not investing any of the money we're giving you to prevent child-maternal transmission. We're going to move that money unless you fix it," said Mark Harrington, a longtime HIV/AIDS activist who was on the Scientific Advisory Board of the Office of the Global AIDS Coordinator when Birx took over. "And then they'd fix it." Harrington worked with Birx to get PEPFAR to improve the monitoring of its TB/HIV programs.

But her willingness to set ambitious targets and rescind funding from governments that didn't comply with her dictates wasn't popular. In an audit of PEPFAR released in February 2020, an independent watchdog found her leadership to be "dictatorial," "autocratic," and "directive" and stated that more than 70 percent of the feedback the inspector general had received about the leadership had been negative. Were some of the criticisms in the PEPFAR report sexist? Probably. Harrington said that the only way to run a program like PEPFAR and maintain bipartisan support in Congress was to demand and enforce tight standards. And a lot of people were uncomfortable because Birx did that. No one had ever dealt with a public health figure like her before.

She was the kind of AIDS street fighter that AIDS activists had dreamed of for years, having built a reputation of her own independent of those of the men she had worked for or with. AIDS activists adored her and admired her dedication to fighting the disease not only in the United States but in the countries people often forgot about. She was willing to roll up her sleeves and do the work, no matter how unglamorous. (They also loved that she was one of the most stylish public health officials around, another leading AIDS activist, Peter Staley, recalled. "There was a gay male thing of adoring her style," he said. "We loved her shoes and scarves.") By the time the coronavirus began to crack the United States open, Birx had become, by some accounts, one of the most powerful public health officials on the planet.

By February 2020, Matt Pottinger was increasingly concerned that the combination of the dysfunctional task force and the completely disorganized administration would lead to a repeat of the 1918 flu outbreak, the last mass-casualty virus event in the United States. He reached out to Birx and pleaded with her to come help. She politely said no. Pottinger kept asking, and she kept refusing.

Every year since Trump had taken office, his administration had proposed cutting PEPFAR's budget. Birx had been able to maintain the program's funding levels by providing Congress with concrete data demonstrating its success. She had spent the last three years trying, in effect, to hide the program from the White House so as not to attract unwanted attention. She had been working hard on a program that addressed structural prevention for young women with HIV, and she wanted to make sure that the financial support for that program continued.

She was also making a political calculation. She had been in government long enough to know how to read the tea leaves. Even though the Democratic primary season was still under way, she believed that Biden could come out on top because he was the safest choice. And if he did win the primary, he could beat Trump. If she were to work in the Trump White House, it could be fatal for her federal career. She wasn't ready for that.

But by late February, she had become increasingly distraught. She had spent most of the month in South Africa working on HIV and tuberculosis, but even from thousands of miles away she could see the US COVID-19 response taking a tragic turn. Why were Fauci and Redfield not publicly demanding that people prepare? Why was Trump acting as if the virus would disappear on its own? She kept reaching out to Pottinger, telling him that the government would not be able to contain the virus. He needed to do more to convince the government to ramp up testing. The White House team was too focused on trying to track down people with symptoms, the same mistake made in the early stages of the AIDS crisis. That meant that people who weren't exhibiting symptoms or were hiding them could fall through the cracks and continue to spread the virus undetected. She feared that an "iceberg" was waiting for them under the surface.

Pottinger made his final plea to Birx. "If you don't come and get people to change their minds about this, Americans are going to die," he said.

She told Pottinger that she needed to think about it overnight. She realized that all the downsides she feared were personal; the upside was that she might be able to help battle what she felt would be one of the worst events in US history. She had more-than-capable subordinates in PEPFAR who could run the program effectively. She couldn't justify turning the request down on the grounds that she was needed elsewhere.

On the long flight back to Washington from Johannesburg, she wrote up a list of all the things that needed to be done. She would have to convince political officials to stop comparing the disease to the flu. The government would have to set up a massive testing infrastructure. And the administration's message that the risk to Americans was low would have to be changed. It wasn't low at all.

Birx believed that she was going to Washington to run the pandemic response. She was given an office on the White House ground floor, the room the White House impeachment lawyers had used for weeks. It was the White House's newest nerve center, the crisis response office. That made sense. She thought she would be the one giving orders and making final decisions, and she struck that tone with task force members during her first meeting.

By that point, Fauci was well respected for his years of experience and media prowess. But he ran his own agency. He had a day job, and he couldn't run the response. He could certainly serve as a principal adviser, but he wasn't going to coordinate across agencies and the enormous federal bureaucracy. Birx, who would be dedicated to her new role, would help figure out what everyone else should be doing. She embraced being the agenda setter.

"We need better data," she said her first time at a task force meeting, exerting the kind of leadership and organization that the group had so far lacked. Its members didn't have a concrete understanding of the severity of the outbreak, and she explained to them how to organize a response. Her approach mirrored her strategy at PEPFAR. Everything revolved around data; the only way to solve a problem, she told them, is to first identify what you are dealing with.

Birx was assiduous and thorough, keeping copious notes of everything. Within days of her arrival, she helped arrange a White House meeting with commercial testing developers, many of whom she knew from her HIV days. The administration needed to get them fully engaged and review their timelines. The only way the government was going to get more tests up and running was to have the commercial manufacturers launch into action. Birx wrote down the details of every meeting she attended and each evening put together summations of the day's events, then circulated her materials to senior leaders.

It was the kind of discipline that had been lacking in the White House up to that point—one central person trying to bring the whole response together. By the second week of March, she was able to bring people from her PEPFAR program to help part-time and had some officials detailed over from other agencies. She assigned a small team responsibility for tracking down disparate streams of data—testing, hospital capacity, supply availability—and to put them all into one place. She wanted to get away from models and instead have real-time information comparable to the European statistics she had collected. The government needed to know what was happening every day. That way, they could figure out which populations were being hit hardest and where to direct resources. It did not make sense, she argued, to distribute limited resources evenly. Accordingly, the second point she raised at the initial meeting was that COVID-19 was "hurting the elderly more than anybody else."

With her concise points and authoritative tone, Birx made an immediate impression on the task force. Many of its members had been desperate for someone besides Azar to take charge. Maybe she was the one they had been waiting for.

Birx's gut instinct was right. The task force had been a mess when she had arrived. No one was really in charge, in part because that was the way Trump had wanted it. The president eventually began to refer to it internally as "that fucking council that Mike has," a signal that he wished it would go away. He didn't want anyone to exert leadership, and many on the task force didn't want the responsibility, either, fearful of the consequences. What if they made a decision he didn't like? With Birx now in charge, other members eyed her with some relief, but warily. How long would she last?

Birx instantly sussed out the new chain of command. The only person outranking her on the task force was Pence; everyone else was fair game. It didn't take long before she began marking her turf, unafraid to call out the men—Azar, Redfield, even Jared Kushner—when she believed that they were wrong. She was direct but often brash with her criticisms and directives in a way that made people uncomfortable. And she sometimes made accusations before taking the time to speak with people and understand where their disagreements might lie.

In one such instance, she was angry that diagnostic tests were being sent to CVS, Walgreens, and other retail stores rather than to hospitals and clinics. Before trying to sort out the disagreement, she accused officials of being unethical and asked if they had some sort of arrangement with the retailers or the companies.

And although Redfield and the CDC had already lost much of their credibility with the task force, Birx's attacks on her former boss and the agency in task force meetings made some people squirm. The CDC was able to get data about twice a week from hospitals with varying levels of completeness, but Birx wanted data every single day and felt the CDC was falling far short. "There is nothing from the CDC I can trust," she said at one task force meeting. She was referring to the completeness of the CDC's data, having determined that more than 70 percent of it was missing age, race, and/or ethnicity. Her steely determination caught everyone flat-footed. But she seemed to know what she was doing, so they went along with her.

In early March, Birx would prove to be an assuring and comforting figure to millions of Americans. She stood next to Pence—and then Trump after he decided to command the briefings out of annoyance that other people were getting so much attention—and walked through detailed charts and slides. She spoke calmly and confidently from the White House podium, explaining to Americans the virus's course through the country and where it was going. She often spoke in such detail that her explanations went over people's heads, including those of the president and the White House aides standing next to her. In fact, she was so deeply ensconced in the minutiae that the vice president's communications team often did not make her available for interviews, believing that she "scared people."

But then something changed: Birx overplayed her hand. In a late-March interview with the Christian Broadcasting Network, she described a version of Trump that simply did not exist. "He's been so attentive to the scientific literature and the details and the data," she gushed. "I think his ability to analyze and integrate data that comes out of his long history in business has really been a real benefit during these discussions about medical issues. Because in the end, data is data and he understands the importance of the granularity. And I think he's been really excited about finding the level of detail that we've been able to now bring over the last few weeks."

What on earth was she talking about? It was the kind of sycophancy one expected from Mike Pence or Steven Mnuchin, not a government scientist.

Then she began highlighting small bright spots in the data in what many people interpreted as an attempt to reinforce Trump's assertion that things weren't as bad as they seemed. By the end of March, the United States had surpassed China as the country with the most confirmed infections. The news was only getting grimmer, but at the March 26 coronavirus briefing, Birx reminded people that nineteen out of fifty states had fewer than two hundred cases each. "So that's almost 40% of the country with extraordinarily low numbers," she said. In truth, the states with fewer than two hundred confirmed infections represented less than 10 percent of the country's population.

AIDS activists and public health experts took notice. "Dr. Birx, what the hell are you doing? What happened to you? Your HIV colleagues are ashamed," Gregg Gonsalves, an AIDS activist and assistant professor at the Yale School of Public Health, tweeted on March 28, later adding, "The meltdown of #DeborahBirx matters. Because after 30 years in HIV/AIDS, she had built up credibility as someone who followed the science. Now she's saying things that no one believes but her and @realDonaldTrump. It's a problem."

AIDS activists were known for being rabble-rousers. They worked hand in hand with scientists, doctors, and public health experts to advance their causes, but they were unflinching in calling out those who fell short or didn't deliver on their promises. Many had worked with Birx for years, forming close and respectful relationships with her, but now they felt as though they were watching her put on a red MAKE AMERICA GREAT AGAIN scarf. She was being sucked into the Trump vortex, just like everyone else who came into the president's orbit. She was chipping away at the reputation she had fought so hard to build over forty years in service to a man who expected unflinching loyalty but never returned it. Why would she do it? What was there to gain?

Birx was, in fact, taking an extremely dangerous calculated risk. She had known Trump for only a month, and he was actually listening to her. He paid close attention to what people said about him in public. If he saw her praising his attentiveness to the data, she felt, there was a good chance that he would keep listening. She knew that he was under pressure to reopen the economy by Easter, something she was determined to stop. So if he was going to agree to shut down the country for another thirty days when everyone was telling him not to, then, sure, she'd need him to be locked into the data—her data.

For some time, her gamble paid off. Other task force members and White House aides marveled at the way she managed Trump, who thought she was elegant and liked working with her. She knew how to strike a delicate balance with him: she flattered him and told him a little bit of what he wanted to hear before offering her recommendations. And although Short and others in Pence's inner circle believed that Birx was more adept at politics than she let on, she believed she was forming a genuinely close relationship with the vice president. And she was. One official remarked to her that her leadership of the group could lead to another presidential appointment for her one day.

March was almost over. The fifteen-day clock was almost extinguished. The task force was running out of time to convince Trump to hold on for a while longer and extend the shutdown. She needed help, and she teamed up once again with Fauci to make the case. The country wasn't ready to be reopened right away, but Birx began working on criteria that states could use to phase in reopening plans slowly, based on their varying caseloads. She also constructed a model to project the numbers of future cases and deaths in the United States. She guarded the model with her life, knowing that if any of her internal adversaries obtained it, they would poke holes in it and try to destroy her credibility.

Birx's findings, which she presented at a task force meeting in late March, were shocking. Even if the White House did everything perfectly, she said, 100,000 to 220,000 Americans would still die in the first surge. Others on the task force reacted in disbelief. There hadn't been even 2,000 deaths yet. Now Birx was talking about a death toll that was a hundred times as large?

Her presentation got worse. That dire projection was based on the assumption that the first surge would not expand significantly beyond metropolitan areas such as New York, New Orleans, Boston, and much of the northeast corridor. Health officials were hoping to prevent it from spreading into places such as Houston, Dallas, and the heartland. But without mitigation measures, they were looking at 1 million to 2 million deaths.

Other than the task force's other doctors, most of the people in the room did not believe her analysis of the data. The math didn't add up. What model was she using? She wouldn't say.

After the meeting, Birx met with Pence and asked him to let her put together all the documentation so she could make her case directly to the president. Despite the skepticism of others in the room, Pence seemed to believe her projections and agreed to set up a meeting where she and Fauci could present their findings to Trump. In preparation, Birx went back and forth with the president's team, boiling her data down to six or seven slides to present to him. She and Fauci consulted with each other every day as she finalized her presentation.

That Saturday night, just a few days after Trump had declared that he wanted everything to reopen by Easter, Birx and Fauci met with the president in the Yellow Oval Room, an ornate second-floor chamber in the White House's private residence just inside the Truman Balcony. It is steeped in history; it's where John Adams hosted the first presidential reception and Franklin Delano Roosevelt learned that the Japanese had bombed Pearl Harbor in December 1941.

Very few people even knew about the meeting. Azar was completely kept in the dark, having been muscled out of critical discussions by Pence's team. He had no idea that a discussion about extending the national shutdown was under way.

Trump was supposed to be on a high that night. He had just enacted a $2 trillion law to try to save the economy. The law had enjoyed broad bipartisan support. It was as if the country had rallied together, finally. But in fact he was rattled, nervous about the way everything around him was crumbling.

Just a handful of others were there that evening, including Pence and Marc Short. Birx and Fauci were nervous, aware that they would be asking the president to believe their opinions over those of some of his most trusted advisers. By that point, Birx had a sense of the brutal politics of the West Wing and knew that the president's economic aides, in particular, were after her. Treasury secretary Steven Mnuchin and others were astute and would attack her data if they had a chance. She could not afford to underestimate their influence.

Birx and Fauci knew the stakes: either they would convince the president to take drastic action that could save tens of thousands of lives, or they would fail to make their case. Birx sat across from the president, papers in hand. She had printed out her slides so that she could present them as a handout. She had come armed with other analyses and slides in case Trump wasn't immediately convinced or he had questions that she could answer with more graphics.

She hoped that Trump would be able to understand the work she had done and the case she and Fauci were about to make. But with Trump, you never knew what would happen.

The doctors began by explaining to him that if he reopened the country now, the fifteen-day shutdown would have been for nothing. There hadn't been enough time to see the effects of the painful step they had taken. The point of the shutdown had been to "flatten the curve," which meant to slow down the exponential increase in new cases. The only way to do so, they said, would be through measures such as closing businesses and mandating social distancing so that the health care system wouldn't face a crush of patients beyond its capacity. On a chart, the rise in cases would look more like a horizontal line rather than a sharp incline.

Birx had confidence in the accuracy of her models, but she knew that Trump sometimes needed more than that. She was aware that one of Trump's closest friends, Stanley Chera, had recently been admitted to New York–Presbyterian Hospital/Weill Cornell Medical Center in Manhattan. Chera had called Trump just days earlier. "I tested positive," he had told Trump, the president would later recount at a *Fox News* virtual town hall.

"Well, what are you going to do?" Trump had asked him.

"I'm going to the hospital. I'll call you tomorrow," Chera had responded.

Chera didn't call back, so Trump followed up with the hospital. His friend was in a coma and would never wake up.

It wasn't just his friend. There were images on television of Elmhurst Hospital in Queens, where Trump had grown up, overrun with patients and death. There were body bags in the hallway. Freezer trucks had been brought in to store the corpses. Birx sensed that all of that had Trump on edge. He was finally seeing the virus as a real and personal threat.

"You have to understand," she told Trump, Pence, and Short, "this is like a tsunami. But we don't have any early warning out in the ocean because we're not testing, so we can't see it."

Hundreds, sometimes a thousand, people were being admitted into hospitals at once. "When you get a thousand patients crashing into a hospital, that's the tip of the iceberg," she told them. "Underneath that water, there's a hundred thousand more cases."

The ones under the water were the people with mild or moderate cases who didn't know that they had the disease. Government officials just couldn't see them, because they still hadn't established an adequate testing program. They were advising people with mild symptoms to stay home and assume that they had COVID-19, rather than be tested. There simply weren't enough tests—or hospitals—to deal with the scope of what was happening.

Birx detailed to Trump the same projections she had presented to the task force just days earlier. Even with the shutdown and the White House doing everything nearly perfectly, she said, 100,000 to 220,000 people would die in the first surge. She and Fauci believed adamantly that the country needed to shut down for another thirty days. Some task force physicians thought they should advocate for a fifteen-day extension, but Birx and Fauci were undeterred. Based on what she was seeing, Birx believed that thirty days were absolutely critical to protect the country against mass death and devastation, and Fauci agreed.

Trump knew that the crisis was serious, but thirty days? Was it really necessary? he asked them. Why did Birx think it was necessary? Did she really believe that 100,000 to 200,000 people could still die even if the country shut down?

Yes, Birx insisted. Her numbers were not models based on theoretical assumptions, she explained; they were reality-based projections based on what she had learned from the European data.

Trump thought about it. For years, people had tried to convince him to do things he didn't want to do. He usually had no problem ignoring experts and following his gut. But this time was different; his friend was dying, and he saw what was happening to New York. Birx's presentation was not some worst-case theoretical projection, it was real. It was happening.

Birx made her final appeal, aiming it to land with the biggest impact on Trump. What he was seeing at Elmhurst and in New York could be repeated at every single one of the country's large hospitals if the shutdown was not extended, she said. And it would have to be done now. If he reopened the economy too quickly, the consequences would be catastrophic.

Trump called a press conference in the Rose Garden the following day. So much had changed in just the past seven days. Trump had appeared hell-bent on reopening the country, but Birx and Fauci had thrown everything they had into convincing him to hold firm for just one more month. They needed more time.

Trump was expected to announce how much longer the shutdown would last at the March 29 press conference. White House officials had been debating whether to extend it for another week or two. About twenty-five minutes after Trump first took the podium, he made an announcement that would stun and anger some of his advisers: he was extending the shutdown guidelines until April 30. He struck a decidedly different tone from the one only seven days earlier. "The modeling estimates that the peak in death rate is likely to hit in two weeks," he said. ". . . Nothing would be worse than declaring victory before the victory is won. That would be the greatest loss of all. Therefore, the next two weeks, and during this period it's very important that everyone strongly follow the guidelines, have to follow the guidelines that our great vice president holds up a lot. He's holding that up a lot. He believes in it so strongly."

There was another press conference two days later, on March 31, during which Trump, Birx, and Fauci detailed their "30 Days to Slow the Spread" plan. Some of the data from Birx's formal presentation to Trump in the Yellow Oval Room were displayed. Privately, many government scientists and doctors did not believe the statistics. One outside adviser at the time said that the math simply didn't make sense; there was no way the United States could possibly suffer that many deaths.

But Birx and Fauci were right; the tsunami of death was nearing. Over those few days in late March, the two doctors had convinced Trump, a science skeptic, to back away from his impulsive reopening plan. Fauci considered the meeting one of the most important he had ever had with a president. Birx had walked the tightrope masterfully.

They had bought more time for the country, but the reckoning was coming fast.

CHAPTER 8

DR. FAUCI

In the early days of the pandemic, Donald Trump was watching television with an aide in a room off the Oval Office. Anthony Fauci, the seventy-nine-year-old director of the National Institute of Allergy and Infectious Diseases, popped up on the screen.

Trump studied him closely. They were both New Yorkers, both septuagenarians. They had met just once before, in 2019, when Fauci had been summoned to the White House for the signing of an executive order. (Fauci, along with Alex Azar, had been scheduled to brief Trump that same year about an Ebola outbreak in the Democratic Republic of the Congo. An uninterested Trump had canceled the meeting.) Trump had never paid much attention to him until now.

Fauci had suddenly become one of the central characters in the government's response to the pandemic. That was how Trump thought about other people, as characters in his show in which he was both the star and the director. And now Fauci was in the credits. People were hanging on his every word.

"What do you think about this guy Fauci?" Trump asked the aide.

The aide replied that Fauci seemed smart and was good on TV. "What do you think, Mr. President?" the aide asked.

Trump shook his head. "He's really negative."

Trump and his new chief of staff, Mark Meadows, were convinced that the public fallout from the coronavirus pandemic could be addressed through an aggressive, unflinching public relations push by the White House. But running what amounted to a disinformation campaign required everyone to be on board and on message. Most health officials tried to thread the needle by emphasizing the importance of public health measures while praising the government's response. Alex Azar was more than happy to oblige. Deborah Birx, they could tell, was trying. This Fauci guy was a lone wolf, though. He didn't adhere to their talking points, and he couldn't be trusted.

On March 20, Fauci and other members of the task force stood behind Trump during a daily press briefing. Fauci was to Trump's left, next to Mike Pence and right in the camera shot. Trump was fired up, railing against federal workers, and took a swipe at members of the US Foreign Service, calling them part of the "Deep State Department."

Fauci had been a federal employee for fifty-two years. The doctor's left hand immediately went to his forehead to cover his face. He seemed to be stifling something, a snicker or a scowl. The whole world saw it. The doctor didn't utter a word, but it was a classic New York "tell." Using only his hand, he seemed to convey "You've got to be fucking kidding me."

The image ricocheted around the world, appearing on newswires and front pages everywhere. Trump haters rejoiced; they now had someone behind the enemy lines. But social media were swamped with conspiracy theories that Fauci was part of a secret cabal to take down the president. Now there was a hero and an antihero, though Americans were split over who played which role.

Trump demands complete loyalty, but Fauci's loyalty was to science, so he continued to speak plainly, even if it meant being at odds with Trump. That only fueled his stardom and Trump's fury. Trump was big and boisterous; Fauci was lean and nuanced. It was a bizarre power struggle because they appeared to be stuck with each other.

During the Ebola outbreak in 2014, Fauci had explained to Obama aides the way administration officials should talk about the disease to the public. Americans' fears about contracting Ebola had been far greater than the actual risk, but officials also couldn't provide false assurances that there was no risk at all, Fauci had said. He carried with him the lessons he had learned during the height of the AIDS crisis: If you tell people there's zero risk, they know you're lying and they won't trust you. You have to meet people's fears where they are and be honest about what is and isn't dangerous. Only from that baseline can you reassure the public and win their trust.

So Fauci corrected Trump in real time at press conferences and was frank about the threat of the virus. He became a foil to Trump to the half of the country that was desperate for someone they could trust. And he didn't shy from the spotlight.

Retailers started making Fauci merchandise to honor the infectious diseases expert. There were Fauci doughnuts, T-shirts, and socks. By early April, there was a Fauci bobblehead doll. He received the ultimate honor on April 25, when Brad Pitt played him on *Saturday Night Live*. (Trump was especially incensed about that.)

Yet as Fauci's fame grew, so did conservatives' animosity toward him. "Fauci is the villain here," said Stephen Moore, the Trump adviser who had pushed for states to reopen by Easter. "He has the Napoleon complex and thinks he is the dictator who could decide how to run the country."

But here's what few people knew about Fauci. Yes, some White House officials hated him, conservatives loathed him, and plenty of people wanted him dead. But he also had a team of unofficial advisers whispering in his ear. They included grizzled and fearless AIDS activists who had called for Fauci to be fired thirty-five years earlier, only to eventually become his partners on the battlefield of science. They didn't shy away from telling Fauci when he was wrong, when he could do better.

And there was one other person who helped stiffen his spine against all the backlash: his wife, Christine Grady.

Several of the officials on the White House Coronavirus Task Force had served other presidents. Birx was a holdover from the Obama administration and had been a CDC employee during the George W. Bush administration. Azar and Robert Kadlec had also both worked in the George W. Bush administration. Yet no one else came close to having Fauci's government experience. He had advised every president since Ronald Reagan and been in the government since the Lyndon B. Johnson administration.

Medicine was a part of Fauci's life from the very beginning. He was born to first-generation Italian American immigrants in Brooklyn. They lived in an apartment over the pharmacy they ran, where everyone in the family was expected to play a role. His mother helped with the cash register. During his elementary and middle school years, Fauci made pharmacy deliveries on his Schwinn bicycle late afternoons, evenings, and weekends.

During Fauci's childhood in the 1940s and '50s, pharmacists were more than just people who doled out medicine. His father also served as the de facto neighborhood physician, psychiatrist, counselor, and more, Fauci recalled. Almost every day, he watched his father help someone with a problem, whether it was a physical illness or a familial or emotional one. By the time he was a teenager, the importance of helping people through all manner of strife had become ingrained. Delivering prescriptions all around his Brooklyn neighborhood had made him acutely aware of the role medicine could play in aiding the sick. "When you would go to the door with the medicine for someone who was obviously sick and would come to the door and give you your fifteen-cent tip and pay for the prescription, I got a feeling there's illness in the world and people can do something about illness and help people," he said in an interview.

His exceptional career started with his admission to Regis High School, a prestigious Jesuit-run high school on Manhattan's Upper East Side that Fauci credits with having had a major impact on his life. His high school years were also when he became accustomed to extraordinarily long days that would serve as a sort of training for his eventual career. His high school was miles away from his Brooklyn neighborhood of Bensonhurst and required a marathon commute. He had to rise early and take a bus to a local subway train to an express stop before he finally made it to Manhattan. Then he'd change trains again to reach 86th Street and Lexington Avenue, the stop nearest to the school. He also played high school basketball at Regis, with games in the late afternoon and early evening that sometimes took place as far north as Harlem or the Bronx. He would commute home late at night, then wake up the next morning and do it all over again.

It was in high school that Fauci discovered his love of science. But he was also pulled by the humanities and the classics that were a fundamental part of the Jesuit style of teaching. (At one point he even dreamed of becoming a professional basketball player, despite his five-foot, seven-inch frame.) When he began attending College of the Holy Cross in Worcester, Massachusetts, he enrolled in a course entitled Bachelor of Arts–Greek Classics–Premed. In addition to the traditional organic chemistry and biology courses, he took numerous philosophy courses, Latin, and French. He figured that becoming a physician was the perfect blend of both his loves: he would be deeply involved with people while exploring scientific questions.

Fauci spent his college summers doing construction jobs. One summer, he was assigned to work on Cornell University Medical College's new library in New York City, which was being torn down and renovated. One afternoon, he walked past the other construction workers, who were spending their lunch hour whistling at the passing nurses. He went to peer inside Cornell Medical School's auditorium, just a few steps from the library.

As he stood there in his dusty construction boots and dirty clothes, a security guard told him he would have to leave before he dirtied the whole place up.

"You know, one of these days I'm going to be a medical student at this place," Fauci told him.

"Yeah. One of these days I'm going to be police commissioner," the security guard replied. "So get out of here."

Fauci graduated from Cornell University Medical College in 1966 at the top of his class. With the Vietnam War raging, nearly all the graduating medical students would be drafted. They had to pick whether they wanted to join the army, the navy, the air force, or the US Public Health Service. Fauci loved studying infectious diseases, so his first choice was the Public Health Service, and he was placed at the National Institutes of Health in Bethesda, Maryland.

Fauci's bosses quickly identified him as a rising star. He was drawn to serious diseases with enormous fatality rates. "The sicker, the better," Fauci has said of the patients he likes to treat. In the 1970s, he began treating patients with an inflammatory disease called vasculitis, in which the body's immune system attacks the blood vessels, which can restrict blood flow and damage tissues and organs. The disease is rare but at the time was fatal. At the same time, he was treating cancer patients who took powerful, toxic drugs that suppressed their immune systems. In patients with vasculitis, the body's immune system was in overdrive, and Fauci thought that by giving a small dose of the cancer drugs to vasculitis patients, he might be able to help slow the overreaction of their immune systems and mitigate the impact of the disease. He ended up curing vasculitis.

A couple years later, a study about a mysterious new disease landed on Fauci's desk. On June 5, 1981, the CDC published an article in its weekly *Morbidity and Mortality Weekly Report* describing the cases of five previously healthy gay men at three Los Angeles hospitals. They had all presented with a rare lung infection called *Pneumocystis carinii* pneumonia, which had so far been reported only in people with compromised immune systems, such as cancer patients. Even more worrisome, the men had a host of opportunistic infections caused by pathogens that a healthy immune system can normally fight off, a sign that their immune systems were weakened and not working properly. Two of the men had already died by the time the report was published. The other three were dying. The five men seemed like some sort of fluke. Fauci didn't think much of it.

A month later, the CDC published an even more alarming report: twenty-six gay men in New York City and California had presented with a rare aggressive cancer called Kaposi sarcoma. All of them also had opportunistic infections.

"For the first time in my medical career, I actually got goose pimples," Fauci later recalled. "And I said, oh my God, this is an infectious disease, but why is it only in gay men at this point in time?"

As he likes to tell it, he decided to change the direction of his laboratory work later that summer; he would focus primarily on the unusual disease being reported in more and more gay men, almost all of whom ended up dead. His mentors advised against it, cautioning he would not make a career by studying the obscure disease. The handful of doctors in California and New York City who were redirecting their careers to focus on the disease received similar warnings. Like them, Fauci ignored the advice.

In 1982, Fauci published a report in the *Annals of Internal Medicine* in an effort to sound the alarm. The disease required some sort of medical treatment, he argued, and there was no reason to believe it would remain confined to a particular segment of the population. In other words, it wasn't just a gay male problem.

The mysterious disease that affected mostly gay men, however, had emerged in the United States six months into Ronald Reagan's presidency. As the gay rights movement was gaining steam, Reagan endeared himself to the white evangelical voters who had helped power his win by doubling down on his socially conservative bona fides. On the campaign trail, he had once said, "My criticism is that [the gay rights movement] isn't just asking for civil rights; it's asking for recognition and acceptance of an alternative lifestyle which I do not believe society can condone, nor can I."

So it came as little surprise that the Reagan administration largely ignored the crisis. Reagan's press secretary, Larry Speakes, mocked the disease dubbed "gay plague" in numerous press conferences, and Reagan hardly mentioned the disease for several years. (By the end of his second term, funding for AIDS research would significantly increase.) As the politics of AIDS became increasingly fraught, Fauci was caught in the middle, trying to study the disease and find treatments while serving alongside government officials who wanted to ignore it altogether.

In 1983, two years into his AIDS research, Fauci was treating a Brazilian politician with a leg injury. He told the politician via an interpreter that he would be discharged from the hospital only if he promised to keep his leg elevated. The politician refused, but the interpreter, an NIH nurse who could speak Portuguese, assured Fauci that the Brazilian would gladly follow the doctor's orders. Later that day, Fauci asked the interpreter, Christine Grady, to visit him in his office. She thought she was going to get into trouble, but Fauci asked her out to dinner. They would marry in 1985.

That was one bright spot during an otherwise trying period. As the AIDS death toll neared six thousand in 1984, the forty-three-year-old Fauci was named the youngest-ever director of the National Institute of Allergy and Infectious Diseases, one of the largest agencies under NIH with a nearly $6 billion annual budget. NIAID is responsible for researching all manner of infectious diseases and developing treatments and vaccines for them. Fauci and his lab had been studying AIDS for three years but had made little progress on a treatment.

With no effective treatment, AIDS was a death sentence. Gay men were watching their friends and loved ones die in alarming numbers. They were outraged at the seeming indifference of the Reagan administration, which enacted devastating budget cuts to health agencies as the disease spread. Fauci, the head of the agency responsible for researching the disease and coming up with treatments, became the face of the Reagan administration's uncaring and seemingly nonexistent response, inviting the ire of gay activists.

By 1987, about fifty thousand Americans were infected with AIDS, forty thousand of whom had died. Gay activists tried to help ravaged communities by setting up small groups and networks to help those diagnosed with AIDS. They organized grocery runs, took sick men to their doctor's appointments, and made sure they didn't get kicked out of their homes. But they were tired of a government that did not seem to care.

In March 1987, a new group formed to demand action and bring global attention to the AIDS crisis: the AIDS Coalition to Unleash Power, or ACT UP. Its members engaged in unapologetically dramatic tactics to seize the attention of policy makers and the general public, including large demonstrations at New York's City Hall and St. Patrick's Cathedral. They staged national gatherings at FDA and NIH headquarters, in an effort to speed up research and new-drug approval and access. The demonstrations were striking and received significant media attention, but ACT UP's members wanted more. The members of the group's Treatment and Data Committee became well versed in clinical trial design and research so that they could help change policy and enable those with AIDS to take more control of the research process. They wanted to have a voice in clinical trial design, to help accelerate the trials and new drug approvals, and to gain patients with AIDS access to experimental drugs; without those drugs, they had nothing. Even so, as the 1980s wore on and the pandemic deepened, scientists and government officials refused to change the research process out of fear that it would compromise scientific integrity.

Many government officials and researchers saw the activists as a loud annoyance, but Fauci saw them as people justified in their anger and frustration. He would eventually invite some of them to meet with him. "It was like, woah—we got a meeting with the head of AIDS," recalled Peter Staley, the longtime AIDS activist. An early and influential member of ACT UP, he has remained close friends with Fauci for more than thirty years and has continued to hold him accountable even as Fauci became world famous during the coronavirus response.

Fauci, still young and fairly new to the NIAID director job, was initially wary of taking on esteemed scientists and researchers, but after two years of meetings and demonstrations he became convinced that the activists should be granted a seat at the table. Though they still frequently disagreed about how much the government could or should do, they often worked together. In late 1989, for instance, the activists came up with an idea to provide AIDS patients broader access to drugs outside clinical trials. There could be a parallel track to the clinical trial in which patients could get access to experimental medication, they suggested, while the controlled trial went on to determine the drug's efficacy. Fauci agreed and advocated for the parallel track, playing a crucial role in convincing the FDA to adopt the policy that is still in place today. And when Bristol-Myers Squibb had a drug called didanosine (DDI) in clinical trials, Fauci helped thousands of AIDS patients who could not get into the trial get access to the drug. "Tony had become an ally to us twice," said Harrington, then a member of ACT UP's Treatment and Data Committee.

Even though Fauci had helped meet some of the activists' demands, it wasn't enough. They had been pressuring the government—to little avail—to allow AIDS patients to be part of the NIAID-funded AIDS Clinical Trials Group, or ACTG. The group had been set up by NIAID in 1987 to research drugs and treatments for HIV/AIDS and the infections that often afflicted those with the disease. Scientists worried that having patient advocates sit on the group would disrupt the scientific process, while AIDS activists believed that as the ones directly impacted, they should help inform and design the trials.

Fauci first invited the activists to meet with him in his NIH office. Eventually, alongside those meetings there were the occasional dinners at the Capitol Hill home of Fauci's deputy Jim Hill, who as a gay man was sympathetic to the activists. Hill had come out to Fauci in 1984 after Fauci offered him the deputy job shortly after being given the NIAID director position.

But Hill worried that he could pose political problems for Fauci. "I've got to tell you, Tony. I'm gay, and I don't want that to get you in trouble," he told Fauci.

"Jim, I've always known you're gay. It doesn't matter to me at all. Shut the fuck up and say yes."

Hill hosted the dinners for Fauci and a rotating cast of AIDS activists including, over time, Peter Staley and Mark Harrington and later others including David Barr and Gregg Gonsalves.

The wine flowed, and as they drank more, Fauci charmed the activists and negotiated with them. "Tony shrewdly thought it would put us at ease having a gay host and good cook," Staley recalled. "It was neutral territory to debate these issues. Jim was a very close friend, and we'd feel at ease with this Arkansas queen, who's a great host with his southern accent." Fauci was so friendly and open to gay activists and patients, Staley said, that for two years they would speculate about whether Fauci was gay, too. At the earliest of the dinners, in spring 1990, Staley and Harrington delivered some uncomfortable news to Fauci and Hill: ACT UP would march on the NIH campus on May 21. For the last six months, the government had ignored its requests to be part of ACTG, and holding a demonstration was the only way to get its attention. Fauci did not look happy. These demonstrations were more awkward now that the activists were developing friendlier relationships with Fauci and Hill.

"But why?" Fauci asked. "We're having this dialogue."

"Because you're not agreeing to any of our demands," Staley retorted.

On May 21, 1990, more than a thousand AIDS activists marched on the NIH headquarters in Bethesda, Maryland, surrounding the NIH director's office in Building 1 as well as Fauci's headquarters in Building 31. Some of the protests were personal. Some demonstrators chanted, "Fuck you, Fauci!" outside his office, while others staged a "die-in" on the NIH lawn. Staley climbed over the overhang of Building 31 and was tackled by police. A cop was walking Staley through the NIH building after his arrest when Fauci came down the hallway, concerned that his friend Peter might get injured in the chaos of the demonstration.

"Peter! Are you okay?" Fauci asked.

"Yeah, just doing my job," Staley replied. "Are you?"

"Just trying to do my job while you guys are doing your demonstration," Fauci said.

The following month, June 1990, AIDS activists and researchers, including Fauci, gathered in San Francisco for the VI Annual AIDS Conference, held by the International AIDS Society. Before a panel where each was to speak, Fauci pulled Mark Harrington aside. "Look, I told the investigators they're going to have to let you guys in," he said. The meetings would be completely open, he added, and there would be a more open process for creating community involvement in the design and oversight of research studies. Fauci had listened and heeded the group's message. Its guerrilla tactics had worked. And he had earned its trust once again.

No one knows Fauci's political affiliation, a point of pride for him. He regularly reminds people that he is "completely apolitical." It's what has enabled him to get along with presidents as diverse as Ronald Reagan, George H. W. Bush, Bill Clinton, George W. Bush, and Barack Obama. In 2008, George W. Bush awarded him the Presidential Medal of Freedom for his work on HIV/AIDS and his "determined and aggressive efforts to help others live longer and healthier lives." Over his forty-three years leading NIAID, he has also amassed bipartisan credibility on Capitol Hill. "He is the best-connected person in Washington, DC," one former Obama administration official said. Presidential administrations and lawmakers come and go. Fauci stays. "He's the most famous doctor in a town where people love calling famous doctors." He has used his White House and congressional ties to impress on politicians the risks of a health crisis. He once showed a reporter a photograph he keeps in his home of then vice president Dick Cheney, whom he had worked with on an anthrax scare after 9/11. "I convinced him that the greatest terrorist was nature itself," Fauci said.

Throughout roughly forty years of health crises, whenever Americans have been scared of the unknown, Fauci has emerged from his labs and vaccine trials and been beamed into living rooms across the country. AIDS, anthrax, swine flu. After an American nurse, Nina Pham, recovered from Ebola in 2014, Fauci embraced her in front of television cameras. (He also treated Pham himself to show his employees that he would not ask them to do something he wasn't willing to do himself.) He knows that people will listen to advice and information. He understands how people think about diseases, what scares them, and what they need to know.

In March and April 2020, when Fauci was all over television, conservative groups were apoplectic. Someone had finally whipped the president at his own game: message control. And it wasn't just the nonstop television appearances—Stephen Moore at one point groaned that Fauci didn't seem to do anything all day besides give interviews—but what Fauci said. Whereas Birx was clearly, and painfully, tiptoeing around Trump's message, Fauci seemed to show no restraint in correcting the president to reporters.

Some of Fauci's initial pushback was relatively gentle, but it was still surprising. During a roundtable with vaccine makers on March 3, Trump kept prodding the company executives to say that their vaccines would be ready in a matter of months. When one CEO said his company hoped to have a vaccine in later-stage trials in a few months, Trump asked, "So you're talking over the next few months, you think you could have a vaccine?"

When the executive tried to explain that he meant the vaccine would be ready for phase 2 testing, Fauci interjected, "Yeah. You won't have a vaccine. You'll have a vaccine to go into testing."

Trump asked how long that would take, and the executive

explained that it would be another several months before the vaccine candidate would be ready for phase 3 testing, the final stage of trials before FDA authorization. "All right. So you're talking within a year," Trump replied.

"A year to a year and a half," Fauci responded. (Trump would turn out to be right. The speed of vaccine development far exceeded expectations.)

Fauci's real-time corrections became more pronounced as Trump began disseminating outright misinformation from the White House podium. At first, it wasn't clear whether they rattled the president. In the early spring, while Trump was saying the virus was going to just "disappear," Fauci gave a television interview and said in no uncertain terms that the virus was not going to disappear. That garnered headlines because he was the only government official openly contradicting the president. The next day, Fauci was in the Oval Office and braced for a rebuke. But Trump simply walked around the Resolute Desk and didn't even bring it up. He gave Fauci a pat on the back, asked him how his day was, and thanked him for coming.

But other White House officials and Trump's allies outside the government began pushing Trump to fire the doctor. "We were saying 'Why does Trump keep Fauci around?'" Stephen Moore recalled of his conversations with White House officials. "I think Trump felt he was stuck with Fauci . . . but I believe there was talk of getting rid of him. . . . Trump would say 'A' and Fauci would get up and say 'B.' Trump doesn't tolerate that sort of thing. You do that, and you're gone." Moore's views were shared by many White House aides, who were frustrated that they could not rein Fauci in. Some aides said they did not understand the fixation on Fauci, because they didn't know what he did all day. "Fauci's a nice guy. He does absolutely nothing," one senior aide said. "People would be surprised when they heard Fauci say something on CNN for the first time, rather than the task force," a second senior aide said.

For a time, Fauci's popularity made him untouchable. He was

far better liked than Trump among the broader public, and officials knew that firing him would make him a martyr. It wasn't like when Trump had fired FBI director James Comey. Fauci's stature was greater than Comey's. But if the White House couldn't fire him, they could try to muzzle him. Jared Kushner and other top aides quietly made it known that Fauci was being ignored. In April, Kushner began telling business leaders that the White House wasn't listening to Fauci and was going to go ahead and reopen everything.

Throughout the spring, Fauci's schedule, like that of almost everyone else working on the pandemic response, was chaotic. He woke up before 5:00 a.m. and headed to his office at the NIH for the first half of the day, then to the White House for the Coronavirus Task Force meeting and subsequent press conferences, some of which ran over two hours. He was also doing several media appearances a day. Until recently, he had been in peak physical condition, running 3.5 miles every day. Now he was sleeping only four hours a night, and his body was breaking down. Working eighteen- or twenty-hour days seven days a week was taking its toll both mentally and physically.

It was clear that he was pushing himself to the brink because he felt he had to in order to protect the science. But Trump's supporters were taking note every time they viewed him as contradicting or undermining the president; if Fauci was not going to back down, neither were they.

Navigating the Trump administration was unlike anything Fauci had dealt with in his career. As early as mid-March, Fauci's friends and colleagues started seeing menacing online threats directed at him. Some tweets referred to "eliminating" and "getting rid" of the doctor.

Initially, Fauci brushed it off. He was so consumed by the pandemic response that he didn't have time to worry about things written about him on the internet. He didn't even have a Twitter account. But in late March, federal security agents approached him.

He had a real problem, they told him, because some of the threats were credible. On March 28, they made him accept a full-time security detail.

Through it all, he relied on his closest adviser for the past thirty-seven years to make sure he was handling everything correctly: Christine Grady, his wife. A nurse bioethicist who is the chief of the Department of Bioethics at the NIH, Grady endured a lot of the same harassment that Fauci did. The conspiracy theorists and other Trump loyalists also went for her. At one point in the spring, some of these people managed to get hold of Grady's cell phone number, calling her five times on a single day with five different death threats.

She never wavered and urged Fauci to continue defending the science publicly, even if it meant inviting the president's wrath. When Fauci got home in the late evening, he and Grady usually power walked together. Fauci would recount the day's meetings to ask if he had handled things the right way or made the right decision. Grady was supportive but honest and didn't hesitate to let her husband know when she felt he could have done better. And she made sure that Fauci, who could on occasion be sharp with his words and short-tempered, got his point across without unnecessarily upsetting people. Fauci ran his emails by her, and she often modulated their tone, making sure his expressions of frustration or annoyance weren't too harsh.

In the spring, one of Fauci's daughters, Megan, drove up from New Orleans with her dog to stay with her parents for a few weeks. She self-quarantined on the lower level of the house, even after Fauci told her that they could get closer to speak with each other. There's no way I'm going to be responsible for infecting Anthony Fauci right now, she told him. During her two-week quarantine, she and her father spoke to each other from the bottom and top of the stairs on the deck.

But her visit was marred by conspiracy theorists, who managed to get the email addresses and cell phone numbers of the entire Fauci family (except, surprisingly, those of Fauci himself). As the threats grew, Megan began having nightmares about someone shooting her dad. The family became increasingly worried for their safety and weren't sure that Fauci appreciated how dangerous it had all become.

Over time, Trump began to sympathize with some of the internet rage aimed at Fauci, especially when he broke rank. On April 12, Fauci told CNN that an earlier response to the outbreak by the Trump administration "could have saved lives."

"Obviously, it would have been nice if we had a better head start, but I don't think you could say that we are where we are because of one factor," he said on CNN. "It's very complicated." He also confirmed a media story that he and other experts had wanted to implement mitigation measures such as social distancing in February.

Trump soon retweeted a message that included the hashtag "#FireFauci." Had the doctor finally gone too far? He was about to test his limits even more.

Two years before the pandemic struck, Fauci invited former ACT UP members David Barr and Peter Staley to his house for dinner to discuss the future of the fight against AIDS (Fauci was aging, but he told the group that he planned to stay in the job until he was at least eighty-five in the hope that he might see the creation of an effective AIDS vaccine). He made his signature pasta with Italian sausage ragù. He used a stopwatch to ensure that the pasta reached the perfect al dente consistency.

Fauci and the activists had endured the harrowing years of the AIDS epidemic in the 1980s and '90s together, watching scores of their friends die. That shared bond was evident at the 2018 dinner, when Fauci asked if he could read the activists a passage from an unpublished memoir he was working on. They assumed that it would be about one of his first Oval Office meetings. Instead, it was about Jim Hill, his first deputy at NIAID, who had come out to Fauci before accepting the job. Fauci had devoted an entire chapter to Hill, including the day in 1991 when Hill had entered Fauci's office to speak privately. He had closed the door, a rarity for meetings between the two of them. Then he had broken down in tears and told Fauci that he had been diagnosed with HIV. As Fauci read the chapter, his voice cracked, startling the activists, who had never seen Fauci that emotional in their three decades working together. He choked up a second time when recounting the eulogy he had delivered on Hill in 1997.

"It really dawned on me. It just came flooding—it was like 'Oh, of course. Of course this man has the same PTSD from the AIDS years that the rest of us do,'" Staley recalled. "He would do rounds every day at NIH. And for years, he lost everyone. There was nothing to be done."

So when the COVID-19 pandemic began killing with ferocity in early 2020, the AIDS activists immediately had a sense of déjà vu. They were initially hesitant to bother Fauci too much, assuming that they weren't telling him anything he wasn't hearing in government meetings. But as February and March wore on, they could see the gaping holes in the federal pandemic response. They decided to dedicate themselves to COVID-19 activism, as there simply wasn't another group with their network and their experience. And they had an open line to Fauci.

Some of the activists were more outspoken than others. Gregg Gonsalves, for instance, had become a professor and researcher at the Yale School of Public Health but had not lost his activist edge. On March 8, days before Trump would order a national shutdown, Gonsalves sent a plainspoken email to Fauci, Birx, Redfield, Azar, and several other top health officials with the subject line: "We Are Desperate for Advice."

"All we see is genuflection in word and deed from most of you to a White House that wants this all to magically go away," he wrote. "We need vocally, unequivocal leadership now, that offers real guidance to communities about what to do, what might happen next. Your own legacies will be defined by this moment, what you do and what you don't, what you shy away from saying because you fear for your jobs or your short-term fortunes in the eyes of the President." He concluded, "The status quo is untenable. It's going to get people killed by this virus."

Only one person responded to Gonsalves: Fauci. He told Gonsalves that he regularly corrected misstatements by others (including the president) and was speaking forcefully about the science and public health implications.

The activists knew that Fauci was taking the virus seriously but could also tell that he was overwhelmed by both the government's response to the pandemic and having to deal with the politics of the White House. They didn't know how much on-the-ground reporting he was getting. Most of the activists lived in New York and saw a catastrophic response playing out as city and state leaders bickered over how to move forward. In early March, David Barr put Fauci on the phone with Demetre Daskalakis, a deputy commissioner in the New York City Department of Health and Mental Hygiene, so that Fauci could hear for himself how bad things were becoming in New York. Fauci took the information to the White House Coronavirus Task Force and later told Barr that the phone call had been immensely helpful. He didn't have opportunities to get information at that level, he said, and it had helped inform how he should move forward.

The CDC regularly communicates with officials in state and local health departments, but it was clear that none of their concerns were being relayed to the task force. Barr came up with an idea: What if he were to set up a regular call with city health department leaders and health officials around the country so that Fauci could hear first-hand what problems they were experiencing?

"That's a great idea," Fauci replied. "Let's do it."

The calls were held every other Tuesday at 7:00 p.m. For one hour, Fauci would listen to horror stories. One city was running out of personal protective equipment, putting its health care workers into danger. Another didn't have gloves. None had sufficient testing capacity. Several were instructing people not to be tested if they weren't seriously ill. Barr would write up the notes from the call and then send them to Fauci, who would take them to the task force meetings. During one meeting in April, officials were congratulating themselves on the number of tests they had deployed. Anyone who wanted a test was able to get one, one Coronavirus Task Force member said.

"I'm really sorry," Fauci said. "I don't want to be the skunk at the picnic, but these things are really not happening in the trenches."

Fauci knew from his calls that the lack of adequate testing was a huge problem that was masking the severity of the crisis. All of the local health officials were telling him that not only did they not have enough tests, they didn't have enough ancillary supplies or trained professionals to use all the tests they had available. And the federal government wasn't helping them coordinate and resolve the supply issues, leaving the states to compete against one another for limited resources.

There was a reason so many people in the White House were engaging in happy talk about how well the pandemic response was going: no one wanted bad news to trickle up to Pence and Trump out of fear it might affect his or her standing or influence. Fauci felt that it was his responsibility to call out what was blatantly untrue. (Birx was also pulling together data on the severity of the crisis that seemed to be going largely ignored.) His interjections would catch Pence's attention, and he would thank Fauci for his input and then move on to another agenda item. Sometimes Pence would even tell Fauci that he had raised a good point. But the most common theme at the task force meetings in April was how successfully the response was going and that the virus was receding. Most of the task force members didn't want to hear Fauci's challenges to that narrative, and he increasingly felt that he was being placated and ignored.

That was how it went, week after week, month after month. Fauci knew that the virus was only becoming more aggressive. If the White House wouldn't listen, maybe Americans would.

CHAPTER 9

OF MASKS AND MEN

April 3, 2020
CONFIRMED US COVID-19 CASES: **270,000**
CONFIRMED US COVID-19 DEATHS: **7,000**

Back in February, Matt Pottinger had relayed what he had hoped would be received as good news by the Coronavirus Task Force. His contacts in China had found a way to significantly slow the virus's spread: face coverings.

Other than urging people to wash their hands and practice "social distancing"—a phrase that made little sense to most Americans going about their daily lives—the White House had offered little guidance about how people should protect themselves. The virus lived in the respiratory system; an infected person would exhale it, whether through breathing, talking, sneezing, or coughing, and his or her respiratory droplets would linger in the air long enough for the virus to find its next victim. Respiratory viruses are among the most difficult to stop, because everyone is constantly breathing and talking. Around the globe, there were reports of horrifying "superspreader" events, where dozens or even hundreds of people became infected. All it took was a single infected person packed closely together with others in a confined space.

A mask, however, could significantly stem transmission, Pottinger argued. If people's noses and mouths were covered, they would emit far fewer respiratory droplets, lowering the risk of infecting others.

Pottinger began wearing a mask to work in early March. But he didn't wear a simple cloth face covering; he wore what other White House aides thought was a gas mask. He looked like a lunatic, some snickered, and it reinforced his reputation as an alarmist. One staffer described him as "being at a hundred" as early as January (on a scale of 1 to 10 in terms of concern).

Having lived in China during the SARS outbreak, he saw the importance of the speed with which Asian countries had mobilized. In early February, he recommended that NSC staffers who traveled outside Washington—even to other parts of the United States—quarantine before returning to work. He also wanted NSC staff to telework when possible, limit in-person meetings, restrict the number of people who could be in a room at one time, and be required to wear masks. That struck many White House aides as absurd. There were just a handful of known cases at the time; the virus was barely a blip on most people's radars. No one else was changing their workplace standards.

"We didn't want people to think NSC was doing more to protect its people than the rest of the White House," one aide recalled. "We were like, why wouldn't we be doing this for the rest of the country?"

One reason Pottinger's push fell flat with health officials in early February was that they were focused on N95 masks, the medical-grade face coverings that are fitted to a person's nose and mouth and seal tightly around the cheeks and chin to make sure no droplets get in or out. They did not yet know whether a simple cloth face covering would offer any real protection against the virus.

Pottinger pointed to a handful of Asian countries where the use of face coverings was universal. The governments in China, Taiwan, and Hong Kong had ordered their citizens to wear masks with seemingly indisputable results. Within weeks, it looked as though those countries had dramatically stemmed the virus's spread. Mask wearing had already been common practice in many Asian countries even before the pandemic, so it was not hard for the governments to convince almost all citizens to wear them. The rapid decrease of COVID-19 cases in mask-wearing countries couldn't have been a coincidence, he argued.

But many on the White House task force were skeptical that mask wearing would make a difference. Some thought Americans didn't even know how to wear masks properly and would likely keep touching their faces, bringing virus particles closer to their mouths. Part of the skepticism came from an old-school view of simple face coverings. Many scientists believed that there wasn't convincing evidence that they made a big difference in seasonal flu transmission. Compared to the US, there were relatively similar rates of flu every year in Asian countries. During one task force meeting in early March, Anthony Fauci and Jerome Adams, the surgeon general, explained this view.

And there was a bigger problem: government officials wanted to preserve the dwindling supply of N95 masks for hospital workers, police officers, and ambulance drivers. They didn't want Americans to panic buy them. "If you look at the masks that you buy in a drug store, the leakage around that doesn't really do much to protect you," Fauci told *USA Today* in an interview published February 17, explaining why masks that were not N95s were unnecessary. "People start saying, 'Should I start wearing a mask?' Now, in the United States, there is absolutely no reason whatsoever to wear a mask." In the same interview, Fauci said that the risks posed by the virus were "minuscule," but warned the situation could change rapidly and the country needed to be prepared.

On February 29, Surgeon General Adams tweeted an even more emphatic message: "Seriously people—STOP BUYING MASKS! They are NOT effective in preventing general public from catching #Coronavirus, but if healthcare providers can't get them to care for sick patients, it puts them and our communities at risk!"

Mike Pence doubled down on the message during one of the first task force briefings: "Let me be very clear—and I'm sure the physicians who are up here will reflect this as well—the average American does not need to go out and buy a mask."

Pottinger's heart sank as he saw the tweet and the ensuing messages. What was the downside in having people cover their faces while they waited for more data and research about how effective masks might be?

By early March, as the shortage of masks was becoming a global crisis, the government doctors only pushed back harder, trying to deter panicked Americans from binge buying. "There's no reason to be walking around with a mask," Fauci said in a *60 Minutes* interview broadcast March 8. "When you're in the middle of an outbreak, wearing a mask might make people feel a little bit better and it might even block a droplet, but it's not providing the perfect protection that people think that it is. And, often, there are unintended consequences—people keep fiddling with the mask and they keep touching their face."

Despite the government's pleas, many Americans began hoarding masks. A black market quickly developed; the normally inexpensive N95 masks sold for huge markups, and the hospitals and health care workers who needed them most could not get enough to protect themselves.

In an effort to codify some sort of official policy, CDC director Robert Redfield offered a garbled suggestion at one task force meeting: public health professionals and first responders, but not regular people, should be urged to wear masks. Redfield's reasoning was that doctors and health care workers walk around a lot, which exposes them to more respiratory droplets that can carry the coronavirus. But that didn't make any sense to others on the task force; doctors and health care workers were more at risk for the simple reason that they treated sick patients and were therefore far more exposed than everyone else. The task force had a number of libertarians who were opposed to encouraging people to wear masks, and they immediately pounced on Redfield's wishy-washy explanation. Everyone seemed to have an opinion. Even Trump's counselor Kellyanne Conway, who wasn't on the task force but had caught wind of the mask debate, entered the room and argued about the communications mess it was creating. She believed this was a medical issue—not a political one—but the doctors themselves had been inconsistent about the efficacy of masks. Why should some people wear masks and not others? Did masks work or not? Yes or no?

Redfield couldn't explain his rationale to the group in a way that made sense. That led some people on the task force to wonder whether he was bullshitting them. Did he really know whether masks would work? And if he wasn't being straight with them on masks, what else might he—and the other doctors—be misleading them about?

"It was when he started tanking," a member of the task force recalled. Redfield would never regain the trust or confidence of many in that room after that episode.

In truth, government officials were completely unprepared as they wrestled with the decision of whether to mandate mask wearing or not, one that likely altered the course of US history. First off, they genuinely did not know how helpful a cloth mask would be. The conventional wisdom was that without the protective seal provided by an N95, masks did not make people significantly safer but instead created a false sense of security. They also still did not appreciate the role that asymptomatic transmission played in the spread of the virus, something that was unprecedented. In retrospect, several health experts have said, they should have paid more attention to the signs that the scale of asymptomatic transmission was significant. In late January, for instance, there was a report of an asymptomatic patient in Germany who had infected several colleagues. But they had no idea that at least half of transmissions were occurring from an asymptomatic or presymptomatic person to an uninfected person.

Based on how previous coronaviruses behaved, they still believed the role of asymptomatic transmission was relatively small.

The federal officials, particularly the members of the health team, were also concealing a critical piece of information from the American people: that the United States did not have nearly enough N95 masks to protect health care workers throughout a sustained public health crisis. The United States' manufacturing capacity was unequal to the production of anywhere near the number needed. Communicating that publicly would be perilous. The government would look unprepared for the inevitable crisis, and the public would panic even more. All the health officials agreed that they needed to prioritize sending masks to hospitals that were treating infected patients and somehow quell the broader public demand. So rather than telling the public the full truth—that they still did not know how helpful a cloth mask would be and did not have the supply of medical-grade masks needed—government officials and scientists including Fauci ended up confusing Americans, who were already on edge. "There was a rationale to not have people try to buy all the N95s and masks at Home Depot and building supply stores because of the need to preserve those for health care workers," one official involved in the response said. "It would've been admitting there were shortages of PPE [personal protective equipment]. It would've been an admission of 'We're not where we need to be.'"

It had been more than a hundred years since the US government had seriously considered imposing a mask mandate. The 1918 Spanish flu outbreak, also known as the Great Influenza, had been the last virus to rip through the United States with a ferocity similar to that of COVID-19. That influenza strain had been one of the fastest-moving viruses doctors had ever seen. Influenza, like COVID-19, is a respiratory illness that typically latches on to human cells after entering through the nose and mouth. Back then, health officials had advised Americans to wear masks, but the federal government had not set a uniform policy. Some local governments, though, had cracked down hard. In certain places, a person who didn't wear a mask had been referred to as a "mask slacker"—an insult. " 'Open-Face' Sneezers to Be Arrested," one newspaper headline read.

On October 24, 1918, San Francisco passed an ordinance requiring all people within the city limits to wear a mask when out in public. Debate over the new rule was fierce. The masks were basic and not especially effective, in part because they were made of gauze, which is porous. Still, many people strongly believed that they were better than nothing.

"Three Shot in Struggle with Mask Slacker," read a headline in the *San Francisco Chronicle* five days after the rule went into effect.

Opponents of the ordinance raised such a ruckus that the city quickly backpedaled and struck it down. "San Francisco Joyously Discards Masks in Twinkling; Faces Beam as Gauze Covers Come Off at Time Fixed," a front-page *Chronicle* headline read on November 22, 1918.

The celebrations didn't last long. Thousands of people would die of the flu in San Francisco after the mask rule was revoked, leading city officials to require masks again in January 1919. But a group called the Anti-Mask League formed to fight the ordinance, and 4,500 people showed up at the Dreamland Rink on Saturday, January 25, to protest the new rule. Some argued that the masks weren't effective. Others argued that the mandate infringed on their civil liberties. The local government flinched, and the city ordinance was struck down once more. The antimask rebellion was too much for the politicians to stomach.

In 2020, an almost identical debate would play out.

The government was supposed to have a stockpile of emergency medical equipment for a crisis like the coronavirus.

The Strategic National Stockpile had been established in 1998 under President Bill Clinton so the country would be ready for chemical, biological, radiological, and nuclear threats. Overseen by the CDC, the stockpile's mission had grown over time to include preparations for emerging infectious disease threats and natural disasters. That meant the stockpile's needs often far exceeded the budget set by Congress. And only two years before the coronavirus outbreak hit, there had been an ugly internal feud over control of the stockpile. The Office of the Assistant Secretary for Preparedness and Response, led by Robert Kadlec, had assumed control of the stockpile after twenty years under the CDC. (The transfer of the stockpile was initiated by Trump's first health secretary, Tom Price, shortly before Kadlec was nominated. The policy review continued after Price resigned and Azar completed the transfer.) Kadlec's team said it was an effort to "streamline" decision-making, because ASPR was responsible for deciding which private biotechnology companies won government contracts to develop and manufacture medications, vaccines, and other essential medical tools for the stockpile. Both Democratic and Republican lawmakers raised concerns that the move to ASPR would disrupt the relationships and processes CDC had established.

By the time the pandemic hit, the stockpile of N95 masks had not been replenished substantially since 2009. Over the next decade, trade and public health groups had repeatedly pressed Congress and the administration to restock the masks, but officials in both the Obama and Trump administrations, in part limited by the stockpile's $600 million annual budget, had focused instead on stockpiling lifesaving drugs and vaccines to fight biological and chemical threats such as smallpox and anthrax. The government is often the only purchaser of these types of treatments, and they are difficult to procure quickly. The government had been overly confident of its ability to scale up the production of protective equipment in the event of a pandemic.

In early 2020, N95s were manufactured by only a handful of companies, with a large concentration in China. In fact, the Trump administration had shipped large numbers of masks to China in

January, when the Chinese government had been scrambling to respond to the crisis in Wuhan. So experts in pandemic preparedness already knew that the United States would soon be facing a supply crisis. Michael Osterholm, the director of the Center for Infectious Disease Research and Policy at the University of Minnesota, met with executives at 3M, a Minneapolis-based manufacturer of personal protective equipment and other basic supplies, in late January to warn its executives that a pandemic was coming and to urge them to increase the company's production capacity to 100 percent. Osterholm was well connected to HHS, the CDC, and the NIH and sent the same warning to his colleagues there. 3M increased its production capacity shortly after meeting with Osterholm.

By early March, with the coronavirus burrowed into the lungs of thousands of Americans, the mask crisis had turned into a global calamity. With simultaneous coronavirus outbreaks in dozens of countries, all of their governments were trying to procure masks. The World Health Organization said that mask production needed to increase by at least 40 percent to meet the global demand, but US factories simply weren't equipped to manufacture N95s on a mass scale. Most countries relied on Chinese products, and China had tight control over exports.

The US decision to send masks to China in January had infuriated US health care workers, who by March were being advised to reuse N95 masks as much as possible and use homemade bandanas if they could not get medical-grade masks. (In normal times, N95s are discarded between patients.) The lack of guidance from the White House only exacerbated the situation. People were still binge-buying masks, willing to pay up to $200 or more for a pack of ten N95s. All of those factors caused severe shortages in hospitals, which were soon bidding against one another for the paltry available supply.

Deborah Birx, Fauci, and Redfield knew that the public health measures in place were nowhere near adequate. Americans would have to do more to blunt the virus's spread. So in March, they decided to begin writing guidelines, or a set of "best practices." Some of the recommendations were stark, advising against gatherings in groups of more than ten and discouraging people from eating indoors at restaurants and bars. But others were weak. The guidelines advised people to stay home if they felt sick. When it came to personal hygiene, they listed just four items: wash your hands; avoid touching your face; sneeze or cough into a tissue or the inside of your elbow; and disinfect frequently used surfaces as often as possible. There was no mention of social distancing or mask wearing.

Pottinger kept pushing, and some of the task force's health officials began to support him, especially when the research began confirming suspicions that huge numbers of infected people without symptoms were spreading it to others. They would later find that at least half of the transmissions were from asymptomatic or presymptomatic patients, an astounding discovery. And new studies were becoming available that indicated that cloth masks worked, which meant the concerns over diverting masks away from those who really needed them was no longer an issue. With the doctors now convinced that masks worked, they knew it was time for a new strategy. If some sort of face covering would in fact help slow the virus's spread, it could help alleviate the extraordinary pressure that health care providers were facing in trying to treat the crush of patients. The doctors were going to strongly advocate for universal mask wearing.

It turned out that Robert Kadlec had been working on finding a way to produce enough cloth masks for every American. He had studied protection against respiratory viruses and aerosolized threats back in the 1990s, when he had been a career officer and physician in the US Air Force. He began referencing decades-old studies showing that cloth masks provided some protection against aerosols that were 1 to 10 microns in size. (A human hair is about 100 microns.) The coronavirus was smaller than that, but the size range depended on whether the person wearing the mask sneezed, coughed, breathed, or talked. In February, he reached out to Jerry Cook, a vice president at the underwear manufacturer Hanes. Could the company repurpose some of its facilities to manufacture three-ply cloth masks for every household in America? he asked.

Cook contacted a handful of other underwear and garment manufacturers, and together they came up with a plan to manufacture 650 million three-ply masks over the next couple of months. The middle layer of the mask was impregnated with a microbiocide that was capable of killing the virus to further protect people in case they did come into contact with the virus. The goal was to send a pack of five masks to every household in the United States to make it easy for everyone to start wearing one.

In March, when Kadlec pitched his idea to other health officials, all of them endorsed it enthusiastically. They were already leaning toward encouraging Americans to wear face coverings. And more and more studies and anecdotal evidence were demonstrating their effectiveness. People could even make their own. Anything was better than nothing. Not everyone was fully convinced just yet. Redfield, who was adamant that the CDC was the gold standard of public health and should not be eclipsed, repeatedly issued the same warning. "We can't get ahead of the data," he'd say. (The CDC was conducting its own study on masks, and Redfield wanted to wait for its results.)

Kadlec's initiative would have the advantage of ensuring that every American had a mask and remove any barriers to complying with the new guidance. And if the masks were coming from the US government—and by extension the president—a debate over whether people should wear them might be avoided. Kadlec first took the idea to a unified command group at the Federal Emergency Management Agency, which unanimously endorsed it. The next step was for Alex Azar, Kadlec's boss, to take the idea to the task force.

At a subsequent task force meeting, Azar modeled for the assembled group the Hanes mask. He was immediately ridiculed. Some task force members hated the fact that the mask was white. Health officials said they could have the masks made in other colors, but these were white because they would show dirt and remind people to wash them. (The company would eventually manufacture some skin-colored ones at Birx's request.) "We can't send these out," Domestic Policy Council director Joe Grogan told Azar. "It looks like you have a pair of underwear on your face." Pete Gaynor, the FEMA administrator, who had already endorsed Kadlec's initiative, joked that the mask looked like a jockstrap. Another official said it looked like a training bra. Marc Short, the vice president's chief of staff, intervened in the midst of Azar's presentation. He felt that the plan was half baked and that the answers to basic questions, such as how much the plan would cost and how the masks would be delivered, were unsatisfactory. Short and other officials were also annoyed that Kadlec tried to purchase the masks without OMB's signoff, and felt he was freelancing because he had already crafted an entire communications plan around the effort. (There were also concerns from some political officials that Trump would oppose having a US Postal Service he despised playing an integral role by being responsible for shipping all of the masks.) Short went over to Pence. "This isn't ready," he told the vice president. "We're pulling it off the agenda." Grogan agreed.

Kadlec was dismayed when no one spoke up to defend the initiative or even devote a full discussion to it. He had prepared a full slideshow presentation to sell the task force on the idea and thought he had figured out how to market it to the skeptical White House. He had initially considered—and written up—one presentation that would effectively kiss up to the White House by making the initiative center around Trump and how much he cared about the American people. But then he had landed on something else to appeal to the White House's sensibilities: that having everyone wear masks would allow the country to reopen economically and get people back to work. People would still need to take precautions such as social distancing, but wearing masks would assure them of some level of protection.

Kadlec never gave either presentation. Short yanked it off the agenda and made sure it never got back on.

The underwear and garment companies ultimately manufactured the 650 million masks as planned, enough for almost every American to have at least two. The health officials hoped that the initiative would send a clear message from the US government: wear a mask and protect your fellow neighbor; help the country get back to normal safely. But instead of being sent to households across the country, boxes and boxes of masks sat untouched for months. (HHS ended up sending many of them to health care centers that served low-income patients and other places in need.)

The government could not reach a consensus on masks, and the bitter split on the task force worsened. Libertarians such as Marc Short and Chief of Staff Mark Meadows were adamantly opposed to actively promoting the use of masks, and face coverings began turning into a partisan Rorschach test of whether you were with Trump or against him.

Yes-or-no questions consumed the White House task force for months. Should flights from China be blocked or not? Should sick cruise ship passengers be sent to Guantánamo Bay or not? Should the economy be bailed out or not? Some approached the mask debate the same way: Should people wear masks or not? As the weeks dragged on, it became clear that the task force members simply didn't know.

The reality was that the virus was moving much faster than academic science was, and the task force members couldn't wait for perfect data; they had to make the best decisions they could and update their guidelines as the scientific understanding grew.

Science, by its very nature, is iterative. Researchers learn bit by bit and then adjust. This is especially true with a new disease. The coronavirus had been in the United States for only two months, and US officials had learned about its global presence just three months before. They had been arguing about it almost as long as they had known about it. What they didn't know far eclipsed what they did know, even if they were learning a little bit more every day.

But with Trump determined to brush aside the virus's threat, the shifting stances of the scientists on masks gave people like Meadows the ability to cast doubt on the doctors' credibility altogether. There were legitimate reasons that doctors did not yet know whether masks would work, including the degree of asymptomatic and presymptomatic transmission, but some White House officials didn't care about such nuances. (When all the doctors emphatically endorsed mask use in late March, economic adviser Larry Kudlow vocalized the way many people were feeling: "Well, you guys said they don't work, and now you're talking about whether we should recommend them.")

Some political officials could not believe that more than a hundred years after the Spanish flu pandemic, scientists and doctors still did not have a consensus about whether masks were effective.

"When it's all said and done, we can bitch and moan about the president's messaging, but we were learning far too much in real time about how to intervene," said Joe Grogan. "We should have known about these goddamn masks."

And other political officials, including Pence's team, were frustrated that the doctors did not offer some sort of mea culpa after they changed their position on masks. The doctors tried to explain to the task force why their view had changed—namely, that there was now a more complete understanding of the role of presymptomatic and asymptomatic spread and that cloth masks were effective outside of a hospital setting. But the officials felt that the doctors owed them and the American public an apology for why they had been wrong before and an explanation of why people should trust them now. Many outside scientists and public health officials would later agree that a fuller accounting of the shifting recommendations on masks was needed to shore up public trust.

Instead, the doctors and scientists on the task force failed to convince economic officials, budget officials, and political libertarians that they knew what they were talking about. Trump wasn't yet involved in the mask discussions, but his proxies knew he would be suspicious of the doctors. Trump was obsessed with his appearance. There was no way he would wear something over his nose and mouth. If the scientists wavered, recommending one thing one day and another thing the next, he would dismiss them out of hand. He didn't want to listen to them anyway, and that would give him a reason to ignore them. That fumbled opportunity created lasting damage to the task force and left a catastrophic legacy.

"We basically gave every single person in the room the license to have a view on masks and divorced it from public health," one member of the task force said, adding that the mask debate had marked the beginning of the end of the task force in terms of the officials' willingness to work together. The hand-wringing and fighting over the issue had led to deep polarization among the members that would manifest in even deeper political divisions across the country. The entire dynamic of the group changed. Instead of trying to come up with a solution that everyone would support and promote, the mask-wearing debate became a philosophical one: one group thought that masks represented public safety; the other group that they represented tyranny.

The American meteorologist Edward Lorenz is considered to be the father of the "Butterfly Effect," a term he coined in 1972. The idea is that the flap of a butterfly's wings in Brazil can lead to a tornado in Texas several weeks later. Is it true? Can something so small, so slight, lead to something so consequential, so monumental, so calamitous?

If Fauci had not been so forceful when he had told Americans not to buy masks in February, would more people have later followed his recommendations that people wear masks as the death toll mounted? If Redfield hadn't stumbled through his explanation of why doctors needed masks, would others on the task force have listened to him more closely? If Azar had tried on a black mask and not a white one that some of the others thought looked like a jockstrap, would the White House have greenlighted Kadlec's initiative and sent masks to every corner of the country? Would lives have been saved? Would the outcome of November's presidential election have changed? There is no way to know.

Some of the most powerful people in the White House—Trump, Short, and Meadows—were adamantly against any sort of mask mandate. Maybe there was never going to be enough science, enough evidence, enough proof to convince them otherwise. But there were several fatal moments in the debate about masks. The consequences would haunt the White House—and the country.

While the White House task force spent days locked in an argument about face coverings, relations between Trump and Chinese officials deteriorated rapidly.

On March 12, Zhao Lijian, the deputy director of the Chinese Ministry of Foreign Affairs Information Department, alleged that the virus might have originated in the United States, not China. "When did patient zero begin in US?" he tweeted. "How many people are infected? What are the names of the hospitals? It might be US army who brought the epidemic to Wuhan."

He posted a video of Redfield testifying before Congress and admitting that some people had died of the virus even though US officials had initially thought they were suffering from influenza. Zhao was alleging that the virus could have been in the United States for many months and been brought over to China by the US military, the way many believed the Spanish flu had originally spread from a military base in Kansas in 1918. "Be transparent!" he wrote. "Make public your data! US owe us an explanation!"

Around that time, the state-controlled China Global Television Network published a six-minute, twenty-seven-second report for audiences in the Middle East suggesting that the virus had originated outside China and been carried to Wuhan during a military exercise in October 2019. The report also seemed to imply that the virus could have originated in the United States.

White House officials were seeing a government-run disinformation campaign take place before their very eyes. Apoplectic, they began tracking the campaign closely. They noted that Twitter accounts linked to Russian bots began spreading the name of a US service member, an army sergeant based in Fort Detrick, Maryland, alleging that she was the one who had taken the virus to Wuhan. US officials believed that she was in danger and gave her a special security detail. The allegation was sensitive; Fort Detrick houses the US Army Medical Research Institute of Infectious Diseases, and the biological lab had reported major safety issues in 2019 before the coronavirus outbreak in China.

How could the Chinese so swiftly turn the tables on the United States and blame the United States for the virus? No one was as furious as Trump. Four days after Zhao's comments, Trump attacked China in a Twitter post: "The United States will be powerfully supporting those industries, like Airlines and others, that are particularly affected by the Chinese Virus. We will be stronger than ever before!"

Only two words in that tweet really mattered: "Chinese Virus." Conservative activists and some Republicans had already begun calling COVID-19 variations of that, but Trump had not directly endorsed its use until that point. (Attempting to give the virus an ethnicity would unleash a wave of racist verbal and physical attacks in the United States. From March through June, there would be 2,120 hate incidents directed at Asian Americans, according to the Asian Pacific Policy and Planning Council and Chinese for Affirmative Action. They included verbal attacks, with innocent people accosted simply because of their race. Many of them were told that they were responsible for bringing the virus to the United States.)

When asked about his use of the "China virus" or the "Chinese virus," Trump said that it was in response to Zhao's allegation:

"Well, China was putting out information, which was false, that our military gave this to them. That was false. And rather than having an argument, I said I have to call it where it came from; it did come from China. So I think it's a very accurate term. But, no, I didn't appreciate the fact that China was saying that our military gave it to them. Our military did not give—give it to anybody."

He didn't relent over the next several days.

March 18: Trump was asked if calling it the "China virus" was racist. "It's not racist at all. No, not at all. It comes from China, that's why. It comes from China. I want to be accurate."

March 19: "We continue our relentless effort to defeat the Chinese virus."

March 20: "I'd like to begin by providing an update on what we are doing to minimize the impact of the Chinese virus on our nation's students."

March 21: "We've also reached agreements with Canada and Mexico on new travel rules at our northern and southern borders to halt the entry of the Chinese virus while continuing trade and commerce."

March 22: "As we continue to marshal every resource at America's disposal in the fight against the Chinese virus, we are profoundly grateful to our nation's state and local leaders, doctors, nurses, law enforcement and first responders who are waging this battle on the ground."

The diplomatic disconnection was a dangerous turn for both countries. Officials in Beijing summoned representatives from the US Embassy to a meeting to talk about Trump's attacks. They wanted him to stop.

Trump loved engaging in a war of words with his adversaries. It was one of his greatest skills. But there were consequences to doing so, and some aides were growing alarmed. They told Trump that they were having a hard time getting the Chinese to export any masks, gowns, or other protective equipment and US hospitals were only weeks away from running out. Trump should consider toning his rhetoric down so that China would release the supplies that the United States needed, they told him, according to one person involved in the intervention.

Around the same time, some of Trump's closest friends in New York, ones with extensive ties to China, also called him to ask him to lower the temperature. Trump begrudgingly agreed to do so, but he didn't want to look as though he was capitulating to the Chinese demands.

On Monday, March 23, he walked to the lectern in the White House briefing room and began his remarks with a markedly different approach. He promised that he would do everything he could to protect Asian Americans, and he (temporarily) stopped referring to the coronavirus as the "China virus" or the "Chinese virus." When he was asked what had prompted his change in tone, he said, "because it seems that there could be a little bit of nasty language toward the Asian Americans in our country, and I don't like that at all. These are incredible people. They love our country, and I'm not going to let it happen."

Trump's shift was immediately noted in Beijing. On March 27, just after midnight in Washington, Trump and President Xi Jinping spoke on the phone. Trump told Xi that China had to stop claiming that the virus had originated in the United States. In return, Xi asked Trump to stop referring to the pandemic as the China virus. They reached a delicate truce and pledged mutual cooperation. It would be the last known time the two leaders would speak in 2020.

"Just finished a very good conversation with President Xi of China," Trump tweeted after the call. "Discussed in great detail the CoronaVirus that is ravaging large parts of our Planet. China has been through much & has developed a strong understanding of the Virus. We are working closely together. Much respect!"

On March 28, a day after he spoke with Xi, a large plane landed in New York after a nonstop flight from China, carrying 130,000 N95 masks, 1.8 million surgical masks and gowns, more than 10.3 million gloves, and 70,000 thermometers. The plane would be the first of many organized through an effort spearheaded by Jared Kushner called "Project Airbridge."

A few days later, the White House task force began receiving a flood of data that showed beyond doubt the effectiveness of mask wearing in preventing the spread. On April 2, the World Health Organization revealed that people could spread COVID-19 five or six days before they started developing symptoms; in some cases, they could do so even fourteen days beforehand. That meant people could be contagious for a long period of time without knowing they were sick. The only way to try to stop the spread was to have everyone, even those who felt fine, wear a mask when in public.

The day after the WHO research was released, the CDC finally changed its recommendations. For the first time, it advised Americans to wear nonsurgical cloth masks to prevent the spread of the disease. That abruptly undid more than a month of pleading with Americans not to wear masks.

During much of that confused period, Trump was holding daily press conferences at the White House, so it fell to him to announce the change. That would prove to be a fatal mistake, as he had no intention of following the new guidelines himself. On April 3, in a blue suit, white shirt, and red tie, he stood at the White House briefing room lectern and provided the new CDC guidance. He announced the mask guidelines but quickly offered a caveat rendering the whole thing meaningless. "So with the masks, it's going to be, really, a voluntary thing," he said. "You can do it. You don't have to do it. I'm choosing not to do it, but some people may want to do it, and that's okay. It may be good. Probably will. They're making a recommendation. It's only a recommendation. It's voluntary."

Later in the briefing, Trump was asked why he wouldn't wear one.

He responded quite simply that he didn't like the image it portrayed. And besides, he felt fine. "I just don't want to wear one myself," he said. "It's a recommendation. They recommend it. I'm feeling good. I just don't want to be doing—I don't know, somehow sitting in the Oval Office behind that beautiful Resolute Desk—the great Resolute Desk—I think wearing a face mask as I greet presidents, prime ministers, dictators, kings, queens, I don't know. Somehow I don't see it for myself. I just—I just don't. Maybe I'll change my mind, but this will pass and hopefully it'll pass very quickly."

Trump's resistance was driven entirely by his obsession with his personal appearance. Masks look ridiculous, he told aides. When people walked into the Oval Office wearing one, he ordered them to take it off.

Even Azar had repeatedly urged Trump to wear one. "Wearing a mask is a sign of weakness," Trump responded on several occasions. "You look weak if you wear a mask."

Trump was not a student of history, so he would not learn any lessons from the 1918 debate over masks. Instead, he channeled anti-mask skepticism, and his followers fell into line. He wasn't just indifferent to masks; he reviled them and encouraged similar contempt among his staff. It was another example of the bully culture he created. Aides were strongly discouraged from wearing masks if they were to be captured in a photograph with him. People were largely not allowed to stand behind him when he spoke if they were wearing a mask. He didn't want to see a mask or be seen wearing one.

Many Republican state governors immediately adopted Trump's resistance to masks, some moving to block local ordinances that required face coverings. County and city officials who did push for mask mandates were harassed and mocked. And a significant number of Republican lawmakers in the House of Representatives and Senate followed Trump's lead, some of them equating masks with tyranny.

Just like that, masks became a political cudgel, one that scientists

on the task force didn't appreciate until much later. They had assumed that most Americans would follow the CDC's recommendations, not realizing how much pull Trump had with the millions of
people who made up his base, a base who had been told that news
was fake, that science was fake, and that Washington elites wanted
to control their lives. A simple piece of fabric three inches high by
six inches across was the easiest way to slow the virus's spread. Instead, it would become a symbol of a fiercely divided United States,
a symbol that would lead to fistfights, arrests, and even violent incidents resulting in death.

For Fauci, the mask debate would linger in a much different way.
His critics multiplied exponentially as the year went on, continu-
ally on the lookout for ways to undercut the world-famous doctor.
They decided that his reversal on mask wearing was the quintessen-
tial sign of his arrogance and fallibility. He wasn't as smart as he
thought, they gloated. And they believed that it gave them license to
question everything that came out of his mouth for months to come.

CHAPTER 10

"LIBERATE"

April 15, 2020
CONFIRMED US COVID-19 CASES: **640,000**
CONFIRMED US COVID-19 DEATHS: **31,000**

The economic devastation in late March and early April occurred on an unfathomable scale. During much of that period, US companies shed a total of 1 million workers each day. (For comparison, during a good stretch, the economy usually *adds* 1 million jobs in the course of 150 days.) Many laid-off employees were sent home with no severance pay or knowledge about when the next paycheck would come. Macy's furloughed most of its 125,000 workers. Disney World closed indefinitely. Major League Baseball delayed its season. Ford, General Motors, Honda, and Fiat Chrysler shut their US factories. Just 87,534 people went through the Transportation Security Administration's travel checkpoints on April 14, down from 2.2 million a year earlier. COVID-19 was strangling everything.

In March, Anthony Fauci and Deborah Birx had convinced Donald Trump to support broad lockdown guidelines through the end of April, but the resulting economic misery was shattering the president's reelection message. In 2016, he had promised to rebuild the US economy, and four years later it was crumbling beneath him. So in early April, he tried to reverse course. But he ran into opposition from an unlikely force: state governors, many of whom wanted to keep their lockdowns in place regardless of what the White House said.

The president didn't do well when he wasn't in control, and some of the governors were creating major headaches for him. He began saying that he could force states to reopen if he wanted to because he was the president.

"There's a debate over what authority you have to order the country reopened," Reuters's Steve Holland told Trump at an April 13 briefing. "What authority do you have on this one?"

"Well, I have the ultimate authority," Trump replied.

Trump's point—which was false but was believed by many of his supporters nonetheless—was that the president had power to overrule every governor and every decision made at the state level. It was an affront to the federalism that Republicans had rallied behind for years, but Trump didn't seem to care. "When somebody is the president of the United States, the authority is total," he said. "And that's the way it's got to be. It's total."

In mid-April, the scale of the virus was still unknown. There weren't enough tests to determine how many people were sick, but the death numbers were climbing precipitously. Some of the tests took more than a week to produce results, making them essentially useless. Someone who was sick wouldn't know it and could be out in the community during that week. Alternatively, someone who was healthy could contract the virus in the period between the time they were tested and the time they received the results, requiring them to be tested all over again. Up to that point, labs had tested 3.3 million Americans, with about 146,000 tests done per day in mid-April. Health experts had hoped that the country would be conducting millions of tests each day by the time the country was ready to reopen. But the administration was nowhere close to that target.

Governors demanded more help from the White House and kept up pressure for a national testing strategy. It made no sense for each state to be doing its own thing. States were actually competing against one another for the limited available masks and tests—and the supplies needed to actually use the tests—driving up the costs of everything. (Reagents and swabs were some of the materials needed to run the tests, and those conducting them needed personal protective equipment such as N95 masks and gloves.) As for a national testing strategy, that remained a no-go for Trump. He didn't want to admit that there was a problem and he didn't want to own it. At the same time, he blustered about exerting federal control over state reopening plans. The conflict was irreconcilable; either Trump was in charge or the governors were.

In the end, no one was in charge.

As the hand-wringing in the West Wing intensified, conservative groups across the country mobilized and fanned out. Organizers in Lansing, Michigan, launched Operation Gridlock, an effort to snarl traffic around the state capital so state officials would have to rethink Governor Gretchen Whitmer's "Stay Home, Stay Safe" executive order, which she had just extended through the month of April. Per Whitmer's order, it was illegal for businesses to require employees to go into work, and the number of people who could enter certain stores was limited. All public and private gatherings with non–family members were prohibited, as was vacation travel.

So on April 15, thousands of people descended on Lansing in cars, vans, and trucks. They gathered in large groups, conservative activists and right-wing militia members, trying to clog traffic and attract media attention. Their signs ran the gamut from the relatively peaceful ALL WORKERS ARE ESSENTIAL poster on the side of a van to the

more apocalyptic warning offered by a man in a red MAKE AMERICA
GREAT AGAIN hat:

The media & Govt. are
LYING to you!
This "crisis" is a FARCE
to usher in horrific
TYRANNY
DO NOT COMPLY

Some of the militia members had rifles slung over their shoulders,
but the event remained peaceful and attracted national media coverage, which had been one of the primary goals.

Similar protests cropped up around the country, particularly in
states led by Democratic governors such as Minnesota and Virginia.
On the same day as the protests in Michigan, Kentucky's Democratic governor, Andy Beshear, held a press conference to explain
the lockdown orders he was keeping in place. A large group gathered
nearby, shouting at him to reopen immediately. "They believe we
should open the economy," he said, acknowledging the protests. "It
would absolutely kill people. We know we're not to that point. My
job isn't to make the popular decision, but the right decision."

Some of the protests were promoted by gun rights groups, warning that the business restrictions were the beginning of some sort of
big-government takeover. Stephen Moore, the conservative econo-
mist with close ties to the White House, helped advise protest organizers and even spoke at a couple of the events. He received phone
calls every day from conservative activists outraged about the influence Fauci appeared to have on business closure rules. "I would
get so many calls every day with people saying 'What's wrong with
this fucking Fauci?'" he said. "Sometimes they'd call him Fucky, not
Fauci."

Moore later claimed that the protesters demanding that state
governments reopen were modern-day versions of Rosa Parks, the

iconic civil rights figure who had helped end bus segregation in the South. The comparison drew widespread scorn.

The day of the Michigan and Kentucky protests—three days after Easter—was one of the deadliest of the pandemic so far. More than 2,700 people died that day, a greater toll than from the Pearl Harbor attack in 1941. But for many of the protesters, it was time to rebel. Despite the grim statistics, millions of Americans believed the president's proclamations that the threat of the virus was overblown, and still others were no longer willing to sacrifice their personal freedoms for something that hadn't yet impacted their lives.

In March and April, Birx's days sometimes began as early as 4:00 a.m. As had become their custom, she and her team worked incessantly to collect and analyze as much data as possible. Unbeknown to most of the task force, Birx was still drafting "gateway criteria" that would provide states with step-by-step instructions for how to reopen. The secrecy was deliberate. She had quickly learned from the mask debate that all those on the task force thought they were an expert on everything and that vetting proposals produced by a bunch of people only led to acrimony and finger-pointing. She knew that the only way for the country to reopen safely was to do it gradually, with stringent precautions in place.

So when Birx finally presented the reopening criteria at a White House news conference on April 16, one day after the Michigan protest, she caught many officials on the task force by surprise. It was the first time most of them were seeing the guidelines. (All the doctors, however, had seen them.)

The guidelines encouraged state leaders to use statistical benchmarks to decide when and how to roll back restrictions on restaurants, bars, gyms, and schools, among other venues. She outlined different phases of reopening. To get to phase 1, for instance—in which a state could return people to work in stages and open large venues with strict social distancing protocols, but would still have to keep bars closed—the state would have to have a downward trajectory of cases over a two-week period. Although the gateway criteria were, in theory, supposed to be an encouraging sign that reopening could begin, the reality was that no state was anywhere close to meeting the benchmark for even phase 1. No one said it out loud, but the doctors believed that the states wouldn't begin hitting the benchmarks until later in the summer, around August. They thought they still had plenty of time to bring things under better control.

The states would also have to establish "core preparedness responsibilities," including sufficient testing and contact tracing, as well as the ability to ramp up their ICU capacity and provide personal protective equipment in the event that there was a major outbreak or surge. Few states were prepared for an onslaught of cases.

Governors and state health officials worried most about the country's pitiful testing capacity. Trump's desire to evade responsibility for a national testing strategy left federal bureaucrats to try to fill the holes where they could, and, over time, the government did increase the number of tests. Ironically, Trump and his aides fixated on the improved numbers for weeks, looking for every opportunity to tout how many tests the United States was conducting compared to other countries. But the numbers didn't take into account that the country's testing capacity was still far behind those of other countries, given the number of cases the US was grappling with. Also left out of their self-congratulatory statements was the fact that they weren't helping states use the tests they were given. Because of the federal government's refusal to help coordinate testing, some states were getting shipments of tests without the supplies and materials to run them; other times, supplies and tests went to the wrong places and not to the states and regions that needed them most.

With no guidance from the White House, career officials inside the FDA and other agencies were scrambling to try to resolve some of the issues, but it was a patchwork effort. "In the absence of a national strategy and all the coordination that goes with that, you have now individual labs, cities, states all scrambling to get tests and the test supplies to run them. Very quickly, we were running into shortages," one senior official recalled. "You had no one coordinating on logistics to make sure supplies were going where they needed to go and tests went where they needed to be. You control that at a national level." Even worse, major diagnostic manufacturers had developed machines that could run hundreds of tests—but many of the machines were sitting idle, simply because there weren't enough supplies or technicians who actually knew how to use them.

Despite all the problems, Birx's reopening guidelines deferred to states as to how to handle their plans. When Trump held a conference call with governors to go over the guidelines, he backed away from his edict just three days earlier that he could override any state directive. "You're going to call your own shots," he told the governors. It was a tactical retreat. Once again, he didn't want to take responsibility for what might happen.

Meanwhile, the protesters in Michigan and elsewhere who were demanding that governors reopen states had caught Trump's eye. They were his supporters, gathering in large groups, the kind that had used to pack his rallies. Oftentimes, they were waving Trump flags and wearing red hats.

On April 17, one day after the guidelines were released and two days after Operation Gridlock in Michigan, Fox News ran a segment at 11:19 a.m. about the protests and how they were spreading across the country.

Two minutes later, Trump announced his unfettered support.

"LIBERATE MINNESOTA!" he tweeted at 11:21 a.m.

"LIBERATE MICHIGAN!" he tweeted at 11:22 a.m.

"LIBERATE VIRGINIA, and save your great 2nd Amendment," he tweeted at 11:25 a.m. "It is under siege!"

Trump's Twitter tirade was enough to throw the barely one-day-old reopening guidelines into the digital toilet.

Those three tweets, sixteen words in total, were the point of no return. With the 2020 election looming (in March, Democratic voters began to coalesce around Joe Biden as the party's nominee), the stock market beginning to rebound, and his supporters' frustration over the lockdowns intensifying, Trump was over the coronavirus, and he had given millions of Americans a reason to move past the crisis, too. Fauci's and Birx's continuing efforts to convince Trump to support the reopening guidelines were no match for cable television, which the president was plugged into for hours at a time. In a span of just a few minutes, it became clear to the doctors that the tide had turned. How could their message, backed up by science that the president didn't believe, compete with the things that really resonated with him, such as Trump flags and red MAKE AMERICA GREAT AGAIN hats?

It couldn't.

The doctors had worked so hard to convince Trump to put broad restrictions into place just a couple weeks ago and had been spending almost every day trying to convince him he had made the right decision. Now he was leading the charge to reopen. The day before his "LIBERATE" tweets, he had brushed aside the idea that the virus might return in the autumn, saying that if it did, he would "stamp it out."

Part of the problem was that he believed that the unprecedented step he had taken—shutting down the entire country for six weeks— would blunt the virus's spread. Birx and Fauci's opinions had carried enormous weight in March and a good bit of April; Birx had briefed Trump multiple times a week, and he had generally listened to their advice, despite often contradicting it in public. But in Trump's mind, Birx and Fauci had led him to believe that after a painful few weeks, the pandemic would be over. So when he realized that the six-week shutdown wasn't the end, he decided that he was done with the doctors and their advice.

"People thought, 'Okay, this is a drastic step but if we take it, it'll be over.' And then it wasn't over," one senior official on the task force said. "It undermined their credibility."

Fauci, in particular, had worked with other presidents during health crises before and knew that there was a delicate balance to maintain between public health and politics. But until then, he had not grasped the fervor with which Trump's core supporters hung on his every word. He hadn't foreseen that Trump would be able to snap his fingers or fire off a tweet and marshal an army of people to do exactly as he said. When Trump made clear to his supporters— and his subordinates—that it was time to reopen, they followed in lockstep. "I knew we were in serious trouble," Fauci said in an interview. "We were fighting a losing battle of people who were looking for an excuse to make out there was no outbreak. I think that was a defining moment there. It was smack in the face waking me up."

The death threats against Fauci picked up precipitously from that point onward. The next day, in Austin, the far-right conspiracy theorist Alex Jones led a protest demanding that Trump remove Fauci from office. "Fire Fauci! Fire Fauci!" they screamed.

Georgia announced that it was going to reopen first, on April 20, even as the number of coronavirus cases spiked across much of the United States. (That defied the White House's reopening guidelines, but Trump didn't raise major objections.) The state's Republican governor, Brian Kemp, wanted to reopen almost everything: gyms, massage parlors, nail salons, hair salons, bowling alleys, tattoo parlors. They were hardly "essential businesses."

Fauci and Birx were dumbfounded but stopped short of openly criticizing the Republican governor. In task force meetings, though, they said they couldn't comprehend why people would have a burning desire to patronize those businesses when the risk was so high.

"What is up with these people in Georgia who want to do massages and go to beauty salons and nail salons?" Birx asked the other task force members during a meeting in April. "Who are these people?"

Fauci agreed, adding sarcastically, "I'm just itching to get a tattoo."

They understood that people were restless and wanted to go back to normal. But the prepandemic "normal" didn't exist at a time when the virus was still spreading so aggressively. In retrospect, some officials concede that the health experts didn't appreciate that the virus wasn't spreading everywhere evenly and that many people in lower-risk states were resentful that they had had to make such a huge personal sacrifice for what felt like a distant threat.

At a Coronavirus Task Force briefing shortly before Georgia's planned reopening, Birx was asked how the state could open safely if it allowed people to congregate in settings where people inherently had to be close together, such as tattoo parlors. Georgia was acting in complete defiance of reopening guidelines that she had set out days before. But Birx continued to try to walk the tightrope in public, stopping short of expressing her beliefs in a way that might seem to be an affront to the president. "If there's a way that people can social distance and do those things, then they can do those things. I don't know how, but people are very creative," she said. The comment stunned outside public health experts, who knew that Georgia's reckless action would cause a spike in infections and deaths.

Birx decided to share her concerns directly with Trump soon afterward, telling him the opposite of what she had said at the press conference. No matter how much the president wanted to see a "big, beautiful reopening," she said, it simply wasn't possible for Georgia to do it safely. Georgia had gone too far, she explained, and the president needed to make that clear so other states didn't pursue such ill-advised plans. It was clear that Trump was torn. There was his Twitter persona, the one most deeply connected to cable news and perhaps his id, that was barking for states to reopen immediately. And then there was the Trump who on occasion actually did heed the advice of his medical advisers, despite his growing mistrust of them. Birx's appeal worked; once again she had gotten through to the president—for a short time, anyway.

"I want him to do what he thinks is right, but I disagree with him on what he is doing," Trump said of Kemp at a press conference on April 22. "I think it's too soon." He tried to encourage people to be patient for just a short while longer. "I love those people that use all of those things—the spas, the beauty parlors, barbershops, tattoo parlors. I love them. But they can wait a little longer, just a little bit—not much, because safety has to predominate."

The mood in the White House was shifting, though. As some of Trump's top aides sensed that the doctors were losing their influence, there was growing talk of the outbreak being over in short order. At one point in late April, Vice President Pence and White House economic adviser Larry Kudlow sat in the Situation Room, waiting for a task force meeting to begin. Both men exuded optimism about the country preparing to reopen, believing that it would lead to an explosion of growth and activity (and no doubt be a boon to the president's electoral prospects).

"Maybe I'm a glass-half-full kind of guy, but I think the country is ready to reopen," Pence said. "And when it's ready to reopen, we are going to really take off."

Kudlow emphatically agreed. "There's a lot of pent-up demand out there."

At the same time as Birx was working on her gateway criteria, the CDC was hard at work drafting detailed guidance that states could use to decide how to safely reopen all manner of businesses— restaurants, churches, summer camps, preschools, workplaces, and other public facilities. Each entity posed its own set of challenges. That was core to the agency's mission: helping the public understand how they could live their lives while protecting themselves and their loved ones. The CDC is not a regulatory agency; it provides guidance that no one is bound by law to follow. But because of its standing as the nation's premier public health agency, state and local leaders usually follow the agency's advice, though to varying degrees.

The problem was that the effort was coming after CDC director Robert Redfield had already—in the eyes of White House officials and HHS secretary Alex Azar—screwed up two other initiatives: testing and masks. People inside the White House had grown wary of him. And because of the testing debacle and the brutal media coverage that had followed, it was becoming easy to blame the CDC for every problem, even when multiple people or agencies were at fault. Redfield, with his nonconfrontational and affable manner, was an especially convenient target. White House and HHS officials believed that he was unwilling to push back seriously and was therefore easy to steamroll. When they heard about the CDC's reopening guidelines, they demanded to scrutinize every word before the agency published anything.

The CDC is typically walled off from the worst of partisan politics. It typically does not send guidance to the White House Office of Management and Budget; CDC guidelines usually go through an internal review process made up largely of career scientists and civil servants and then are released to the public. During health emergencies, the agency does have to work more closely with the White House, which sometimes reviews guidance and recommendations, especially when something as drastic as school or business closures is involved. But the Trump White House, eager to reopen with as few restrictions as possible, was interfering to a degree never before seen in the agency's seventy-four-year history.

CDC scientists were working eighteen- and twenty-hour days trying to prepare nearly a hundred pages of guidelines, hoping to release them in April to inform the states how they could reopen. The agency sent the documents to HHS, which then sent them to the White House. That was when the chaos began. Rather than a small number of health and political officials reviewing the documents and offering targeted suggestions, hundreds of people weighed in, ranging from Ivanka Trump to a low-level political appointee at the

Department of Education. But everything ground to a halt when the document reached the Office of Management and Budget, led by Russell Vought.

Pence's chief of staff, Marc Short, and Trump's chief of staff, Mark Meadows, were bitter rivals, but they were unified when it came to watering down the CDC guidelines as much as possible. Short felt that some of the restrictions represented a dream scenario for liberals, allowing the government to dictate what people could and couldn't do. They funneled most of their opposition to the proposals through Vought, who nitpicked the CDC's guidance with agency officials. Short and Meadows thought the doctors were incapable of seeing the bigger picture.

Redfield had emailed a draft of the CDC's initial proposal to White House officials on April 10 and then again on April 24, asking when the White House would sign off on them so he could post them online. But OMB officials never signed off, only telling Redfield under no circumstances to post the proposal, according to emails obtained by the Associated Press.

Some White House officials used the time to see how far they could push the CDC to water down its guidelines, a process the agency's career scientists took as a personal affront. They were the experts, the ones who had spent their careers dedicated to health crises just like this one. Now people with no public health background were telling them how to do their jobs.

The CDC's chief of staff, Kyle McGowan, pushed back against many of the suggestions. It was a slow dance, a staring contest to see who would break first before the hammer came down. After enough back-and-forth, Vought, the OMB director, would get onto the phone with McGowan or someone else at the CDC and tell the person to get into line.

In one particularly acrimonious encounter, OMB and the CDC were at odds over restaurant reopenings. The CDC recommended that all tables be placed at a socially distant six feet apart and that all waiters wear masks. OMB wanted the agency to remove the definition of social distancing as being six feet apart. The agency dug in, arguing that social distancing was a well-defined term, appearing in dozens of places on the agency's website and in other documents. If it changed the definition in one document, it would have to change the definition everywhere else.

Vought and Paul Ray, the administrator of OMB's Office of Information and Regulatory Affairs, requested a phone call with Redfield and McGowan to work through the issues. The OMB officials argued that the guidance, as it stood, could open restaurants up to lawsuits if tables were, say, five and a half feet apart, rather than six feet. They kept insisting that the CDC take the term "social distancing" and any reference to patrons and tables being six feet apart out of the guidelines. Redfield and McGowan resisted, arguing that the guidelines would be worthless without that advice. All that would be left was the recommendation that waiters wear masks, which most were already doing anyway.

Eventually, they reluctantly came to a compromise: the agency would take out the recommendation that tables be six feet apart but would hyperlink to the term "social distancing" on its website, where the agency explained what it meant. Ray followed up in an email after their call. "Good chatting just now. We propose the following edits," he wrote. They included replacing the term "social distance" with "enhance spacing" for restaurants and workplaces. Political officials wanted to tout a roaring comeback, and they couldn't do that if businesses were half empty or weren't recovering. "You had the head of OMB telling the CDC director what he wants changed in a scientific CDC document," McGowan said.

OMB launched similar fights with the CDC on the reopening of day camps and churches. Vought was particularly aggressive on that matter, berating CDC officials into changing their proposals. In fact, he was acting on behalf of other people in the White House. Meadows and Short had made clear to OMB that those guidelines needed to be as loose as possible. They feared that tough restrictions on churches, for example, would offend Trump's conservative base. In some instances, the CDC capitulated.

"They got a lot of pressure and they caved," said Olivia Troye, who was a top Pence aide at the time and was working with Redfield on scaling back several of the recommendations.

Still, the process that had begun in April dragged into May and then into the summer without any clear guidance from the Trump administration or the CDC. So on May 14, the CDC simply posted a six-page outline of guidelines on its website without the White House's permission. The guidelines were scant, but they were something, and making them public without Vought's sign-off was a major act of defiance by the CDC.

The guidelines said that schools, day care centers, and summer camps should not reopen unless the people running the entities ran rigorous checks and screening to monitor children, teachers, and counselors. Coming just days before summer camps were set to begin, the guidance appeared to recommend canceling camps across the board.

Pandemonium ensued. A number of Trump's wealthy friends in New York called him to complain. They had been planning to send their children to expensive sleepaway camps in New York and Pennsylvania for the summer. Trump didn't know anything about the camp guidelines and excoriated Meadows for allowing the posting to happen. (Trump had never been the outdoorsy type, but he often reacted instinctively when his wealthy friends called to complain.) Meadows then exploded at Vought, who in turn exploded at the CDC officials.

The whole pandemic response was managed through power, intimidation, and bullying. Meadows, as Trump's enforcer, often punctuated angry phone calls with comments to this effect: if things aren't resolved quickly, you will have to clean out your desk at the end of the day. Everyone knew that when Meadows was screaming on the phone, it was a threat, either explicit or veiled.

For White House officials, the ultimate lesson was that despite the pushback, there was a point at which the CDC would give in and break. Consequently, some of the other reopening guidance wasn't made public until July or August, months after most states were well into their plans. Dozens of officials weighed in, knowing they had carte blanche to bully the CDC until they got their way. In the absence of concrete federal recommendations, the states fended for themselves without the advice of the nation's top public health experts. That led to disorganized and often dangerous reopenings. Some of the states that reopened the fastest and didn't have access to the CDC's guidance, including Florida, Texas, Oklahoma, and Arizona, saw the biggest spikes in summer cases.

People close to Redfield said that the whole experience had crushed him and he was beginning to unravel emotionally. As the year went on, friends and colleagues watched him become a shell of himself. His shoulders hunched. His voice lost its pep. He told one close friend that he was planning to quit by the election and not serve out the remainder of Trump's first term. (He never followed through, in part because he was afraid of whom the White House might select to replace him if he left.) He had spent his whole life trying to follow in his parents' footsteps and had attained one of the most powerful positions in public health, only to be torn apart by politics. To some, it seemed he was betraying the very scientists and experts he had wept before on his first day in office.

Michigan governor Whitmer's emergency order was set to expire at the beginning of May, so the protesters returned to Lansing on the last day of April. This time, though, many of them were armed and entered the capitol building chanting, "Lock her up!" The protest did not have the peaceful feel of the one that had taken place two weeks earlier. One person speaking at the rally told others that by supporting conservative political candidates, the protesters could effectively "slap Gretchen Whitmer right across the face."

The rally had been planned in part by several militia groups. One had even labeled the event "judgment day." People with firearms showed up in droves. And they weren't content to stand outside on the lawn. They wanted in.

As the protest picked up steam, a group of men with rifles stood in the gallery above the legislative chamber while others tried to barge into the chamber, held back by police. Unmasked militia members screamed in the police officers' faces, comparing Whitmer to Adolf Hitler.

Trump made it clear whose side he was on. The next morning, he attacked Whitmer and told her to negotiate a "deal" with the rioters, tweeting "The Governor of Michigan should give a little, and put out the fire. These are very good people, but they are angry. They want their lives back again, safely! See them, talk to them, make a deal."

Whitmer stood her ground and extended the restrictions, a move that helped slow the spread of the virus in her state. Animosity toward her would not go away, however. Trump attacked her again and again. Several months later, the Justice Department and Federal Bureau of Investigation would announce multiple arrests as part of a planned attempt to kidnap Whitmer. Six of the people involved in that plot had marched inside the Michigan capitol on April 30 and were among the group Trump had cheered on.

Armed militias became a prominent part of antimask rallies over the next several months, as many Trump supporters equated face coverings with a hostile government takeover. At times Trump seemed to revel in the paranoia and would only egg it on further as the election neared.

PART II

CHAPTER 11

PHARMACIST IN CHIEF

April 23, 2020
CONFIRMED US COVID-19 CASES: **843,000**
CONFIRMED US COVID-19 DEATHS: **47,000**

Even though much of the administration was focused on the COVID-19 response, there was a certain insularity that came with working within the walls of the White House day in and day out. The people responsible for leading the nation through a war with a virus were in many ways shielded from the unfathomable carnage taking place across the country. On March 31, there were 520 COVID-19 deaths nationwide in a twenty-four-hour period. By April 14, the deadliest day in the first seven months of the pandemic, the number of deaths had more than quadrupled, to 2,967. It was a mass casualty event day after day after day—a Pearl Harbor or 9/11 attack almost every day of April.

"The monster is still loose and it's going to be out there in Ohio and across the country until we get, you know, the shot that will take care of and will protect us," Ohio governor Mike DeWine said on *Fox News* in April. "So we've got to continue to be very, very careful."

What does a tidal wave of death look like?

In a hospital, a nurse holds a smartphone up to a dying patient's face so that family members can say goodbye from afar. No one is allowed at the patient's bedside for fear of spreading the virus.

New York City sets up forty-five mobile morgues and allows crematoriums to run twenty-four hours a day.

Lorna Breen, a New York City emergency room doctor, is so distressed by the chaos and death she witnesses during the worst of New York's outbreak that she kills herself on April 26. "I couldn't help anyone. I couldn't do anything. I just wanted to help people, and I couldn't do anything," she told a friend, according to the *New York Times*.

People protest the presence of a refrigerated trailer outside a funeral home in Hialeah, Florida, complaining that the dead bodies inside could pass on COVID-19 to people in the community.

The state of Minnesota purchases a former grocery storage facility for $5.5 million to serve as an emergency morgue.

Many Catholic priests administer last rites over the telephone, unable to anoint dying Catholics with oil as part of the sacred ceremony.

In order to make room for a crush of new corpses, the Maricopa County Medical Examiner's Office in Arizona moves twenty-two bodies into rented coolers that look as if they were designed to store bags of ice.

Hospitals quickly run out of supplies as they treat far more patients than their facilities can handle. Health care workers wear homemade masks and garbage bags to try to fill the gaps, putting themselves at immense risk. Hundreds of the workers trying to save patients succumb to the disease themselves.

Critically ill patients struggling to breathe are placed on gurneys in hospital corridors, as there are no beds for them.

St. Louis officials spend $2 million to renovate a portion of a refrigerated warehouse to store as many as 1,300 bodies until they can be properly buried.

Two trucks parked outside a Brooklyn funeral home give off such a stench that someone calls the police. Dozens of decomposing bodies are found inside. The funeral home operator says he simply has nowhere to put them. He has never before had so many bodies to take care of at one time.

On Sunday, April 26, the *Boston Globe* runs twenty-one pages of death notices, up from seven pages at the same time a year earlier.

Fifty freezer trucks holding 650 bodies are parked beneath the 39th Street Pier in Brooklyn, where they will stay for months because the families of the deceased can't afford to bury them.

More than two thousand nondescript wooden caskets are buried on Hart Island in New York, a place where people are put to rest when their families can't pay for services or their bodies are unclaimed. It is the same place where some of the first victims of AIDS were buried.

After 58,000 Americans have died and Trump says the pandemic will end soon, the Pentagon purchases 100,000 additional body bags to help deal with the continued toll.

The state of Maryland uses an ice skating rink as a temporary morgue.

The city of Chicago uses a massive refrigerated warehouse as a "surge center" to store bodies, swapping out cargo for corpses.

A seventy-six-year-old California woman contracts COVID-19 at a funeral and then dies. Family members don't get out of their cars at her funeral, driving through instead.

After Washington state bans funerals, a family holds an open-casket viewing at the side of a road so mourners can pay their respects.

By May, 100,000 people have died from the coronavirus; 200,000 by September; 300,000 by December. The time it takes to reach another 100,000 deaths gets shorter and shorter as the year goes on. More than 3 million people die in the United States in 2020, an increase of 400,000 from one year earlier. The 15 percent jump is the biggest one-year increase in deaths since 1918.

Alex Azar's black limousine sped toward the White House on the morning of March 18. The streets were eerily quiet, as many of the office buildings were vacant. The scene was dystopian. The HHS secretary noticed his phone light up. It was Donald Trump on the line. "Testing is killing me!" Trump exclaimed, screaming so loudly that Azar's staff in the limo could hear every word of the conversation. "I'm going to lose the election because of testing! What idiot had the federal government do testing?"

It was an awkward question. It was actually Trump's son-in-law, Jared Kushner, who just five days earlier had said he would be rolling out a huge national testing strategy with the help of the private sector.

"Uh, do you mean Jared?" Azar asked, trying to stay out of a family drama.

No, not Jared, Trump said. It was the CDC test that had incensed Trump. Why was the CDC creating tests in the first place? The CDC should have never taken on testing. That had put the whole issue into the federal government's lap, and the federal government was Trump. Azar tried to explain that that was what the agency did during every new public health emergency, only this time the CDC's network of public health labs hadn't been enough to keep up with a fast-spreading respiratory virus. Trump didn't care. The news media were obsessively covering the lack of coronavirus tests, and everyone was blaming Trump. The CDC should never have been involved, Trump said. States and private businesses should be responsible. Azar kept trying to explain that this was what the health agencies did in every emergency. "This was gross incompetence to let CDC develop a test," Trump seethed. Azar had been yelled at by Trump plenty, but this was a new level of anger. Trump asked Azar who oversaw the CDC. Azar said he did. So Trump held Azar responsible for the testing mess.

Without warning, Trump pivoted the conversation. Larry Ellison, the cofounder and executive chairman of Oracle, who had recently held a fundraiser for Trump, had called the president to tout remdesivir, a drug designed to treat Ebola that the NIH was studying to see if it could help treat coronavirus patients, the president said. Trump said that Ellison was one of the smartest people on the planet. "Larry

Ellison called me and said remdesivir works," he said. "I'm ordering you to have FDA approve it today."

Trump had another order for Azar. Laura Ingraham, the *Fox News* firebrand, said that the old antimalaria medication hydroxychloroquine worked as a cure against coronavirus. Trump told Azar that Ingraham had taken hydroxychloroquine while traveling in Africa and had not become ill. It had worked, Trump said. He ordered Azar to approve the use of hydroxychloroquine immediately.

Azar tried to explain that the FDA had to approve drugs based on clinical trials and data, and it didn't have either of those yet. It could not approve a drug based on the anecdotal reports of a political supporter and a *Fox News* host. "It doesn't matter," Trump responded. "These are very smart people, Larry Ellison and Laura Ingraham, and they say they work, so just approve them." Azar consulted with his general counsel later that day to see if HHS did, in fact, have the authority to order the FDA to approve the drugs. The president had given him an order, and he wanted to give him an answer one way or the other.

That afternoon, Trump was meeting with a number of health officials, including Hahn, Fauci, and his former FDA commissioner, Scott Gottlieb, who was dialed into the meeting by phone. Trump again floated the idea of having the FDA immediately approve the two drugs. Gottlieb and Fauci told the president that it was a terrible, potentially dangerous idea and strongly advised against it. About fifteen minutes into the meeting, Azar, who hadn't been invited, stormed in, breathless. He told the president he had conferred with his lawyers and could order the FDA to approve the drugs. The authority of the FDA commissioner was vested in the HHS secretary. Or, if Hahn did not want to approve the drugs, Azar said he could do so on his own. (A senior administration official said Azar was providing options on how to implement the president's priorities, and was trying to be helpful and responsive.) The other health officials were stunned that Azar would even entertain the idea and pushed back fiercely. Trump eventually backed down. But it helped set off the mad scramble to try to appease his insatiable appetite for hydroxychloroquine within the bounds of the law.

Chloroquine and its cousin hydroxychloroquine were traditionally used to treat malaria, lupus, and rheumatoid arthritis. But a handful of early trials, studying very small groups of people, had suggested that chloroquine might help prevent COVID-19 from killing people. The trials had been scattershot and largely anecdotal rather than the kind of randomized, controlled clinical trials that can provide a more definitive answer to whether a drug works.

But it had been enough to pique a few people's interest. There were no particularly effective treatments for coronavirus, and scientists and the federal government had a responsibility to screen as many current medications as they could to see if a drug already in the US arsenal might work. What health officials did not appreciate was that Trump valued information and anecdotes from outside friends and advisers as much as, if not more than, briefings by scientists armed with data and peer-reviewed research. A call from Larry Ellison or Laura Ingraham carried more weight with Trump than a briefing by Fauci or the FDA commissioner.

The advocacy by Ellison and Ingraham coincided with increased hydroxychloroquine frenzy on social media. "Maybe worth considering chloroquine for C19," Elon Musk tweeted on March 16, linking to a hydroxychloroquine "study." The linked study was a Google document written by two cryptocurrency investors, one a lawyer and the other a nonpracticing ophthalmologist. They were not virologists or infectious diseases experts. Nor was Musk, the founder of the breakthrough electric vehicle company Tesla. Although his scientific acumen is considered to be top notch, he was repeatedly mistaken when it came to judging cures for COVID-19.

The study Musk cited in his tweet said, "Recent guidelines from South Korea and China report that chloroquine is an effective antiviral therapeutic treatment against Coronavirus Disease 2019. Use of chloroquine (tablets) is showing favorable outcomes in humans infected with Coronavirus including faster time to recovery and shorter hospital stay."

The authors alleged that the paper had been written "In consultation with Stanford University School of Medicine, UAB School of Medicine and National Academy of Sciences researchers," references that gave it an aura of legitimacy. In fact, all three organizations would deny any involvement.

With Trump, that was often all it took. It was how a molehill could become a mountain. With this much desperation, with this much death, many latched on to the idea that chloroquine would be the miracle treatment to defeat the strange new virus. It's unclear exactly how the hydroxychloroquine mania first made its way to Trump. But it did, and there would be no truer believer than the president.

Three days after Musk's tweet, Trump publicly endorsed using the drug, startling aides and horrifying health officials, who could not believe that an unproven drug was being pushed from the presidential bully pulpit. "Now, a drug called chloroquine—and some people would add to it 'hydroxy-.' Hydroxychloroquine," he said. "So chloroquine or hydroxychloroquine. Now, this is a common malaria drug. It is also a drug used for strong arthritis. If somebody has pretty serious arthritis, also uses this in a somewhat different form. But it is known as a malaria drug, and it's been around for a long time and it's very powerful. But the nice part is, it's been around for a long time, so we know that if it—if things don't go as planned, it's not going to kill anybody."

Fauci in particular was appalled. It was one thing for Trump to misunderstand the virus; it was a whole different matter for him to act as a doctor or pharmacist, encouraging people to take a drug for off-label use.

"The answer is no," Fauci said emphatically the next day when asked whether there was any evidence to suggest that hydroxychloroquine would work against the coronavirus.

And so Trump and Fauci squared off for their most public showdown yet, like two cowboys in a Western on either end of a dusty street. People peered out of the saloons to watch.

Support for hydroxychloroquine would become yet another litmus test for loyalty to Trump. And it would teach Fauci and other doctors on the task force a new lesson: Trump wasn't only willing to ignore science, he was prepared to reinvent it, and many of his enablers would bend to his will. After all, he was credulous of things he read in dark corners of the internet, and was often skeptical towards scientists and pharmaceutical companies. Maybe the cryptocurrency investors and Musk had discovered something that Fauci and the other doctors were too timid to appreciate.

"I think, without saying too much, I'm probably more of a fan of that than—maybe than anybody," Trump said after Fauci's initial rejection of the drug. "But I'm a big fan, and we'll see what happens."

That was how things had gone throughout Trump's presidency. When he had wanted to build a wall along the Mexican border, his aides had diverted money from the Pentagon budget to build it. When he had wanted to purchase Greenland from Denmark, his aides had begun studying how to pull it off. When Trump wanted something, many of his advisers lived in fear of his wrath if they didn't accede to his desire, no matter how outlandish. So when he wanted a drug to be pumped into Americans, dozens of his aides dropped whatever else they were doing and tried to buy every antimalaria pill on the planet.

The debate over hydroxychloroquine was a strange one. Since the drug had already been approved by the FDA to treat malaria, lupus, and rheumatoid arthritis, doctors could already prescribe it for other ailments if they thought it might help. And that was exactly what some doctors around the country decided to do. There were no available treatments for COVID-19, and if their patients were willing to accept the risk that came with taking the drug, there didn't seem to be a lot to lose.

Yet as Trump began touting the drug, pharmaceutical companies took notice. Several offered to donate tablets that would amount to 30 million doses, including the pharmaceutical companies Sandoz and Bayer, which wanted to donate 3 million tablets of a chloroquine medication to the Strategic National Stockpile. Bayer's pills, however, came from plants in India and Pakistan that had not been inspected by the FDA. In order to distribute the pills to doctors and allow doctors to prescribe the donated drug to patients, the FDA would need to issue an emergency-use authorization.

Pressure increased on health officials to find out whether hydroxychloroquine actually worked. And there were legitimate reasons to study it. In the face of a new disease, researchers have to study the existing arsenal of drugs to see if something already available might work. But Trump's fixation on the drug, which translated to an almost cultlike obsession, led to a disproportionate amount of time and resources being spent—and ultimately wasted—on it.

Oracle, for instance, was trying to set up a website and mobile app with the federal government to collect data on doctors' use of the drug, an idea promoted by Ellison that several health officials eventually helped kill.

On March 17, Robert Kadlec's office began working with Bayer to secure its donation of 3 million doses of the drug. Kadlec's division was responsible for the Strategic National Stockpile.

"This can be a BIG immediate win," Kadlec's manager of strategic innovation and emerging technology, Joseph Hamel, wrote in an email to Christopher Houchens, the acting director of the Division of Chemical, Biological, Radiological and Nuclear Medical Countermeasures at the Biomedical Advanced Research and Development

Authority (BARDA), an agency under HHS that is responsible for protecting the United States against emerging biological threats.

Career scientists at both BARDA and the FDA raised a number of concerns about the donation, including the fact that the safety of the pills was unknown. In an internal email to Rick Bright, the BARDA director, Houchens wrote that "there are safety liabilities associated with the drug . . . accepting the donation could send a signal that we are not concerned about the risk." He added, "I do not believe we should accept the donation until we have an understanding on the clinical utility of the drug. Accepting the donation could lead to widespread use that is not supported by any clinical data."

But HHS officials, at Azar's direction, pressed BARDA to accept the donation. Some officials also pushed for a Nationwide Expanded Access Investigational New Drug protocol, which would allow for much broader use of the drug and for it to be prescribed outside of hospitals. Bright would later detail in a complaint that HHS's general counsel, Robert Charrow, an Azar loyalist, had instructed him to "drop everything and make the chloroquine donated by Bayer widely available to the American public." HHS dismissed Bright's complaint, with both Trump and Azar stating he was a disgruntled employee.

"I am not sure who has the background on this, BARDA does not yet and [is] playing catch up with little to no details. . . . Who has talked with Oracle? Where is the drug coming from? Has FDA cleared?" Bright wrote to Kadlec and several others at BARDA.

Kadlec responded, "Bob Charrow asked that BARDA lead this. Please identify a team to support."

The career scientists stiffened. On March 21, Janet Woodcock, a well-respected veteran of the FDA who was the agency's director of the Center for Drug Evaluation and Research, penned a cautionary note to a number of HHS officials: "We must be really carefully [sic] not to be seen as endorsing an off label use. We prosecute companies for this. It is CDCs job to give advice on medical practice decisions." She and her colleagues eventually convinced HHS to ask the FDA for an emergency-use authorization for the donation that would allow the Bayer pills to be used only in a hospital setting, where patients could be closely monitored by a doctor.

On March 29, the Food and Drug Administration issued the authorization, and usage of the drug almost instantly soared. In February, before Trump's comments, the CDC recorded 383,435 prescriptions of the drug. In March, the number jumped to 759,186 and remained elevated for months, in large part because of Trump's boosterism. Just thirteen days after Musk's tweet and ten days after Trump had first mentioned the drug at the press briefing, the White House was trying to snap up every pill it could get its hands on.

Florida's Republican governor, Ron DeSantis, who had been elected in 2018 largely because of Trump's support, decided to follow the president's advice and sought a large amount of the drug for his state. He ran into a problem, though, when he reached out to an Israeli company that sold the drug, Teva Pharmaceutical Industries. It turned out that the pills were made in India, which had blocked shipments to other countries. So DeSantis persuaded Trump to intervene with India's prime minister, Narendra Modi, and Modi made an exception for Florida. It was an extraordinary presidential intervention for a medication that had no proven track record in treating the new virus.

And it played out like this again and again, all over the country. Republican officials and many Trump advisers, most with zero medical expertise, did whatever they could to get their hands on the drug. On April 4, Brett Giroir, the assistant secretary for health at HHS and the administration's testing czar, wrote to several colleagues that he had received a call from the White House. "Really want to flood Ny [*sic*] and NJ with treatment courses. Hospitals have it. Sick out patients don't. And can't get." Pete Gaynor, the FEMA administrator, wrote back that FDA commissioner Stephen Hahn had called him and he and another official were "on it." (Hahn was not told to flood New York and New Jersey per se, but officials were all trying to increase the supply, especially for those who needed the drug for its approved uses.) Even the Department of Veterans Affairs authorized the use of hydroxychloroquine and gave it to 1,300 veterans who had contracted the virus.

Hahn told Giroir to supply pharmacies all over the United States with the drug as quickly as he could. Steven Adams, the deputy director of the Strategic National Stockpile, warned Giroir that the FDA's emergency-use authorization covered only hydroxychloroquine's use in hospitals, not in pharmacies or outpatient settings.

"NOPE," Giroir wrote back. "Needs to go to pharmacies as well. The EUA matters not. The drug is approved [and] therefore can be prescribed per doctor's orders. That is a FINAL ANSWER." (Increased use of the drug to treat COVID-19 meant that people who needed it for its intended uses, including lupus and rheumatoid arthritis, often couldn't get it in pharmacies.)

There was so much pressure to advance hydroxychloroquine as a COVID-19 treatment that resources were pulled away from studying other potential treatments. STAT, a health and science–focused news organization, found that 237,000 patient volunteers had signed up for clinical trials of the drug by mid-2020, a figure that represented 35 percent of all volunteers for any treatment. Clinical trials for other COVID-19 treatments had a hard time recruiting participants because so many people were participating in hydroxychloroquine studies.

No one inside the White House latched on to the drug as fiercely as Peter Navarro. When Trump embraced something, Navarro made it a personal crusade. He had seen how Fauci had tried to humiliate Trump in a press briefing, by daring to question the efficacy of hydroxychloroquine. Navarro had become fixated on Fauci back in January, repulsed by the know-nothing doctor who seemed to undermine the president at every turn. Navarro could shut that down. If this was going to be a test of loyalty to Trump, he was intent on acing it.

———

Peter Navarro had long since developed a reputation as a trouble-maker. An ambitious kid with a chip on his shoulder, he was raised largely by a single mother in Florida and Maryland. After winning a full scholarship to Tufts and doing a stint with the Peace Corps in Thailand, he got a PhD in economics from Harvard University. In 1989, he was hired by the University of California Irvine to teach economics and settled down in San Diego, almost ninety miles from campus.

An ardent environmentalist who railed against the city's greedy developers, he was recruited into Democratic politics, running for mayor of San Diego in 1992. He lost, due in part to his surly temper-ament and a series of negative campaign ads that ended up backfir-ing on him. Then he lost a race for city council in 1993. Then he lost a race for county supervisor in 1994.

"He burns inside intellectually that his brilliance isn't accepted and appreciated," said Larry Remer, a San Diego political consultant who helped run two of Navarro's campaigns. "It just burns him."

Still, each loss seemed to embolden Navarro. In 1996, he decided to run for Congress. He shuttled back and forth to Washington, working the circuit with political action committees, groveling for money, and cutting deals with Democratic power brokers, asking for help and attention. In one of his proudest moments, he claimed that in exchange for $200,000 in fundraising, he had been able to bring Vice President Al Gore to San Diego for an event to draw at-tention to Navarro's candidacy. Navarro even secured a speaking slot for himself during the 1996 Democratic National Convention in Chicago.

Still, he lost his congressional race by 10 points. It was all for nothing. Five campaigns. Lost them all.

Navarro couldn't win at politics, but he also couldn't sit still. En-vironmentalism wasn't the only issue that had caught his eye as he campaigned and taught. He had noticed that a number of his night school students were losing their manufacturing jobs, displaced by companies moving operations to China.

China fit neatly into the big-bad-wolf, David-versus-Goliath prism through which Navarro viewed life. And so he began a spastic decade of launching himself in a full-throated attack against China, its military, its industrial policy, its (lack of) environmental regulations, its currency manipulation, the Communist Party. Navarro wasn't really a Democrat anymore. He didn't need a political party. He was a nationalist fighting for manufacturing jobs and blue-collar workers.

He began writing books about China. In 2006, he published *The Coming China Wars: Where They Will Be Fought, How They Can Be Won*, about the looming economic and military tensions with China and how the United States must confront and combat it. He alleged that US consumers were being lulled to sleep through their addiction to cheap Chinese merchandise and that that was funding China's military. He also warned that a deadly virus strain could emerge from China because of a combination of factors that many people often ignored. "The resultant 'cross pollution' creates a 'soup of chemicals and viruses' that now threatens the world with the possibility of a pandemic in which tens of millions of people may die," he wrote.

It was that book, Navarro would later tell people, that had caught Trump's eye several years later. The two exchanged written correspondence, and Navarro thought he had a fan in high places.

Navarro kept writing. His most prominent book, *Death by China: Confronting the Dragon*, was coauthored with a USC business professor, Greg Autry, and published in 2011. But a book wasn't enough for him; he also made a documentary with the same title, narrated by Martin Sheen, and wrote a song about China stealing US manufacturing jobs. The documentary has a gory animated scene in which a graphic of the United States comes into view and then a serrated knife, labeled MADE IN CHINA, comes onto the screen and plunges itself into the US Midwest, red blood spilling everywhere.

Navarro has claimed that because his books had already drawn Trump's attention to him, he was asked to join the presidential campaign. At first, he was seen as a bit of an oddball. A lot of the staffers were from the Republican National Committee or New York City, and Navarro was a fish-out-of-water surfer guy. But Trump loved him and kept him around. Navarro never quite made it into the inner circle, though, which rankled him.

The Trump team was unprepared to win the election, so they had no plans for what to do after November 8, when Trump shocked everyone—even himself—by winning. Navarro was asked to join the transition team, where he quickly learned that his role could be as big as he wanted. There was no one to stop him. Trump needed something to do, something to *announce*, after his inauguration to make it look as though he was getting things done. So Navarro began drafting executive orders that Trump could sign that would, in Navarro's view, promote US manufacturing and send warning shots at China. He was closely paired with Trump's longtime friend Wilbur Ross, who was seventy-nine at the time and prone to falling asleep in meetings. The alliance, though, gave Navarro credibility within the team.

Navarro could be abrasive and stubborn, but the president-elect liked having a little bit of "crazy" around to keep adversaries on their toes. So he created a new office, the National Trade Council, an entity that hadn't previously existed, and appointed Navarro as its director.

Chinese officials immediately expressed displeasure that Navarro was going to be part of Trump's White House, which of course thrilled the president-elect. Navarro was given a first-floor office in the Eisenhower Executive Office Building adjacent to the White House with a single staffer; the "council" wasn't so much a "council" as it was a "Peter." He launched himself at his work, looking for ways to help US companies that had for years lost out to foreign competitors. He was particularly focused on reviving the beleaguered US steel and aluminum industries. He had left behind his wife and their six cats, Bob, Jack, Nike, Luna, Pumpkin, and Shadow, in Laguna Beach.

In those early days, Navarro found himself boxed out by Treasury secretary Steven Mnuchin and National Economic Council director Gary Cohn, Wall Street veterans who had a more global worldview and generally supported getting along with other countries to promote US trade. Navarro, who referred to China supporters as "fucking panda huggers," would find himself excluded from meetings. In late 2017, Cohn successfully reorganized the White House structure to make Navarro report to the National Economic Council. The idea was to cut off his access to Trump. Navarro fumed.

But he had a few people looking out for him in the White House, notably Stephen Bannon, Trump's chief strategist, who shared the view that China was trying to destroy the US middle class. Through Bannon, Navarro developed a network of spies inside the White House who alerted him when a key trade or economic meeting was on the agenda. Navarro would miraculously appear, sit against the wall, and chime in when he felt compelled to. He also had the most important protector in the White House. Trump seemed to rely on him for counsel. When issues pertaining to China came up at meetings, Trump would often look around and, if Navarro wasn't there, ask, "Where's my Peter?"

"The president told me to hang in there, and the president told me my role was to be the one who calls bullshit," Navarro confided to a colleague.

That role, of internal brawler, would become Navarro's primary job. Republican lawmakers, many of whom were free traders and didn't like Navarro's protectionist bent, couldn't stand the guy, and he was never able to build a political critical mass behind any of his ideas. So he spent much of his time working with companies and unions and fighting with other White House officials about the direction of the White House's policy.

The conflict came to a head in May 2018 when Trump sent Mnuchin, US trade representative Robert Lighthizer, and Larry Kudlow, who had replaced Cohn as director of the National Economic Council, to meet with Chinese officials about a possible trade deal. Mnuchin wanted to cut a deal and make the trade tension go away so that the economy wouldn't be affected. Trump's warmonger rhetoric had already hammered the stock market, and companies had halted making investments until they knew how things were going to shake out.

Navarro didn't trust Mnuchin to deal with the Chinese and carry out the president's best interests, so he found a way onto the plane to Beijing. At first Navarro was on his best behavior. But then he found out that Mnuchin was headed to a private meeting with China's vice premier, Liu He. Private meeting? Without Navarro? Navarro went ballistic, screaming at Mnuchin, first in the courtyard and then later in the Great Hall of the People. It was quite a scene to have the members of the US negotiating team at each other's throats in public when they were supposed to be conveying a unified front to the Chinese. Lighthizer broke up one shouting match between Mnuchin and Navarro, saying, "We're not having this discussion here." When the US officials looked around, they saw that everyone in the room was staring at them.

Navarro wasn't in Beijing to make friends. He wasn't even in the White House to make friends. There seemed to be only one relationship he cared about, and that was his bond with Trump. When the US officials boarded the government plane to fly home, dejected because they were returning to Washington without any firm results, Navarro seemed unfazed.

Navarro learned a couple things in those first two years. He knew that Trump didn't like long dissertations or lectures. He wanted people to agree with him and back him up. He also knew that Trump loved being praised and loved when people attacked his enemies, the more viciously the better. Navarro also knew that the best way to appeal to the president was directly in the Oval Office or during buzzworthy television appearances.

That June, Trump flew to Canada for the Group of 7 summit. It was the first time in his presidency that he was spurned by other world leaders. He was trying to bully Canadian prime minister Justin

Trudeau into making major concessions as part of an updated North American Free Trade Agreement, and the usually mild-mannered Canadian was resistant. Trump threw a hissy fit and left the summit early. As Air Force One was in the air, Trudeau gave a press conference and pushed back sternly against Trump's meltdown. "Canadians, we're polite, we're reasonable, but we also will not be pushed around," he said.

That was seen by White House aides as a huge slight. Trump was apoplectic that a foreign leader would dare call his bluff. He was on his way to Singapore to meet with North Korean dictator Kim Jong-un, and that type of knee to the groin made him look weak.

Back in Washington, Navarro was watching closely. His nationalist plan would never work if other world leaders began ganging up on Trump. Navarro needed everyone on the defensive. He booked himself on television to rush to his boss's defense. "There's a special place in hell for any foreign leader that engages in bad faith diplomacy with President Donald J. Trump and then tries to stab him in the back on the way out the door," he said on *Fox News Sunday* the day after Trudeau's comments. "And that's what bad faith Justin Trudeau did with that stunt press conference."

White House officials couldn't believe it. What the hell was Navarro doing? White House staffers don't talk about the leaders of other countries like that. Navarro would later apologize. Even he knew that he had gone too far, but he would do whatever it took to defend his boss.

Navarro wasn't an official member of the White House Coronavirus Task Force, but he did have a knack for sidling into meetings when he wanted to make a point. As the government struggled with the pandemic, he regularly reminded people that he had predicted an event like this in his books. He had been right in January and February, when he had warned about supply shortages and the lives that would be lost. If people still weren't listening to him now, he would make them do so. And that was what he did on Saturday, April 4.

Jared Kushner and a broad range of top advisers were at the meeting, which eventually turned to Stephen Hahn, the FDA commissioner, who began discussing the results of hydroxychloroquine treatment in clinical trials and health care settings.

As if on cue, Navarro stood up, dramatically waving a packet of papers. "I'm hearing that people are saying that it's only anecdotal," he began. "I have, in my hand, fifteen articles, which prove the efficacy of hydroxychloroquine." He thwacked the papers down on the table for people to pass around.

Fauci, who picked up some of the papers, saw instantly that every one of the articles Navarro had clipped was bullshit. So did the other doctors. There were no randomized, controlled clinical studies or anything else beyond anecdotal evidence that supported hydroxychloroquine's use in treating COVID-19.

"Uh, Peter," Fauci began, "I'm sorry, but I've read those articles, and they are all noncontrolled, non-placebo-controlled, nonrandomized, anecdotal cohort studies that most of the scientific community doesn't believe."

Fauci could see Navarro's anger building. Navarro believed that his PhD made him just as qualified as any doctor to evaluate scientific studies, and he had long suspected that Fauci was full of shit. "That's science, not anecdote," Navarro shot back.

Navarro's resentment and hatred of Fauci had begun building almost two months earlier, when Fauci had raised questions about the China travel ban at the end of January. (Fauci ultimately supported the ban.) But after Fauci questioned the hydroxychloroquine studies he had come armed with, Navarro made him public enemy number one. Some thought Navarro had gone too far, too many times, in trying to swat down his enemies. They would watch him do the same with Fauci.

Navarro had recently found himself going nose-to-nose with

almost everyone in the West Wing, challenging even Jared Kushner. On several occasions, when he heard someone in the Oval Office dismissing COVID-19 as the "flu," he leaped out of his chair, got into the person's face, and said, "This is very serious."

So Navarro wasn't intimidated by Fauci one bit. And when word leaked out about their confrontation, he seemed thrilled. He began attacking Fauci in a series of television appearances, trying to exaggerate his own credentials to make himself appear to be Fauci's equal in the medical profession.

"Doctors disagree about things all the time," he said on CNN two days after the meeting. "My qualifications in terms of looking at the science is that I'm a social scientist. I have a PhD. And I understand how to read statistical studies, whether it's in medicine, the law, economics or whatever."

Navarro took it upon himself to track down as many hydroxychloroquine tablets as possible to add to the Strategic National Stockpile. The government already had 30 million, but he thought it needed more. In part because of Navarro's pressure, the stockpile eventually amassed close to 65 million pills.

Navarro wasn't the only person with little medical experience to shill for hydroxychloroquine from late March into mid-April. A steady stream of Fox News personalities also pushed the drug, both on television and directly to Trump in the Oval Office. No one was more supportive than Laura Ingraham, who had risen to prominence on the network with her unwavering support of Trump's every decision. Ingraham called it a "game changer" and described one doctor's view of it as helping save patients "like Lazarus, up from the grave." Ingraham and her "medicine cabinet," two doctors who regularly appeared on her show to tout the drug, were regular visitors in the Oval Office for several weeks. She and several other hosts mentioned the pill more than a hundred times from late March until April 13, before dramatically cutting back after evidence began to emerge that the pill was not only ineffective but was unsafe for some patients. An early study of 368 Department of Veterans Affairs patients who had taken the drug had found that those who took it faced a higher risk of death than those who did not.

The fixation on hydroxychloroquine marked a dangerous opening into politicization of the FDA and health agencies more broadly. The speed with which it was dumped into the Strategic National Stockpile and became a national point of discussion emboldened Trump and some of his top aides to meddle in the agency's affairs. At the same time FDA, BARDA, and HHS officials were trying to figure out what to do about the demand for hydroxychloroquine, a small group of FDA officials was exchanging skeptical emails about oleandrin, a plant extract that could be poisonous, which was being pushed by Mike Lindell, the chief executive officer of MyPillow and another frequent White House visitor.

"I think the only reason this is being passed around is because at some point it was forwarded by Congressman (chief of staff now?) Mark Meadows. Also forwarded through Debbie Birx's assistant. So apparently there is some connections at that level. But in my opinion, this sounds really sketchy. I doubt there is scientific merit," one official wrote.

Another official passed the note along to a larger group: "I am reluctant to bother you with this, but the company (which claims to have a drug that was used to successfully treat a child in Mexico) has made a number of political contacts and suggests that the President of Mexico may contact our President about the drug. It is not clear what we are being asked to do about this at this point." (The FDA never endorsed it or authorized its use in any way.)

Peter Navarro seemed to feel especially free to terrorize Hahn and other FDA officials. He communicated with a group of researchers in Detroit who had been pushing the FDA for an application to study hydroxychloroquine in twenty-six Michigan hospitals, as well as Detroit first responders; Navarro remained obsessed with the research group for months. And he began sticking his fingers into all sorts of issues, aided by his temporary hire of a conspiratorial pharmacist who berated FDA officials to move faster.

As the agency reviewed the data on hydroxychloroquine over the next several weeks, more and more evidence indicated that the drug wasn't effective against COVID-19. In fact, the agency found that the drug appeared to cause severe heart problems in some patients. "The FDA determined that chloroquine and hydroxychloroquine are unlikely to be effective in treating COVID-19 for the authorized uses in the EUA. Additionally, in light of ongoing serious cardiac adverse events and other potential serious side effects, the known and potential benefits of chloroquine and hydroxychloroquine no longer outweigh the known and potential risks for the authorized use," agency officials wrote in a news release on June 15. The drug's emergency-use authorization was revoked.

Just like that, the US government was left with 63 million doses of hydroxychloroquine and 2 million doses of chloroquine in its stockpile. The pills would be largely useless unless there was a sudden epidemic of malaria—which wasn't likely to happen.

Trump would continue to promote the drug, but the formal government support for the medication was over. Still, thousands of people would take hydroxychloroquine because Trump swore it would work, and they would follow his advice wherever it led them. In May, Trump stunned Hahn and almost everyone else when he announced that he was taking hydroxychloroquine as a precautionary measure.

Trump and many of his top aides were infuriated at Hahn for revoking the emergency-use authorization. They felt he was no longer on the team and had betrayed them. Hahn was being hit on both sides, by Trump and many White House aides, and by career and outside scientists who were angry that the FDA had been used as a prop in political theater and believed he had been too deferential to Trump. (Some FDA officials remarked that Hahn seemed to love going to the White House.)

Navarro, who never missed an opportunity to ratchet up the strife, took it upon himself to write to Hahn personally, attaching a twenty-five-page screed about why his decision had been a betrayal. "I strongly urge you to monitor the EUA situation carefully. The FDA has had a tremendous negative effect on the ability to do clinical trials and advance use of HCQ as a prophylactic and therapeutic. The latest proposed action is OUTRAGEOUS," he wrote, then instructed Hahn to call a researcher in Michigan. "Let's talk tomorrow about the direction things need to go. This latest news is BAD based on BAD science."

There was yet another ill effect of Trump's obsession with hydroxychloroquine: it signaled to aides that he wanted to hear about any and all potential treatments, no matter how potentially ridiculous, no matter how wasteful of time and resources. Touting miracle cures was a surefire way to get into his good graces, and his aides had permission to bypass the scientists and come straight to him. All that would lead to the most notorious of Trump's proposed magical fixes for the disease.

William Bryan, the acting undersecretary for science and technology at the Department of Homeland Security, was conducting two preliminary studies at the agency's laboratory in Fort Detrick, Maryland. The first study found that the virus didn't survive as long on surfaces that were exposed to direct sunlight or in humid conditions. For example, a virus particle on a grocery cart sitting in the blazing sun would not last as long as a virus particle on a grocery cart inside a store. A second study found that rubbing alcohol and disinfectant could be used to clean surfaces in a way that made it harder for the virus to spread.

Bryan briefed the DHS brass on his initial findings, and Acting Deputy Secretary Ken Cuccinelli—who had largely been banned from attending task force meetings—saw an opening. He said they would have to take the information to Pence immediately. The findings had not been reviewed or analyzed, but Cuccinelli wanted the White House to know about them anyway.

On April 22, Cuccinelli took Bryan to the Situation Room and introduced him to the vice president and others on the task force. Bryan tried to explain that he had conducted the research in a type of scientific cylinder, leaving many confused. He said that the cylinder was comparable in size to an orange Home Depot bucket, an analogy that startled others in the room, who thought that DHS was doing research with equipment purchased at a hardware store. Why was DHS even involved in this? some of them wondered. What did it know about this sort of thing?

Bryan's research had been focused on what conditions could keep people from contracting the disease from surfaces such as doorknobs and tabletops. It had nothing to do with a treatment for the disease; that was far outside his expertise. But Pence was enamored with the finding, knowing that Trump wanted to hear anything that resembled good news. The daily press briefings also put pressure on Pence and others to regularly have something new to announce. So he told Bryan to come back the following day to brief the president.

Bryan appeared slightly nervous when he entered the Oval Office but gave the president the same explanation: the virus can't live long on a surface if it's exposed to direct sunlight, and bleach and disinfectants are good ways to kill the virus on surfaces so that people can't pick it up as easily. (Several aides would later lament that someone with no experience briefing Trump should never have been brought in. There was an art to doing so.)

"When you spray bleach, it dies immediately," Bryan told the president. "COVID is very sensitive to bleach."

Trump paused, as if to absorb the information, and then his eyes widened. He turned his head, pursed his lips in a smile, and looked around the room, trying to make eye contact with each person individually. It was a Eureka! moment. Trump acted as if that was it.

They had found it: the cure. He wanted Bryan to join him during the press conference. They were going to tell the world about the new discovery.

Trump, Pence, and other members of the task force marched up to the White House briefing room. Birx took a seat against the wall over to Trump's right, where White House aides usually sit. Trump had Bryan regurgitate his findings for the press in an attempt to show that new discoveries were being made.

Bryan told reporters that the "virus dies the quickest in the presence of direct sunlight" and talked about his experiments with disinfectants. Of course, he was talking about disinfectants on surfaces, and he didn't even mention the bleach experiment, but Trump could hardly contain himself as he began riffing on the possibilities with the reporters in front of him:

> "A question that probably some of you are thinking of if you're totally into that world, which I find to be very interesting. So, supposing we hit the body with a tremendous, whether it's ultraviolet or just very powerful light, and I think you said that hasn't been checked, but you're going to test it. And then I said supposing you brought the light inside the body, which you can do either through the skin or in some other way. And I think you said you're going to test that too. Sounds interesting, right? And then I see the disinfectant, where it knocks it out in a minute, one minute. And is there a way we can do something like that by injection inside or almost a cleaning, because you see it gets in the lungs and it does a tremendous number on the lungs. So it'd be interesting to check that. So that you're going to have to use medical doctors with, but it sounds interesting to me. So, we'll see, but the whole concept of the light, the way it kills it in one minute. That's pretty powerful."

Birx, sitting twelve feet away in a navy sweater with a pastel scarf around her neck, stared at the president, her lips pursed tight. She inhaled briefly, as if she'd seen a ghost, then exhaled. As he kept talking, she finally looked away to a spot across the room, listening to his voice but no longer looking at his face. Bryan, sitting two chairs away from Birx, was also dumbfounded, aware that what the president was saying was not even remotely close to what his research had been about.

After Trump finished, the stunned Birx walked back into the White House, away from the reporters and cameras. When she turned to Olivia Troye, the Pence aide, it was clear that she was appalled. "I can't believe that just happened," she told Troye.

The public blowback was ferocious and humiliating for the president. Clorox and the parent company of Lysol swiftly issued statements warning people not, under any circumstances, to ingest disinfectant or bleach. The White House went into bunker mode, and the episode marked the end of Trump's daily briefings, a relief to some aides who thought they were hurting the president. Trump had finally gone too far. A few days later, he tried to tell reporters that he had just been joking, "asking a question sarcastically to reporters." But everyone knew it wasn't true. Trump had been doing that sort of thing for years, making stuff up on the fly. And he had always gotten away with it—until now.

The government's top health officials testify before Congress on February 26, 2020. *From left to right:* Dr. Anthony Fauci, director of the National Institute of Allergy and Infectious Diseases; Stephen Hahn, commissioner of the U.S. Food and Drug Administration; Alex Azar, secretary of the U.S. Department of Health and Human Services; Robert Kadlec, assistant secretary for preparedness and response at HHS; and Robert Redfield, director of the Centers for Disease Control and Prevention.

Chip Somodevilla/Getty Images

White House Acting Chief of Staff Mick Mulvaney (*left*) shares a laugh with Representative Mark Meadows (R-NC) on February 6, 2020, one month before Mulvaney was fired and replaced by Meadows.

Drew Angerer/Getty Images

Deputy National Security Advisor Matthew Pottinger was a key player in the debate about shutting down flights from Europe and China.

DREW ANGERER/GETTY IMAGES

Vice President Mike Pence speaks on March 2, 2020, during a briefing on the administration's coronavirus response. Standing with Pence are (*from left to right*) Robert Redfield, Dr. Fauci, and Dr. Deborah Birx, the White House coronavirus response coordinator.

DREW ANGERER/
GETTY IMAGES

Alex Azar (*left*) watches as President Trump holds up a picture for reporters during a visit to the headquarters of the Centers for Disease Control and Prevention in Atlanta on March 6, 2020.

JIM WATSON/AFP VIA GETTY IMAGES

President Trump departs the dais on March 9, 2020, as his advisers look into the crowd of reporters. *From left to right:* White House adviser Peter Navarro, Treasury secretary Steven Mnuchin, Dr. Fauci, Alex Azar, and Robert Redfield.

DREW ANGERER/GETTY IMAGES

Dr. Birx and Dr. Fauci listen as President Trump speaks to the media on March 20, 2020.

JABIN BOTSFORD/ THE WASHINGTON POST VIA GETTY IMAGES

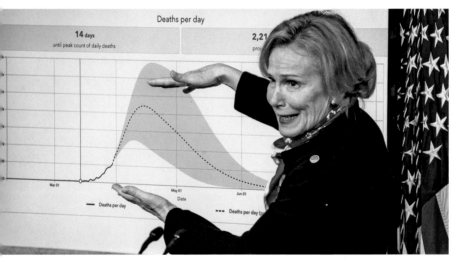

During a briefing on March 31, 2020, just days after convincing President Trump to keep restrictions in place, Dr. Birx shows the media a model of projections of future deaths.

JABIN BOTSFORD/THE WASHINGTON POST VIA GETTY IMAGES

Omar Rodriguez organizes bodies in the Gerard J. Neufeld funeral home on April 22, 2020, in the Elmhurst neighborhood of Queens, New York.

Spencer Platt/Getty Images

Kellyanne Conway, the senior counselor to the president, confers with Joe Grogan, the White House Domestic Policy Council director.

Chip Somodevilla/Getty Images

To protest Governor Gretchen Whitmer's stay-at-home order, demonstrators hold a rally on May 14, 2020, in front of the Michigan State Capitol in Lansing.
Scott Olson/Getty Images

Peter Navarro speaks to reporters outside the White House on June 18, 2020.
Jabin Botsford/The Washington Post via Getty Images

President Trump addresses his supporters during a Make America Great Again rally at the BOK Center in Tulsa, Oklahoma, on June 20, 2020.

JABIN BOTSFORD/THE WASHINGTON POST VIA GETTY IMAGES

White House senior adviser Jared Kushner, Press Secretary Kayleigh McEnany, Alex Azar, and CEO of U.S. International Development Finance Corporation Adam Boehler walk on the South Lawn toward Marine One on July 27, 2020.

ALEX WONG/GETTY IMAGES

Dr. Fauci throws out the ceremonial first pitch prior to the game between the New York Yankees and the Washington Nationals at Nationals Park in Washington, DC, on July 23, 2020.

Rob Carr/Getty Images

Marc Short (*center*), Vice President Mike Pence's chief of staff, watches as his boss responds to a reporter's question during a meeting in the White House's Roosevelt Room on September 17, 2020.

AP Photo/Andrew Harnik

White House physician Sean Conley (*right*) speaks with Chief of Staff Mark Meadows before an update on the condition of President Trump on October 5, 2020, at Walter Reed National Military Medical Center in Bethesda, Maryland.

SAUL LOEB/AFP

In a grand photo-op from the White House balcony facing the South Lawn, President Trump removes his mask upon return from Walter Reed Medical Center on October 5, 2020.

WIN MCNAMEE/ GETTY IMAGES

Dr. Scott Atlas, a member of the White House Coronavirus Task Force, points to his watch as he walks to the White House on October 12, 2020.

NICHOLAS KAMM/AFP VIA GETTY IMAGES

CHAPTER 12

REMDESIVIR

May 1, 2020
CONFIRMED US COVID-19 CASES: **1,000,000**
CONFIRMED US COVID-19 DEATHS: **63,000**

The bleach debacle occurred around the same time as NIH research-ers were conducting a clinical trial on an existing antiviral drug that showed promise. Early findings suggested that remdesivir, developed by the pharmaceutical company Gilead several years earlier to treat Ebola, could help treat the sickest COVID-19 patients. Those who received remdesivir were recovering faster than those who did not. As it always did with clinical trial results, NIAID, the division run by Fauci, put out a press release on April 29 stating the initial results. Unlike the proclamations that came from the White House podium, the statement gave only the simple facts, with no hyperbole.

That same day, Fauci was called to the White House for a sepa-rate press event; Louisiana governor John Bel Edwards was visiting, and reporters gathered in the Oval Office to listen to Edwards and Trump discuss the response. Fauci was seated next to Birx on a gold couch, with Trump just a few feet away. A reporter asked Trump about what seemed like "good news" on the treatment front, and Trump turned to Fauci to ask him to elaborate. Fauci felt ambushed with the cameras there, but he figured the news would be better coming out of his mouth than someone else who knew less, so he went ahead. He ended up breaking with protocol by getting ahead of the press release. "What it has proven is that a drug can block this virus," he said, his voice hoarse. Remdesivir, he later added, "will be the standard of care." Trump's eyes glazed over as Fauci detailed the scientific process through which his agency had come to its conclusions but heralded the development as "good news."

To people watching, it looked like Fauci deliberately used the Oval Office event to make a press announcement and like he had jumped the gun. His comments at the White House event unnerved many, including the AIDS activists who believed that the doctor was the last line of defense preventing Trump from acting upon his worst instincts. Fauci's off-the-cuff comments were not the way scientific studies were normally announced, the activists and some outside scientists thought. An outside board, not Fauci, would be the one to decide whether remdesivir would be the new standard of care. They also believed that Fauci had grossly overstated the early results of the study. The trial had shown that it was moderately effective, but it was also a preliminary analysis. Was Fauci finally caving in to political pressure to offer a rosier-than-reality outlook? Why hadn't he just let the press release speak for itself, as NIAID had always done?

Matters got worse. Later that night, articles were published in *Science* and *Politico* detailing how, at Trump's direction, the NIH had abruptly terminated a grant for a study examining how coronaviruses spread from bats to humans. It was an area of research that had renewed importance given the pandemic. The study's sponsor was a New York–based research nonprofit called EcoHealth Alliance, but reports linked the grant to the Wuhan Institute of Virology at the same time as right-wing media were seizing on the theory that the coronavirus had either escaped from or been engineered in a lab in Wuhan, China. (Peter Navarro, characteristically, was the most bullish of those inside the White House peddling the Wuhan lab theory. He even suggested that the virus could have been designed by the Chinese military as a type of biological weapon, an argument in line with his 2011 book, *Death by China*.) A reporter from *One*

America News Network, a tiny conservative outlet that was even more loyal to the president than *Fox News* was, asked Trump about the grant during a briefing one week before it was terminated. "We will end that grant very quickly," Trump replied.

AIDS activist Peter Staley texted Fauci the next morning. "WTF?" he wrote with a link to the *Science* article. Fauci called him right away.

The peer-reviewed NIH study had already come under scrutiny within the federal government as soon as officials realized that the Wuhan Institute of Virology had a subgrant under the contract. The institute had the most expertise in studying which bat viruses might be the next to come out of China and pose a major threat. But with questions swirling about the origins of COVID-19—experts had determined that the virus was not man-made but could not rule out that it might have slipped out of a lab—the NIH had gone to the principal study investigator on April 19 and asked that payments be halted to the subcontractor in Wuhan until it had more answers.

A few days later, the relatively small grant had garnered new attention. The chatter by Navarro and the other White House hawks who were convinced that China had deliberately unleashed the virus on the world had found a welcome audience among right-wing conspiracy theorists. On the afternoon of April 24, NIH director Francis Collins and Fauci received notice that Trump wanted to formally announce in a 5:00 p.m. press conference that the grant had been terminated. Collins and Fauci told the White House and HHS that they were not sure the NIH actually had the authority to terminate a peer-reviewed grant in the middle of a budget cycle. The HHS general counsel told them to do it anyway and made clear it was a direct order from the president, implying that their jobs were on the line if they didn't comply. Fauci and Collins reluctantly agreed to cancel the grant.

Fauci related the series of events to Staley.

"What do you mean?" Staley asked. "You can't cancel a grant like this."

"What do you want me to do?" Fauci said.

"Can't you and Collins threaten to resign over this?" Staley suggested.

"You want us both to resign over a $3.7 million grant?" Fauci snapped back.

Staley instantly backed down. "You're right, you're right," he said. "That's not what you resign over." (Collins and Fauci heard from many members of the scientific community that they should have resigned. The HHS general counsel later found that the agency probably had not had the authority to terminate the grant. NIH had to reinstate the grant but stopped all of its funding.)

It was the second time in a matter of days that it looked as though Fauci was being bullied by political forces at the White House, and Staley thought it was a worrisome trend. "You combine this with what happened with your Oval Office remdesivir announcement—and I know this doesn't matter to the country. We're not talking about Trump and politics and Fox and the whole country. We're talking about the fact that you are now our leader in AIDS, in public health advocacy," he told Fauci, his voice rising with emotion. "In the scientific community, you are our leader. And in the course of forty-eight hours, you have broken two major tenets of how the scientific community does things. We have these rules for a reason, which you've been a major defender of your whole life."

Fauci said he understood but explained that he'd had to make a split-second decision about how to make the announcement, and he'd thought it would be better if the news came out of his mouth than someone else's.

Staley told Fauci that he had more power than he was giving himself credit for. If he explained to the people at the White House that NIAID and the scientific community had a specific way of doing things, they would understand.

"I hear you," Fauci said. "I'm only human."

Staley's words clearly resonated with him. Two days later, on May 1, Gilead's chief executive officer, Daniel O'Day, visited the White House to announce that remdesivir had received an emergency-use authorization from the FDA and that the company was donating 1.5 million vials of the drug to the government. It was a big development; the recovery time of patients who received the drug through an intravenous tube was shortened on average from fifteen days to ten days. Trump and his aides praised the company in the Oval Office that day and leaned hard into the FDA's blessing of the drug.

As the event took place, Fauci called Staley. "Are you watching the news?" Fauci asked him. He told Staley that there was an Oval Office meeting with Gilead's chief executive officer in which officials were spinning the news of the company's donation and Fauci wasn't there, in part because of their conversation the other day. Earlier that afternoon, Fauci had attended a task force meeting in which top aides had been in a "full spin cycle" discussion of how they would present the Gilead announcement. As the meeting wore on, Fauci realized that in light of recent events, it would look terrible for him to stand alongside O'Day and praise the company. As aides began to head to the Oval Office for the event after the meeting, he pulled Mike Pence's chief of staff, Marc Short, aside and explained that he could not attend because he had already upset the scientific community with his remdesivir announcement. Could Short help get him out of it? Surprisingly, Short was amenable and told Fauci it would be fine as long as he told Pence. When Fauci pulled Pence aside to explain, Pence, too, told him he understood.

But afterward, Deborah Birx, Robert Redfield, and Stephen Hahn let Fauci know that they did not appreciate his breaking off from them. The four doctors were supposed to present a united front, and they could have all attended the Oval Office event together and ensured that they stuck to the facts about remdesivir. Instead, Fauci had peeled off from the group on their way up to the Oval Office, rather than discussing it with them in their weekly meeting (he had made the decision at almost the last minute, though). They were already beginning to feel that Fauci was going rogue with his statements in the press; people close to Birx and Redfield said they had begun to resent Fauci's hero status while the two of them were being pummeled—a sentiment shared among several members of the task force and government officials involved in the response more broadly—considering that Fauci had also made mistakes and they were fighting in the trenches together. Trump was putting enormous pressure on them to approve drugs, and things would only get worse later in the year, when they would be dealing with the results of the vaccine trials. They had thought the four of them were a team of doctors who would stick together. But Fauci felt he had to draw the line somewhere. He needed to take more risks, even if that meant alienating himself from the other doctors even more.

Now that the FDA had authorized remdesivir and the government had a limited supply to dole out, officials needed to distribute it quickly to the hospitals that needed it most. The distribution would be a sort of trial run for vaccine distribution, which would be an exponentially more complicated task. In the event, the government proved to be woefully unprepared and disorganized. Some hospitals that were overrun with sick patients couldn't obtain a single dose. In the first tranche of 607,000 doses donated by Gilead, the US government sent some doses to the wrong hospitals, others to hospitals with no intensive care units and thus no eligible patients, and even some to hospitals that couldn't refrigerate the medication and had to send it back.

It turned out the FEMA officials tasked with the initial distribution had used faulty and possibly outdated data to figure out which hospitals needed the drug most. Birx ended up working with Kadlec, who oversaw the Office of the Assistant Secretary for Preparedness and Response, and his chief medical officer, John Redd, to re-do the distribution and ensure the drug got to the hospitals that needed it most.

But media stories soon identified massive issues with the remdesivir distribution. The government had unilaterally decided which hospitals should get the drugs, rather than consulting with the states, which had a better understanding of which facilities needed it. Kadlec was communicating with state health officials and trying to manage one piece, while FEMA and its logistics group had another team working on the same problem. With so little coordination and communication, the whole effort was a disaster waiting to happen.

After it became clear that the initial distribution of the drug—one of the administration's few chances to have some good news to share—had been botched, White House officials were incensed. Over the weekend, Kadlec received a call on his cell phone from a White House number. He barely had time to answer before the voice on the other end ripped into him. "I'm going to fire your ass if you can't fix this! What the fuck?" the voice bellowed.

"Who is this?" Kadlec asked.

"This is Chief Meadows. Don't you know who this is?" Mark Meadows yelled back.

That was what the response had turned into: a toxic environment in which no matter where you turned, someone was ready to rip your head off or threatening to fire you. There was no sense of a team effort; you could either kill or be killed. Several officials recalled that other than Pence, who was compassionate but did not seem willing or able to act on the advice he was given, no one in the White House was asking: What's the right thing to do for patients? What's the right thing to do for America?

The episode showed how ill equipped the White House—and the administration more broadly—was to execute on some of the hardest parts of responding to a pandemic. Too much attention was being paid to Trump's mood and announcements from the Oval Office. The knifing, turf wars, and petty rivalries that had begun in January were now manifesting themselves in even more dangerous ways. Fighting a virus on such a large scale required trust and teamwork; it required a complex logistical operation, with many people acting together as a team.

The fatal flaw in the effort had been exposed. And the situation would become much worse.

CHAPTER 13

JARED'S SHADOW TASK FORCE

Aside from the president, only one person in the White House stood above everyone else, was more powerful than the rest, untouchable, unquestionable: Jared Kushner.

The president's son-in-law, who served as Trump's de facto top diplomat, de facto chief of staff, and de facto campaign manager, was simultaneously responsible for everything and nothing. He was somehow seen as both liberal and conservative. Or maybe neither. Some aides thought he tried to have it both ways all the time and always got away with it. That bred immense resentment among others in the White House, many of whom felt that they had to work harder than he did and still ended up on the wrong end of Trump's ire.

Kushner was the rare kind of person who elicited extreme emotions from virtually everyone who worked with him: jealousy, hatred, disgust, admiration, awe, infatuation. Some people harbored all of those feelings about Kushner at once.

When it became clear that the COVID-19 pandemic was subsuming Trump's final year in office and therefore threatened his election prospects, Kushner stepped in. But he didn't step into the Coronavirus Task Force; he stepped over it.

In March, as the government was proving embarrassingly ill equipped to test the millions of possibly infected Americans, Pence's office enlisted Kushner's help, knowing that if the president's son-in-law became engaged, everyone else would follow. Initially, Kushner did not have much information about the virus because he wasn't included in the early task force meetings. Some people thought he was too dismissive of its risks, equating COVID-19 to the flu. He also thought that Anthony Fauci and Deborah Birx lacked an appreciation of the larger economic and political landscape. He felt that there were too many voices competing for attention and no one coordinating a unified response. He knew what a shit show looked like, and this was a shit show.

Kushner possessed a self-proclaimed "extraordinary ability to cut through red tape," a skill he regularly reminded bureaucrats of. The government, in his view, was moving too slow, was too wedded to its processes and rules. It needed someone like Kushner to come in and break the logjam. So Kushner sought to form a "shadow task force" with Azar's consult and the help of two of his friends, Adam Boehler and Brad Smith. Boehler had been Kushner's roommate one summer during college and had previously worked at HHS before being appointed as CEO of the US International Development Finance Corporation. Smith was the director of the Center for Medicare & Medicaid Innovation, part of HHS's Centers for Medicare & Medicaid Services, and had cofounded a palliative care company called Aspire Health with former Tennessee senator Bill Frist. While the White House task force sat around and squabbled, Kushner's task force was going to get shit done. Kushner would end up using FEMA as a way to carry out his directives and get around the White House task force.

Much of Kushner's work in the White House so far had similar characteristics. He would take on big issues—Middle East peace, the opioid epidemic, the United States' relationship with Mexico—and then deliver what appeared to be some sort of "deal" to the president. Very often those deals, over time, were not as impressive as they had initially looked. And by the time people realized that he had left a mess behind, he had bounced off to something else. Trump, who didn't have an appreciation of details or nuances either, didn't much care. Kushner was clever enough to give his father-in-law something to announce, then disappear. It was an impressive skill. He ruled the White House with a cockiness and swagger that few had seen before. It wasn't that he ignored government knowledge and expertise; he just wasn't burdened by them.

Kushner's first real foray into the coronavirus response was helping Trump write the bungled Oval Office address on March 11. The next day, his shadow task force sprang to life. A group of about fifteen officials from across the federal government—HHS, FEMA, the US International Development Finance Corporation, the White House, and elsewhere—convened on the ground floor of the West Wing and outlined their mission. They were going to tackle testing and supplies, the two most vexing and complicated challenges facing the country.

Kushner disdained the slow, meandering protocol that many government civil servants abided by. Instead, he revered the brutal efficiency of the private sector. In his view, what the response needed was a businesslike approach to replace the outdated, lackadaisical government processes. Kushner had graduated cum laude with a degree in government from Harvard University in 2003, then enrolled in a joint Juris Doctor/Master of Business Administration program at New York University, from which he had graduated with a JD and MBA. He was captivated by those with similar MBA and business backgrounds, convinced that theirs were exactly the minds the federal bureaucracy needed.

During the March 12 West Wing meeting, Kushner popped in and out, never staying for long, as the group toiled away until 3:00 or 4:00 a.m., debating how to engage the private sector and which were the right partners to create more testing across the country. Eventually they determined that FedEx and UPS would be best able to send tests to labs nationwide, while a drive-through testing model at retailers such as CVS, Walgreens, Rite Aid, and Target would enable people to be tested close to home. Kushner called several company executives and convinced them to come to Washington on Friday,

March 13, for a meeting with the president. Like a bunch of MBA students pulling an all-nighter on a case study, the team was going to try to get the strategy up and running by the weekend, whether it was ready or not.

After the meeting with the company executives, Trump held a news conference in the Rose Garden—an event Kushner orchestrated—flanked by the industry officials and members of the White House Coronavirus Task Force. There he proceeded to make a series of announcements that would prove to be inaccurate and deceiving. He said that there would be pop-up testing sites at Walgreens and CVS stores across the country so that Americans could go to their neighborhood pharmacy and quickly find out whether they were infected. And there would be a streamlined website, developed by Google, into which people could input their symptoms, determine if they needed a test, and, if they did, be directed to one of the retail sites to get one.

"Google is helping to develop a website. It's going to be very quickly done, unlike websites of the past, to determine whether a test is warranted and to facilitate testing at a nearby convenient location," he said. ("Unlike websites of the past" seemed to be a dig at the problems that had plagued the Obamacare website launch several years earlier.) "We have many, many locations behind us, by the way."

That all seemed genius. Kushner had come in just a few days earlier, and now an incredible announcement, with some of the top companies in the country mobilizing to combat the coronavirus, was already being made. The thirty-nine-year-old whiz kid, whom other officials referred to as the king of the "slim suit crowd," had tossed aside the slow, lumbering government process and solved every problem with a snap of his fingers.

Only a couple hours passed before it became clear that it was all an illusion. There weren't thousands of pop-up testing sites at CVS and Walgreens stores ready to go. Not even one had been set up. There was no website. There weren't even, it turned out, enough tests to make the plan work. Google quickly tweeted that its sister company Verily (formerly Google Life Sciences) was "in the early stages of development" of the promised website and that it was beginning with a Bay Area pilot project "with the hope of expanding more broadly over time"—hardly the thousands of locations Trump had announced were imminent. The retailers who were supposed to host the drive-through testing sites said they still did not have basic information about how they would work, including when and where they would begin. And the state and local officials who would be responsible for operating the sites seemed to have heard about the plans for the first time during Trump's speech.

Kushner's team quickly realized that the test rollout was going to take more work and what they needed to do was to somehow obtain tests, hundreds of thousands of them. They began pushing people at FEMA and ASPR (Robert Kadlec's agency, which managed the Strategic National Stockpile) to get the drive-through testing initiative off the ground. Officials at ASPR asked what they thought was a basic question: Had they made sure to obtain all the supplies they needed to launch such an ambitious project? They didn't just need tests; they needed reagents, swabs, and other materials to conduct the tests, in addition to personal protective equipment such as N95 masks, gowns, and gloves for the thousands of health care workers who would be administering the tests in close contact with potentially sick people.

We're working on it, the Kushner team assured them. But in fact, they hadn't sorted out the supply issues. Instead, they commandeered the already limited supplies by getting their hands on whatever swabs were available—diverting them from companies trying to send their tests to hospitals and doctor's offices—and ransacking the Strategic National Stockpile for N95 masks, surgical masks, gowns, and other equipment. The Kushner team would end up using 30 percent of "key supplies" from the Strategic National Stockpile to operate forty-four drive-through testing sites for five to ten days, according to an internal document. Meantime, the CDC was advising doctors to use bandannas and scarves as face coverings if they could not access medical-grade masks, an astonishing recommendation just as hospitals were anticipating a crush of patients.

"When [the drive-through testing initiative] first rolled out, it was not a clean rollout, so they created a shortage of testing supplies by default of rushing in and trying to solve it," one official involved in the effort said. "And that was Team Jared."

Swabs were an integral part of the tests; they were what health care workers would stick up a patient's nose and toward the back of his or her throat to collect viral material. But after a huge portion of the available swabs in the United States had been diverted to the drive-through testing initiative, there was only one manufacturer the US government could turn to for more: Copan, which had a plant in the Lombardy region of Italy. The coronavirus had hit Lombardy hard, and Italy had implemented severe flight restrictions that made it extraordinarily difficult to get access to the swabs. The officials needed to come up with another plan fast. Somehow they would have to find a plane that could get into Italy, load up quickly, and airlift the swabs back to the United States. Otherwise, the entire testing initiative in the United States was likely to fail. And then there would be no stopping the virus.

A top FDA official received a call from two top officials at BARDA. Was the FDA aware of any issues with supply shortages, and could BARDA help with anything?

"We have an issue," the FDA official told the pair. "We may not be able to get swabs out of Italy."

The BARDA officials said that the agency had helped orchestrate airlifts of vaccines in the past with the military. Would something like that be helpful here?

BARDA helped connect the FDA with the military, and the FDA helped the government connect with Copan. Now even more agencies were involved in trying to secure a single airplane that could make a boomerang trans-Atlantic flight. It was far outside the remit of some of the health agencies involved, but the situation was dire.

As the air force colonel flying the plane prepared to depart for Italy, no one had authorized him to take off. He emailed a number of officials, informing them that he didn't have clearance to leave yet. ASPR was also involved in the mission, and Kadlec, who had spent twenty years in the air force before retiring as a colonel, took matters into his own hands. "If you don't take off now, we're not going to get these swabs," he told the pilot. "I'm authorizing you to go. Go." ASPR officials had no idea who was supposed to authorize the flight, probably someone at the Department of Defense. It didn't matter anymore.

The plane flew to Italy and returned with the swabs—at least 20 million of them, along with 10 million units of the transport media needed to submit the swabs to laboratories. It was a risky but ultimately successful mission, a rare bright spot in the otherwise dysfunctional and leaderless pandemic response. But the effort underscored the extraordinary lengths government officials had to go to simply because Kushner and his team were determined to establish testing sites, no matter the cost. They had made a big announcement, and now everyone else had to scramble to make it happen and fix whatever mess was left behind.

Despite Kushner's promise that thousands of retail testing sites would be created all over the country, in the end only seventy-eight materialized. In March, an internal planning document about the drive-through testing effort blamed the whole problem on ASPR's procurement process. Blame never fell on Kushner. "When asked for help procuring the supplies necessary to operate the drive thru testing sites that were not in the stockpile, ASPR said they were not able to procure those supplies through existing relationships in the timeframe required," the document stated.

With fingers pointed at Kadlec and ASPR, Kushner's team began instructing people to find other ways to get the supplies they needed. Kushner, Boehler, Navarro, and other aides proceeded to call up companies directly, hoping to strike a deal on the phone as though they were buying a car. Kushner was correct that the normal processes for procuring supplies were cumbersome and slow. But circumventing those processes risked wasting taxpayer money, buying faulty supplies, or running afoul of government contracting laws. There were protections in place to try to prevent the government from overpaying for products or supplies and to try to ensure that companies did not receive unfair advantages due to personal relationships, among a host of other potential problems. "It can be onerous and time-consuming. That's what they didn't want to do—anything that would slow them down from doing it," one official involved said of Kushner's team's circumventing the normal process. "People say the federal acquisition regulations are very onerous, but it's done so that you don't buy a $600 or $800 toilet seat."

All of a sudden, the effort to procure supplies was a free-for-all. Navarro was trying to buy supplies. Kushner's team was trying to buy supplies. FEMA was trying to buy supplies. Private companies were trying to buy supplies and donate them to the government. With no central clearinghouse for what was going on, everyone was trying to strike deals from the White House, putting those involved into legally dubious territory.

One FDA official, for instance, received a call late one night from a White House official with a possible lead on masks in China. What did the FDA official think of the masks? The official replied that he knew nothing about them and could not make a determination over the phone. At the time, China was hoarding much of its mask supply and sending counterfeit products to the United States, making it essential that the FDA be able to properly test and evaluate the data on possible leads. The White House official offered to connect the FDA official with someone in China in a haphazard effort to get sign-off with virtually no proof or evidence that the masks worked or were not fraudulent.

"That's not how you go about buying product," a person familiar with the exchange said. "This is what happens when you don't have things coordinated in a systemic fashion."

As Kushner assembled his shadow task force, he brought in a couple dozen volunteers from the business world, a group of mostly twenty-somethings from private equity firms and consulting companies to bring "entrepreneurial special sauce" to government.

Max Kennedy, Jr., a grandson of Robert F. Kennedy and a former consultant at the venture capital firm Insight Partners, arrived for his first day as a volunteer on Monday, March 23, unsure of what exactly he would be doing or where to go. He walked into FEMA without having to show an ID or go through a security check. He had assumed that he would be helping fill in and manage spread-sheets or doing some other menial task that would free up time for the government officials who were trying to keep up with the crisis. He heard from two of his Insight colleagues, who had started a few days earlier, that the team of volunteers had been reorganized three times in three days, moving from the White House to HHS before it was finally settled that the volunteers would work out of FEMA, foreshadowing the chaos that lay ahead.

On his first day, about forty people gathered inside Conference Room A inside FEMA headquarters in Washington, D.C., a win-dowless basement room with long tables and television screens tuned to CNN and Fox News. A significant number were in military uniforms, about a dozen were volunteers who had come down to Washington from New York City, and the rest were government of-ficials. There were bottles of hand sanitizer on all the tables but few efforts at social distancing, Kennedy said. A FEMA official told the volunteers that their goal was to "end bad news cycles." Another official told them that their job was to "get the stuff and get it as fast as possible," referring to supplies such as masks, gowns, and other critical protective equipment.

Kennedy was assigned to a team responsible for following up leads on personal protective equipment (PPE). The effort was disjointed and scrambled, without a single person or agency clearly in charge of coordinating matters. With the US stockpile of PPE nearly depleted, the team needed to find more quickly. Without a central clearinghouse, numerous people across the country—members of Congress, senators, governors, and others who thought they had leads on equipment—got in touch with their own contacts inside the federal government, creating chaos. Some members of Congress saw an opening to try to push products from questionable companies, several officials involved said. A handful called government officials several times a day. "Everyone was coming thinking they had the answer, someone in their district or state," one government official said. "We were hearing from everyone coming out of the woodwork." None of the volunteers was given a government email address; instead, they had to use their personal email addresses, a hurdle Kennedy cited in a whistleblower complaint he later filed with the House Committee on Oversight and Reform. Vendors understandably could not be sure that the messages coming from the volunteers' personal email addresses were not spam or fraudulent. The personal email addresses also unnerved government employees, who were suddenly seeing sketchy-looking emails pop up in their inboxes with issues related to the response.

"God knows who some of these folks are," one senior administration official said. "It's a hornet's nest of people that are nongovernment that are giving direction to government employees."

The volunteers were well intentioned but wholly unprepared to tackle the colossal task in front of them. They sent basic questions to the FDA about whether supplies and equipment met the agency's standards, often irritating FDA employees who were bogged down in work of their own. And the volunteers who were vetting the leads often didn't know what to do next or how to resolve minor technological issues, such as looking up a company's DUNS number—a unique nine-digit identifier—or confirming their contractor registration in a federal database.

Kennedy recalled that Trump administration officials were

"extremely dismissive" of FEMA procurement officers, whose job is to procure critical supplies for the US government. "We'd sometimes say, 'Why are we here? When should we send things to procurement?' And they'd say, 'Don't send things to procurement until they're literally ready to wire the money. Government folks are slow,'" he said. "The whole reason we were there was a belief the government would move slowly."

That was coupled with deference to the private sector. Kushner's ally Brad Smith told the volunteers that the federal government should be "the buyer of last resort" and avoid stepping on the toes of the private market. The Kushner team felt that if the federal government attempted to purchase massive amounts of equipment, it would drive up the cost for companies and hospitals because there would be more demand and less supply. But that attitude led to states' competing against one another and often grossly overpaying for the materials, rather than the federal government purchasing them at a fair price and making sure they were distributed to the hardest-hit regions.

"It highlighted their overall attitude about the US government's role in the process. The buying arm of the country with by far the most COVID patients was ten volunteers in a basement ordered not to buy unless they were sure otherwise it would not get into the US," Kennedy said.

A couple weeks after the effort began, a number of the volunteers were taken to meet Trump. "How do you like your first few weeks working in government?" Trump asked them. "It doesn't work too well, does it?"

The government officials and volunteers worked long hours, often beginning the day at 7:00 a.m. and not leaving until the early hours of the morning. Many of the volunteers soon grew intensely frustrated that they were being handed enormous responsibilities for which they did not have the training and having to work at a punishing pace without any sense that they were making a difference. The volunteers often vented their frustration to each other.

When it became clear that the government had a paltry stock of supplies to send out to the states, Trump decided to change the message. For weeks, he had been fixated on how to absolve the federal government of responsibility for the crisis. On April 2, he tweeted, "Some have insatiable appetites & are never satisfied (politics?) Remember, we are a backup for them. The complainers should have been stocked up and ready long before this crisis hit." Kushner reiterated the message at a White House briefing later that day. He blamed the states for failing to build up their own stockpiles, adding, "The notion of the federal stockpile was it's supposed to be our stockpile, it's not supposed to be states' stockpile that they then use." HHS's website, which had previously stated that the Strategic National Stockpile existed to support states and localities when they requested federal assistance, changed its description the next day to match Kushner's statement. "The Strategic National Stockpile's role is to supplement state and local supplies during public health emergencies," the new statement said. "Many states have products stockpiled, as well."

There were parts of the pandemic response that resembled a friends-and-family operation, with preferential treatment for those close to Trump or Kushner. According to Kennedy's whistleblower complaint, that was clear in the volunteer effort, which was instructed to prioritize VIPs, including conservative journalists, and others with ties to high-level government officials. Jeanine Pirro, a Fox News firebrand who was incredibly loyal to Trump, called and emailed repeatedly because a hospital she knew needed masks, Kennedy wrote, adding that no checks had been done to ensure that the hospital was in particular need of PPE. One suggestion from Tana Goertz, a former *Apprentice* contestant and the Trump Team coordinator at Women for Trump, was passed on to a volunteer with the note "Please prioritize this one. Thanks!" Others whose suggestions were given top priority included Brian Kilmeade, a cohost of *Fox &*

Friends; Charlie Kirk, a young Republican activist; and Albert Haz-zouri, a dentist who frequented Mar-a-Lago.

"This prioritization caused significant issues as it forced the team to spend time on low quality leads from VIPs and because it gave a leg up for potentially hundreds of millions of dollars in spending to those who had a connection to officials or journalists," Kennedy wrote.

Special treatment for VIPs ended up becoming pervasive in the government response. Kushner had also helped set up a friends-and-family email account at the White House, with leads apportioned to the appropriate agencies. (They often landed at the FDA because many of them were tips about "new and exciting" technologies.) Once again, the VIP leads consumed an inordinate amount of time; whether real or perceived, those who received them felt pressure to drop what they were doing and prioritize any request that seemed to have the approval of Kushner. Trump's second ex-wife, Marla Maples, also came through on the White House email address, advocating for a company, according to an official who received the email. At a time when the FDA should have been singularly focused on clearing new diagnostic tests, as well as new treatments and vaccines for COVID-19, officials instead found themselves scrambling to respond to all sorts of harebrained requests and ideas.

"They're calling and pushing the FDA commissioner around, asking 'Can you talk to this company or that company?'" one senior administration official involved in the efforts said. "You were like, 'What the fuck do these people have to do with anything?'"

Government officials were deeply divided over whether Kushner's involvement was a good thing. On the one hand, Kushner's stature in the White House and relationship to Trump meant he could get things done when he wanted to with a single phone call. Some governors from both parties appreciated his help, because they knew their requests or messages would get to the right place. On the other hand, many thought Kushner didn't hesitate to overstep his authority (his authority, actually, remained murky), and he rarely briefed others in government on what he was doing. Someone who worked closely with Kushner throughout the process said that his key motivator was "being in control." Kushner's defenders, though, said he was particularly attuned to trying to help the president respond to the crisis of the day.

But no one, it seemed, was ever actually in control.

One of Kushner's biggest sources of pride was Project Airbridge, an initiative that sought to move "heaven and earth" to drastically cut the time it took to get medical supplies into the United States from overseas. The effort tasked the federal government with partnering with a handful of medical supply companies that could purchase masks, surgical gowns, and gloves in Asia. Then the government would pay for the supplies to be flown to the United States to avoid shipping delays and ensure that at least half of the products went to COVID-19 hot spots around the country. Taxpayers footed the bill for at least $91 million worth of cargo flights. The White House boasted that Project Airbridge had helped bring nearly 1 billion pieces of PPE to the front lines.

Yet a subsequent investigation by the House Committee on Oversight and Reform, during which members of Congress interviewed representatives from six large medical equipment distribution companies that were taking part in the government response, found that Project Airbridge was mostly full of hot air. The Trump administration did not purchase PPE directly, instead providing the (very expensive) transportation for equipment already purchased by private companies. The congressional report detailed yet another instance of the way the administration's decision not to create a federal effort to directly procure PPE had forced state and local governments, as well as hospitals and other facilities, to "compete for scarce supplies." Because the contracts did not require distributors to report information about the prices they were being offered on PPE and because the government did not serve as a central purchaser, states and hospitals often massively overpaid for basic supplies. Often, state governments tried to work directly with brokers in China, which led to a plethora of other problems.

As numerous shady contracts and deals emerged, the federal government often punted on doing due diligence, passing them on to states with less robust systems to vet them. The costs of that were evident when a Silicon Valley engineer made an offer to FEMA to procure thousands of ventilators from China for the United States but requested cash up front. The offer went nowhere inside the federal government but was passed on to New York State officials, who put $86 million of taxpayer money at risk before terminating the contract, according to the *New York Times*. The private-sector volunteers helped sort through such offers, usually tossing aside the ones that seemed too good to be true. In another example, a man from Panama badgered federal officials several times a day, claiming that if they gave him cash up front, he could procure 2 million masks from a warehouse in Panama and bring them to the United States. But state governments were sometimes hoodwinked by such scams in their desperate search for scarce supplies.

Like many of the deals Kushner had struck as a senior White House aide and son-in-law of the president, Project Airbridge sounded and looked good on its face. Some officials point to that initiative as evidence of the value Kushner brought; it was a program built up from scratch. But others point to it as a classic example of the way Kushner operates: it gave the president something impressive sounding to announce, then underdelivered. A *Washington Post* investigation found that Project Airbridge had vastly overstated the amount of supplies it had brought in and what it had been able to accomplish.

Still, even those who don't like Kushner concede that he was trying to help. And he did speed along certain initiatives and get some states the supplies they needed. Government procedures and rules are often archaic, and there were certainly processes that needed to be expedited and handled differently during such a crisis. But the effort could have been more successful, several government officials argued, if they had been consulted and brought into the fold. Instead, they were viewed as roadblocks, and many were ultimately cast aside.

"These guys were trying to 'get things done,' " one senior administration official involved in the effort said. "Okay, got it. But not only what they were trying to do but how they were trying to do it was really circumspect."

Like Trump, Kushner chased good headlines and tried to swat down bad ones. His shadow task force was no different. Kushner and Boehler often let news reports dictate where they should focus their efforts. When the media said there was a test shortage, they tried to obtain tests. When the media said there was a mask shortage, they focused on masks. And in the spring, a potential ventilator shortage dominated the news, so they shifted their efforts accordingly.

The sickest coronavirus patients often suffocate or effectively drown to death. The pneumonia caused by COVID-19 causes air sacs in the lungs to fill with fluid, making it difficult for patients to breathe normally. Some patients improve if they are given oxygen, but in the most dire cases, they end up on a ventilator.

As the virus ravaged New York, Governor Andrew Cuomo projected at the end of March that the state would need up to forty thousand ventilators and asked the federal government to help. That was more than double the number of ventilators the United States had in the Strategic National Stockpile. ASPR officials had no idea where New York's projections were coming from. That would mean forty thousand people—simultaneously—would be on the brink of death in just one state. There was no way a single state could possibly need that many ventilators, they thought. And the state's outbreak was concentrated in New York City, which meant that hospitals upstate could transfer unused ventilators to city hospitals most in need.

Robert Kadlec knew the State Health Official at the New York Department of Health from their days together in the Bush administration. Kadlec wanted to understand firsthand what Cuomo's projections were based on and found out that they had been put together and analyzed by experts at Weill Cornell Medical College, McKinsey & Co., and the CDC. The New York state official told Kadlec that there were high utilization rates of ventilators in metropolitan New York City. But when Kadlec pressed him about how many the state *really* needed right now, the state official told him seven hundred. Fine, Kadlec responded, and ordered the transport of seven hundred ventilators from the stockpile to New York City.

Trump also publicly cast doubt on Cuomo's request for ventilators during an appearance on Sean Hannity's Fox News show. "I don't believe you need forty thousand or thirty thousand ventilators," he said, launching one of the first grenades into what turned into a public war between the two.

But Kushner, determined to tamp down the headlines predicting mass death due to a ventilator shortage, was angry at Kadlec for his actions, especially after Cuomo continued to insist that the state needed forty-three times as many ventilators as the federal government had sent. Kushner demanded that the government send four thousand ventilators to New York state, amounting to a quarter of the entire US stockpile. (Trump had called Kushner a "hoarder" for not sending more ventilators to the state.) Kadlec insisted that that was too many to send to a single state and pointed out that the issue wasn't just the ventilators themselves; the officials needed to think about the total supply and the staff and medications needed to run them. "You don't know what the fuck you're talking about," Boehler and other aides told Kadlec. In the end, four thousand more ventilators were sent to New York state. Few, if any, of them were used to treat patients, government officials said.

Further fueling the ventilator hysteria were catastrophic models from outside groups and government officials predicting that the country would need 200,000 or 300,000 ventilators at the peak of the outbreak. At that point scientists still had little understanding of why many people with coronavirus ended up so severely ill as to require a ventilator. But huge numbers of people in China had been on ventilators, and ICUs in Italy had become overwhelmed. People were scared, and the country seemed to be wholly unprepared in almost every aspect. It didn't need to add lack of ventilators to its list of problems.

So Kushner, Boehler, Navarro, and other aides began an all-out effort to get their hands on to every ventilator available. They began personally calling up ventilator manufacturers, striking deals over the phone, then instructing subordinates to carry out or finish the deals. "They would toss it to people to say, 'Manage this,'" one official involved said. "They put people in great jeopardy, legal and otherwise." The three regularly pushed government bureaucrats to move in "Trump time," deriding those who raised concerns about how the deals were being made. (Navarro would use the phrase "Trump time" throughout the pandemic; it meant "as soon as fucking possible.")

Once again, Navarro, Kushner, and Boehler were making commitments for the US government without going through the traditional process, leading some government officials to allege that they massively overpaid for products. In one of the most egregious examples, Navarro and other senior White House officials made a new deal with Philips Respironics, a US company. The Obama administration had negotiated a contract with the company in 2014 to supply ten thousand ventilators to the Strategic National Stockpile by June 2019. The date had been pushed back several times, once under the Obama administration and several times under Trump, according to a Democratic congressional report. The ventilators were supposed to be delivered in June 2021, but the company approached the Trump administration in late January 2020, after the first US case of coronavirus was diagnosed, about accelerating the timetable under the existing contract. The administration ignored the offer for six weeks, according to the report, until March, when the pandemic had become a full-blown crisis.

That was when Navarro and other White House aides stepped in to negotiate a new contract. The new ventilators were virtually identical to the ones the company had agreed to make in 2014 except for some small ancillaries. But the administration agreed to pay Philips $15,000 per ventilator, up from about $3,000 per ventilator agreed to in 2014. The congressional investigation estimated that the deal had meant up to $500 million in wasteful spending. In response to the investigation, the company denied any wrongdoing and said on "no occasion has Philips raised prices to benefit from the crisis situation."

Navarro, Kushner, and Boehler also struck deals with a number of other ventilator companies and helped Trump make another announcement with bells and whistles: some manufacturers would shift part of their production lines to ventilator production. It was one of the most ambitious ways the federal government engaged the private sector, pushing companies to help in a time of crisis. And the companies delivered. The federal government ultimately contracted with several companies to produce about 243,000 ventilators, far more than the country needed (but around the number the most catastrophic models predicted would be needed). Trump began referring to the United States as the "King of Ventilators."

The enormous focus on the machines showed how single-tracked the Kushner effort could be: ventilators were not going to cure COVID-19, and they were only one of hundreds of supply problems the administration was facing. Ventilators were not even going to stop everyone from dying of the disease, but they likely did save lives. In the spring, with little known about how best to treat COVID-19 patients, they were an important part of the treatment process for people who were deathly ill. But the reality was that nearly half of the people who went on to a ventilator alive came off it dead.

Some of the ventilator deals had political overtones. One of the participating companies was Spirit AeroSystems, a Kansas-based firm that was partnering with the medical equipment manufacturer Vyaire Medical to produce almost 40,000 machines. By that point,

Kadlec had determined that the government had ordered far too many ventilators and the cost of maintaining them in the Strategic National Stockpile would be astronomical—roughly $100 million to manage and store 250,000 of them. Over the summer, he canceled orders for about 90,000 so that the United States would end up with about 150,000 in the stockpile, the number required for a virulent flu pandemic. Among the canceled orders were the ones for many of the ventilators that Vyaire Medical and Spirit AeroSystems had been contracted to deliver.

The cancellation caused an uproar in Kansas that boomeranged back to Washington. Spirit, which had undergone massive layoffs at the beginning of the pandemic, said it had been able to retain a thousand jobs because of the contract. Kadlec received a call from Kansas senator Pat Roberts. The state's other senator, Jerry Moran, toured Spirit AeroSystems' facilities in early September—almost exactly two months before the presidential election—and claimed to have reached out to the White House to ask why the contract had been canceled. "I know there is plenty of work and there's plenty of folks that need them. So we're not understanding why the work has stopped," he said during the tour.

Navarro and other aides couldn't believe that Kadlec would make such a decision on his own and put jobs at risk so close to the election. Navarro told Kadlec that he was hurting the Trump brand. He had no qualms about saying, even to other White House officials, that they had "blood on their hands" if they didn't do what he thought was in the best interest of Trump and the country.

Kushner's team and Navarro didn't have much in common, and they often disagreed, but periodically they formed alliances. They knew how to play hardball and were adept at arm-twisting. They didn't do it in unison, though. There wasn't always a plan. They made things up as they went.

Some White House officials saw Navarro as a missile: pointed in the right direction, he could be extremely effective; if he missed the target, well, things could get messy. Navarro saw things differently. As highly critical of the Chinese government as he was, he liked to reference versions of the Chinese idiom "Sometimes you have to kill the chicken to scare the monkey." In other words, sometimes you have to make an example of one person in order to scare someone else into action.

General Motors was the chicken.

On March 27, Trump invoked the Defense Production Act and ordered GM to manufacture ventilators after a tense back-and-forth. Failure to comply with the DPA can bring the prospect of a year in prison for a company's chief executive officer, and GM was now in Trump's crosshairs. But the White House didn't just need ventilators. It also needed N95 masks.

Around this time, Kushner invited Kadlec and several others into his office to talk about the plan for procuring masks. Kadlec assured him it was all taken care of. He had purchased 600 million masks. That's great, Kushner told him. When will they be here? June, Kadlec responded. Kushner exploded, throwing his pen against the wall.

"You fucking moron," he said. "We'll all be dead by June." Kadlec tried to explain that his team had looked at the burn rates for masks to determine how many they would need over the next few months. It's going to be tight, Kadlec said, but once we get to June we're going to have more masks than we need. Kushner was not convinced Kadlec knew what he was doing.

Kushner, Boehler, and Navarro then began an aggressive effort to track down as many N95s as possible. They needed tens of millions to ensure that hospitals didn't run out. Navarro worked closely with Honeywell to ramp up its production in the United States, but even more were needed.

There was one US company that had the capacity to produce even more of the highly-sought-after masks, and White House officials thought it wasn't playing ball: 3M. It produces masks in the United States, China, and at least two other Asian countries. The company has a diverse portfolio of businesses, and more than $30 billion in sales in 2019. It is a multinational firm with huge reach, and a huge client base. The whole world wanted their N95 supply.

Boehler and Navarro simultaneously reached out to 3M, with Boehler tracking down chief executive Mike Roman and Navarro connecting with Omar Vargas, 3M's head of government affairs. Boehler and Navarro wanted as many of 3M's N95s as they could get their hands on—every last mask.

Roman told Boehler that the company had begun working on expanding production since January but demand was overwhelming from countries around the world. 3M was doing everything it could. Roman also told Boehler that the masks made in the Asian factories were made for export to Asian countries and Asian customers. He then raised the question of whether the masks made for the faces of Asian people would fit adequately on the faces of Americans. (Boehler couldn't believe what he was hearing and told others that this sounded fishy.) But there was another problem. Roman did not think the Chinese would let 3M move N95s out of the country. They were stuck there. Boehler told Roman he'd figure that part out, and Roman told Boehler to connect with Vargas and work through the logistics.

Vargas, a former Justice Department official who had served as president of the Hispanic National Bar Association Legal Education Fund, was already getting an earful from Navarro, who still hadn't made up his mind as to whether 3M would be another chicken or the monkey. At this point, the company was getting completely jerked around by this new shadow task force. The White House didn't have a designated point person to deal with 3M. The company was getting inundated with questions and demands from multiple people with seemingly no coordination.

The next day, when Boehler was in an Uber riding to work, he and Vargas connected by phone. Boehler wanted to go through the numbers again of how many masks could be exported as soon as possible to the United States so they could try to plan distribution. Vargas immediately interjected. "No, that's business confidential," he said. Boehler was outraged. Business confidential? This was a global pandemic. Vargas said they were shipping masks from China to other clients and they couldn't reveal the numbers. Boehler tried to interrupt. "I don't think you understand . . ."

"Who the fuck are you?" Vargas said to Boehler.

Boehler paused.

"Who the fuck are you?" Vargas said again, adding that he had already talked with Navarro.

Vargas was, in fact, getting whiplash from Navarro and Boehler berating him and his CEO for masks. It was unclear what authority they were acting with, and the conversations had become suddenly hostile. The call ended shortly after that.

Navarro, meanwhile, had given up on Vargas and had started calling 3M's CEO as well. Now Roman was hearing separately from both Navarro and Boehler. Navarro told Roman he was done dealing with Vargas and would be speaking with Roman directly from now on.

"People are dying," Navarro said he told Roman. "Get your act together or we are coming after you."

Stories about Boehler and Navarro taking on 3M—a huge US company—began circulating in the West Wing and through the White House task force. Some senior US officials were mortified and thought Boehler, Navarro, and Kushner were acting like thugs, strong-arming a huge US manufacturer that was getting pulled in many different directions. The federal government had an ongoing relationship with 3M, and several people thought it was reckless to try to bully them like this. They needed to be able to work with the company after the pandemic, too. Few people outside the White House even knew who Navarro or Boehler were.

Soon after his standoff with Vargas, Boehler was in a meeting in Kushner's office when Pence walked in. Good news, Pence said. I just spoke with 3M and they are going to give us 10 million more masks. Boehler and Kushner looked at each other. They were incredulous. The company was going around Boehler and Navarro and trying to cut a deal with Pence, who didn't know any of the back story. Now some people wondered whether 3M was playing rope-a-dope with the Trump administration.

Boehler and Kushner marched into the Oval Office and told Trump what happened. They told the president that 3M was "playing games." 3M officials had insisted that they were doing everything by the book and honoring their existing contracts.

Trump pounded the table with his right fist.

"Bring me the DPA," he said, using the acronym for the Defense Production Act. If 3M wouldn't sell the government the masks the easy way, then they would have to do it the hard way. Trump signed an order that day allowing FEMA to block 3M—or any other company—from exporting N95s without the government's approval.

"We hit 3M hard today after seeing what they were doing with their Masks," Trump wrote on Twitter. He added that the company "will have a big price to pay!"

The language in the government order was stark. "In addition to an injunction, failure to comply fully with this rule is a crime punishable by a fine of not more than $10,000 or imprisonment for not more than one year, or both," it read.

The choice was clear. If 3M didn't comply, Roman could go to prison. Again, other White House officials were flabbergasted that it had come to this, that the CEO of a Fortune 500 company was being threatened with prison because Boehler and Navarro had set their sights on him. Roman called Boehler to protest but it was too late. And the White House was preparing to bring in its closer: Jared Kushner.

Trump's son-in-law called Roman a few days later with a directive. He said he would be sending 3M a purchase order for 55 million masks per month for three months. 3M needed to sign it, Kushner said. This was not a negotiation.

Roman raised a big issue. He said he didn't think the Chinese government would allow them to ship 55 million N95 masks a month out of China. Kushner told him to let the White House worry about that, and Roman agreed to sign the contract.

Kushner and Boehler then connected to a top official in the Chinese government. They told him that there was a lot of anger building in the United States and that they needed to release these masks. Soon after that call, the Chinese government agreed to do so. This version of events was confirmed by four people directly involved in the back-and-forth.

In an interview, Vargas told a much different story. He denied ever using vulgarity in a conversation with the White House and said his conversations with Kushner, Boehler, and Navarro were unemotional exchanges of information about how mask exporting works. He said he had no idea where Trump's tweet about hitting the company "hard" had come from. Asked about Navarro, Vargas said, "Peter is Peter."

Kushner exited the coronavirus response around the middle of the year, leaving government officials to try to explain some of the questionable decisions. When coronavirus cases started spiking again, he was nowhere to be seen, infuriating some top White House aides. By then, he had shifted his focus to trying to secure several Middle East peace agreements that he believed would be an important part of Trump's reelection message. During a swing through the region in September, he worked on normalizing relations between Israel and several Gulf countries. Boehler went back to his position at the US International Development Finance Corporation over the summer and accompanied Kushner on several of the Middle East trips.

On the rare occasions when the pair would drop back into the fold on the pandemic response, eyebrows were raised. In one instance, they met with senior Indonesian government officials. They placed a call to a senior US health official involved in the vaccine effort, wanting to know if he could help cut a deal to secure vaccine doses for Indonesia from a pharmaceutical company the United States had partnered with. The US government had little, if any, control over which countries the vaccine makers sold their doses to. And it was still trying to do everything it could to secure enough doses for US citizens. Why did Kushner want vaccines to go to Indonesia? That struck the US official as just another in the long list of head-scratching interventions by the president's son-in-law. It wasn't the first. He hoped it would be the last.

CHAPTER 14

THE DOWNFALL OF THE HEALTH AGENCIES

It didn't take long for the Trump administration's coronavirus response to resemble a dysfunctional middle school band. They were a rivalrous, out-of-tune orchestra with broken instruments and each person playing their own song, as loudly as possible. A primary reason that they weren't in harmony was because few health officials had much respect for someone who was supposed to be their leader: HHS secretary Alex Azar. So by mid-April, several White House aides decided they had had enough of Azar. Enough of the drama, enough of the infighting, enough of the news stories they were convinced that Azar and his team were planting to make himself look good. It was time for him to go.

He had already been marginalized for weeks. Since the day back in February when Mike Pence had replaced him as the head of the task force, the HHS secretary had hardly been present at the daily White House briefings. When he did make an appearance, he was often instructed to stand at the end of the stage, out of the camera shot. While all that was happening, his father, who lived more than two hours away on Maryland's eastern shore, was dying. Azar had last seen his father on Presidents Day in mid-February and couldn't drive back and forth to see him because he felt he had to spend every weekend fighting negative stories about his management and leadership. He missed two task force meetings, on April 6 and 13, the day his dad died and the day he was buried. HHS received questions about why Azar had been a no-show. Someone had leaked even that.

The White House had effectively taken over HHS, which is supposed to oversee the CDC, FDA, CMS, and NIH, by having those
agencies' leaders report directly to the vice president's office instead
of through Azar. He had virtually no control over the massive health
agency anymore. The ramifications of that shakeup were tremendous. The agencies were now subject to direct political pressure from
the White House. That meant Donald Trump's inner circle was exerting control over the CDC and FDA, institutions Americans were
supposed to trust with the most crucial, life-and-death decisions.

But even though they had clipped his wings, Azar was still fluttering around.

During the first two weeks of April, both the *Washington Post* and
the *New York Times* published lengthy investigations that detailed
missed and ignored warnings about the coming pandemic, including
warnings from Azar. Trump was especially angry about the story in the
New York Times, his hometown newspaper, whose approval he constantly sought (even though he dismissed its reporting as "fake news").

Kellyanne Conway, senior counselor to the president, called Azar
shortly after the *Times* story came out. "You're looking pretty good
in that *New York Times* story," she remarked, noting that Azar had
been the recipient of a deluge of bad press, leaks, and anonymous
quotes both before and after the *Times* story. Azar insisted that he
hadn't been behind it. He told Conway that the fact that the White
House had ignored warnings in January and February was already
public because of statements various officials had made at the time.
Still, White House officials remained convinced that Azar and his
team had been key sources for the story.

Trump decided to take matters into his own hands. One way to
muzzle Azar, he felt, was to change the communications team at
HHS. (For Trump, the pandemic was often a "messaging" problem,
not a public health crisis.) Days after the story ran, the president
called Michael Caputo, who had been Trump's personal driver decades before, and had worked on Republican campaigns since the
1980s. A fierce Trump loyalist and longtime associate of Roger Stone,

Caputo had worked on Trump's campaign and was interviewed as part of the Robert Mueller investigation, but was not charged with any crime (he had once advised former Russian leader Boris Yeltsin). He had no health background or experience, but that didn't matter; Trump appointed him assistant secretary of public affairs at HHS. The White House made it clear that Caputo would report directly to Trump. It looked as though Azar was about to be fired.

The following weekend, on April 25, White House staffers began drawing up a list of potential replacements for health secretary. They floated the name of Deborah Birx, but another obvious choice was Seema Verma, the CMS administrator, whose feud with Azar only five months earlier had gotten so bad that Trump had asked Pence to intervene. Even though she was Azar's subordinate, she was a long-time protégée of Pence's, having worked for him during his time as governor in Indiana. Azar had kept Verma off the task force, but Pence had included her and the White House went directly to her for CMS-related issues. Azar felt she was regularly going around him. The heads of HHS's largest operating divisions traditionally vetted everything through the health secretary. But as Azar was feuding or had strained relationships with Stephen Hahn, Robert Redfield, and Verma, they were being called directly by Pence's chief of staff, Marc Short, as well as by Mark Meadows, Domestic Policy Council staffers and members of the National Economic Council. That only made the group dynamics worse.

As the list was being drawn up, media outlets began reporting that Azar could be on his way out. He initially tried to ignore the reports, but they intensified as the day wore on. Finally, he called Mark Meadows, his closest political ally in the White House, to complain. (The two had a relationship that predated Meadows's tenure as chief of staff.) Meadows told Azar that the reports were false and suggested he was almost certain who was leaking the stories. Kushner also called Azar to tell him the stories weren't true. Pence, meanwhile, spoke to Trump, cautioning him that a big personnel move like this would be difficult and unwise during a crisis.

Trump called Azar the next day to reassure him, dismissing the reports of Azar's imminent ouster as fake news. But he also mentioned the *Times* story. "You leaked that *New York Times* story," he told Azar.

Azar replied that HHS had received questions and had answered them. And he pounced on the opportunity to get rid of his biggest enemy in the White House once and for all. "Mr. President, you have a cancer on your presidency, and his name is Joe Grogan. He's leaking constantly," he said. Azar and Meadows were convinced that the domestic policy adviser was behind the media reports that Azar was about to be ousted. "All these stories about the failed response are coming out of the White House, and you're the collateral damage because of this pathological need to destroy me."

Azar was wrong; in fact, the leaks were coming from everywhere. Many people, both inside and outside the West Wing, had turned on him. Indeed, Trump's closest advisers had decided that the HHS secretary was damaged goods. Few people trusted him or listened to him anymore, they believed, and that hurt the president. He was essentially a dead man walking. But firing an HHS secretary in the middle of a pandemic wasn't ideal. They would have to make a decision one way or the other. Azar was on thin ice; they needed to either push him under or rescue him.

That weekend, Jared Kushner called Azar to schedule a meeting to "map out a path for success." What Kushner meant was map out whether Azar would have a job on Monday. So on a rainy, dreary Sunday, Azar and one of his deputies pulled up to the gated Washington, D.C., mansion of Adam Boehler, Kushner's closest ally inside the administration, who wasn't afraid to crack skulls. The gates swung open as if Azar were being taken into a secret fortress. At first they snacked on gluten-free fries that Boehler's wife had made in an air fryer for Azar, who has celiac disease. Then the tone shifted. Boehler made it clear that if Azar was to continue to lead HHS, things would have to change dramatically. Kushner's other close ally Brad Smith was there, too. Azar was essentially being put in the position of making a business pitch to business executives who would decide his fate.

Earlier that morning, Azar had drafted a game plan with two of his closest advisers. At Boehler's home, he promised to resolve the disagreements with Verma and find a way to make it through the election with her remaining in charge of CMS. But he refused to stay in his position if Joe Grogan remained in government, alleging to Boehler and Smith that Grogan had been the source of daily leaks and "made-up stories" about him. He also laid out five actions he would deliver on by the end of the year, including a multibillion-dollar effort to deliver a COVID-19 vaccine and develop a "next-generation" Strategic National Stockpile, so the United States would be better prepared for future health crises. And he would double-down on a number of the president's priorities, including the tortured effort to claim a win on lowering drug prices.

In theory, the person who should have led the emergency response to the coronavirus was Robert Kadlec, the assistant secretary for preparedness and response. But Kushner, who often made snap judgments about people, had lost faith in Kadlec in February after being unimpressed by some of his briefings, thinking he did not have enough "operational experience." Kadlec had clashed with Kushner's team multiple times and alienated Kushner himself. Azar knew that if he was going to succeed in his rebirth, it was not politically viable to have Kadlec running the pandemic response. He told Boehler and Smith that he needed someone from the military, preferably the Coast Guard. (Kadlec and Azar had previously been allies. A senior official said Azar did this in spite of his long-standing respect for Kadlec.)

Trump would later tell one task force member that a big part of the reason he hadn't fired Azar that weekend was because of the election; it would have looked like an admission, about six months before November 3, that he had picked the wrong leader. "He was in trouble and I saved him," he said of Azar. The president and his aides were in the midst of their push to reopen the economy; they needed to beat down media reports that the government's response to the pandemic had been disorganized and the COVID-19 outbreak was still out of control. "To then fire Azar didn't fit in with his narrative," the task force member said.

The meeting at Boehler's house marked the start of a dramatic turn for Azar and the health agencies. Azar, a frequent punching bag for Trump, was willing to go to extensive lengths to preserve and improve his standing with the mercurial president. In the following months, he would demonstrate his loyalty by effectively becoming a campaign surrogate for Trump by traveling to swing states and defending the administration's pandemic response. It meant upending the traditional role of an HHS secretary and in many ways, negating the independence of agencies that had been designed to be largely free of political interference. Americans needed to be able to trust the agencies to give them scientific, apolitical advice on how to navigate the pandemic. But with Azar now running roughshod over the agencies, which were often reporting directly to a White House focused on the election, and Kushner breathing down the secretary's neck, could Americans trust them anymore?

The cost to Azar of keeping his job was enormous. It didn't matter; it was a price he was willing to pay.

The newly emboldened Azar went gunning for Joe Grogan as never before. In the event, Grogan proved an easy target. By late April, he was approaching burnout, exhausted by all the turmoil. On Wednesday, April 29, he walked into a meeting in the Roosevelt Room with Birx and other aides about CDC reopening guidelines for schools and child care centers. The arguing was incessant. Why does the CDC even need to issue guidelines? White House aides asked. What is the CDC's role? What should the guidelines say? It was as if the same arguments that had been playing out for months—about flights or cruise ships or masks—just kept repeating themselves on a nonstop loop.

Grogan was in the meeting for only ten minutes before he picked up his papers and walked out. He was done. Trump had begun treating him differently that week, too, asking questions about him behind his back. Something had changed. All the complaints from Azar had skewed Trump's perspective on the Domestic Policy Council director. He had joined the White House as a close ally of Mick Mulvaney, and Mulvaney had been jettisoned more than a month before. As Grogan silently walked out of the Roosevelt Room that day, Birx could see the look on his face and said, "Oh, dear."

He announced his resignation a few hours later. One of Azar's longest-sought wishes had finally come true.

Azar now thought he was rocking and rolling, having just escaped a figurative death. He was convinced that Kushner, Boehler, and Brad Smith had a new respect for him and wanted him to stay. In reality, Kushner seemed to view Azar as an easy way to exert control over the health agencies. Kushner in fact told one associate that he knew the HHS secretary was a weak performer and part of the administration's problems. But, he added, "Why would I fire him when he does everything we ask him to do?"

Several health officials were expecting Azar to be fired that weekend and didn't understand how he had survived yet again. They, too, almost immediately noticed changes in his behavior. Birx grew alarmed at the number of times Azar mentioned the president in his public remarks, going to ever-further lengths to lavish praise on Trump. And numerous White House officials noticed that Azar was much quicker to deflect blame onto others when something went wrong. Azar was fed up with the agencies underneath him; they were all working independently and taking orders directly from the White House. Why would he accept blame for their missteps when he was so often out of the loop on what they were all working on? His strategy seemed to be to get to Meadows before anyone else could, which usually resulted in Meadows's berating someone else over the phone. The finger-pointing became incessant.

"He was a beaten dog, and he didn't want to get beaten again," one person close to Azar said, adding that the HHS secretary had tried to "coerce and cajole people to do their jobs in an environment where it was highly politically charged."

Azar had been under unrelenting pressure for months. He was the nation's top health official during a public health catastrophe. His father had just died. His job was under constant threat. He knew that several people in the White House wanted him gone and were undermining him at every turn. And after every piece of bad press (and there was a lot of it during this time, often multiple times a day) he would receive an irate phone call from someone at the White House. He would try to talk the person off the ledge by assuring him or her that the story was no big deal and he'd figure it out. Then he'd call Redfield or Hahn. "I just got this call. What the fuck is this?" he would ask. It further fueled his anger that he had to ask his subordinates about various media stories. Why didn't he know about these issues before they were in the press?

His key ally remained Mark Meadows, who loathed the task force's doctors and often called them screaming about their statements and decisions. He would not let the likes of Redfield, Hahn, Birx, Anthony Fauci, or NIH director Francis Collins keep him from delivering for Trump. He regularly called the agency leaders on their cell phones to chastise them for public comments they had made or for moving too slowly on something the White House wanted. When he didn't feel he was getting what he wanted, he would call Azar. "Get your boys in line!" he would tell him, and Azar would oblige. He was grateful for his relationship with Meadows, after all; it had helped him keep his job.

Ever eager to please Trump, Azar publicly accepted Michael Caputo when he arrived as the new communications head of HHS. On April 15, Azar posted a photo on Twitter of the two men sitting at a conference table working, with the Health and Human Services logo visible in the background. "I'm delighted to have Michael Caputo join our team at @HHSGov as our Assistant Secretary for Public Affairs, especially at this critical time in our nation's public health history," he wrote. (Several White House officials who had been gunning for Azar took delight in watching him try to make the best of a situation that had clearly been created as a way to control him.)

Caputo's brash, unapologetic, and abrasive public persona discomfited health agency officials. He also identified clear problems behind the scenes. Caputo thought he could help repair the relationships between Azar and his operating division heads. But as he studied the group dynamics further, he discovered that they were irreparably broken. He dubbed Hahn, Redfield, and Verma the "three musketeers" because the trio met weekly to coordinate various aspects of the pandemic response and commiserate about Azar. Hahn and Redfield felt as though they were under relentless attack and sought Verma's advice about how to survive what they felt was abuse from Azar and his team.

That was the toxic dynamic of the nation's top health officials, who were supposed to work together to help lead the country out of the crisis. Instead, Verma, Redfield, and Hahn felt that their boss was against them, trying to elevate himself at their expense. For his part, Azar felt he couldn't catch a break. The others were holding meetings at the White House that he wasn't privy to, yet he was the one constantly being yelled at for problems that were their agencies' responsibility. White House officials—especially Trump and Meadows—usually directed their anger at the various health agencies toward Azar, frustrated that he could not seem to control them. The end result was that Hahn and Redfield felt constantly harassed by Azar, while Azar's dissatisfaction with the two increased as he felt they were overpromising and falling short.

"The secretary not only did not help Bob Redfield, Seema Verma, Deb Birx, or Steve Hahn. He actively worked against them with the White House," one task force member said. A spokesperson for

Azar said that he was often the recipient of complaints about various officials and agencies from the White House, and relayed those to his subordinates without always mentioning they originated with the White House. "As a seasoned business and government leader, Secretary Azar demands performance, accountability, and integrity in his teams. Individuals who are not able to meet these high standards may find this culture uncomfortable," Azar's office said in a statement.

The CDC and Redfield often bore the biggest brunt of the White House's pressure campaigns, with Azar taking the lead. Despite their initial skirmish over Redfield's salary, the two men had worked fairly amicably for the first two years of their tenures. But their relationship had gone sideways after the CDC testing debacle. Redfield felt betrayed by media stories that blamed it all on the CDC, which he thought both HHS and the FDA were leaking. After the fiasco, there were discussions between Azar and top White House officials about firing Redfield, as well as uncomfortable confrontations between Azar and Redfield. "That fucking CDC" became a common refrain of Azar, Meadows, Trump, and other top White House officials when they were frustrated by leaks and guidance coming from the agency. The discussions about replacing Redfield never became too serious, but the incident convinced Azar and White House officials that Redfield could not control or manage his agency.

The continued White House interference in the CDC's reopening guidelines especially unnerved the career scientists, who began to look for other ways to preserve the agency's independence and integrity. In late May, a rancorous battle ensued over the CDC's guidelines on reopening houses of worship. The agency wanted to place certain restrictions, including against singing in church choirs and taking Communion, which the White House saw as an outrage, not least because Trump was heavily reliant on an evangelical base of supporters. Never mind the recent CDC report detailing a

COVID-19 outbreak at an Arkansas church that had killed three people and infected dozens. Or the one that had found that after a two-and-a-half-hour choir practice in Skagit County, Washington, more than fifty people (thirty-two confirmed cases and twenty probable secondary cases) had become infected, three of whom had been hospitalized and two of whom had died. "Transmission was likely facilitated by close proximity (within six feet) during practice and augmented by the act of singing," the report stated.

The White House argued that telling people not to share Communion chalices was a violation of the Constitution. CDC officials said they had evidence that sharing chalices was a method of transmission. But White House officials successfully pressed the agency to take out the reference to Communion by broadening the reference, advising that no one share cups rather than singling out churches. The acrimony between the CDC and the White House over how to treat religious houses of worship resulted in Redfield, a devout Catholic, being called into the Oval Office to meet with Trump and Pence, who pressed him directly to loosen the restrictions. People couldn't be banned indefinitely from attending churches, synagogues, mosques, and the like, especially not a few months before the election (that was never stated out loud, but the reasoning seemed clear to some CDC officials). White House officials were also concerned because some states had deemed religious houses of worship "non-essential," or had pushed them to a lower tier in their reopening plans. It was always easier to get Redfield to fold when he was by himself, White House officials felt, without someone else present to help him defend his positions. He would push back, but only so much; the constant conflict and backbiting were sapping him of his will to fight.

Redfield and Kellyanne Conway worked through an agreed-upon document on guidance for churches and religious houses of worship to operate in a COVID-safe manner. They wanted to make it clear that houses of worship could open and follow public health guidelines based on their individual situation. (Some houses of worship are very large, for instance, which would make social distancing easier, while some were in regions of the country with lower rates of infection.) But the process for getting CDC guidance cleared had become so confusing and bogged down that CDC officials didn't know what White House suggestions they had to accept and which ones they could reject. So they went ahead and posted the document with some changes intact and others ignored.

It took until the following morning for someone to notice; two White House aides alerted Conway that the CDC guidance was different than what she and Redfield had worked on. Material that had been negotiated out of the guidance had made its way back in. Conway called Redfield. "What are they doing? They need to take it down," she told him. Redfield quickly instructed the officials in Atlanta who managed the CDC's website to do so. White House officials were convinced that career CDC officials took out their suggestions as a sort of political stance, and wanted people fired as a result. Caputo called the communications operation to find out who had posted the original guidance, but the agency's career officials refused to out one another, and Caputo never found out who was responsible.

As it became clear that the CDC's guidelines were being subjected to unprecedented political interference, public health officials and scientists bemoaned the fall of the world's premier public health agency. But the agency still had its famed *Morbidity and Mortality Weekly Report* (MMWR), the CDC's weekly scientific digest. The studies in the publication are not peer reviewed in the same way that submissions to medical and scientific journals are, but they undergo a rigorous clearance process within the CDC and have always been completely independent from outside pressures. Even the CDC director does not review or approve *MMWR*.

Pence and his team made it clear early on that they did not want *MMWR*s, press releases, or statements from the CDC going out without review by his office; Birx was the proxy. But a study published on the *MMWR* website on May 1 threatened to elicit even further politicization. Anne Schuchat had penned the report herself and alone—an unusual occurrence, as most reports were written by teams of lower-level scientists—detailing how the coronavirus had spread undetected in February. The article was fairly benign, but it seemed to suggest that opportunities to slow the virus's spread had been missed. Schuchat also gave an interview to the Associated Press around the same time in which she stated that the US government had been slow to recognize the impact that travelers arriving from Europe were having on the US outbreak.

When the White House saw the AP headline—"Health Official Says US Missed Some Chances to Slow Virus"—along with top-line findings from the report Schuchat had written, Meadows called Azar to unload the administration's anger. Why the hell had Anne said that stuff? Why had she given the interview? Who had signed off on it? Given that Schuchat was the agency's second-highest-ranking official and had taken the rare step of authoring the report herself, White House officials believed that she was "speaking her truth" out of political motivation, as one official put it. How could Azar have let it happen? Meadows wanted Schuchat's cell phone number. Azar told Meadows to hold off on calling her; he would investigate himself. (Meadows would later ask for Schuchat's cell phone number a second time, and Azar agreed to give it to him. Meadows ended up calling her directly.)

Azar called Redfield and related the discussion he had had with Meadows. Redfield didn't yet know about the study published in *MMWR*, so he read it and then called Azar back. He told his boss that it was highly unusual—maybe unprecedented—to have a single-author piece in *MMWR*. But he reminded Azar that *MMWR* was an independent publication with its own editorial board. He could not, and would not, influence it.

You're the CDC director, Azar and one of his aides told Redfield. You own *MMWR*. This is a scientific document, he told Azar and the aide. I don't see these until they're written and about to post, and I don't make changes to them.

You can do whatever the hell you want, the aide told him. You're the director.

MMWR was a treasure in the scientific world, and the studies published in it were considered integral to the nation's public health work. They were a chance for public health officials across the country to understand what some of the country's top scientists were learning in real time and had become particularly valuable during the pandemic. The reports were typically closely held by a small group of CDC officials until publication, and any sort of interference in them was unfathomable. But during the pandemic, the agency began sending full summaries of upcoming reports to a small group of HHS and White House officials, including Birx, Caputo, and Brett Giroir, the coronavirus testing czar. Caputo would have his scientific adviser, Paul Alexander, who held a doctoral degree in methodology, review the reports for him. Alexander was fiercely loyal to Trump and ended up berating CDC officials for months to change the content of reports in the *MMWR* that he viewed as undermining the president. The content never changed—though there were occasional changes to wording—but the whole episode underscored the politicization that could occur as soon as the process was opened up to more officials. When *Politico* and other outlets reported Alexander's interference in the reports, Azar had him fired.

The constant pressure, abuse, and criticism were becoming too much for Redfield. He was vehemently loyal to the chain of command, but he felt that his boss was ripping him apart. A toxic cycle began to emerge. Redfield would avoid communicating with Azar unnecessarily and grew reluctant to brief him on problems he or the CDC might be facing, expecting to incur Azar's wrath if he did. Azar, in turn, would often learn about problems with the CDC in the press or from angry phone calls from the White House, which only fueled his frustration and anger at Redfield. On several occasions when Redfield had pushed back on Azar's demands, Azar hadn't just shouted but screamed at him. The relationship between the two men—the nation's top health official and the top public health official—had become completely dysfunctional in the middle of a raging pandemic. The consequences of this were catastrophic. They could not work together effectively to craft health policy and help protect the public.

Redfield ended most work days exhausted and feeling personally hurt by the public and private attacks. He thought about resigning so many times he lost count. Then he'd survive another day and go home to a late dinner with his wife. They'd look at the television and see a headline on cable news claiming that he was on the brink of being fired. It was depressing. On the one hand, the scientific and public health community wanted him to resign and stand up to Trump. On the other hand, he felt Azar and Meadows were bullying him and on several occasions wanted him to resign. If he quit, what would happen to the government response to the pandemic? What would happen to the CDC? He had the most important public health job in the country during the worst public health crisis in a century. He wasn't an especially strong leader and had made serious mistakes. But he wasn't going to quit now. "That was the saddest thing for [Redfield]," one person familiar with his thinking said. "It's a hard job, but you don't expect yourself to be shot in the back from the guy above you."

Redfield was in a bind, but it turned out that he wasn't the only one. And he and the others would form an alliance that would create major headaches for both the White House and Azar.

Over the months of the pandemic, a small group of doctors had banded together, united by their feeling that they were under attack, whether by Azar or by the White House: Birx, Fauci, Hahn, and Redfield. There wasn't always bonhomie among the four, but their weekly doctors' meeting became a kind of group therapy session, a place where they could debate complex medical and scientific questions and also support one another as they navigated the varying degrees of political pressure. They were careful not to include others in their group whom they viewed as being close to Azar, including HHS assistant secretary for health Brett Giroir, Robert Kadlec, and NIH director Francis Collins. They feared that information would make its way back to Azar, who would then call Meadows and give him more ammunition with which to attack the health professionals.

Fauci was a career official who could not be directly fired by the president and who had some insulation because his boss, Collins, fully supported him. Birx was also a civil servant but was serving in a political position, having been appointed by former president Obama, whereas Hahn and Redfield had been appointed by President Trump and could be fired at any moment. All three had thought about resigning several times throughout the year and discussed it with one another.

They all harbored the same concerns about who would replace them if one of them left: Would the White House install someone at CDC who would more easily acquiesce or someone who shared their worldview? Would it pick an FDA commissioner who would rubber-stamp all of Azar's proposals that would slowly strip the agency of its autonomy? Would there be anyone left in the White House voraciously collecting data, trying to understand where the outbreak was headed and what people could do about it?

At that point, their influence was greatly diminished and they certainly did not have the ear of the president anymore. Birx had stopped briefing him, and on more than one occasion, Trump had tried—and failed—to force Redfield to walk back public comments he had made, telling reporters that the CDC director was "confused." But they all agreed that their presence mattered, that their staying was better than their being replaced by sycophants.

During one meeting in Birx's office, the four doctors made two pacts. The first was that an attack on one of them was an attack on all of them. They would defend one another to the White House and Azar if they were privately or publicly criticized, and they would push back against lies and mistruths about one another that their adversaries were feeding to the media and other officials. When it became clear that Hahn and the FDA would be heavily criticized in an upcoming media story, Redfield, Fauci, and Birx all spoke to the reporter in his defense. When Birx was urging states experiencing outbreaks to close bars and impose mask mandates, drawing the ire of White House officials, Hahn spoke to the vice president's office to defend her recommendations.

The second pact, among Birx, Redfield, and Hahn, was more drastic: they agreed that if one of them was fired or forced to resign, the other two would immediately quit in protest. They were, in effect, chaining themselves to one another. Individually, they might seem expendable to Trump, who had already pushed out Mulvaney, Grogan, and his press secretary in the short period since the task force had been formed. They knew he wouldn't think twice about firing any single person. But Birx understood the politics of the moment. The president was hurtling toward election day and could not afford to lose three doctors from his task force all at once. That would reveal a pandemic response in disarray. She made the doctors' pact clear to Meadows and to Pence's office: if you fire one of us, you fire all of us.

"Having Steve Hahn, Bob Redfield, and Debbi Birx leave simultaneously would be crushing," one task force official said. "It was common knowledge that there was that coalition."

When the perceived bullying by Azar became "outrageous," Birx let Pence know and asked him to call Redfield and Hahn to assure them that they were valued. She kept up the doctors' meetings through the duration of Trump's term, in large part because "the psychological trauma that Redfield and Hahn were under was unrelenting," one official familiar with the group said.

Their efforts weren't always successful. On several occasions, either together or separately, they approached Pence's office to let the vice president and his aides know that Azar was causing untold numbers of problems. They kept hoping that Pence would intervene, that he would help rein Azar in. Instead, Azar gained more power over the pandemic response as Trump and Pence turned their attention to the campaign trail.

The high-risk pact, though, stifled the ability of Trump and Meadows to fire any one of them during an angry outburst. It was a risky game of politics by the three doctors. But it worked.

Spring was turning into summer, and there was still virtually no effective treatment for COVID-19. The administration and the NIH had gone big on the development of a vaccine but didn't pay nearly as much attention to treatments at every level. (There was remdesivir, which wasn't superb but appeared to help severely ill COVID patients. Its availability, however, was limited. And there was dexamethasone, an inexpensive steroid that also seemed to be effective with some of the sickest patients.)

The FDA had encouraged the academic world to begin conducting clinical trials on a century-old treatment: convalescent plasma therapy, which involves infusing a sick patient with the liquid portion of the blood of another person who has recovered from the infection. The idea is that people who have been infected with and recovered from an infection have developed the antibodies needed to fight it off; an infusion of antibody-rich blood might therefore help a sick person recover.

Despite the FDA's request, the academic world was either very slow to get organized, or in some cases resistant to studying convalescent plasma therapy in a randomized, controlled clinical trial, the gold standard of scientific research. Doctors and scientists worried that only a small number of hospitals would be able to conduct rigorous trials, thereby limiting the number of people who could access the treatments at a time when thousands of people were dying every week.

So instead, the Mayo Clinic—one of the country's top hospitals—agreed to set up a so-called expanded-access program, which enables doctors and patients to access experimental drugs and treatments outside of clinical trials. If people wanted to try the treatment, they could do it through Mayo's program; it was initially meant to treat five thousand patients but eventually treated about ninety-five thousand.

In July, the FDA began reviewing the Mayo Clinic's data from the program, which were unrefined and hard for officials to make sense of. The level of antibodies in the patient blood samples hadn't been measured, making it impossible for the FDA to determine whether the treatment was effective or not. If the agency could see which groups of people had been given plasma with high levels of antibodies and whether the patients in that group had recovered faster than those in the group that had received plasma with lower levels of antibodies, maybe the data would be suggestive enough to meet the bar for an emergency-use authorization. But Mayo Clinic was transferring data to the FDA in real-time, so it was not cleaned up in the same way clinical trial data normally would be.

Emergency-use authorization is not a full approval but allows the FDA to sign off on treatments and vaccines during a public health emergency. Convalescent plasma therapy appeared to be safe, but it was still unclear whether it was effective. Government scientists then looked at a subset of the data that included people who were under eighty years old and not on a ventilator. Among that group, there appeared to be a modest difference: those who had received convalescent plasma with a high level of antibodies had done moderately better, if they had received it early.

When Hahn presented the data to the doctors on the task force, including Birx, Redfield, Kadlec, and Giroir, they all told him that the FDA needed to move forward with the emergency-use authorization. You can't wait any longer, they said.

Decisions made by the FDA can literally make the difference between life and death. Its process for screening drugs and vaccines is supposed to be ironclad, so that Americans can trust that the pills they take and the needles doctors stick into their arms are safe. If the FDA cuts corners, the consequences can be disastrous and deadly.

The FDA made a presentation to several members of the task force and top White House aides during a Zoom call on July 29. Peter Marks, the director of the FDA's Center for Biologics Evaluation and Research, went through the results, convinced that the agency had enough evidence to show that convalescent plasma therapy met the relatively low bar for an emergency-use authorization. It was safe, and it looked as though it could benefit patients.

But Collins objected. It was bad enough that they hadn't been able to conduct a randomized, controlled clinical trial. Now it would look as though they were cherry-picking the data to show that the therapy worked best by excluding some patients with more advanced disease from its analysis. A participant on the phone call paraphrased Collins's warning to the FDA: if you do this, you are going to bring down the wrath of the academic world.

There was silence on the call. Then Birx interjected. "Francis," she said, "it sounds like you're threatening the FDA."

Marks, a career scientist unaccustomed to the rough-and-tumble of White House politics, was taken aback by Collins's forceful response. He knew it would be a disaster if he couldn't bring the NIH on board. He said he could enlarge the data set and try to get better answers, hoping that that would be enough to convince Collins.

The White House was livid, not least of all at Collins. So was Azar, who felt that the emergency authorization was ready to go and that the FDA had already been sitting on it. They believed that Hahn and the FDA were letting the NIH push them around when the decision was FDA's to make. One senior official involved in the discussions said that he understood Collins's objections but added, "This is one of the things [conducting clinical trials and evaluating data] NIH is good at. But in the middle of a pandemic, standing on academic purity and saying we need additional data was a mistake."

An outside review board, which is required under FDA regulations for experimental treatments involving human subjects, allowed the Mayo Clinic to extend its expanded-access program until August 24, the same day the Republican National Convention kicked off. In the meantime, pressure was building on the FDA to approve the treatment. Some White House aides were still bitter at the agency's decision to revoke the emergency-use authorization for hydroxychloroquine, making them even angrier that Hahn was delaying a decision on convalescent plasma treatment because of Collins. With the election quickly approaching, the White House needed wins. There had been so little good news on treatments and so few reasons to give people hope other than the promise of an eventual vaccine. Kushner's allies Adam Boehler and Brad Smith called Hahn and others at the agency, including Marks, repeatedly, asking them when they would have a decision.

By August 12, Marks had reviewed additional data from the Mayo Clinic and believed the FDA now had enough to move forward with the emergency-use authorization. But Collins still did not think the data were sufficient, resulting in a tense exchange between Hahn and the NIH director. Hahn asked Marks what he thought they should do. If we get even further data that helps answer your questions, Marks asked Collins, will that help? Collins said yes. But gathering it would take another seven to ten days.

Just days before the FDA and NIH expected to be able to review Mayo Clinic's additional data—and days before the start of the Republican convention—Collins received a phone call while trying to take a short vacation in Chincoteague, Virginia. It was the president. "You know, my polling numbers are looking really good," Trump began. "But you doctors are killing me!" He then launched into a tirade about convalescent plasma therapy and accused Collins and the NIH of standing in the way of its authorization. Didn't Collins and other scientists recognize they were hurting people? "People are dying," Trump told him.

Collins could barely get a word in but tried to reassure the volatile president, saying, "You know, Mr. President, you don't want to make a decision on data that turns out to be wrong. It'll come back to haunt you."

Trump then went on another rant, this time about the way the doctors had killed hydroxychloroquine. Even though the FDA had revoked its emergency-use authorization two months earlier and it was clear that the drug did not work—and could actually cause heart problems in some COVID-19 patients—he had never given up on it, even if he was talking about it less in public.

Collins found another opening. "We are within a week of having a much larger data set where I know I can trust the antibody levels," he explained. "Can we please just put this off until next week?"

"No. Absolutely not," Trump said emphatically. "We've gotta have the data on Friday, or it doesn't matter." Friday was August 21, three days before the Republican convention. The implication was that the treatment would have to be approved before the huge political rally; otherwise it would be of no value to Trump.

The larger data set came in on Saturday, August 22. By then, Trump had lost all patience for what amounted to a scientific disagreement between two agencies. The same day, he fired off a tweet: "The deep state, or whoever, over at the FDA is making it very difficult for drug companies to get people in order to test the vaccines and therapeutics. Obviously, they are hoping to delay the answer until after November 3rd. Must focus on speed, and saving lives!"

The president had ensnared himself in a scientific debate, and his aides followed suit. Boehler continued calling incessantly, as did Brad Smith. "What are you waiting on?" Smith asked Hahn in a phone call. "You're letting NIH manipulate you." Meadows also called Hahn, telling him to get a move on. The president just wanted the damn thing done, he told him.

Once again, the additional data were raw and unrefined; when the data came in, it had not yet undergone intense quality control, given the urgency of the situation. But FDA officials decided that they would move forward with the emergency-use authorization because the data did not show any safety problems and earlier data tranches had suggested that convalescent plasma therapy could provide a modest benefit to some patients.

The agency wanted to put out a press release and brief reporters on a call, as it did with most authorizations. The announcement should be rolled out of the FDA as a small win, career officials thought, nothing more. But Trump had called Azar on Saturday to yell at him about the delays on convalescent plasma, and Azar informed the president it was about to be authorized and announced by agency officials on Sunday morning. When Trump learned about this, he demanded that he announce it himself, ordering his press secretary, Kayleigh McEnany, to return to Washington from Florida for an announcement on Sunday afternoon.

On Saturday night, Marks emailed Hahn his team's findings from the new Mayo Clinic data set: convalescent plasma therapy was most effective in patients not on a ventilator, younger than eighty years old, who were treated with plasma with a high antibody level within three days of their diagnosis. That group had showed a 35 percent improvement in survival after seven days. "From my perspective it is a definite go," Marks wrote in his email.

"Thanks, Peter. I completely support your conclusion. Please give my thanks to your incredible team," Hahn wrote back.

On Sunday, Hahn, Azar, Collins, Marks, and others met at the White House for the planned announcement, gathering in the Roosevelt Room. It was the last place Marks and Collins wanted to be. They had both tried to avoid going to the White House after realizing that Trump was focused on touting "wins" ahead of the election whether they were real or not. Yet after being asked to attend the event, the two were left out of the announcement. Hahn and Azar took the stage with Trump, who began by touting the news as a "truly historic announcement." Azar followed Trump, praising the president's "bold leadership" for helping to bring about the emergency authorization.

"We saw about a 35 percent better survival in the patients who benefited most from the treatment," Azar said, adding that those patients had been younger than eighty years of age and not on artificial respiration. ". . . We dream in drug development of something like a 35 percent mortality reduction. This is a major advance in the treatment of patients. This is a major advance."

Hahn then parroted Azar's statement: out of one hundred patients, he said, thirty-five would be saved by the administration of convalescent plasma.

Collins and Marks watched the press conference on Caputo's cell phone, and "both immediately had their hair on fire," one senior administration official recalled. Hahn, Azar, and Trump had completely misrepresented the data, which indicated a *relative* reduction in mortality, not an *absolute* reduction. There had been a 35 percent improvement among patients who had received plasma with a high level of antibodies compared to a group that had received plasma with a low level of antibodies. That was not at all the same thing as saying that thirty-five out of a hundred patients would have been saved. A result like that simply didn't exist. Marks and Collins were in disbelief that Hahn, an oncologist, could have misunderstood the data so horribly. The politicization of the FDA had reached its nadir.

The scientific community quickly lambasted Hahn for making such a gross misstatement, especially on the eve of the Republican National Convention. Between Trump's Saturday tweet, the timing of the event, and Hahn's error, the FDA looked as though it had succumbed to White House pressure yet again, only months before it was expected to make a decision on whether to authorize a coronavirus vaccine. It was looking increasingly like a prop in Trump's reelection campaign.

The authorization of hydroxychloroquine as a COVID-19 treatment had been an ugly chapter in the FDA's history and had only paved the way for even more interference by the White House. It looked as though the White House could railroad the agency's officials anytime it seized on a new miracle cure, real or not. Public trust was integral to the FDA's survival, and the appearance of its politi-cization was just as bad as actual political interference. The agency Marks and other scientists had dedicated much of their careers to was supposed to be an independent regulatory body and had been the envy of the world. The FDA seal of approval carried enormous weight. But the reputation the agency had spent 114 years building and maintaining had been shattered in a matter of months. Would it ever recover? If it signed off on a vaccine—and one that would be developed in record time, no less—would people want to take it?

As FDA officials watched the dismal coverage the following day, Wayne Pines, a former FDA official and now a communications con-sultant to Hahn, advised him to correct his error. The statistic Hahn had used was misinformation, Pines argued, and the fact that the FDA had provided misinformation from the White House podium needed to be rectified. Pines helped Hahn write a series of tweets that he sent out beginning around 9:36 p.m., including "I have been criticized for remarks I made Sunday night about the benefits of con-valescent plasma. The criticism is entirely justified. What I should have said better is that the data show a relative risk reduction not an absolute risk reduction."

Hahn hadn't told anyone that he was going to issue a public apol-ogy. It was what he had to do to try to rebuild the FDA's reputation and his own, and he didn't want to be talked out of it. Not sur-prisingly, HHS and White House officials were outraged when they saw his tweet. Azar thought Hahn's apology tour was overwrought. Caputo, in particular, viewed Hahn's apology as undermining both Trump and Azar. But Caputo was also sympathetic to Hahn's plight. His agency was in full revolt in the wake of the convalescent plasma debacle. Hahn could either regain control by siding with the career staff, or the FDA would be torn apart just before the vaccines arrived for the agency's sign-off.

Hahn was over it. As he pieced together the series of events, he felt bullied and manipulated by everyone—by Trump, by Meadows, by

HHS, and by the NIH. Trump's tweet on Saturday made it look as though he had strong-armed the FDA into the decision, even though the agency had already planned to authorize convalescent plasma therapy. And before the announcement on Sunday, Meadows told ABC News that the FDA had to be pushed to make a decision and "feel the heat."

The whole affair was a brutal lesson and a warning to Hahn and the FDA: letting the White House get so involved in a scientific disagreement had been an error. The convalescent plasma emergency authorization could have been a win and an event that attracted the attention of only the medical and scientific press if it had been rolled out as a modest advancement by the FDA, as initially planned. "This is a dress rehearsal for the vaccine," Marks told Hahn afterward.

The episode was a turning point for the commissioner. He was not going to be manipulated anymore. He was almost certain he would lose his job after he publicly apologized—but he didn't. The White House wasn't going to get rid of him so late in the game. But he needed to earn back the respect of FDA career officials, many of whom felt he had not protected the agency against political interference. He would stand with the agency's Office of Vaccines Research and Review in whatever decisions it made on whether and how to authorize a COVID-19 vaccine, perhaps the most important and consequential decision in the agency's history. (The top officials in that office had also made clear that they wouldn't be pushed around and would resign if they were subjected to inappropriate pressure.) And he was sick of feeling harassed by Azar, who, he felt, was trashing him behind his back.

In the following weeks and months, Azar had discussions with top White House officials about whether Hahn needed to be replaced as frustration grew over his handling of vaccine and treatment authorizations. Hahn would eventually find out about the discussions, expediting the breakdown in their relationship.

Hahn was not a fighter in the way that many other Trump officials were; he generally didn't yell or get in people's faces. But he set about forming a protective barrier around the FDA to restore its independence. He would handle calls from the White House; the career officials were not to be bothered. If they got a call from the White House, they would have to let Hahn know so he could step in. The FDA would get scientific consultation from the NIH, but the NIH wasn't going to call the shots. Hahn had been hoodwinked numerous times. He was no bureaucratic ninja, certainly nowhere near the level of Meadows and Azar. But he was ready to fight back. And he would hold tremendous power in the months to come: there would not be any coronavirus vaccine until he signed off on it.

CHAPTER 15

FROM BAD TO WORSE

May 25, 2020

CONFIRMED US COVID-19 CASES: **1,657,000**

CONFIRMED US COVID-19 DEATHS: **98,000**

Days had turned into weeks. The school year was ending, and children headed home with nothing to do, nowhere to go. In Boston, 20 percent of high school students didn't log on at all in May. College students graduated at home and stumbled into a terrible job market. Many summer camps were canceled. Businesses kept closing. Millions of Americans remained unemployed, and layoffs continued.

The nation was shaggy—literally, as people weren't getting haircuts—and unkempt. Americans had stopped going to the dentist. Stopped going to the doctor. Stopped going to the gym. They were stress baking and stress eating and stress drinking. They were stressed, disillusioned, lost.

Some members of the task force, including Deborah Birx, expressed optimism that the sacrifices weren't being made in vain. The data suggested that the lockdown measures and restrictions were working; infections and deaths were being prevented. Hospitalization rates appeared to have fallen by 50 percent. It looked as though the effort to "flatten the curve" that Anthony Fauci and Birx had preached in March and April was finally showing results.

But they had only a limited understanding of what was happening.

There was a major blind spot: a number of the testing centers set up in the first few months were drive-up sites that allowed people to be tested inside their automobile. That meant they were mostly testing people who had cars and could take time off work. Large numbers of low-income Americans without these advantages were excluded from the tallies. Those workers were disproportionately Black and Hispanic. And many of them were really sick.

Compounding matters, Black and Hispanic Americans were at a greater risk of having one or more of the underlying health conditions that made COVID-19 more lethal: obesity, diabetes, hypertension, and cardiovascular disease, among others.

The task force was so overwhelmed in March and April with trying to wrap its arms around the pandemic and addressing issues like testing and supplies that it missed another calamity: the disproportionate impact the virus was having on people of color.

In Black and Brown communities, testing was inadequate. Those households were also hit disproportionately hard by the economic fallout. Millions of Black and Hispanic Americans had jobs that could not be performed remotely, including in grocery stores, construction sites, and meatpacking plants, where they were exposed to lots of people every day. Many of them also had to use public transportation to get to and from work. While many Americans were hunkered down, safe at home, those workers had to continue putting themselves at risk. And if they spoke up about having symptoms, they could lose their income. The paid leave policy approved by Congress earlier in the year was not as effective as envisioned. Some White workers who were initially laid off found it easier to obtain another job within weeks. For Black workers, it was much harder.

The virus's uneven impact in those early months was unmistakable. In the records of 600,000 US COVID-19 victims between January 22 and May 30 that included details on race and ethnicity, 33 percent were Hispanics and 22 percent were Black. In other words, more than 50 percent of the cases affected groups that represented roughly 30 percent of the US population. And in some places, the disparities were extreme.

At one point, 80 percent of Georgians hospitalized by the virus were African American.

In Milwaukee County, Wisconsin, Black Americans make up 26 percent of the population but accounted for 81 percent of the coronavirus deaths in the early weeks of the pandemic.

More than 70 percent of the coronavirus deaths in Chicago were among African Americans, even though they make up just 33 percent of the local population.

More than 76 percent of the people hospitalized with coronavirus in one Louisiana health care system were Black, even though they make up just 31 percent of the local population.

Ultimately, CDC data would find that African Americans and Hispanics were roughly three times as likely to die from coronavirus as Whites.

President Trump acknowledged the disparity at a press conference in early April, identifying it as a major conundrum that he couldn't comprehend. Could Black and Hispanic Americans really be three times as likely to die? "Well, we're helping them a lot," he said falsely of his purported assistance to minorities. "But what's happening is we're trying to find out why is it that it's three and four times? Now, maybe that's not going to be the final number, but why is it three or four times more so for the Black community as opposed to other people? It doesn't make sense, and I don't like it."

As news outlets began to bring attention to the problem, the task force found itself scrambling. Surgeon General Jerome Adams, one of the only high-ranking Black officials in the entire Trump administration and the only Black health official on the task force, had been raising the issue of racial disparities in the disease's impact internally and warning officials that it could become a problem. He found a sympathetic ear in Mike Pence, with whom he had worked when Pence was the Indiana governor. At Pence's encouragement, Adams began to speak publicly about the issue, becoming a regular presence on cable television and something of a rising star. But Adams and other officials felt that the White House was only paying lip service to the problem and not thinking seriously about ways to address it.

"We were reactionary," one task force member said. "It came from the outside and people were reacting. We had started looking at the data, and we didn't have enough."

Three days after Trump spoke about the high infection rates among Black Americans, Adams tried to take matters a step further. At a press conference with Trump, Adams took the microphone to implore Black and Hispanic communities to be careful about contracting the virus. "Avoid alcohol, tobacco, and drugs. And call your friends and family; check in on your mother; she wants to hear from you right now," he said. "And speaking of mothers, we need you to do this, if not for yourself then for your abuela. Do it for your grand-daddy. Do it for your Big Mama. Do it for your Pop-Pop. We need you to understand—especially in communities of color, we need you to step up and help stop the spread so that we can protect those who are most vulnerable."

Adams was making a direct appeal to Black and Hispanic families by invoking a vernacular that he thought would connect with them. But for much of the public, it came across as wildly insensitive and disconnected. Why was the surgeon general telling Blacks and Hispanics but not White people to avoid drugs and alcohol? His folksy nicknames for Black elders, "Big Mama" and "Pop-Pop," also landed with a thud. When pressed by PBS reporter Yamiche Alcindor, who told him his comments had offended some people, Adams said he had simply been using the same language he uses with his own family and drawing from his own experiences. Adams has a brother who has been into and out of prison for crimes related to substance abuse problems, an uncle who died of cancer in prison because of crimes related to substance abuse, and another uncle who is an alcoholic.

Anthony Fauci leapt in to defend Adams. "Jerome, you did it beautifully. You can't do it any better than that," he said at the

White House podium. "I know Jerome personally. I can just testify that he made no—not even a hint of being offensive at all with that comment."

Yet Adams's comments continued to generate more controversy in the days that followed. It became clear that he would be asked about it every time he went on television, making Adams the story. "If you put him out there, he would've had to defend himself," one task force member recalled. "We needed to just focus on the issues of coronavirus. He had a gaffe."

The White House mostly kept Adams off television as a result. It was a lose-lose situation. Adams would later say that he had stayed on the task force because otherwise a person of color would have had no input whatsoever into the task force's response. "That's a heavy cross to bear," he tweeted in early 2021.

Trump did little to focus on racial disparities in the weeks to come. Health data collection systems are archaic and slow, so getting racial breakdowns was no simple task. Meaningfully addressing the issue would have required a significant financial investment and sustained focus. Outside scientists, public health groups, and medical associations were calling, emailing, and texting administration officials, telling them they had to get the data out. To make matters worse, the White House blocked efforts to crack down on meatpacking plants and other firms that had stayed open and put their workers at a heightened risk of infection. The majority of those workers were Black and Hispanic.

By late May, the focus in the White House was clearly on reopening. In a pre–Memorial Day press briefing, Birx encouraged people to go outside, play golf, play tennis, go to the beach. Things appeared to be headed in the right direction, and Trump had lost so much interest in the virus that he considered disbanding the task force once and for all. It was rarely meeting anymore anyway. The administration anticipated a summer lull that health officials hoped to use to stock-pile supplies and tests.

Data in May showed that there were roughly twenty thousand new cases of the virus each day, down significantly from the April peak but still quite elevated. Some top health officials pleaded with people to continue to take the virus seriously and warned that the situation could spiral out of control again as soon as just a few people let their guard down. There was finally a chance to crush the first wave. But people wanted to resume their precrisis lives. Everyone was fatigued after two months of canceled trips and dinners and parties. Many people wanted to move on.

Americans were about to learn a terrifying lesson: the virus didn't get tired, and it didn't take breaks.

On the Saturday of Memorial Day weekend, throngs of people congregated at beaches, pools, and bars in nearly every pocket of the United States. Hundreds of people in swimsuits and bikinis, none wearing masks, packed into the pool at Backwater Jack's in Missouri's Lake of the Ozarks. Close to seven hundred thousand people went to the Lake of the Ozarks that weekend, crowding into bars, boats, and everywhere else. The sight of that many people all together, all at once, was jarring, like something from the beforetimes. The images ricocheted around the country and sparked significant outrage and reproach among the half of the country that had been heeding regulations scrupulously. When a lawmaker later asked Redfield about the photographs, he simply shook his head. And it wasn't just in Missouri; similar scenes unfolded in Florida, Maryland, Virginia, and elsewhere. Many Americans had had enough of the lockdowns and the lecturing. They were busting loose. The collective sacrifice that many Americans had endured was over, and the country was tearing in two.

A clerk at Cup Foods, a south Minneapolis market, called the police at 8:01 p.m. on May 25 and alleged that a customer had used "fake bills" to buy a pack of cigarettes. Several police officers responded and approached a blue Mercedes-Benz parked outside. They pulled out a forty-six-year-old Black man, and within seconds George Perry Floyd, Jr., was facedown on the street.

But it wasn't an ordinary arrest. One of the officers, Derek Chauvin, pinned Floyd to the ground, keeping his left knee on Floyd's neck for more than nine minutes. Floyd gasped, "I can't breathe" and "Please don't shoot me." He called out for his mother. Anxious onlookers pleaded with the police officer to stop. A bystander videoed the whole scene as Floyd slowly, tragically died, then uploaded the video to the internet. In a matter of hours, millions of people had watched Floyd's murder. It resembled a modern-day lynching.

The next day, four Minneapolis police officers were fired, but the city exploded with violence as protesters vandalized a police station and the police responded by firing tear gas. The protests spread all over the country, then all over the world. A new civil rights movement had been born.

Fueling the movement was an anger about what felt like willful ignorance toward the way the pandemic was ravaging Black and Brown communities. There was little targeted outreach; few federal officials publicly acknowledged what was happening, and there were no real resources being directed to help. But that all came as little surprise to communities that were used to being left behind and forgotten.

A number of horrific things happened in 2020, things that would have been terrible in isolation. But they didn't happen in isolation. They were intertwined, interlocked. That made it all so much worse. Shortly before he died, Floyd had lost his job as a bouncer at El Nuevo Rodeo, a nightclub, after Minnesota's governor had issued a stay-at-home order. His autopsy would later show he died with coronavirus. Floyd's life, in many ways, was a microcosm of what was playing out nationally. Did those factors play a role in the chain of events that led to his death? It's unclear. But Americans were on edge before he died, and they went over the edge in the days that followed. All of the frustration and resentment of the past few months, and of centuries of injustice, finally bubbled up to the surface and exploded. Angry Americans poured into the streets.

Floyd's death had snapped the country awake again. The police killings and racial injustice that had chronically haunted the United States were now center stage. In 2020, everything seemed bigger, deadlier, more important. The presidential election was less than six months away. The new awakening drew Americans out of their homes en masse. But not just protesters; many others flocked to beaches and boardwalks, convinced that the pandemic was over. Bars began to fill up. Masks began to come off.

And so as May bled into June, the two crises moved in tandem, sometimes together, but always moving. The protesters moved through the streets. The virus moved through the air. Both were spreading fast. Both were impossible to stop.

And in Floyd's killing and the protests that followed, Trump saw a way to change the subject.

The president, who had elevated the practice of grievance politics to an art, recognized right away the golden opportunity to rile up his core conservative supporters before the election. He set about rebranding himself as something of a cop in chief, calling for violent crackdowns on protests around the country. And he showed no restraint.

He retweeted a video of someone saying "The only good Democrat is a dead Democrat."

A few days after protests had swept the country, he tweeted at 12:53 a.m., "When the looting starts, the shooting starts."

It was clear, based on when he was on social media, that Trump wasn't sleeping much, and his rhetoric showed he was consuming a tremendous amount of conservative cable television such as Fox News. He embraced his new image of saber rattler. Not only did he threaten Democrats and protesters; his language toward China turned darker as well. He had resumed referring to the pandemic as the "Wuhan virus" and pinning all the blame on the Chinese government.

No matter how viciously Trump threatened to crack down on protesters, the protests spread. There were Black Lives Matter events in nearly every corner of the country, even deep red pockets of Appalachia and Texas. He was unable to snuff them out. Following his instincts only made things worse. The more he threatened people, the more the protests grew.

A few days after Floyd's death, a sustained, vocal, defiant protest began gathering near Lafayette Square, just north of the White House in Washington, D.C. It was so loud that the protesters' chanting could be heard inside the West Wing. People from all walks of life were gathered there: grandmothers and grandchildren; preachers and teachers. And as the protest dragged into the night, a small but violent group of people broke off and began looting parts of downtown Washington. At one point some of them even burned a section of St. John's Church on Lafayette Square, roughly a hundred yards from the White House's north gate. Since his first day in office, Trump had been obsessed with crowd sizes. And these crowds were enormous.

On Friday, May 29, just four days after Floyd's killing, the protests outside the White House were so thunderous that the Secret Service moved Trump into a secure bunker under the White House for protection. Trump was livid when that was disclosed by the *New York Times*, fearing the optics made him look like a shivering coward rather than the fearless Winston-Churchill-in-the-rubble image he wanted to project. He tried to explain it away, saying that he had simply been inspecting the bunker. But the damage had been done.

Humiliated and refusing to read the mood of the country, Trump didn't reverse course. Instead, he doubled down. He spent the night of May 31 gorging on conservative cable networks, which were playing nonstop footage of looters and protests. He tweeted that he might unleash dogs on protesters if they came back to the White

House, and he called for his supporters to launch a counterprotest. The counterprotest never materialized, and he realized that he'd have to do something himself.

The next day he hatched a plan, prodded by his daughter Ivanka. He needed to show Americans that he wasn't cowering in the White House's bunker. He needed to show his bravery.

What unfolded next was a carefully choreographed chain of events that shocked even some of his closest aides and would become a defining image of his presidency. At 6:43 p.m., Trump delivered remarks in the White House Rose Garden on the White House's south side, vowing to lead a major federal crackdown on the protests:

> These are not acts of peaceful protest. These are acts of domestic terror. The destruction of innocent life and the spilling of innocent blood is offense to humanity and a crime against God.
>
> America needs creation, not destruction; cooperation, not contempt; security, not anarchy; healing, not hatred; justice, not chaos. This is our mission, and we will succeed. One hundred percent, we will succeed. Our country always wins.
>
> That is why I am taking immediate Presidential action to stop the violence and restore security and safety in America.

As the words were leaving his mouth, federal forces moved against protesters near Lafayette Square, just minutes before the city's newly instituted 7:00 p.m. curfew. They used flash grenades, gas, and rubber bullets to clear the crowds. Children and elderly people who had come to protest in solidarity ran from the scene screaming. The government's crackdown was an astonishing act of violence against its own citizens.

Trump wrapped up his remarks in the Rose Garden and soon emerged from the White House's north gate, striding across Lafayette Square. He was surrounded by his top aides, family members, Defense Secretary Mark Esper, Attorney General William Barr, and

General Mark Milley, the chairman of the Joint Chiefs of Staff. The group made it all the way to H Street NW, which runs along the north side of Lafayette Square, and then turned to face the media. Trump, standing in front of St. John's Church, held up a black Bible for the media to see.

"It's coming back strong," he said to no one in particular, his voice uncertain. "It'll be greater than ever before."

He was trying to pose for a photograph, but he was clearly searching for words. He beckoned several staffers to join him for a photo before they returned. The tear gas drifted up to the church's patio, and burned a clergy member's eyes. General Milley patrolled the streets of Washington in his combat fatigues that night like a commander inspecting the battlefield. It was as if the military had invaded its own country.

The United States that had existed four months earlier had faded in everyone's memories. There were two crises now, interlocked. It was during this period that the one hundred thousandth American died of COVID-19. But hardly anyone noticed because everyone was shocked at how the country was unraveling. The president was trying to run the pandemic response and beat back the protests through rhetoric, fear, and tribalism. People had to pick sides: either you were with the protesters, or you were with Trump; either masks stood for safety, or they stood for tyranny. There was no middle ground.

Trump was threatening a police state, martial law. White House officials said that dramatic action was needed to counter "anarchy" in the streets. People were buying guns at a furious pace. There was a growing sense that something terrible was going to happen. And terrible things did happen; numerous protesters and police would be killed in the coming weeks, with Trump's rhetoric egging on the violence.

"The slide of the United States into illiberalism may well have begun on June 1, 2020," retired marine general John R. Allen, the president of the Brookings Institution and a member of the Homeland Security Advisory Council, wrote in *Foreign Policy* two days later. "Remember the date. It may well signal the beginning of the end of the American experiment."

All through those events, the virus continued to move, regenerating itself, growing stronger. It took two weeks for the number of coronavirus infections to accelerate again. (Some cities that had seen large protests, however, did not see significant upticks of the virus in the weeks that followed, likely because people were outside and wearing masks, health experts would later say.) Testing had slowed, and just as Trump had lost interest, so had many other Americans. Fauci and other health experts watched the protests with apprehension, fearful about what would happen when so many people gathered together shoulder to shoulder during a deadly pandemic, just when things had appeared to be improving. The country had finally had a chance to flatten the curve, to get out of the first wave of infections. Instead, it would never emerge from the first wave, and the virus ravaged the country in one continuous stream, taking no breaks.

As Americans burst out into the open during the hot and dangerous summer, the virus burst out, too. "The only way you are going to get through the outbreak is if we all pull together," Fauci told others at the time. "This is the antithesis of us all pulling together."

Just a few days after the Lafayette Square incident, the president went to Maine to meet with a group of lobstermen. He threatened new tariffs against foreign countries if they somehow disadvantaged US fishermen. He took Peter Navarro with him. "Peter Navarro's going to be the lobster king now, okay?"

His jaunt to Bangor occurred just as the Dow Jones Industrial Average fell 600 points because investors were on edge about what Trump might do next. It reinforced the fact that the work the task force was doing was increasingly meaningless. Trump didn't believe any of it. He didn't listen to any of it. He was mainly following his instincts now and taking cues from what he saw on cable television. One member of the task force watched his performance that day and said it seemed darkly comical, like a *Saturday Night Live* skit.

"If we lose the November election, we literally issued a lobster executive order in the middle of a Great Depression and a pandemic," that person said.

CHAPTER 16

THE SECOND WAVE

June 15, 2020

CONFIRMED US COVID-19 CASES: **2,100,000**

CONFIRMED US COVID-19 DEATHS: **116,000**

In other countries, the virus appeared to be vanishing. In Europe and Asia, people were eating out at restaurants and children were preparing to return to school. That gnawed at Donald Trump. Why did his health advisers still want the United States to be cautious when everyone else was moving on?

"Corona is cancelled!!! Enough already," Trump's son Donald Trump, Jr., tweeted on June 15. He was reacting to a huge demonstration in support of Black Trans Lives Matter in Brooklyn that showed pictures of people packed together, the types of large crowds that the task force and Democratic governors had warned against for months. Here, for many on the right, was liberal hypocrisy in action. Conservatives were sick of the double standard they believed had set in. Liberals wanted to shame people who wanted to gather together, eat at a restaurant, or open schools, but they also supported mass gatherings of protesters all over the country. Many conservatives believed it validated their view that Democrats were trying to make a power play. Their policies weren't just about the virus; they were about control.

The daily number of deaths had fallen from its peak in April. But there were still twenty thousand new cases a day, a phenomenon that was driving the president crazy. More and more, he was convinced that the fault lay in all the testing that was being done. If the US would only stop testing people who didn't have symptoms and who didn't seem to be sick, the number of new cases would disappear. Then the virus would be gone, and life could go back to normal. It was time to get on with the presidential campaign. All the protests and all the new cases made him look weak, as though he wasn't in control. A new poll was about to show that Americans were the most unhappy they had been in fifty years. Trump needed to change the message.

He convened his top aides for a meeting in the White House Cabinet Room, an important projection of power. He wanted the press to see him in charge. He sat between Mike Pence and Ben Carson, the HUD secretary. In front of the president was a single red folder containing a single white piece of paper announcing World Elder Abuse Awareness Day. But his focus was on something else. He wanted to explain why there were still coronavirus cases in the United States. "That's probably the downside of having good testing is you find a lot of cases that other countries who don't even test don't have," he said. "If you don't test, you don't have any cases. If we stop testing right now, we'd have very few cases, if any. But we do. We're at a level that Mike is going to talk about that's so high. But we will show more—more cases when other countries have far more cases than we do. They just don't talk about it."

His explanation was nonsensical. Other White House aides didn't necessarily believe that the number of tests should be reduced, but Trump's comments reflected a growing sense of skepticism among some aides about the value of testing. (Trump was also beginning to tell aides privately that he wanted fewer tests done.) Most people who visited the White House were tested every day, and it didn't seem to be preventing infections from spreading or even indicating to people when they had first gotten sick, several aides thought. Mike Pence's newly promoted communications director, Katie Miller, tested negative one night and was then confirmed to have the virus only a few hours later. So what was the point of the tests?

Trump also refused to accept the embarrassing reality that other countries were in fact doing more testing and had far better testing capabilities relative to their populations. The idea he was trying to convey was that many Americans who were testing positive for the virus weren't *really* sick. They had no symptoms or only mild ones. It wasn't that big a deal. But because the United States was finally testing people on a larger scale—the country conducted nearly 450,000 tests on June 15, up from about 10,000 per day in mid-March—more cases were being diagnosed that previously would have been missed.

Something strange was happening: the number of new cases of coronavirus had fallen in New York City, which had been the epicenter for much of the spring, but now the virus was sinking its teeth into other states—Arizona, Florida, Georgia, Texas, Oklahoma— that were harder for Trump to explain away. They were states with large numbers of Republicans who hung on his every word and mirrored his disdain for mask wearing. That started to worry White House officials, who saw the citizens of those states as being more "their people."

To show the country that he was moving on, Trump planned a big campaign rally in Oklahoma for that weekend. He and Meadows believed that talking about the pandemic was a losing proposition and the rally would give the president a major platform to change the message. Local leaders openly expressed fear that Trump's visit would overburden their already taxed hospitals. But the president's campaign aides had convinced him that the indoor arena would be pulsating, with every seat full and a spillover crowd outside. People all over the country would see that he was back.

Ahead of the Tulsa rally, Pence's staff began writing an op-ed for the *Wall Street Journal* assuring Americans that the pandemic wouldn't ever again get as bad as it had in the spring. They felt the new uptick in cases in some states was blown out of proportion by the media. Doctors had a better understanding of the disease now, and there were drugs that could treat the sickest patients. A speechwriter conferred with Olivia Troye, Pence's homeland security, counterterrorism, and coronavirus adviser, about what should be said.

Troye agonized over the request. Maybe if they wrote an op-ed that stuck strictly to the facts, they could achieve their goal without misleading the public. She tried to offer some guidance about how it could be worded. But she didn't see the final draft until it appeared in the newspaper with the headline "There Isn't a Coronavirus 'Second Wave.'"

"With testing, treatments and vaccine trials ramping up, we are far better off than the media report," Pence wrote.

Troye was floored. The headline was completely off base. She slammed her door and threw a pen against the wall. Then she marched into the speechwriter's office. "Are you fucking kidding me?" she fumed. "Do you know how stupid this makes [Pence] look?"

The op-ed was immediately panned by public health experts for its inaccurate and dangerous claims, especially as the number of those infected with the virus had begun a new climb. And it was dramatically overhyping the US government's response. For example, it claimed that Project Airbridge, Jared Kushner's initiative to secure protective equipment, had obtained more than 143 million N95 masks and 598 million surgical and procedural masks. In fact, Project Airbridge had helped bring only 1.5 million N95 masks and 113.4 million surgical masks into the country. The op-ed proved to be a public relations disaster that would haunt the administration right up to the election. The serene confidence of Pence's optimistic projections was not just misguided, but tone deaf.

"It's a virus, Mr. Vice President," Anthony Fauci told Pence at the next task force meeting. "We don't know where it's going to go."

———

Unlike some of Pence's other top advisers, Troye had taken a winding career path to the vice president's inner circle. She had started at the Republican National Committee and then joined the Pentagon after the September 11, 2001, terrorist attacks. Focusing on intelligence and counterterrorism issues, she had moved over to the Department of Homeland Security in the first year of the Trump administration. In May 2018, she had been dispatched to Pence's team as homeland security and counterterrorism adviser and had quickly become one of his more trusted aides, briefing him on everything from hurricanes to domestic security threats.

Troye was a Republican, but not a "Trump Republican." Her mother was a Mexican immigrant, and she cringed at some of the president's statements and directives. She thought that by working directly for Pence, she could help influence policy and promote better outcomes. It also let her avoid having to directly carry out some of the president's actions that she found objectionable, such as the child separation policy for migrant families.

Troye established an immediate rapport with the vice president, whom she thought polite and courteous. He was always asking people about their families and thanking them for their service. It made Pence's deference to the president all the more confusing to her. The two men seemed like polar opposites. Pence believed strongly in states' rights and the importance of governors; Trump acted as though he were king. Pence was a throwback to civility; Trump was brash and crude. When Trump said something bombastic or inflammatory or insulting, Troye would look for Pence's reaction. She was always amazed. He wouldn't even flinch. Never rolled his eyes or stifled a gasp. Pence consistently deferred to the president's whims and was especially cognizant of Trump's obsession with public image and photo ops. In late April, Pence visited the Mayo Clinic in Minnesota to spend time with doctors and coronavirus patients. Despite the hospital's requirement that everyone wear a mask, Pence did not.

"Since I don't have the coronavirus," he said, "I thought it'd be a good opportunity for me to be here, to be able to speak to these researchers, these incredible health care personnel, and look them in the eye and say 'thank you.'" The comment was ludicrous, and he later admitted that not wearing a mask had been a mistake. It ended up becoming the dominant story from his visit, rather than the Mayo Clinic's convalescent plasma program that Pence was hoping to highlight.

He would justify his attitude toward the president based on his reading of history. After Trump asked him to be his running mate in 2016, Pence studied several biographies of figures who had served as vice presidents. Two books in particular, about George H. W. Bush and Calvin Coolidge, emphasized the importance of advocating the president's policies. The two men had never, ever contradicted the president in public, even in cabinet meetings. If they wanted to challenge the president, they did so in private. Pence stuck to the same modus operandi.

Still, the Mayo Clinic flub reflected the hyperpartisan advice that Pence often received from his other top aides, including Marc Short and Katie Miller. In addition to being skilled political infighters, they were unapologetic about their strident conservative views. (Part of the reason Miller was skeptical about the effectiveness of masks was that Democratic-led states with mask mandates were struggling with coronavirus outbreaks just as Republican-led states were.) Troye felt constantly undermined by Short and Miller and couldn't understand why Pence took direction from people she thought were so ideological. She thought it was, in part, because the conflict-averse Pence didn't want to crack down on his staff. Trump, Short, and Miller tried to exert power by controlling everyone around them. Pence, by his own volition, was sandwiched in the middle of it all.

Pence briefed the president regularly on the virus and often did so with a positive spin. He would seize on the good news in Deborah Birx's briefings, even if it sat atop a dumpster fire of terrible statistics. If Birx said that things were worsening in forty-six states but improving in four states, Pence would highlight the four states with encouraging news.

But in private, he was much more concerned. Back in March, one of his best friends, Tom Rose, his chief strategist and senior adviser, had become infected. The entire speechwriting team had immediately been sent home because of possible exposure, giving Pence a firsthand glimpse at how quickly the disease could spread. Later, the father of one of his aides contracted the virus and became critically ill; he ended up on a ventilator for seventy days. Pence checked in with the staffer about his father almost daily.

Then, on Friday, May 7, Pence prepared to fly to Iowa to tout the state's coronavirus response. His flight was delayed, though, and eventually Miller and several other aides were pulled off the plane. Miller had tested positive for the virus, and now much of the senior White House staff was at risk.

Miller's diagnosis rattled Pence. He had spent a considerable amount of time with her and was worried that he might have contracted the virus, making him the next superspreader. He wouldn't let Short into his office. He told Troye, "I could have it and give it to you."

"His face when he looked at me and said that was heartbreaking," Troye recalled. "He looked visibly shook."

Pence continued to stand alongside Trump at press conferences and not blink when the president waved the threat of the virus away.

Miller's diagnosis had the knock-on effect of upending the task force. Because she was omnipresent at the meetings, often ricocheting around the room, virtually everyone present had been exposed. Fauci and Stephen Hahn went home to quarantine, taking themselves out of the White House's orbit for more than a week. But it also had the effect of forming unexpected bonds between people who had been at odds. Fauci called Miller each day to check in. Her condition, after all, was concerning. She hadn't told many people, but she was nine weeks pregnant and the virus's impact on expectant mothers was still unknown.

———

Trump's campaign manager, Brad Parscale, had promoted the June 20 Oklahoma event as perhaps the biggest campaign rally of all time, with more than 1 million ticket requests to see the president relaunch his campaign at the BOK Center in Tulsa. Trump's family was ecstatic to see the patriarch reboot. His son Eric tweeted, "TULAS OKLAHOMA HERE WE COME!!!" (He would later fix the spelling.)

The optics were striking. The country was still struggling to contain the virus in the South and Southwest. When the *Daily Beast* asked Fauci just days before the rally whether he would attend, Fauci was blunt: "No. I'm in a high risk category. Personally, I would not. Of course not."

But Oklahoma was Trump country. He had won the state in 2016 by 36 percentage points. He needed a place where he had adoring fans. And he needed a place that would let him pack the house. Despite the surging number of cases in the state, Oklahoma had lax rules about large indoor gatherings. The BOK Center had posted signs inside the arena encouraging social distancing, but Trump aides swiftly removed them. They wanted the place to be packed to the gills; they wanted it to look like 2019.

The day before the rally, via Twitter, Trump implicitly threatened violence against anyone who threatened to protest or cause trouble before the rally: "Any protesters, anarchists, agitators, looters or lowlifes who are going to Oklahoma please understand, you will not be treated like you have been in New York, Seattle, or Minneapolis. It will be a much different scene!"

So it was with horror on Saturday afternoon that Trump's aides realized that nowhere near 1 million people were actually showing up to the rally. Nowhere near 100,000. Or 50,000. Or 10,000. Just an hour before Trump was scheduled to speak, the streets of downtown Tulsa were dead. Around 6,200 people ultimately attended, the Tulsa Fire Department later said, filling just one-third of the seats.

Trump wore his trademark blue suit, red tie, and white shirt. When he took the stage, he tried to avoid acknowledging the lackluster turnout and scores of empty blue seats. He launched into a two-hour riff of grievances and complaints: about Democrats; about the media. But there was something *off* about him, something rawer and meaner. It was almost as if he had to try harder to impress the smaller crowd. The laugh lines weren't landing as cleanly, so he had to go to a darker place. And he did.

First he claimed that he had told his aides to order testing to be scaled back so that the number of new cases would not be as high. "When you do testing to that extent, you're going to find more people, you're going to find more cases," he said, moderating his voice in a way that made it hard to tell whether he was joking. "So I said to my people, 'Slow the testing down, please!' "

Then he uncorked one of the most racist tropes of his presidency: "It's a disease, without question, has more names than any disease in history. I can name—" The first name that came to mind—in fact, the only name he would use for it then—spilled out of his mouth next: "Kung flu."

When it came to blatantly racist remarks, Trump often skirted around the edges. But now he leaned hard into the phrase, stunning some aides. He would invoke "kung flu" again in the coming days. The rhetorical tiptoeing he had done in March was long over.

His comment about testing caused heartburn in the White House. His aides didn't know how to defend it. Hundreds of people across the government had worked tirelessly for months to try to help scale up the country's testing capacity, without much direction or leadership. Some agency staffers were logging hundred-hour weeks; at least two FDA employees had been hospitalized possibly due to overwork. In ad-libbed comments, Trump was undercutting their months of hard work. He made it all sound political.

Peter Navarro, appearing on television the next day, said Trump was just joking around. "Tongue in cheek," he said. Trump was asked about his remark a few days later in Arizona. Had he been joking, as Navarro had suggested? "I don't kid," the president responded.

People close to the president said they had no recollection of his explicitly telling aides to order testing for coronavirus to be slowed down but confirmed that he had thought for weeks that the tests were causing more problems than they were worth. It was no secret that he didn't want more testing. He didn't even think the tests were accurate to begin with.

A new Fox News poll had Trump trailing Joe Biden 50–38, an enormous gap for any candidate, let alone an incumbent president less than six months before an election.

White House and campaign aides had witnessed the way Trump kept oscillating during the pandemic. Sometimes he acknowledged the severity of the crisis; other times, he tried to brush the problem aside. He could never seem to commit to either belief, thus hamstringing his own response.

But something changed after that rally. Some speculated that Trump could see the country and the election—which to him were inseparable—slipping away. Many Americans had mostly tolerated three years of his bellicose behavior, but in this fourth year, with the pandemic causing so many deaths and so much economic carnage, it seemed too much. Trump wasn't going to change who he was, though. That meant there was only one path to reelection: he needed to electrify the people who just wanted the pandemic to be *over*. They hadn't shown up in Tulsa, but they would show up the next time.

They included his hard-core base of supporters, as well as the many exasperated Americans who had lost their jobs and were hurting financially and who resented the government overreach in the national shutdown. There were signs suggesting that the latter group was larger than many had thought. Los Angeles County had recently reopened its bars, and half a million people had gone to them the next day. There were potentially a significant number of like-minded citizens who were craving a return to their prior lives if only the government would get out of the way. If every one of those people voted, Trump still had a chance. He needed to align himself with them.

Trump had to commit to that approach, though. He couldn't equivocate anymore. He couldn't be held back by the doctors and have people chirping about masks and social distancing on television. He needed to lean in hard to the idea that the pandemic was in the rearview mirror and it was all China's fault and he would make China pay.

So Trump kept going, demanding that the country reopen and saying that all would be fine if the doctors would just knock it off with all the tests and the masks. He kept holding events, packing together maskless, cheering crowds. At a rally at Dream City Church in north Phoenix, *Washington Post* reporter Anne Gearan observed that one of his three thousand supporters tried to start a chant of "No more masks!"

"The stock market in the last 50 days is the best stock market in history," Trump told the crowd. "And it went up today again, by the way. Think of that. Think of that. Go back a week—50 days, the strongest 50 days in stock market history. This is during, hopefully, the end of the pandemic."

It was a terrible, tragic, deadly miscalculation.

The Pence op-ed, the one insisting that there was no "second wave," could not have been timed any worse.

For starters, the United States still hadn't made its way out of the first wave. The country never got the daily case rate low enough. And the crest of the next wave was just forming. JPMorgan analysts had noted that restaurant activity picked up markedly several weeks earlier, something that had proved to be a precursor of the new outbreak. When people packed indoors did not wear masks, the virus spread fast. As the summer wore on, new cases cropped up everywhere. In the spring, the cases and deaths had largely been concentrated in certain parts of the country, but now the virus was spreading across the country like a bucket of water poured onto a linoleum floor.

Eighty people who had visited a bar in East Lansing, Michigan, tested positive for the virus, leading local officials to ask anyone who had visited the bar to self-quarantine for two weeks. The number of new cases in California spiked. Intensive care units at Houston hospitals reached 97 percent of their patient capacity. The Republican governor of Texas, Greg Abbott, declared that there was a "massive outbreak" in the Lone Star State as it logged ten thousand new cases a day, ordering bars to close early and cutting restaurant capacity. Florida had ten thousand new cases a day, then several weeks later the state was up to fifteen thousand new cases a day. The state's Republican governor, Ron DeSantis, shut down all the bars.

The economy was walloped again. Another 1.5 million people filed for unemployment the week after Trump's Tulsa speech, and the parent company of Chuck E. Cheese filed for bankruptcy. Macy's kept laying off workers. United Airlines announced that it might have to cut half its workforce. The virus and the economy were in a new death spiral—except for the stock market, which was feeding off the Federal Reserve.

Goldman Sachs analysts noted that states containing 40 percent of the US population had put their reopening plans on hold and states containing 30 percent of the US population had reversed their reopening plans. The reopening push by Trump and Pence was reversing itself.

All Trump could do in response was complain about the tests. He was convinced that the large numbers revealed by testing were scaring the economy into a depression.

In truth, the virus was spreading so fast over the summer that it rendered the tests almost useless. The enormous surge in cases meant that labs were being sent more tests than they could handle. But instead of pouring resources into alleviating the testing backlog,

Trump was obsessed with finding a reason to deflect the blame for high case counts.

On July 9, he tweeted, "For the 1/100th time, the reason we show so many Cases, compared to other countries that haven't done nearly as well as we have, is that our TESTING is much bigger and better. We have tested 40,000,000 people. If we did 20,000,000 instead, Cases would be half, etc. NOT REPORTED!"

The strident, combative atmosphere Trump fostered in public also played out inside the White House. From the earliest days of the task force, a rivalry had developed between Mike Pence's staff and the new chief of staff, Mark Meadows, that intensified as the election neared.

When Pence had taken over the task force in late February, he had mostly allowed the doctors to speak freely at press conferences. By mid-March, when Trump began taking the virus more seriously and Pence was conducting daily briefings, 60 percent of Americans said they approved of the way the president was steering the country in response to the pandemic, and Trump's approval rating hit 49 percent, among the highest of his presidency.

But Meadows and others close to Trump were beginning to worry that Pence was outshining Trump, so the president soon commandeered the briefings. Meadows also seemed to resent the fact that Pence listened to the doctors. Even though Pence was the head of the Coronavirus Task Force, some White House officials saw Meadows trying to box the vice president out, arguing that he didn't need to be part of certain decisions and meetings. And he increasingly saw the Coronavirus Task Force—which he wasn't officially part of—as a waste of time anyways. So one morning in April, he called a meeting of senior staff at 8:00 a.m.

Marc Short showed up, puzzled as to the purpose of the meeting. "Why are we doing this?" he asked.

"The task force is useless and broken," Meadows said. He wanted to create a new group of people who would be more focused on messaging and reopening the economy.

Meadows also announced that he would be the main person in charge of dealing with Capitol Hill. He had left Congress only a few months earlier, and he liked the power that came with negotiating with his former colleagues on behalf of the White House. Accordingly, he wanted Pence to check with him before heading up to Capitol Hill for any meetings. The vice president needed permission to go up to Capitol Hill, where he had also once been a member of Congress? Short said absolutely not.

One member of the task force said that the relationship between Meadows and Short after that went "nuclear holocaust." Meadows would tell Short that he was the "chief" and he would "call the shots here."

Pence was too polite to challenge Meadows directly, but Short was furious on his boss's behalf. He was having none of it. "Who is the chair of the task force?" he would ask in front of others. "Is it Mark Meadows or the vice president of the United States?"

The seemingly endless turf wars among the White House players were symptomatic of a larger problem. Too many people thought they were in charge of coronavirus messaging. Meadows was trying to infuse politics into the way they talked about the economy and schools, but the vice president was beholden to the task force. He had earned almost everyone's trust by listening to the input from Fauci, Birx, and others, then relaying their concerns to the president, even when he didn't agree with them. Meadows, by contrast, couldn't care less what Fauci and Birx thought. Olivia Troye was trying to referee it all, as White House staffers and agency leaders and officials went to her with complaints. But they were going to Short with their complaints, too. The doctors complained about Azar and Meadows; staffers complained about the doctors. It was a circular firing squad.

Trump's comments, meanwhile, were becoming increasingly delusional, if not dangerous. He had pivoted hard to the "happy days are here again" theme even in the midst of the latest surge, and there was no turning back. Fauci and Birx feared that things were spinning out of control. States had reopened too quickly—very few had followed the gateway criteria Birx had presented just a few weeks earlier—and the United States had completely lost its grip on the virus. It appeared to be the only major country where the government was in denial about what was unfolding.

Sensing a rebellion brewing, Pence hastily called another public task force briefing. Pence and his aides believed if they weren't talking about the virus, it looked as though they weren't taking it seriously. But Meadows wouldn't let them hold a briefing at the White House, so they held the briefing at HHS headquarters instead.

Trump's economic adviser, Larry Kudlow, asked Olivia Troye if he could attend the HHS briefing, and she told him of course. But before everyone gathered, she knew she needed to pass along some scuttlebutt she had heard about Birx to Marc Short and Katie Miller. It sounded as though the doctor was planning to use her time at the press conference to present an extensive slide deck of data to reporters. Aware of Short's and Miller's need to control all messaging, Troye sensed that they might not like what Birx was going to say. But when she finally connected with Miller, the communications director seemed distracted and Troye felt she couldn't relay her concerns. Well, this could get interesting, Troye thought.

A few hours later, the task force members gathered at HHS. Kudlow told them that the economy was at risk of backsliding if they didn't do something soon and that there seemed to be one obvious solution: "If we want to prevent another shutdown, then everybody needs to wear a goddamn mask."

The doctors agreed with the view Kudlow expressed in private. And they were about to take their complaints public.

———

"I want to proudly say of the entire federal team under the leadership of President Trump, we have made truly remarkable progress in moving our nation forward," Pence said, kicking the press conference off. "We've all seen the encouraging news as we open up America again, more than 3 million jobs created in the last job report, retail sales are rolling." He spoke for twenty-five minutes, and near the tail end of his remarks he noted that the virus was picking up in some parts of the country and people should heed the guidance of their local officials. He then handed things off to Birx, unaware of what she had planned.

Miller thought Birx was only going to present five or six slides. But when she took the microphone, she unloaded a visual presentation with more than twenty slides to show reporters the severity of the outbreak all over the country. Now that Pence had handed off the lectern to her, she wasn't giving it back. "If we can go to the first slide, please, and start where the vice president left off," she began, and proceeded to deliver a massive data dump, a Birxian broadside.

She would say "Next slide" or "Next slide, please" twenty-two times over the next eleven minutes, instructing her aide to keep the data rolling. Her slides were a devastating portrait of what was happening across the country. There was little to celebrate; cases were going up dramatically. Birx also poured cold water on Trump's argument that more testing was the reason for more cases. She showed that yes, the number of tests was increasing, but so was the percentage of people who were testing positive.

"This gives you a map of Texas, or it shows where the cases are and where they're rising the most rapidly."

Next slide.

"Same situation that we're showing here with Arizona; rising number of tests being performed, but also rising test positivity, rising cases."

Next slide.

"So this is California. So you can see California over the last week has had that increase in test positivity."

Next slide.

Troye watched the statistics unfolding. Then, out of the corner of her eye, she saw Short storming over to her. The look on his face conveyed one mood: apoplectic.

"Where the hell did those slides come from?" he asked her, stomping off before she could answer.

"Jesus Christ, I can't catch a break," Troye muttered under her breath.

The slides continued, and Short was back. "Well, Marc, this is why I called you and Katie," Troye told him. "Because I heard there was a slide deck."

When Birx was done, the ambush by the doctors had only begun. Fauci was next, and he was similarly riled up. His voice was hoarse, but there was an edge in it. He said he had never before seen a disease that had such a wide range of outcomes. He said that some states had opened up too early and they needed to "drop back a few yards," using a football analogy. Pence was talking about going full steam ahead; Fauci was talking about going in reverse. He said that Americans needed to unite around a greater civic purpose, to rally together for the broader public good. "You have an individual responsibility to yourself," he said. "But you have a societal responsibility. Because, if we want to end this outbreak, really end it, and then hopefully, when a vaccine comes and puts the nail in the coffin, we've got to realize that we are part of the process."

Next came Azar, who tried to pivot back to Pence's optimism. "America has never been readier to combat COVID-19," he said. He even used a phrase from Pence's opening remarks, saying that there had been "remarkable progress." He also emphasized basic public health measures.

During the press conference, Trump was nowhere to be seen. In fact, in the middle of it, he tweeted an FBI wanted poster asking for clues related to the vandalization of a statue of Andrew Jackson.

Two weeks after the Tulsa rally, there was a spike in coronavirus cases in Tulsa. Some attendees would later end up very sick, including Herman Cain, a seventy-four-year-old Republican pizza magnate who had once run for president and whom Trump had once proposed for the Federal Reserve. He was hospitalized in Atlanta and never recovered. He died of COVID-19 on July 30.

On July 20, Trump huddled with campaign advisers in the Oval Office to look at his prospects for the election in four months. Trump, in a navy suit and bright pink tie, sat behind the Resolute Desk with a stack of new polls in front of him. Public polls showed that Trump's disapproval rating was near an all-time high, but the group looked relaxed. As Trump sipped from a large glass of Diet Coke with ice, his aides tried to gently nudge him to accept one of their key findings: that masks weren't as viscerally offensive to Republicans as Trump had been led to believe.

A top campaign pollster, Tony Fabrizio, and Trump's campaign adviser Jason Miller sat across the desk from Trump and presented the data showing that 81 percent of Republicans were supportive of some kind of mask requirement. Mask wearing was not the political anvil Trump had feared, they told him, and if he reversed course, it would show leadership heading into the election.

Other Trump advisers also appeared to be softening on mask wearing. Kushner weighed in. He thought embracing mask wearing was a no-brainer. It made people *feel* safer and could actually help address some of the tension boiling up in the country. Besides, they had plenty of masks at this point. The ground was shifting on masks, right there in the Oval Office. Maybe many Republicans would follow suit if they saw Trump was behind it.

But that balloon quickly popped. From the back of the room, Mark Meadows interjected. Absolutely not, he told them. "We can't do the masks. The base will just turn on you." His statement shattered the argument that the campaign advisers were trying to erect in front of the president. Trump agreed with Meadows: no masks.

Trump was obsessed with placating his base of supporters, the red hat–wearing throngs that packed his rallies and represented about 30 percent of the electorate. He couldn't risk alienating them, but Trump and Meadows didn't seem to be considering the vast majority of Americans who would support some version of a mask mandate, especially if it was presented as a means of reopening the economy. Instead he immediately agreed with Meadows and brushed aside all the polling. There wouldn't be any mask mandate.

In the summer, still doing damage control after the *Wall Street Journal* op-ed, Olivia Troye was helping to write Pence's remarks about reopening schools in the fall, but then the comments were rewritten by Short and Katie Miller. In the revised comments, Pence said that the risks of keeping kids home from school outweighed the risk of spreading the virus if they returned, a view shared by many conservatives but something at the time that government scientists did not have the answer to. There was significant concern about young children spreading the virus to older and at-risk relatives and of schools becoming superspreader sites. CDC scientists were still trying to determine the risk posed by school reopenings, and the White House had frittered away the summer without investing money or coming up with a plan for schools to reopen safely. When Pence realized that his remarks had strayed from what had been verified, he was upset and asked Troye what had happened.

At the next staff meeting, Troye noticed that Short had brought a new policy adviser to the room. And it struck her: This is how it ends. This is how they always do it. They don't fire people or counsel them or try to smooth things over. They bring someone else, someone new, in to squeeze whatever morale is left out of an aide. Short was replacing her and doing it in the most painful way.

She demanded a meeting with retired lieutenant general Keith Kellogg, Pence's national security advisor. She told Kellogg she was concerned about the way Short and Miller were undermining both her and the vice president. Pence had told her to be the fact-checker before he said things, and she couldn't fact-check things if Short and Miller rewrote his remarks. "You are not going to do that to me," she said. "I have worked so hard to gain his trust." She then told him that the White House's focus was all wrong. "We're going to get to the point where we are going to lose thousands of people every day," she said. "It's only going to get worse."

There are different accounts of what happened next. Troye said that Kellogg and Pence had asked her to stay, but others insist that she was pushed out. Either way, it was an inglorious departure for someone who had played a central role in the government's pandemic response. By August, she was gone. But she didn't disappear.

CHAPTER 17

OPENING DAY

July 23, 2020
US CORONAVIRUS COVID-19 CASES: **4,000,000**
US CORONAVIRUS COVID-19 DEATHS: **143,000**

Sean Doolittle drove to Nationals Park, weaving through the quiet streets of Washington, D.C. It was opening day for Major League Baseball. Normally the streets would be pulsing with people dressed in red, one of the Nationals' team colors. Today, they were mostly empty. The T-shirt and peanut vendors were gone. Opening day was supposed to have been almost four months earlier. The virus had wrecked that. People were still stuck at home. Fans were not allowed inside the ballpark.

Doolittle, a thirty-three-year-old left-handed relief pitcher, liked to ride his bike to the ballpark before day games, a thirty-minute tour through the nation's capital. But that morning he was nervous that if he worked up a sweat—it was July, after all—he would fail the temperature test at the front door. And then he would be barred from the stadium and prohibited from playing. It was the Nationals' first game together since winning the World Series in October 2019, in the beforetimes. And Doolittle was supposed to catch the ceremonial first pitch thrown by one of his personal heroes: Anthony Fauci.

When he arrived at the clubhouse, he was stunned to see the news on social media that the team's star hitter, Juan Soto, had tested positive for the coronavirus and wouldn't be able to join the team. Doolittle had expressed reservations a few weeks earlier about playing the season, concerned about much of the country's refusal to wear masks and the rising case numbers. More than a thousand people were dying of the coronavirus each day, one death every ninety seconds. "We haven't done any of the things that other countries have done to bring sports back," he had told reporters then. "Sports are like the reward of a functioning society. And we're trying to just bring it back, even though we've taken none of the steps to flatten the curve."

Spring training had begun in February, as normal; then the players had suddenly been sent home in mid-March with no expectation as to when they'd return. Over the next few months, Doolittle had worked closely with the players' union to improve testing protocols and safety measures for the teams. Now they were trying to play baseball again in empty stadiums. But with the country on edge because of the social unrest and the unemployment and the pandemic, he wondered, was it too soon?

Just three days earlier, the Nationals had announced that Fauci would throw out the first pitch, calling him "a true champion for our country." (Donald Trump was so insanely jealous of Fauci's selection that an hour before Fauci was set to throw out the first pitch, the president announced that he had been invited to throw out the first pitch at the Yankees' home opener on August 15. According to someone close to Trump, Yankees president Randy Levine later rescinded the offer because of all the blowback.) When Doolittle saw the news about Fauci, he immediately texted one of the Nationals' public relations officials. "Let me catch this," he requested. "I want to catch this." The official instantly agreed.

"I can't imagine the position that he was in," Doolittle said of Fauci in an interview, "this being a novel virus. We're finding things out in real time as the situation develops and there's already scientists and doctors . . . and all that stuff is under attack thanks to this administration that's peddled conspiracy theories and allowed those conspiracies to blossom and develop in certain groups around the country."

Being invited to throw out the opening pitch was a rare bright spot in an otherwise brutal and unrelenting few months for Fauci. The doctor had become a resistance hero, the defender of science in an administration waging a war against it. By that point he was rarely at the White House anymore, having worn out his welcome long before. Still, he had taken on a sort of outsized importance in people's minds. They thought he had more power than he did, and his stardom had bred resentment and anger among much of the White House staff (and even among some health officials).

In early July, just a couple of weeks before opening day, a *Washington Post* story detailed the deteriorating relationship between Trump and Fauci. The White House usually responded to palace intrigue stories by trying to swat them down, but this time it took a highly unusual and controversial tack: instead of claiming that the president and Fauci had their disagreements but respected each other, the usual method of deflecting bad press, the White House press office sent out what amounted to a campaign opposition file on Fauci. It detailed about a dozen times the White House claimed that the infectious diseases doctor had been wrong about the pandemic, all of which were missing important pieces of context or used quotes of his that were selectively cut. "Several White House officials are concerned about the number of times Dr. Fauci has been wrong on things," a White House official wrote in response to a request for comment.

The White House circulated the list to a number of news outlets in the next twenty-four hours, which amounted to an unprecedented assault on Fauci and his credentials. The scientific and medical community jumped to his defense, as did those who had worked with him in previous administrations. Fauci couldn't believe it. The list hadn't come from Peter Navarro or some anonymous official who might have disliked him; the White House communications office had put the list together and was disseminating it widely. He knew that wouldn't have happened without sign-off by Mark Meadows, who had installed most of the aides there.

A day before the *Washington Post* article came out, Fauci and Mike Pence had a long talk over the phone. Pence asked Fauci what he could be doing better, and seemed to genuinely want to know. Fauci gave Pence a one-on-one about how to talk to the public about epidemics. Fauci told Pence, on more than this one occasion, that it was always important to level with the American people, even if it meant telling them an inconvenient truth. In this case, Fauci said, the truth was that they were in serious trouble with the pandemic, and they could not just do happy talk. Once you deny reality and spin happy talk, Fauci continued, then you lose all credibility and your message loses all impact. Pence seemed sympathetic to Fauci's argument, but his loyalty to the president always prevailed. Still, Pence managed to remain respected and well-liked by Fauci and the other doctors.

A few days later, after the White House circulated its "oppo list," Fauci had a very different conversation with Mark Meadows. The *Post* article included one detail that particularly irked Meadows: three of Fauci's scheduled television appearances had been canceled by the White House after comments he had made during a Facebook Live event. Fauci told Meadows that he had no idea how that detail had gotten out but that he knew the "oppo list" could not have gone out without Meadows's approval. Meadows denied it but told Fauci that White House officials were sick of his "talking out of turn" and contradicting the president.

"All I'm doing is describing what's really happening out there. You can't expect me not to do that," Fauci kept insisting. At a certain point, he offered Meadows a warning: if the administration didn't change its strategy soon—if it didn't provide a consistent message on masks and work to ramp up testing—Trump was "going to lose the election."

It was a frustrating conversation, though Meadows assured Fauci that the campaign against him was over.

But the following day, Navarro tried to finish Fauci off, writing an op-ed in *USA Today* under the headline "Anthony Fauci Has Been Wrong About Everything I Have Interacted with Him On." Navarro, who did not have to go through normal White House channels, had had the op-ed published on his own and was publicly criticized by other White House officials for having done so.

The message from that week was unmistakable. It was already clear that the White House had been muzzling Fauci. Now it had fired a warning shot of what else could be in store if he did not get into line.

Doolittle was a relief pitcher. He had made a career entering games in high-pressure situations, when the game is on the line, when everything is tense. He knew what it was like to face a torrent of criticism and negative venom, though admittedly on a much different scale. He admired Fauci's toughness, and he wanted to stand with him.

Catching the first pitch can be an inglorious affair, squatting behind home plate for someone who isn't a pro. You never know where the ball is going to go. But Doolittle saw it as a big moment. This game would be nationally televised. Doolittle wanted to stand on the baseball diamond with Fauci to show his support—not just for this man, this seventy-nine-year-old doctor, but for what he represented: a dedication to truth and science.

Doolittle had caught many ceremonial first pitches before (it was his tenth season, and he had played in All-Star games twice). Relief pitchers are quirky. They have routines, even for things like this. He liked to greet the person shortly before the game and talk to them, try to calm their nerves. He had thrown almost four hundred innings from a big-league mound, but he knew how nerve-racking it could be for a person who had never stood on that mound of dirt to stare at home plate. It was just sixty feet, six inches away, but it could look like so much more.

So Doolittle, with his scratchy red beard, in a crisp white uniform, red socks up to his knees, red hat, and dark navy mask, waited for his cue from the top step of the Nationals' dugout. He had never met Fauci before and knew he had just a tiny window to connect with the famous doctor before the pitch, to try to help him relax.

Then the public address announcer (why was there even a public address announcer at a game with no public?) introduced Fauci, and the doctor emerged from a gate across the field, from the other side of home plate. He wore black suit pants, black shoes, and a white Nationals jersey with his name and the number 19, for COVID-19.

There was so much going through the doctor's head, so much the public couldn't know.

There were two critical people in Fauci's life who advised him on the political minefield he was navigating: his wife, Christine Grady, and Peter Staley, the longtime AIDS activist who had become one of his closest friends.

After Fauci's agonizing several days with the White House, Staley had raised a drastic idea. Staley had been largely supportive of Fauci all year, believing he was a necessary bulwark against misinformation in the task force and the White House. But it looked as though Fauci had lost his influence in the late spring, and Staley often pressed him to justify why he was still trying to walk on the knife's edge. After the public attack by the White House, Staley wondered, what was Fauci accomplishing by staying? Was it time to resign from the task force, to speak out and tell the public everything he had seen and knew?

"It's clear you have spoken the truth publicly on the podium, which has generated the ire of the president and the president's people," Staley told him. "But the fact is that you're just standing there when there's stuff that's being said that clearly you can't object to because it doesn't have to do with you." If the president started talking about the magic of hydroxychloroquine, for instance, and didn't explicitly ask Fauci to weigh in, Fauci could look complicit by simply standing alongside the president and saying nothing.

Fauci had no serious plans to quit or resign his position. But the conversation with Staley was enough to take the question to Grady, his closest adviser. So one evening, he and Grady sat at their kitchen table, where all the difficult family discussions tended to take place. "If I leave, they'll say that was another great Fauci statement," Fauci said, aware of the lore that had built up around him. "Not only is he courageous enough to contradict the president, but he's not going to stand for this nonsense."

That would send a message that Fauci had drawn a firm line. It would be something.

But . . .

"There wouldn't be my capability of publicly setting the record straight when things are said that are not true," he countered.

He feared that if he left, there wouldn't be anybody who would go to the microphone and say unequivocally that hydroxychloroquine doesn't work, that the virus won't magically disappear, that people must wear masks, that the battle would be long and hard.

Grady initially agreed with Staley, convinced that the task force had become a waste of time for her husband. She felt that the White House task force was toxic and he should get out of there. But after she heard Fauci's list of pros and cons, she agreed his voice pushing back against the Kabuki science and political theater was still needed, even if the president was attacking him.

They decided he would stay. Fauci had wanted to go into the conversation with an open mind. But deep in his gut, he knew there was no way he was ever going to walk away despite how ugly it had all become. He didn't even need to sleep on it.

Doolittle sprung from the Nationals' dugout, and the All-Star relief pitcher and world-famous doctor met for a brief moment near home plate, tapping gloves. "Hey, I'm really glad you're here," Doolittle said, trying to speak clearly through his mask. "I'm really excited about this. Thanks for being here."

Even though there were no fans present, the stadium was surprisingly noisy. The public address announcer was still talking, and his voice echoed through the stadium. It was unclear if Fauci said anything back to Doolittle before he started striding toward the mound. "I couldn't hear if he responded, which gave me the impression that he was pretty nervous about it," Doolittle said.

Doolittle's advice to people throwing out the first pitch was always this: slow things down. Soak it in. Take a deep breath. Don't rush. Don't. Rush.

"I could see in my head, I think he's going too fast," Doolittle recalled. "He's kind of rushing through this. It's normally better when people take a second and look around and soak in the moment."

What Fauci hadn't told anyone was that he had spent the previous few days trying to stretch out his arm. He had been a star athlete in Brooklyn sixty-five years earlier, playing shortstop on the St. Bernadette youth team alongside future Yankee World Series champion Joe Pepitone. But he hadn't thrown a baseball in years. And his attempts to loosen up his arm had the opposite effect: he had shredded his shoulder. So when he went to the mound at Nationals Park, he didn't have a prayer of throwing the ball straight. He would be lucky to throw it at all.

Fauci rushed a quick windup and hurled, the ball fluttering out of his hand. Instead of traveling sixty feet, six inches, it went about thirty feet. And it went nowhere near Doolittle, landing halfway between first base and home plate.

Oh, no, Doolittle immediately thought. *He's probably going to get some shit for this.*

Fauci threw up his hands in a sort of New York "whaddya-gonna-do" motion and started to walk away. Doolittle stopped him so they could take a photo together—socially distant—and then Fauci disappeared and Doolittle briefly returned to the clubhouse. His teammates ribbed him about the pitch. "Some guys were kind of cracking jokes," Doolittle said. "It was all in good fun. They were giving me shit. 'You should have dove for that. Come on, that's your guy!' It's kind of understood I'm the token liberal or leftist in the clubhouse."

Doolittle didn't pitch that game, as storms rolled in and umpires ended it in the sixth inning. The Nationals lost to the New York Yankees 4–1. When he does pitch, Doolittle refuses to check social media afterward as a way to screen out the hate. But because he hadn't pitched and knew it had been a big moment for the country, he peered at his phone that evening in the clubhouse and was shocked at what he saw.

Some conspiracy theorists were alleging a deep, dark plot by Doolittle and Fauci, as if they were in cahoots somehow and the fact that the ball had gone to Fauci's left and Doolittle's right was a premeditated symbol. Others alleged that the letters in "Doolittle" could be sorted through English gematria, which assigns a number value to each letter and then reveals a secret code. "It was claiming that my name was a code for 'Drain the swamp,'" Doolittle said. "And that I was part of the deep state as well. I've gotten a lot of crap online for various things, being outspoken. Pitching poorly. You see it all. I thought I had seen it all. This was next-level stuff. It was very surreal. It was a little scary."

Doolittle had interacted with Fauci for just a few minutes in a mostly empty baseball stadium on a hot July day before a game that hadn't even lasted nine innings. But his brief moment with the doctor had opened a window for him into the darkest parts of the United States, to the conspiracies and hate that were somehow tilting the White House's response to the pandemic and trying to undercut Fauci.

Doolittle's memory of Fauci's brief moment on the mound—and the vitriol that had followed—would sear into his brain. He felt terrible that the pitch had gone so poorly. But not everyone felt bad for Fauci; some were thrilled at seeing the doctor look fragile and hapless. One person in particular was ecstatic, a person who was watching from the White House, several miles away: the president himself.

CHAPTER 18

ATLAS, SHRUG

"Tony, something's wrong."

Deborah Birx had called Anthony Fauci one day over the summer, unnerved by some recent statements by Donald Trump and Mike Pence. They were back to saying that the virus would somehow magically vanish on its own. Trump was continuing to deny the efficacy of mask wearing. Some of his recent remarks had been such fantastical bullshit, Birx told Fauci, bearing no resemblance to the guidance and data she had been providing the White House. She couldn't figure out where it was coming from.

The bizarre comments reached an apex on August 3, when HBO broadcast an interview that Axios journalist Jonathan Swan had conducted with Trump. Birx watched in astonishment.

Swan pressed Trump on the surging number of coronavirus deaths in the United States, which had recently eclipsed more than a thousand per day. Trump swatted the question aside, insisting that things weren't as bad as Swan made them sound. "Take a look at some of these charts," he responded, picking up several pieces of paper to show Swan.

Charts? Birx thought. Who gave him new charts? She had provided the White House hundreds of charts in the past six months, but Trump and many others had paid little attention. Now Trump had *new* charts? His own charts?

As the camera zoomed in on Trump, he held up the first chart and couldn't seem to make sense of what it said. "The United States is lowest in numerous categories," he told Swan, studying a chart with four lines on it. "We're lower than . . . the world."

"Lower than the world?" Swan repeated, incredulous. "What does that mean?"

"We're lower than Europe," Trump said. "Take a look. Take a look. Right here."

"In what? In what?" Swan asked.

In what? Trump didn't know, so he handed Swan the piece of paper, which the reporter proceeded to examine more closely than Trump had. It was a chart that showed deaths as a proportion of total cases. In other words, because there were more cases in the United States, the proportion of deaths didn't seem as high. But that masked the reality of the situation. There were still more than a thousand deaths per day—a fiasco despite Trump's attempt to sugar-coat it. Earlier in the interview, Swan pressed Trump further about the rising death toll, asking him how he could say that the virus was under control when more than a thousand Americans were dying of COVID-19 every day.

"They are dying, that's true. And you have—it is what it is. But that doesn't mean we aren't doing everything we can. It's under control as much as you can control it," Trump said. It was one of the most startling admissions yet that Trump had thrown up his hands and somehow found a way to justify the high death count—or even declare victory—just as the virus was surging again.

Birx had sacrificed so much to join the Coronavirus Task Force in February. She was sixty-four, and this might be the last stop on the path of her illustrious government career. It was increasingly clear that her reputation, everything she had worked for, was being swallowed up by the White House's bungled response. She couldn't go back to PEPFAR; she had alienated too many people at the CDC in her push for better data. She now felt physically ill when she went into the West Wing each morning. Fauci and FDA commissioner Hahn had mostly stopped coming to the White House, especially since it seemed as though someone new there caught the virus every day. Birx didn't feel safe inside the West Wing, both because there seemed to be a never-ending outbreak and because she was worried that behind every wall, someone was conspiring or leaking damaging stories about her to the press.

The interview with Swan seemed to be the nail in the coffin. Trump had found an alternate data set, an alternate reality, a counternarrative of "facts" that reinforced his belief that the pandemic had been blown all out of proportion. It was never clear who exactly had given him the charts, but it was apparent that Trump was now going to listen only to those who said what he wanted to hear. Birx could never quite wrap her head around the logic of that. It didn't matter how you tried to manipulate the data; the truth was going to come out anyway. Like Trump, some Republican governors and lawmakers alleged that some deaths that had been labeled as COVID-19 deaths had really been due to something else. But excess deaths were excess deaths. She reminded the governors of that all the time. No matter how hard they tried, no one would ever be able to successfully hide the evidence or the objective data: those people were dead, and they were dead because of COVID-19.

To compound the situation, for months she had been receiving death threats, between ten and twenty letters a week sent to her home. Some threatened to kill her; others told her to kill herself. At first she had turned the letters over to the State Department's security team—she had been a State Department employee before joining the White House—who wanted her to keep sending them along. But at a certain point, the letters started coming too often for her to keep up. "I don't have time for this," she thought. Some sick people had obtained her daughter's cell phone number and texted her all sorts of terrible, crude things. She was putting herself through all this, and for what?

She had gone from meeting with Trump three times a week and dictating most of the administration's policies in the spring to rarely seeing him. Fauci, through it all, had remained beloved by much of the public, viewed as a necessary counter to the misinformation and distortions coming from the White House. But for Birx, the reputation as a data-driven, dedicated, hard-charging doctor, scientist, and public health official she had spent more than forty years building was in tatters, yet another tragic case of a person undone by Trump and his orbit. Around that time, House speaker Nancy Pelosi publicly attacked Birx, arguing that she had aligned herself too closely with the president. Did Pelosi not realize that Trump wasn't even speaking to Birx anymore?

Taking a calculated risk, Birx decided to respond to Pelosi's remarks. During a CNN interview in early August, a rare national television appearance for Birx, she said she had "tremendous respect" for Pelosi and that the pandemic was becoming much worse. She went on to say the crisis was entering a new stage, where it was becoming "extraordinarily widespread" in urban and rural areas. Well aware that she served at the president's will, she had been careful never to stray too far from Trump's message. Her statements on CNN marked a stark departure from the president's insistence that the outbreak was in the rearview mirror.

On the same day the Axios interview aired, Trump lit into Birx on Twitter, calling her "pathetic" and accusing her of taking the "bait" from Pelosi. He had had enough of Birx and the other doctors. And he was preparing to finish them off.

Trump had long made clear to aides that he needed a doctor's viewpoint in the room that matched his own, someone who had a medical degree but who understood the enormous economic and political costs of shutting down, someone with indisputable credentials. It was too close to the election to get rid of key advisers, and the resignation pact of Birx, Stephen Hahn, and Robert Redfield had complicated things. Fauci couldn't be fired because he was a career government employee with extensive legal protections, and aides had already concluded that dismissing him would only make him more of a martyr. But that didn't mean that Trump had to listen to them or even look at them anymore. He wanted someone else.

Some aides had noticed a doctor making the rounds on Fox News. Like Trump, he was convinced that the virus's impact was being blown out of proportion and kept warning about the economic consequences of prolonged shutdowns. The doctor, sixty-five-year-old radiologist Scott Atlas, had ties to Stanford University. He was just what Trump was looking for.

Back in March, Atlas had floated the goal of "population-based immunity," which was widely viewed as "herd immunity," the idea that once enough people in society have either been infected with a disease and developed immunity or have developed immunity through vaccination, the rest of the population will be protected from contracting the disease at high rates. The faster that happened, he argued, the faster the United States could move past the virus. The United States had never tried to reach herd immunity through natural infection; most doctors, scientists, and public health professionals found the idea reprehensible and cruel, as enormous numbers of people would have to die to achieve it. For a highly contagious virus such as coronavirus, experts predicted that a herd immunity strategy would amount to hundreds of thousands or even millions of excess deaths.

But Atlas and other conservatives were inspired by the example of Sweden, which, unlike its European counterparts, had decided not to impose lockdown orders and had kept most schools and businesses open. What the advocates of the Swedish model did not mention was that the Swedish government recommended social distancing and mask wearing and the country still had among the world's highest infection and death rates. Atlas's embrace of these measures was viewed by other medical experts as extremely controversial and dangerous. A neuroradiologist by training, he had no experience in infectious diseases, but he wasn't afraid of going toe-to-toe with other doctors and scientists.

A fellow at Stanford's conservative Hoover Institution, he had spent the last several years arguing against Obamacare and advocating a fiercely libertarian view of health policy. He proudly considered himself a "contrarian" and, later, the "anti–Dr. Fauci." He thought that the media were "contaminated" and that had led to "contaminated public policy and science." He said that major science journals such as the *Lancet* and the *New England Journal of Medicine* "feel compelled to be politically visible" and that had "contaminated the discussion." He called some of their peer-reviewed scientific articles "garbage science."

On April 22, when 2,282 people died of the virus and New York's hospitals were overwhelmed, Atlas penned an op-ed for *The Hill* website stating the following:

> The tragedy of the COVID-19 pandemic appears to be entering the containment phase.
> . . . We know from decades of medical science that infection itself allows people to generate an immune response— antibodies—so that the infection is controlled throughout the population by "herd immunity." Indeed, that is the main purpose of widespread immunization in other viral diseases—to assist with population immunity.

In early July, as the number of new cases eclipsed seventy thousand a day, Atlas said on Fox News that "most of the cases are in healthier, younger people" who can "generally deal with this and recover fine." In a *Fox News Radio* interview that month, he said, "These people getting the infection is not really a problem, and in fact, as we said months ago, when you isolate everyone, including all the healthy people, you're prolonging the problem because you're preventing population immunity."

When Democrats raised concerns about reopening schools, Atlas called their argument "ludicrous" and said that children were at almost no risk of becoming seriously ill or spreading the virus to their parents or grandparents. He blamed part of the summer surge on people he alleged were flooding into the United States from Mexico. In other words, the virus was coming from Mexicans and Central Americans who were crowding into hospitals in California, Texas, and Arizona. He claimed to have data that refuted almost all of Birx's and Fauci's pronouncements.

That was all catnip for Trump. White House aides printed out transcripts of Atlas's television appearances and presented them to the president. Trump, a voracious consumer of Fox News programs, had seen some of Atlas's appearances and liked them. Atlas had a knack for sounding authoritative as he echoed things that Trump had believed all along about the virus. The White House quietly brought him in as a senior adviser in late July.

The day after Trump called Birx "pathetic," the task force gathered for another meeting in the Situation Room. Alex Azar, Fauci, Birx, and several others sat at the large table, waiting for Pence. When he was more than thirty minutes late, they wondered whether something was wrong.

In fact, Pence was in the Oval Office listening to Trump vent his frustrations about the doctors and health officials. He hated their public messaging and didn't want them spreading fear about the virus. He felt out of the loop, with no idea of what the doctors were thinking or what they would say out on television.

Pence knew that the doctors were equally frustrated at their diminished access to Trump. Why don't you come down to the task force meeting today, Pence suggested, and talk to everyone directly? Trump liked the idea, but he wanted everyone to come up to the Oval Office instead.

Marc Short eventually went down to the Situation Room to corral the group. "Everyone at the table, up to the Oval Office right now," he barked.

"Uh-oh," one of the attendees said. "This can't be good."

When they walked into the Oval Office, they saw Trump sitting behind the Resolute Desk, seething. Several chairs were set across from him. Birx took the chair in the middle. Fauci was to her left, Brett Giroir to his left. Pence and Azar sat in the other chairs. There were some seemingly random attendees, including Secretary of Agriculture Sonny Perdue.

"I am sick and tired of how negative you all are," Trump began. "I am sick and tired of your speculations. I spend half of my day responding to what Tony Fauci has to say, and I'm the president of the United States!"

Then he began peppering the room with insults, like a marksman moving from one target to the next with precision. First he turned to Fauci, pointing a finger at him. "You've got to stop being so negative!" Then he turned to Birx. "Every time you talk, I get depressed. You have to stop that."

Trump was furious that they wouldn't do the same sort of upbeat messaging that he himself was doing, the sort of messaging that Azar had been all too eager to do, though he lacked the credibility of the others.

For the doctors, it was unclear what Trump was trying to accomplish. It was, in a way, an opportunity for him to clear the air. He really didn't have much face time with the doctors anymore, in part because Meadows had prevented it. But surely the president couldn't expect them to hold back their assessment of the worsening pandemic. In fact, when Trump began unloading on the doctors, Fauci instantly realized what was happening and knew he was about to see more bluster.

It was like an unhealthy marriage that had gone on too long, that was held together by convenience and the fact that it would be too messy to break it off. What Trump was doing was showing them, once and for all, that he was done with them. He might not be able to fire them, but he could ignore them. And he could replace them.

In fact, he already had.

———

A few weeks before Atlas's arrival, Meadows asked Short what he thought about bringing him in. Short thought it was a bad idea and told Meadows so. There was already a team in place that had been working together for months, and this wasn't the time to bring in someone new. But, Short argued, if you are going to bring Atlas in, he should be on the task force. The last thing the pandemic response needed was some rogue player with a separate line to Trump and Pence, not coordinating with everyone else.

When the task force met again a few days after the Oval Office meeting, Pence took his seat at the head of the table. Birx sat to his right, next to Fauci and Redfield. Seated to Pence's left was Atlas. He was slight, with closely cropped white hair capped on top by a puffy curl. Pence introduced Atlas, and then Birx began her presentation. She said that cases were spreading in many parts of the United States and the situation was becoming grim.

Atlas interjected, speaking in a tone that was somewhere between polite and impolite: "But what's happening with deaths? Because deaths are what really matters."

Birx was puzzled but kept going. "Well, let me finish," she said.

But Atlas wouldn't let her finish. "Well, deaths are the only thing that matters. Why are we so focused on cases? And don't forget, testing is up."

"Well, there's a lot to correct about that, Dr. Atlas," Birx replied.

Pence stepped in. "Okay, Scott, welcome to the task force," he said, trying to make light of the situation. "This is a place where we want all views held. Deb, thanks, and Scott, keep it up."

The meetings continued like that for days. Birx would begin her presentation and Atlas would keep interrupting her, challenging her on virtually every fact she brought forward. "How do you know that?" he often asked her.

Atlas was convinced that people who had tested positive but didn't have symptoms of the virus didn't need to have their lives disrupted and shouldn't have to abide by the quarantine rules. The lockdowns and business restrictions were destroying the economy, he told the task force.

Birx's anger grew. This was precisely the reason she had flown back from Africa in February, to convince the White House that asymptomatic carriers posed a tremendous risk to everyone else. "Yeah, the asymptomatic person transmits to your grandmother, who then dies, okay?" she shot back at Atlas. Unconvinced and undeterred, he kept trying to poke holes in her data.

At one point, when she said that few people were wearing masks in a certain part of the United States, he asked her how she knew. She replied that she had recently been there, meeting with people. She had driven twenty-five thousand miles over the course of the spring and summer, visiting state capitals and talking with governors and local health officials. She had pulled over at rest stops and truck stops to try to monitor mask usage. But Atlas wasn't impressed. Had she met with *everyone* in those states? Birx couldn't believe the nerve of the guy.

"I've talked to a lot of people," she said.

Birx felt trapped. Not only did she feel sick to her stomach every day when she walked into the White House, but Trump had now brought in someone with views antithetical to those held by the vast majority of the scientific community, who wanted to completely reopen the economy, who dismissed the consequences she had warned about. She didn't have the access to Trump she'd previously had. She still spoke with Pence, who had been relaying the doctors' advice and input to the president. But that didn't seem to work anymore, either. She would present one set of facts, and then Atlas would walk into the room and present a completely different set, one that Trump was more inclined to believe. And it was those "facts," the graphics that

Trump was now holding up, that reaffirmed his belief that the virus was disappearing. They undermined all of her work.

As soon as it became clear that her influence with Trump was vanishing, Birx leaned harder into her strategy of visiting individual states and delivering her recommendations in person. She would go on local news broadcasts, hold press conferences (always calling on female reporters first), and methodically move from town to town, from state to state, urging residents to mask up and socially distance.

Even so, some of her public comments still seemed, to some scientific and public health experts, painstakingly crafted not to counter Trump's message. It was at that point that Fauci tried to press Birx to further change her public positioning. You've got to get away from the happy talk, he told her privately, and start telling it like it is. Birx was doing good, important work that he felt was being distorted.

It's unclear whether the conversation with Fauci influenced Birx in any way. But as Atlas consolidated his control, Birx became more outspoken, both in public and in the daily reports she sent to top administration officials and to state officials across the country, which amounted to around a thousand people. If she was worried, she wanted the states to know she was worried. She put all the information she wasn't allowed to say in public into the governors' reports.

She also helped pave the way for Hahn and Redfield to use state and local media as a way to break loose of the White House's control. Redfield was forbidden to host CDC briefings in Washington or Atlanta, but he occasionally hosted something similar in Utah, North Carolina, or whatever other state he might be traveling to. The White House paid little attention to the regional press, and the doctors were pleasantly surprised when they saw their comments picked up by the *Philadelphia Inquirer*, the *Washington Post*, CNN, and other major media outlets. The doctors' group was still talking and meeting regularly, so they would often agree on a message that Birx would take out on the road. They were dividing and conquering.

The state strategy felt like the most effective way for the doctors to make a difference. The task force had become a den of dissent, a place for Birx and Atlas—and occasionally Redfield, Fauci, and Hahn—to squabble. They kept fighting to a draw. Oftentimes, their discussions devolved into arguments about what was true and what wasn't. Atlas kept insisting, without evidence, that the United States was approaching herd immunity.

He was careful never to call his strategy "herd immunity," but he advocated most of its elements: the virus should mostly spread freely among the vast majority of the population, so people could develop the antibodies needed for immunity, and the administration should be concerned only about the most vulnerable: those in nursing homes and in high-risk settings, such as prisons and meatpacking plants. That was where the tests and other resources should be directed, he argued. He wanted schools to be fully reopened and believed that mitigation measures such as mask wearing and social distancing were pointless. Sure, you can wear a mask if you want, he would say, but it doesn't do any good. He was convinced that places that had been hit hard by the virus, including New York City, Chicago, and New Orleans, had already reached herd immunity. It wasn't the mitigation measures that had brought the numbers of cases and deaths down, he postulated, but rather the fact that enough people had contracted the virus to protect the rest of the population.

Atlas infuriated the doctors because he wasn't some idiot who could be easily dismissed. He was a smart guy—smart enough to know just how to advocate his point to a White House eager to believe what he was saying. Still, the other doctors would push back on most of what he said. What evidence was there that any part of the country has reached herd immunity? they'd ask. Several regions had experienced bad outbreaks after relaxing restrictions too quickly, undercutting Atlas's argument. And no one knew what proportion of the population had to be infected to reach herd immunity. What evidence did Atlas have that definitively showed children did not spread the virus? How did he not understand that those who were considered vulnerable extended far beyond nursing homes? He was forgetting the millions of those who were obese, diabetic, Black or Brown, undergoing chemotherapy, or facing a whole host of other underlying medical conditions.

The doctors thought that Atlas cherry-picked data to support whatever point he wanted to make. He regularly cited at least two doctors with impressive credentials—Martin Kulldorff, a professor of medicine at Harvard Medical School, and Jayanta Bhattacharya, a professor of medicine at Stanford University—who shared his belief that the cost of lockdowns outweighed the public health considerations. There were also many issues on which the scientific evidence was mixed, but Atlas selected the studies that supported whatever point he wanted to make.

"Instead of looking at the data and making a conclusion, he makes a conclusion and picks the data to fill in," Fauci said in an interview.

As the media attention on Atlas increased, he became more defensive. He insisted that he wasn't advocating herd immunity. But he argued against any sort of intervention to slow the virus's spread, including mask wearing, which he compared to the old myth that wearing a copper bracelet would cure arthritis. And his arguments were clearly working. At one point, Trump asked Birx if she thought that New York and New Jersey had reached herd immunity. She couldn't believe he was asking her that.

Scott Atlas had risen to the top ranks of Stanford University Medical Center, serving as chief of radiology at the hospital from 1998 until 2012. He had edited a top textbook, *Magnetic Resonance Imaging of the Brain and Spine*, and trained more than a hundred residents. His list of speeches, published articles, and experience fills 159 pages. He had delivered speeches in India, Russia, Singapore, the United Arab Emirates, Switzerland, Vietnam, Indonesia, Brazil, Argentina, and Canada and all over the United States.

But at some point the Illinois native began drifting further and further into conservative policy and punditry. That made him a perfect fit for Stanford's conservative Hoover Institution. In 2006, Atlas wrote his first article for the opinion page of the *Wall Street Journal*, entitled "Health Care for 1.3 Billion People? Leave It to the Market." There were other articles for the *Washington Times* and FoxNews.com, and a piece for the *Orange County Register* in 2007 with the headline "Oh, Canada, We Don't Want Your Health Care." That year, he supported Rudy Giuliani's run for the Republican ticket in the presidential race.

Five years later, in 2012, he became one of a team of health advisers to Republican presidential candidate Mitt Romney. Romney's campaign aggressively criticized the Affordable Care Act, President Obama's primary health care achievement (which people often pointed out was similar in design to the health care plan Romney had instituted as governor of Massachusetts). Romney's aides wanted to collect anecdotes about people in England or other countries with various iterations of government-run health care who couldn't access doctors or cutting-edge treatments. They also wanted anecdotes that would illustrate Medicare's shortcomings as a way to argue against more government intervention in the US health care system.

Atlas wrote back with a link to a column he had published in *Forbes* after Senator Ted Kennedy's death in 2009. In the email, Atlas argued that Kennedy's own experience with brain cancer could be an anecdote the campaign used:

> Senator Kennedy is a very powerful and compelling anecdote—he was being treated by chemo that was approved in the US years before it was available in the UK (I know because I was interpreting all of his brain MRI studies after his scans were acquired in Washington and Boston). Not only that, he was exercising his full individual choices and liberty in scouting out the best doctors and best medical diagnoses and treatments when it counted the most.

That brazen invocation of the dead Democrat's brain scan shocked some of Romney's aides.

Atlas was staking out a position as a doctor who wanted a very limited government role in health care and a very big role for the private market. He wasn't your typical doctor, though. During that time, he called himself an "invited professor" and traveled the world, lecturing on health care in various countries. Some of his work was funded by GE Healthcare Systems, including a 2013 trip when he trained 150 radiologists during a one-day seminar in Kuala Lumpur. Between 2015 and 2018, he was paid or reimbursed more than $100,000 in total by GE Healthcare Systems for consulting, speaking fees, or travel, according to records obtained by ProPublica.

Atlas's views were not backed up by the vast majority of the infectious disease and public health community. Maybe that was because he was a radiologist, Fauci thought, and not an infectious diseases guy. Maybe he and Birx could talk to him and explain where they were coming from. If they could agree on a set of facts and data, they could all work together to fight the pandemic. It was worth a try. He floated the idea with Birx.

"Maybe we should sit down with him," Fauci told Birx. "What I heard him say is so ridiculous, but why don't we give him the benefit of the doubt?"

That was a nonstarter for Birx. "This guy is fucking crazy," she said. "We can't deal with him. He's a nutcase. He's impossible."

"Deb, we gotta give the guy a chance," Fauci said. "He's a physician. He's one of us." Like Birx, Fauci, Hahn, and Redfield, Atlas was supposed to have spent his life helping people. Where was all the nonsense coming from? Maybe he just needed help understanding their perspective.

"Absolutely not. We're not going to give this guy a chance. I've been dealing with him," an exasperated Birx told Fauci. "He's been undermining me at every single step of the way."

Birx explained to Fauci that she had sat down with Atlas at the end of July, when he had first arrived at the White House. Aides had requested that she go over all her data with Atlas, and she had obliged. She had explained to Atlas in detail how she was triangulating data from various sources so that she could not only get a snapshot of what was happening but also understand what was *going* to happen. But it had all been for naught; Atlas was completely set in his views, and nothing would change his mind. Worse than that, many officials felt that he had kept working to undermine Birx's data, despite her careful explanations of where it was coming from.

Fauci could try to talk to Atlas if he wanted, Birx told him, but she wasn't going to try to convince him anymore. Fauci still wanted to give it a shot, so he reached out to Atlas on his own. "Scott, let's see if we can come to some sort of agreement of what it is that we agree on and what it is we disagree on," he told him on the phone.

Atlas was defensive and strident from the start. "I only want to do what's best for the country," he countered before explaining that he actually knew more about the virus than Fauci did because he knew the literature better than Fauci did. Well, that's not a good starting point, Fauci thought. He could tell by Atlas's tone that there was no way they were going to come to any sort of agreement. This was never going to work. And it wasn't designed to.

Atlas was given a White House email address and an office on the first floor of the Eisenhower Executive Office Building, adjacent to the West Wing. He had unfettered access to Trump but no real responsibility. "My background is I'm a health care policy person, and I have a background in medical science," he told a British interviewer in October. "My role really is to translate medical science into public policy. That's very different from being an epidemiologist or a virologist with a single, limited scope."

Atlas only grew more emboldened over time and relished the fact that Trump listened exclusively to his medical advice. He doubled down on his insistence that the country was reaching herd immunity, even as cases began a steep climb in the fall. By then he had crafted a new argument to back up his assertion: people who had had other coronavirus infections in their lifetimes, including the common cold, had so-called T-cell immunity that afforded them some protection against COVID-19, meaning that a much bigger share of the population was protected against the virus than previously thought. In fact, immunologists were studying the issue but could find no evidence to support it.

For her part, Birx continued to sound the alarm about regions of the country that looked as though they were on the precipice of huge outbreaks in her daily reports to the states and in task force meetings. Mask mandates work, she told the task force. So does shutting down bars and indoor dining. Florida was on the brink of another catastrophic wave of cases, and Birx had gone down to the state and convinced local officials to impose restrictions to slow the virus's spread.

By that point, Atlas had carte blanche and decided to meet with Florida's leaders himself to undo all of Birx's work. Interventions don't work, he told them, so you might as well keep the economy open. Atlas's message was much more in line with what the state's Republican leaders wanted to do anyway, so they listened.

The tone of Birx's daily reports became increasingly urgent. She and the other doctors warned of a bleak winter if Americans didn't come together and work to blunt the spread of the virus.

Trump and his top aides may have been listening to Atlas and encouraging him to speak out, but others were taking notice that his statements and advice about how to handle the virus were dangerous. On September 11, YouTube removed a fifty-minute Hoover Institution interview with Atlas from June in which he had offered a number of controversial theories, among them that younger people could not transmit the virus. YouTube said that statement violated its effort to prevent the circulation of misinformation about the virus.

For all his bluster, Atlas was thin skinned, and he exploded. In an interview on Fox News, he likened YouTube's decision to the type of action that takes place in "Third World countries—the countries we used to be proudly distinguished from."

Two weeks later, on a flight from Atlanta to Washington, Redfield was bemoaning Atlas's behavior during what he thought was a private phone conversation. "Everything he says is false," he said, speaking about Atlas.

Redfield was unaware that an NBC reporter was sitting nearby on the plane. She introduced herself to Redfield when they landed and said she was going to publish a story about his comments. Redfield was furious, saying that it had been a private conversation and should not be treated as an on-the-record quote. He tried to stop NBC from printing the story, but to no avail. I can't catch a break, he thought at the time. But several months later, he would look back on his comments with pride. He was glad the story had been reported. He wanted people to know how he had felt.

By October, Birx and Fauci had had enough. They felt Atlas was so disruptive to the task force's work that the meetings had become completely pointless. All the team members did was fight, and the doctors felt that Pence and other officials seesawed among the differing points of view.

"They created a false equivalency. They say, 'Well, one smart doctor says this and another smart doctor says that, and so who knows who's right?'" Fauci said in an interview. "That is really dangerous because that's a false equivalency because in reality you may have one smart doctor, or a group of smart doctors who are right and the other smart doctor who is actually dead wrong."

Birx and Fauci decided to sit down with Pence. He needed to understand how dangerous Atlas's ideas were, they thought, and be given a sort of ultimatum. They didn't go so far as threatening to resign if Atlas stayed, but at one point Birx said that if Atlas came to a task force meeting, she wouldn't attend it. As usual, Pence heard them out, but ultimately told them to resolve their issues with Atlas themselves. He didn't want to put his thumb onto the scale. Atlas eventually decided on his own to stop attending the task force meetings; he didn't need to do so anyway, given his access to the president.

The White House never formally adopted a herd immunity strategy, but the stalemate that resulted from the numerous clashes between Atlas and the other doctors amounted to the same thing. As the number of cases climbed again in the fall, there was a clear sense of hopelessness and frustration on the part of top White House officials. The outbreak would never be under control, so why bother? The election was only weeks away, and they wanted the country to feel as though it was back to normal.

Trump was holding rallies attended by thousands of maskless people, proclaiming that the outbreak was over. Few, if any, of the top political officials were talking about mitigation measures or restrictions to help protect against a deadly winter. They were encouraging people to go out and live their lives. The death rate had decreased, and that was all that mattered. And they were beginning to make good on Trump's request at the Tulsa rally months earlier that they slow down testing. Birx and Fauci repeatedly pressed the administration to reverse this, including spending $9 billion of unused congressionally appropriated funds. Atlas shot down their efforts, which never went anywhere. Instead, some tests were directed to nursing homes and testing the broader population was deemphasized.

The strategy may not have been official, but it was clear: the administration had de facto adopted a "let 'er rip" attitude.

CHAPTER 19

A SHOT IN THE DARK

September 10, 2020

CONFIRMED US COVID-19 CASES: **6,400,000**

CONFIRMED US COVID-19 DEATHS: **192,000**

While Donald Trump's aides battled over the virus's lethality, the president knew that there was only one way for him to be reelected: he would have to deliver a vaccine.

The president's advisers had long cautioned him that developing a safe and effective vaccine in time for the election would be nothing short of a miracle. That was in part why he had seized on treatments such as hydroxychloroquine and remdesivir; he was hoping for anything that might vanquish the virus or at least give the illusion of doing so. He had even, at one point, considered touting a botanical extract, oleandrin, which can be poisonous.

Now the president who had eschewed science found himself waiting for a historic scientific breakthrough to end the biggest crisis of his presidency. It was a stark change for Trump, who had long flirted with antivaccination views. Shortly before his inauguration in January 2017, he had met with Robert F. Kennedy, Jr., a prominent antivaccination activist, and asked him to chair a vaccine safety panel.

Trump had been sidelining government health experts and doctors for months. Now everything hinged on them. And pharmaceutical companies, which he had once said were "getting away with murder," were the only ones that could pull off the speedy development of a vaccine. From the start, some of them had been moving through clinical trials with breathtaking speed. Maybe there was a chance for a miracle?

The vaccine's birth encapsulated the whipsaw nature of the government's response to the pandemic. In January and February, while Trump had been saying that COVID-19 would disappear on its own, pharmaceutical companies had begun racing to develop a vaccine against the new virus. They had been able to get to work as soon as Chinese researchers uploaded the virus's genetic sequence to an open-access repository for genetic information on January 10; Moderna, a small biotechnology company, for instance, had partnered with the NIH and gotten its vaccine into the first phase of clinical trials in just six weeks.

Some in the White House had echoed the president's line early on, believing that the virus would evaporate when the weather warmed. One exception was Peter Navarro, who had sent other White House officials a memo on February 9 urging dramatically accelerated development of a vaccine and the need to launch multiple trials at once. It called for a "'Manhattan Project' Vaccine Development." But as Navarro didn't really know anything about vaccine development and was alienating aides left and right with his rants about how China was deliberately using the virus to destroy the United States, no one took him seriously. As the weeks went on, though, more people started to worry. Maybe the virus wasn't going to just go away. Maybe it really was going to kill hundreds of thousands of Americans. A vaccine looked increasingly like the only way to stop it.

As the crisis deepened, Trump tried to have it both ways, brushing aside concerns about the virus's impact while breathing down the neck of virtually everyone around him to make sure needles were jammed into arms before the election. Fauci and other scientists repeatedly told him that the development of a vaccine would take a year to a year and a half, but Trump wanted one faster. And as the months went on and his reelection chances began slipping away, he became more brazen in his predictions, putting government scientists and pharmaceutical companies in untenable positions. By the fall, he had gone from promising one "very soon" to making clear that he expected it before November 3, which was, of course, election day. "We're going to have a vaccine very soon, maybe even before a very special date. You know what date I'm talking about," he said in early September, also accusing the FDA and CDC of trying to subvert his election chances.

Over the summer, the early results of the vaccine trials were proving remarkably promising. Scientific breakthroughs were happening. The United States was on track to have a vaccine by the end of the year, eleven months after it had first learned about the virus, a stunning achievement. Before the COVID-19 pandemic, the fastest vaccine ever to be developed had been one for mumps in the 1960s— and that had taken four years. Several companies would likely now shatter that record, and the federal government was throwing everything it had at the problem to get a vaccine across the finish line.

It didn't matter. For Trump, if a vaccine didn't come in time for the election, it wasn't going to be soon enough. From the testing failures in February to the hydroxychloroquine mess in March, from remdesivir in the spring to convalescent plasma therapy in August, the FDA had been under enormous political pressure all year long. But nothing had compared to the torture the agency endured in September and October over the vaccine and the all-out war that ensued between FDA officials and the White House.

There is nothing easy about vaccine development. It's an inherently risky process that often takes a decade or longer and costs hundreds of millions of dollars, if not more. There are three phases of clinical trials that a company must complete before it can begin to apply for FDA approval or authorization (a lower bar that is used during public health emergencies). Usually it first tests a product on lab animals before moving on to human trials. Then each of the three phases of clinical trials is bigger than the last to establish the drug's safety and efficacy.

A number of companies were able to begin their research in January. But regulators at the FDA were dismayed in March when they realized that the most ambitious companies were not aiming to have their vaccines ready to deploy until summer 2021. One company told the agency that it was aiming for the first quarter of 2022. "That was not so hot to see," one FDA official recalled.

Peter Marks, the director of the FDA's Center for Biologics Evaluation and Research and the country's top vaccine regulator, approached FDA commissioner Stephen Hahn at the end of March with an idea. One of the main reasons vaccine development takes so long is that a manufacturer must complete certain steps sequentially. Even after its vaccine has been tested and approved by the FDA, there is a three- to four-month delay in manufacturing doses of the product that can be injected into arms.

But with the pandemic ravaging the country and no time to waste, Marks had reached out to Robert Kadlec, the assistant secretary for preparedness and response, to figure out how to cut through all the delays and enable companies to carry out the normally sequential steps simultaneously. That would mean not only that the three phases of clinical trials would have to move as seamlessly and quickly as possible but that the companies would need to manufacture doses of their products before they even knew if they worked. That had never been done before in the United States.

It wasn't, however, the first time an idea like this had been floated. It was a key part of the conception of the Biomedical Advanced Research and Development Authority (BARDA), which is under ASPR, when the agency was created in 2006. BARDA's role was to accelerate the development and manufacturing of medical countermeasures for pandemics and other biological and chemical threats. It had done so for dozens of medical products through US government funding, technical assistance, and guaranteed procurement for the Strategic

National Stockpile. Marks and Kadlec were proposing an idea that was on a scale and timetable that had never been attempted.

Companies weren't going to do it on their own and foot the bill. Manufacture millions of doses of their vaccines before they had any idea if the FDA would sign off on them? They could end up throwing millions or billions of dollars down the drain. But, Marks wondered, what if the federal government were to pay for the doses now, taking away any risk? What if the government were to throw money at the companies to move as fast as possible? The FDA would also be in constant communication with them, helping them design their clinical trials and making sure they knew exactly what benchmarks they needed to meet.

Marks and Kadlec took their idea to Alex Azar, who agreed that things had to be done differently this time. Azar had another concern: if China or Russia developed a vaccine before the United States did, it could change the global strategic balance of power for decades to come. The United States prided itself on its immense scientific might. The vaccines were the new space race. Not being first would be humiliating and might push other countries into the arms of Russia and China. That could be a huge geopolitical setback.

Azar received a final proposal from Marks and Kadlec on April 13 and immediately began assessing the political landscape. The effort would require billions of dollars and full White House support. Marks and Kadlec proposed betting on several vaccine candidates by providing their manufacturers huge government contracts in the hope that even one or two would work. The overall concept was based on World War Two's Manhattan Project, a highly focused, tightly managed, and generously resourced effort to build the atomic bomb. If Marks and Kadlec's proposal was successful, they thought the development and production of safe and effective vaccines could have the same global impact.

Azar's critics and allies both said he saw an opportunity to improve his reputation and standing by helping to deliver a vaccine. He was well positioned to play a key role, as he had more than a decade of experience in the pharmaceutical industry and oversaw all of the health agencies. But he knew he was on the outs with the White House and needed political cover to make it all work. He needed someone untouchable. He needed Jared Kushner.

As he was seeking Kushner's support, Azar received an offer from Mark Esper, the defense secretary, to have the Pentagon help with the effort. Vaccinating all of the country's 330 million residents would be possibly the largest and most complex vaccination effort in US history. The military, with its operations and logistics expertise, was well suited to help, Defense Department officials believed. Even better, Esper was well liked by the White House. Now Azar could be paired with Esper's superior reputation, giving the project a greater chance of success.

Everything seemed to be coming together nicely, and it soon came time to brief key White House and health aides. On April 29, several members of the task force gathered in the Situation Room to learn more about Marks and Kadlec's proposal. Marks was a career official who oversaw a 1,100-person division at the FDA and had generally steered clear of politics. Tall, thin, and wiry, with speckled gray hair and thin-rimmed glasses, he was an academic oncologist who had worked for several years in the drug industry before landing at the FDA in 2012. His office was responsible for evaluating data on biological products, including vaccines, and he would have maybe the most important job in the country over the next several months.

He was proud of his proposal—which he had dubbed "Project Warp Speed," a nod to the *Star Trek* television series. (The administration would adopt his moniker for the project with a slight modification, changing it to "Operation Warp Speed.") But it was the first time he had been to the White House during the Trump administration, and he wasn't quite sure what to expect. Some of the people there were the same ones who assailed science and government bureaucrats, dismissing them as the "deep state." Things got off to a strange start when Marks walked into the Situation Room and realized that there was no place for him to sit at the table. Wasn't he supposed to be the main presenter that day? He took a seat off to one side.

Before anyone else could begin, Mark Meadows launched in. There's no plan to manufacture at risk! he yelled. (*Manufacture at risk* meant producing doses of a vaccine before it was known whether it worked.) Why aren't we building any manufacturing facilities? he asked. "Mark, this isn't making widgets," Azar replied. "We're making biologics." He explained that you couldn't just build a bunch of factories to make vaccines. It was an extraordinarily complicated task, and how manufacturing plants were built would depend on a company's specific product.

Then Deborah Birx instructed Marks to sit at the head of the table to begin his presentation. It was the seat the president or vice president occupied when he came to the Situation Room. For a career scientist like Marks, it was a surreal moment. He began explaining his Project Warp Speed proposal and the different vaccines the federal government was planning to bet on. Two of them—from Pfizer and Moderna, which was partnering with the NIH—relied on a new, unproven technology. They were mRNA vaccines, which teach the body how to recognize the spike protein on the coronavirus's surface and defend against it. Researchers had been studying the genetic technology for decades, but it had never been used in an approved vaccine before.

Birx quickly began grilling Marks, her voice rising. You're investing in all these unproven vectors and platforms, she told him. Producing amounts of mRNA vaccines beyond 20 million to 25 million doses per month will be difficult; you need a mix of innovative and proven platforms to give us the best opportunity for success. Birx also wanted the government to bet on so-called subunit protein vaccines, which use fragments of protein from the virus to produce an immune response in the body, that could be rapidly manufactured in large quantities.

Neither Azar nor Hahn interjected while Birx was hammering

Marks. Marks felt helpless, unsure of how to respond to Birx, who also said that HHS had set back the vaccine by three months because there wasn't a shared vision and comprehensive strategy. Why was she tearing into him like this? Why was neither of his bosses protecting him against this tirade?

"Why didn't you do this weeks ago?" Meadows demanded of Marks. He inched closer to Marks, getting increasingly riled up. "Shouldn't you have done this weeks ago?"

Meadows and Birx were leveling one-two punches at the stunned FDA scientist, and no one was stepping in to bail him out. Marks answered their questions in detail and defended his Project Warp Speed vision, but not enough to satisfy Birx and Meadows. At the end of the meeting, Hahn said they would find a way to address the issues raised.

Several meeting attendees remarked afterward that it was one of the most uncomfortable, unprofessional displays they had ever seen. And they were stunned that neither Hahn nor Azar had defended Marks.

Fauci found Azar after the meeting and put his arm around him. "Alex, don't worry. mRNA is gonna work. It's gonna happen," he said in his upbeat Brooklyn drawl.

Marks left the meeting feeling discouraged and downtrodden. Domestic Policy Council director Joe Grogan helped facilitate a meeting two days later between Marks and Birx to help clear the air.

Marks hoped he would lead the initiative he had devised, but Azar and the White House quickly brought in an outside pharmaceutical executive, Moncef Slaoui, a member of the board of directors of Moderna who had played an integral role in the development of more than a dozen vaccines over the course of his career, to run the project, along with Gustave Perna, a US Army four-star general, who would oversee logistics and operations. Marks felt crowded out, and it was clear that he was no longer in control. He decided to remain at his post at the FDA. (He would have had to leave that post if he were to run Operation Warp Speed.)

Kushner and Azar, meanwhile, wanted to keep the effort away from Mike Pence and the task force, which they increasingly viewed as incompetent and inefficient. They decided to put Birx onto the board of Operation Warp Speed, so that the vice president's team would still be involved but would be prevented from further interference.

Sensing that the vaccine could be one of the few bright spots in the otherwise calamitous pandemic response, Kushner, who had no background in drug or vaccine development, infectious diseases, or public health, was eager to maintain his position as one of the board members. When Pence called Azar one Sunday in early May, informing him of his plan to hold a vaccine briefing for the task force at the NIH later that week, Azar sensed a power grab. He called Kushner, who quickly had the briefing canceled.

One of Operation Warp Speed's goals was to have at least 100 million vaccine doses ready by January 2021. Trump and the White House had bought into the idea, with an amendment: they wanted the doses by October 2020.

"Gee, I wonder why that is?" one official wondered.

Most health officials knew that October was an unrealistic deadline but decided to go along with it; it was better to get moving and make sure that the vaccine effort was prioritized than to argue over dates. Besides, some officials thought, you never know when you might get lucky.

But the obsession with getting the vaccine before the election soon became all-consuming. During a task force meeting in May, shortly before Operation Warp Speed was formally announced, officials broke into a deeply contentious argument about the accelerated process. Some health officials were alarmed that there had been no discussion about the scientific issues that needed to be addressed to reach that historic goal. Top White House aides made it clear that the future of the administration depended on the success of the vaccine. Some health officials, including Marks and NIH director Francis Collins, decided that they would try to avoid the White House as much as they could in the coming months to escape political pressure.

When Trump met with Slaoui and Perna in mid-May to sign off on their leading Operation Warp Speed, he didn't even seem to believe that the development of a vaccine in the next several months was possible. "He thought vaccines were too pie in the sky and therapeutics he could get," one meeting attendee recalled. Trump told the officials gathered that he didn't want to make it seem as though everything depended on the vaccine. He asked Slaoui what he thought about hydroxychloroquine and remdesivir as treatments. He was still hoping for a miracle drug, something that could be made available right away, to convince Americans that everything was fine.

Days after that meeting, Azar called Kushner with good news: the drug company AstraZeneca, based in the United Kingdom, was partnering with Oxford University on a vaccine that looked promising. The Operation Warp Speed team was excited about the AstraZeneca product, so Azar had spoken with the British secretary of state for health and social care, Matt Hancock; Operation Warp Speed eventually signed a deal with the company, agreeing that the United States would purchase the first 300 million doses of the vaccine if it secured an emergency-use authorization from the FDA. The United States had even beaten the British government to securing the first doses. A jubilant Azar called Kushner, who put Trump on speakerphone.

"I have incredible news," Azar began. "I've signed a contract for 300 million doses of AstraZeneca's vaccine. We're the first in the world. We've scooped the British." He said that they needed to be careful about the news leaking because the deal would be announced when the markets opened in London the following morning.

"Why London?" Trump asked. Azar explained that AstraZeneca was a United Kingdom–based company.

"This is terrible news. I'm going to get killed. [British prime minister] Boris Johnson will have a field day with that," Trump replied. "Why aren't we doing this with an American company?" He told Azar to not do any press on the contract.

Azar felt defeated. He'd finally had good news to tell the president, and the president was still angry. "I can't do this anymore," he said to his immediate staff. "I've just been chewed out as if I've done the most horrific thing imaginable."

But as Trump's poll numbers kept falling over the next several months, his tune on the vaccine would change. Several vaccines were moving through clinical trials at an unprecedented clip. By midsummer, it looked as though Pfizer and Moderna would soon begin phase 3 clinical trials, the final step before applying for emergency-use authorization from the FDA. A vaccine might really be available by the end of the year.

Suddenly, the idea of a vaccine wasn't theoretical, it wasn't pie in the sky, it was real. Americans weren't buying Trump's promises of miracle cures and a virus that would magically disappear. But they might believe that the pandemic was coming to an end if Trump could show he was on the cusp of delivering a vaccine. He had found his escape hatch.

Delivering a vaccine in a year or less was perhaps the most challenging task in the pandemic response, even harder than creating a national testing program. (Several officials lamented that the administration had not launched an Operation Warp Speed for testing.) It was certainly harder than asking everyone to wear a mask, social distance, and model good behavior.

Despite Trump's disdain for science and those who defended it, he had long been enamored of the United States' technological prowess and its ability to deliver breakthrough medicines. When he railed about high drug prices, he rarely meant the prices of such things as genetic technologies and advanced cancer treatments. So getting Trump and the White House to buy into Operation Warp Speed wasn't hard. The concept aligned with Trump's beliefs and the broader Republican orthodoxy. The federal government would spend a huge amount of money, yes, but it would be in support of the private sector's ability to bring the product to market. The vaccine effort "worked because it was commensurate with what they did well," one senior administration official said. It was also not a novel concept. Global public health leaders had for years talked about using government investments to reduce the financial risks that might otherwise deter companies from developing products without a large market. That had been the idea behind HHS's Biomedical Advanced Research and Development Authority (BARDA): that the agency could work with pharmaceutical companies and help fund the development of drugs and vaccines to biological threats.

The administration ultimately awarded contracts to five companies: AstraZeneca, Janssen (owned by the pharmaceutical giant Johnson & Johnson), Moderna, Novavax, and Sanofi, which partnered with GlaxoSmithKline. Pfizer did not take any money from Operation Warp Speed for research and development but agreed that the federal government would purchase doses of its vaccine if it won an emergency authorization from the FDA. Pfizer wanted more flexibility to forge ahead as it saw fit and did not want Operation Warp Speed dictating the way its trials should be designed or conducted.

That meant the government had less visibility into the company's processes, which led to tension when the company increasingly looked as though it would be one of the first with a vaccine. Pfizer officials were shocked when Operation Warp Speed interfered with some of the company's contracts with outside manufacturers for critical vaccine components. Pfizer had had the supply agreements in place for some time, but Operation Warp Speed diverted some of the contracts to other companies that the federal government was partnered with, including Moderna. US government officials said they were not punishing Pfizer, but rather trying to make sure all of the

Operation Warp Speed companies had equal access to supplies, factories, and other resources. Still, Pfizer officials were shocked. Like everyone else, they were trying to help bring the pandemic under control—just without government money. Why would the federal government want to get into the way of that?

That interference foreshadowed the acrimony that was still to come between Pfizer and the Trump administration.

Stephen Hahn knew he wasn't built for Washington. He was an oncologist and researcher and the chief medical executive at the University of Texas MD Anderson Cancer Center, consistently ranked as the top cancer hospital in the country. Academic medicine was hardly the preparation he needed to survive Trump's Washington.

Hahn was affable and eager to please. He had been FDA commissioner for all of two and a half months when he was added to the task force in late February, and he seemed enamored by White House meetings with the president and vice president. He seemed to love the prestige that came with the position, suddenly receiving direct calls from the White House. And he wanted to deliver on the administration's needs without angering the career scientists in the FDA, who viewed him skeptically. Some officials observed that, as a result, Hahn often told people what they wanted to hear. The hydroxychloroquine debate had been a classic example: Hahn had told Trump there was supportive data for hydroxychloroquine but that the agency needed data from clinical trials. Trump and some of his aides would seize on a statement like this, and then feel Hahn blindsided the White House later when he said or did something that contradicted what he had previously said. In trying to please everyone, he ended up upsetting many of them.

There was painful irony in Hahn's standing. Perhaps no one was weaker in the eyes of the White House than Hahn. But in fact, no one was more powerful than Hahn. No vaccine could receive emergency-use authorization without the FDA's sign-off. The solution to the pandemic would have to go through the bald cancer doctor from Texas whether Trump liked it or not.

During the spring and summer, Hahn made so many miscalculations in his dealings with the White House that he lost the trust of much of his agency.

After the convalescent plasma therapy debacle, which many in the agency had considered a low point in the FDA's history, seven of the top career officials decided they needed to send a clear public message that the agency would not stand to be pushed around anymore.

The FDA has seven main centers, run by career officials, that collectively make the decisions on virtually all products that are regulated by the FDA, whether they be devices, drugs, medical technologies, or vaccines. The center directors hold some of the most powerful, influential posts in the entire federal bureaucracy. Trump's accusations that FDA scientists were part of the "deep state" made them realize that few people understood what they did. Understanding the science and deciding whether to sign off on products wasn't black and white. Throughout the pandemic, the center directors had been pressured to evaluate and rubber-stamp all sorts of shady products and drugs; they had pushed back on all of them. FDA officials weren't getting rich off their jobs in the agency and could have made a lot more money working in the private sector. Instead they had dedicated themselves to public service, which made protecting the integrity of the agency their most important job.

After some discussion, the center directors agreed that they needed to be more transparent around their decisions and how they were made, to assure the public of their commitment to science and that they weren't cutting corners for the sake of political expediency. One of the center directors raised the idea of writing an op-ed that they would publish jointly in a major newspaper. Initially, none of the others liked the idea; they had never done anything like that and feared the blowback from sticking their necks out publicly.

But the center directors later decided to support the approach with one director proposing to write a first draft for their input. They decided to tell Hahn about the op-ed at the last possible minute, so he couldn't get in the way. Some simply didn't want to put him in a difficult position, where he might feel pressured to tell his superiors about the op-ed before it was published. But the secrecy with which they proceeded underscored some officials' lack of confidence and trust in him.

"Maintaining the American public's trust in the FDA is vital," the op-ed, published in *USA Today* on September 10, said. "If the agency's credibility is lost because of real or perceived interference, people will not rely on the agency's safety warnings. Erosion of public trust will leave consumers and patients doubting our recommendations. . . . Protecting the FDA's independence is essential if we are to do the best possible job of protecting public health and saving lives." It was an unmistakable shot across the bow from career FDA officials to the White House. Back off.

Hahn was being criticized from all sides. One of the most stinging condemnations was an open letter addressed to him by Eric Topol, a prominent doctor and scientist who was the founder/director of the Scripps Research Translational Institute and editor in chief of Medscape, a website widely used by doctors and clinicians. It was published on August 31, just a few days after Hahn had misrepresented the data on convalescent plasma from the White House podium. The headline read, "Dear Commissioner Hahn: Tell the Truth or Resign."

"The circumstances of your statements in recent days has led to a crisis in confidence. Not only has your credibility been diminished but so has that of the FDA, its 15,000-plus staff members, and, most importantly, your ability to oversee the health interests of the American people," Topol wrote in his scathing rebuke. Toward the end of the article, he wrote, "We cannot entrust the health of 330 million

Americans to a person who is subservient to President Trump's whims, unprecedented promotion of unproven therapies, outrageous lies, and political motivations."

The letter was stinging, but Hahn understood the criticism. He called Topol to explain his perspective and address the criticisms head-on. He was under enormous pressure from both HHS and the White House to approve a vaccine by November 3, he said, and he worried that Azar, always eager to deliver for the president, would wrest the decision away from him if he did not move quickly enough. He also knew he could be fired if he pushed back too hard against Trump. But he had made a decision: he was going to stand with the career scientists. He was not going to cave in to pressure from Trump or anyone else on the vaccine, even if it meant losing his job.

The convalescent plasma incident had taught Hahn something that others had believed for a long time: many of the people in the White House and throughout the administration really *weren't* trying to do the right thing; they were looking out for themselves, for Trump's reelection, and first and foremost for their own political careers. The sheen and prestige Hahn had once associated with visiting the White House and meeting with the president were gone. In the future, he would avoid going there as much as he could—not least because there seemed to be a constant coronavirus outbreak—and focus on rebuilding trust within his agency.

Several officials, including Azar, took note of Hahn's new posture, which began the rapid deterioration of their relationship. Azar believed that Hahn was abandoning the team to try to restore his reputation. And he didn't think that Hahn was moving fast enough on vaccine and therapeutic authorizations, in addition to causing unnecessary delays in the process. Azar also became so angered by constant media leaks of phone calls he had with Hahn that he began demanding that the two meet in person, just to ensure that no one else from the FDA was listening in without his knowledge.

Trump and Meadows were also beginning to focus their anger

and frustration on Hahn and would regularly complain about his performance to Azar. Azar, for his part, told White House officials that his biggest issue with Hahn was that he seemed disengaged. By the middle of September, Trump started using one of his favored epithets by referring to him as "that fucking Hahn." At one point, one of Trump's most trusted advisers, Johnny McEntee, pulled Azar aside on the driveway of the West Wing. The president really can't stand Hahn, McEntee said. Azar agreed and said if the White House was looking for a better suited option, it could be someone such as Janet Woodcock, an FDA career veteran and one of the agency's top-ranking officials.

Hahn would later be tipped off about such discussions and would feel betrayed by his boss, whom he thought could have been making his life easier by having his back. Instead, he felt, Azar was exacerbating the situation by telling the White House that he was causing delays. Didn't they know that everyone at the FDA was working around the clock and had drastically cut the time it usually took to authorize drugs and vaccines? They couldn't cut corners and put people's safety at risk, Hahn would argue.

Even though Azar wanted to get rid of Hahn, he also felt saddled with him. He knew that firing Hahn just as public trust in the vaccine was plummeting would only further hamper the process. There would be an outcry from the public, as the move would look obviously political. Azar also knew that any vaccine approval had to have the full support of FDA career officials, or else it would only be a pyrrhic victory because no one would take the vaccine. (That didn't stop Azar from haranguing Hahn to move faster.)

Over the summer, Marks's center had begun sending letters to the vaccine developers, explaining what the FDA would require from them before it would issue an emergency-use authorization for a vaccine, which is a much quicker process than a formal approval: the companies would have to follow the clinical trial participants for at least two months after they received their second vaccine shot to see if any of them developed abnormal side effects or complications.

That timing effectively ruled out the possibility of an available vaccine before election day. The agency initially didn't plan to publicize the guidance, but Hahn and Marks had had a phone call with a prominent senator who suggested the agency go forward with the public document. And with the public's trust in the vaccine plummeting, Marks knew it had to. In May, more than 70 percent of people said that they would get the vaccine if it were available. By September, the number had dropped to just over 50 percent.

Azar learned about the guidance when Moncef Slaoui, the head of Operation Warp Speed, told him during a meeting that the FDA had changed the criteria for authorizing the vaccine. One of the companies that had received the letter about the two-month follow-up had alerted Slaoui. During a call the following day, the FDA chief of staff, Keagan Lenihan, informed Azar and Slaoui that the agency was preparing to formalize what was in the letters. Well, Azar thought, the gig is up. There's nothing I can do. FDA career officials have already sent the letters and boxed us in. The guidance was soon reported by the *Washington Post*.

The White House couldn't believe the audacity of the FDA. Why was it suddenly moving the goalposts? Several aides, including Meadows, were now convinced that FDA bureaucrats were intentionally trying to derail Trump's reelection prospects. Meadows called Hahn in a fury, asking what the fuck the agency was doing. Trump blasted the new guidance on Twitter: "When you have great companies coming up with these vaccines, why would they [the FDA] have to be, you know, adding great length to the process? We want to have people not get sick. I don't see why it should be delayed further. That is a lot of lives you're talking about."

In the coming days, Meadows demanded detailed justification from Hahn and the FDA about the agency's decision to publish the guidance. The White House even threatened not to clear the guidance. But Hahn and Marks had already decided that they weren't going to let the administration stop them. Not this time. Top officials at the Center for Biologics Evaluation and Research, including

Marks, had made clear that they would quit if they came under any undue pressure on the vaccine, which would have been a complete public relations disaster. The stakes were far too high.

Marks realized just how much hinged on the FDA's ability to convince Americans that it would authorize only a safe product during a webinar in October. He had done as many webinars and science conferences as he could fit into his schedule in the last several months, hoping to demonstrate to anyone who would listen just how rigorous the FDA's process was and the number of safeguards it had in place. But during that webinar, he learned that only 9 percent of people polled by a Black radio show had said they would take the vaccine. "Oh, crap," he thought. But why should he have been surprised?

The FDA did send the White House more data on why the guidance was necessary, but nothing happened. They were worried that the White House was going to sit on it. Tired of waiting, the agency publicized the guidance on its own by including it as part of a briefing package for a meeting with its vaccine advisory committee.

Finally, FDA scientists thought, Hahn was defending his agency, no matter the cost.

Trump was so fixated on having a vaccine before the election that it came up in almost every meeting, whether it was about the vaccine or not. That was the case on September 24, when a number of top health officials, including Azar, Seema Verma, and Brad Smith, as well as Meadows, gathered shortly before boarding Air Force One for an event unrelated to coronavirus. As officials were discussing the health care executive orders the president was supposed to sign later that day, Trump began talking about the vaccine and railing about the FDA guidance. We need a vaccine before the election, he said, and the FDA guidance is going to delay that.

"Mr. President," Azar began. "I need you to understand this. There is no way there's going to be an FDA-approved vaccine before the election. There may be data, and you can own that. . . . That's your win, as is the fact that you'll have tens of millions of doses by the end of the year." His blunt assessment surprised several officials in the room who were accustomed to the shocking lengths the health secretary usually went to in order to placate Trump.

Once aboard Air Force One, Azar and Meadows discussed what a problem Hahn and the FDA had become. They weren't supportive of the president or anything they were trying to do, Azar thought, and he believed some at the FDA were constantly leaking information to the news media. After the election, there might need to be some changes, Azar and Meadows agreed.

As November approached, the White House anger with Hahn boiled over, culminating in a series of screaming phone calls from Meadows to Hahn, Trump to Azar, Meadows to anyone he believed had a role in getting a vaccine before November 3. Almost every major national poll showed Trump losing to Joe Biden—badly. Trump himself was telling aides and outside advisers that his reelection chances were directly tied to the vaccine. Meadows and Trump were injecting themselves so aggressively into the approval process that prominent Democrats began raising doubts about whether the FDA's decision would be scientifically pure.

"If the public health professionals, if Dr. Fauci, if the doctors tell us that we should take it, I'll be the first in line to take it, absolutely," Democratic senator Kamala Harris said of a prospective vaccine during the vice presidential debate on October 7. "But if Donald Trump tells us to take it, I'm not taking it."

Operation Warp Speed did end up delivering on its promise to produce a vaccine by the end of the year. In fact, two vaccines were available by then, developed by Pfizer and Moderna, the two companies that had relied on the new mRNA vaccine technology; both were more than 90 percent effective. (To put in perspective how spectacular those results were, the FDA had told companies that their vaccines had to be at least 50 percent effective to win emergency authorization.)

The effort was an unambiguous success, one that Trump and his team could certainly take credit for. But Pfizer's results were publicly reported a week after election day, Moderna's a week after that. The news was the first real hope Americans could seize on to that the pandemic would one day come to an end. But it hadn't come when the president needed it to.

CHAPTER 20

LONG LIVE THE KING

October 1, 2020
CONFIRMED US COVID-19 CASES: **7,200,000**
CONFIRMED US COVID-19 DEATHS: **207,000**

HHS Secretary Alex Azar's phone rang with an urgent request: Could he help someone at the White House obtain an experimental coronavirus treatment, known as a monoclonal antibody? If so, what would the White House need to do to make that happen? Azar thought for a moment. The FDA would have to authorize a "compassionate use" of the drug, since it was still in clinical trials and not yet available to the broader public. Only about ten people so far had used it outside of trials. Azar said of course he would help.

Azar wasn't told who the drug was for but would later connect the dots. The patient was one of Donald Trump's closest advisers: Hope Hicks.

It had been a frenzied week for Trump, even by his standards. On Saturday, he had hosted a huge, festive party to announce his pick for Supreme Court justice, Amy Coney Barrett. Hundreds of people, including Azar, had attended the gathering on the White House South Lawn—very few of them wearing masks. The celebrations had continued indoors, where most people remained maskless. By that point, Trump's contempt for mask wearing had turned into unofficial White House policy. He actually asked aides who wore them in his presence to take them off. If someone was going to do a press conference with him, he made clear that he or she was not to wear a mask when he or she was by his side. With just a month to go until the election, he was making a final sprint, seeking to exude enthusiasm and confidence and block the virus out of people's minds.

But the virus had begun a new surge, the one Robert Redfield, Anthony Fauci, Stephen Hahn, and Deborah Birx had been warning about for months. As it turned out, a number of the revelers at the White House party that day were already sick (it turned out that many people had not been tested before they were allowed in). Attendees hugged and kissed and sat packed in tight during the ceremony. It was a superspreader event at the most powerful address in the world: 1600 Pennsylvania Avenue.

A few days after the White House gathering, Trump flew to Cleveland for the first presidential debate against his Democratic challenger, Joe Biden. Incumbent presidents rarely lose reelection, but Trump's poll numbers were weak, in part due to the public's disapproval of how he was handling the pandemic. Trump didn't use the debate to act contrite (which he would never do) or project to wary voters that his administration was doing everything in its power to beat back the virus. Instead, he went at Biden full throttle and from all sides, even attacking his opponent's willingness to wear a face covering. "I don't wear face masks like him," he said with disdain. "Every time you see him he's got a mask. He could be speaking 200 feet away from him and he shows up with the biggest mask I've ever seen."

Trump was erratic during the whole debate, and he seemed to deteriorate as the night went on. The pundits' verdicts were brutal. Even the conservative news outlets thought Trump was acting bananas. Something was wrong; he was acting too desperate, too unhinged.

In fact, he was not well.

Trump had tried to joke about the virus for months, sometimes even mocking people who had become ill. It was part of his false bravado. At one meeting several months earlier, NEC director Larry Kudlow had stifled a cough. The room had frozen. Kudlow was in his seventies and in poor health. Trump had waved his hands in front of his face, as if to jokingly ward off any flying virus particles, and then cracked a smile. "I was just kidding," he'd said. "Larry will never get COVID. He will defeat it with his optimism."

Then he had turned darkly serious. "John Bolton," he had said, referring to his former national security advisor, who had written an explosive tell-all book about his time in the White House. "Hopefully COVID takes out John."

There was another side to Trump, though, that predated the coronavirus crisis: he was a germophobe who hated getting sick. He even had a favored brand of antibacterial hand wipes that he handed to many Oval Office visitors. He had once asked his former acting chief of staff, Mick Mulvaney, to leave the room during a 2019 interview after he had coughed while Trump was answering a question. "If you're going to cough, please leave the room. You just can't, you just can't cough," he had said, shaking his head. "Boy, oh boy."

In 2020, his anxiety deepened. During a meeting at the White House on April 7, an aide approached Trump to tell him that British prime minister Boris Johnson had been admitted to an intensive care unit and it appeared that he might lose his struggle with COVID-19. "That's awful," Trump responded. "I've had friends go into the ICU, and they never come out."

Nearly six months later, the day after Amy Coney Barrett's swearing in ceremony, Trump hosted military families at the White House. They crowded closely around him. At Trump's insistence, few were wearing masks, but they were packed in a little too tight for comfort. He wasn't worried about others becoming sick, but he did fret about his own vulnerability and complained to his staff afterward. Why were they letting people get so close to him? Meeting with the Gold Star families was sad and moving, he said but added, "If these guys had COVID, I'm going to get it because they were all over me." He told his staff that they needed to do a better job of protecting him.

Less than forty-eight hours after the disastrous presidential debate, Azar received the phone call about the emergency treatment for Hicks. She had traveled with Trump on Air Force One and Marine One throughout the week. Among his closest advisers and confidants, Hicks had been by Trump's side before he had run for president and was one of the few people in the West Wing he trusted unconditionally.

Shortly after Azar was contacted about Hicks, FDA commissioner Stephen Hahn was contacted by someone from the White House with a similar request and even greater urgency: could the FDA sign off on a compassionate-use authorization for a monoclonal antibody right away? A compassionate-use authorization is typically reserved for the sickest patients, the ones who usually don't have a lot to lose by taking an experimental drug. There is a standard process at the FDA by which doctors file an application for their patients and agency scientists review it. The difference was that most people don't directly call the commissioner.

The White House wanted Hahn to complete the process in a matter of hours. Hahn, who still did not know who the application was for, immediately consulted career officials. The FDA needs to go by the book on this, the officials insisted. Hahn relayed the message back to the White House. They kept pressing him to speed it up, essentially to cut corners. No, we can't do that, Hahn told them several times. We're talking about someone's life. We have to actually examine the application to make sure we're doing it safely.

A compassionate-use application doesn't require a patient's name. He or she can remain anonymous but the FDA needs all of the clinical information to make an assessment. Agency scientists have to make sure that the experimental medication won't react adversely with other medications a patient is on or cause problems because of the patient's underlying health conditions.

When Hahn later learned that the person the White House was trying to speed up the application for was the president, he was stunned. For God's sake, he thought, it's the president who's sick, and you want us to cut corners? Trump was in the highest risk category—at seventy-four, he rarely exercised and was considered medically obese; he was the type of patient who was most likely to die. As it did with all compassionate-use applications, the FDA made a decision within twenty-four hours. Agency officials scrambled to figure out which company's monoclonal antibody would be the best one given the clinical information they had, and decided on Regeneron's antibody treatment, REGEN-COV.

The White House physician, Sean Conley, would later tell reporters that on Thursday Trump had developed a mild cough, a stuffy nose, and fatigue. But in reality the president's condition that day had deteriorated rapidly. White House staffers didn't know for sure yet whether Trump had the virus, but they were shielding his symptoms and possible diagnosis from the public. That was why they had begun their frantic efforts to obtain every possible measure to treat him. It was only when news dribbled out in the early evening that Hicks was sick—an infection the White House had also tried to conceal from the public—that people began to speculate about the president himself.

At 9:00 p.m., Trump was patched in by phone to Sean Hannity's Fox News program. By that point, Bloomberg had reported that Hicks was sick, and everyone was waiting to see if Trump might be, too. No one knew what he would say. When Hannity asked about Hicks's status, Trump abruptly volunteered that he himself had been tested and was awaiting results (a handful of White House officials already knew the results of an initial test). The event with military families several days earlier continued to rattle him.

"I just went out with a test, because we spend a lot of time and the first lady just went out with a test also," he said, sounding uncharacteristically muted. "So whether we quarantine or whether we have it, I don't know. It's very hard when you're with soldiers, when you're with airmen, you're with the Marines and the police officers, I'm with them so much. And when they come over to you it's very hard to say, 'Stay back, stay back.' It's a tough kind of a situation. It's a terrible thing. So I just went for a test and we'll see what happens. I mean, who knows?"

Maybe Trump had in fact caught the virus from one of the military families. Or maybe he had caught it at the Supreme Court event (several other people who attended that day would test positive around the same time Trump became ill). The White House made no effort to try to trace its spread. Almost everything Trump did was a high-risk event; he could have caught it at any point.

At 12:54 a.m., Trump made it official in a Twitter post: he and his wife, Melania, had tested positive for coronavirus. "We will begin our quarantine and recovery process immediately. We will get through this TOGETHER!"

For months, Trump had dodged the virus. Taunted the virus. Flaunted safety protocols. Held big rallies and packed the White House with maskless guests. But finally, just one month before his reelection, the virus that had killed more than 200,000 Americans was now burrowed inside the most powerful person on the planet.

Only a few hours after his tweet, Trump became terribly ill. His fever spiked and his blood oxygen level fell below 94 percent, at one point dipping into the 80s. Conley, the White House physician, attended to the president at his bedside. An oxygen mask was strapped to Trump's face in an effort to stabilize him. The virus had made its way into Trump's lungs. For many septuagenarian Americans with COVID-19, the administration of supplemental oxygen marked the start of a rapid downward spiral.

The doctors gave Trump an 8-gram dose of two monoclonal antibodies through an intravenous tube. That emergency treatment was what had required the FDA's sign-off.

He was also given a first dose of remdesivir, also by IV.

Typically, doctors space out treatments to measure a patient's response. Some drugs, such as monoclonal antibodies, are most effective if they're administered early in the course of an infection. Others, such as remdesivir, are most effective when they're administered later, after a patient has become critically ill. But Trump's doctors threw everything they could at the virus all at once. His body was bombarded with multiple treatments less than twenty-four hours after he had tested positive. His condition appeared to stabilize somewhat as the day wore on, but, still fearing he might end up on a ventilator, his doctors decided to move him to the hospital. He couldn't stay at the White House any longer; it was too risky.

Many White House officials and even his closest aides were kept in the dark about his condition. But after they woke up to the news that the president had tested positive for coronavirus, cabinet officials and aides lined up at the White House to get tested. A large number of them had met with him the previous week to brief him about various issues or had traveled with him to the debate.

It was unclear even to Trump's top aides just how sick he was. Was he mildly sick, as he and Conley were saying, or was he sicker than they all knew? Trump was supposed to join a call with nursing homes later that day. Officials had been scheduled to do it in person from the White House, but that morning they were informed that the call would be done remotely. Trump's aides insisted that he would still be on the call.

As one aide waited in line for a coronavirus test, she saw Conley sprint out of his office with a panicked look on his face. That's strange, the aide thought. An hour or two later, officials were informed that Pence would be joining the call with nursing homes. Trump couldn't make it.

If there was one moment in 2020 when time seemed to stand still, it occurred that Friday evening at 6:16 p.m. That was when all the pain and agony and lies and desperation and confusion fused into one image that arrested the whole country, and even people around the world. All eyes were glued to the sight of one person walking alone. Was he walking with pride? Was he walking with shame? Was this how it would end, with some sort of Shakespearean death march? Would he ever be seen again?

It took Trump fifty-one steps to walk from the Diplomatic Reception Room, out the White House's southern door, to the giant green-and-white helicopter known as Marine One. He walked alone, carefully, slowly, in a navy suit with a navy mask pressed tight across his nose and mouth—a mask he rarely wore because he thought it made him look weak. But on that early Friday evening, on that walk to Marine One, it wore him.

Could the whole year have flashed before his mind's eyes during those fifty-one steps? He had seemingly fallen so far, so fast. He had forced world leaders to bend to his will and filled arenas with pulsating fans. He had shaken himself free of an impeachment and the betrayal of others. But he couldn't shake himself free of the virus, which had stealthily invaded his presidency like an invisible enemy, killing all those people, including his friends. And now it had somehow lassoed him, not just his reelection campaign but his body. He was physically weak, as weak as he'd been in years. It was a long thirty-second walk.

There were thirty-one days to go before the November elections. His indestructible veneer was gone. He had mocked the virus so many times, called it "the China virus," "kung flu," "the plague," "the sniffles." But viruses don't care about elections, politics, or powerful people; they just keep moving, looking for their next target.

Trump and his inner circle had been warned that this could happen. Given the way they were behaving, it was only a matter of time. It was hardly the first outbreak at the White House. Over the past eight months, Trump had come dangerously close to the virus a number of times, then somehow always escaped its grip. In February, he had been only one degree removed from a man at a conference who had tested positive. In March, he had come into contact with several people visiting him at Mar-a-Lago who were infected as well. Throughout the year, there had been a steady series of White House aides and staff who contracted the respiratory disease, bringing it closer and closer to the president. It had come so close to Trump so many times that it was beginning to look as though he had somehow outsmarted the microscopic villain that had destroyed the lives of millions of Americans.

The repeated escapes made the White House more careless, even brazen in tempting fate. Birx and Redfield wrote to top aides after every White House outbreak, warning them that 1600 Pennsylvania Avenue was not safe. Birx took her concerns to Pence directly. This is not safe, she told him. If you can't or won't wear a mask, you need to be more than ten feet away from people. This is just too risky.

Their warnings had gone unheeded, and now everyone had to pay the price. Trump didn't want to go to the hospital, but his aides had made clear what his choice was: he could go to the hospital now, while he could still walk on his own, or he could wait until later, when the cameras would capture him in a wheelchair or a gurney. There would be no hiding his condition then.

About ten steps along, he turned to the reporters to his right. He hated them. Loved them. Loved hating them. He gave them a thumbs-up with his right hand, then a thumbs-up again, then a half wave. He never raised his hand above his hip. He kept walking.

Twenty steps along.

Trump wasn't a *medical* guy; he had flirted with the idea that vaccines cause autism. He wasn't a *doctor* guy, either. His doctors in the past had had a tendency to gloss over his, well, health. His girth. Like the time in 2018 when the White House physician had said that he could live to be two hundred years old if he had a healthier diet.

He was about halfway to Marine One now. The whole South Lawn was before him. Thirty-six days earlier, he had jammed 1,500 people onto the lush green expanse. He had given his speech accepting the Republican nomination for president here for adoring fans dressed in red, white, and blue. They had cheered when he had stood before them on a stage. He loved crowds, and he loved adoration. He loved noise and primal screams. "Together we will crush the virus!" he had told them that evening, triggering a big round of applause.

Now the lawn was empty except for the helicopter. He climbed in and was gone, airlifted nine miles to the Walter Reed National Military Medical Center in Bethesda, Maryland, where Redfield, Fauci, and Birx had first trained.

At 11:31 p.m., the only sign of life came from Trump's Twitter feed: "Going well, I think!" it said. "Thank you to all. LOVE!!!"

Trump's condition worsened early Saturday. His blood oxygen level dropped to 93 percent, and he was given the powerful steroid dexamethasone, which is usually given if someone is extremely ill (the normal blood oxygen level is between 96 and 98 percent). The drug was believed to lower the risk of death in coronavirus patients who were receiving oxygen. The president was on a dizzying array of emergency medicines. It would have been exceptionally difficult for an ordinary patient to have had access to this combination of drugs. Most of them were in short supply or not yet available to the general public.

Throughout Trump's time in the hospital, his doctors consulted with the task force medical experts whom the president had long ago discarded. They talked to Fauci, Hahn, and Redfield, seeking their input and advice about his treatment. At one point Trump even called Fauci to discuss his condition and stress how great he thought the monoclonal antibody was that he had received. Trump added that it was miraculous how quickly it made him feel much better. White House aides may have disparaged Fauci and resented the fact that they could never get him to stay on script when he went on television, but he was still the doctor they all wanted when they got sick.

People all over the world were watching developments in suspense. Trump supporters set up camp outside Walter Reed, holding signs and praying for the president's recovery. They brought flowers and signs reading FEEL BETTER MR. PRESIDENT and TRUMP WAS SENT FROM GOD!

People close to Mark Meadows said that he was consumed with fear that Trump might die.

On April 3, 1919, another US president had become violently ill due to a global pandemic. He was Woodrow Wilson, who was in France to try to reach a deal with foreign leaders about the post–World War I global order.

He had spent much of the previous year trying to minimize people's attention to the flu, which had ravaged the United States and killed millions of people worldwide. He'd thought that too much attention to the flu outbreak would hurt Americans' morale during the war, and the government had pressured the news media not to cover it.

So when Wilson became sick, the White House revealed little about his illness, instead saying that he was overworked. In reality, he had a high fever and was hallucinating. The disease nearly killed him. Six months later, he suffered a massive stroke from which he never recovered. He finished his presidency essentially as an invalid.

———

Trump's condition was a complete mystery, and no one would give a straight answer as to how long he had been sick. (He had agreed to be tested before the presidential debate five days earlier, but no one would say if he actually had been.)

Conley held a press conference outside Walter Reed on Saturday morning and said that Trump was in "exceptionally good spirits" and was "extremely happy" with the way his recovery was progressing. That upbeat prognosis was strange, considering that Trump remained hidden from view inside a hospital. Conley refused to say how high his fever had been or when he had last tested negative for the virus. He also refused to disclose that Trump had received supplemental oxygen, claiming that he did not know if he had or not. He would later say that he had been trying to be positive so as to aid Trump's recovery; in other words, if he had been more truthful, it might somehow have led Trump to relapse and his condition to worsen. Those who were being briefed on Trump's medical condition were confused and disheartened by Conley's remarks. He was a good physician, they all knew, but the message was muddled, and his public assessment of Trump's condition was not reflective of the reality they were all aware of.

Meadows met with reporters right after Conley spoke and gave a more candid account of the president's condition but did so "on background," meaning that the information could be used but his name could not. "The president's vitals over the last 24 hours were very concerning and the next 48 hours will be critical in terms of his care," he said. "We're still not on a clear path to a full recovery."

But since he was speaking to reporters in view of television cameras, it didn't take long before everyone figured out that he was the "senior administration official" who was saying that Trump was not yet out of the woods. Other White House aides were mortified. The president was sick, and every day, another White House aide was testing positive for the virus. They were supposed to be convincing voters that they had the pandemic under control, that they could be trusted to lead and protect the country. But they couldn't even protect the president or keep their stories straight.

At least two of those who were briefed on Trump's medical condition that weekend said he was gravely ill, and feared that he wouldn't make it out of Walter Reed. He did continue to post on Twitter from the hospital, anxious to convey that he was upright and busy. He called for an economic rescue package and said that his condition was improving. In the Walter Reed presidential suite, he was joined by Jared Kushner, Meadows, and his social media director, Dan Scavino, all of whom wore N95 masks, eye shield glasses, and medical gloves.

It was unclear if one of the medications helped or the combination of them helped, but by Saturday afternoon, Trump's condition began improving. One of the people familiar with Trump's medical information was convinced that the monoclonal antibodies—a drug not yet available to millions of Americans fighting the virus—had been responsible for the president's quick recovery.

Throughout the day on Saturday, the restless Trump made a series of phone calls to gauge how his hospitalization was being received by the public. In all likelihood, the steroid he was on had given him a burst of energy, though no one knew how long it would last.

"This is like a miracle," Trump told his campaign adviser Jason Miller in one of his calls from the hospital. "I'm not going to lie. I wasn't feeling that great."

In order to show that Trump wasn't bedridden, the official White House photographer was summoned in the late afternoon. Two photographs of the president were released later that evening. In the first, Trump—tieless in a navy suit and white shirt—is seated at a circular wooden table, signing a piece of paper with a large black marker. In the second photo, taken just a few minutes later according to metadata imprinted on the image, he is at a different table, this time with his jacket off, reviewing a folder with the marker tucked between his fingers. His face is pinkish, and his golden hair is a bit wavier than normal. Trump is not wearing a mask in the photos, meaning that the White House photographer was highly exposed to the virus.

The photos looked completely staged. But they showed that he was upright and in a suit. He appeared to be on the mend. Later, the White House released a video of Trump speaking from the same chair as the one in the first photo. He appeared a bit winded, but he hinted that there might have been a divine intervention. "We're going to beat the coronavirus, or whatever you want to call it, and we're going to beat it soundly," he said. "So many things are happening. If you look at the therapeutics, which I'm taking right now—some of them and others that are coming out soon that are looking like, frankly they're miracles, if you want to know the truth. People criticize me when I say that, but we have things happening that look like they're miracles coming down from God. So, I just want to tell you that I'm starting to feel good."

Robert Redfield spent the weekend Trump was sick praying: praying that he would recover, praying that he would emerge from the experience with a newfound appreciation for the seriousness of the virus. He prayed that Trump would tell Americans how serious the coronavirus was and that he now understood that it does affect everyone. He prayed that Trump would tell Americans to listen to public health advisers. And he prayed that he would tell the public health advisers to take the lead in the government's response to the virus.

There were few signs that weekend that Trump would have a change of heart. It had already been a battle to get Trump to agree to go to Walter Reed in the first place. Now, Trump was badgering Conley and his other doctors to let him go home early. Redfield heard news that Trump was insisting to be discharged and immediately spoke to Conley on the phone. The president can't be discharged this quickly, Redfield advised Conley. Trump was a high-risk patient and there were no guarantees that he wouldn't have a second backslide, or some kind of organ failure. (That happened with many COVID patients—they seemed to be on an upswing, and then quickly deteriorated.) He needed to stay in the hospital until that risk had passed. Conley agreed, but said that the president had made up his mind and he couldn't convince him otherwise.

If they couldn't keep him in the hospital, the doctors hoped that Trump would at least emerge from Walter Reed a different president. The members of the doctors' group, all of whom spoke that weekend, shared Redfield's hopes. Some of the doctors even began mentally preparing to finally speak their minds, freed from the White House's shackles on their messaging. It would surely be the inflection point, they all thought. There's nothing like a near-death experience to serve as a wake-up call. It was, at the end of the day, a national security failure. The president had not been protected. If this fiasco wasn't the turning point, what would be?

On Monday morning, the White House was strangely quiet. Many staffers stayed home, either sick with coronavirus—including Press Secretary Kayleigh McEnany, First Lady Melania Trump, and senior adviser Stephen Miller—or afraid of becoming infected. Meadows had turned all of his attention to Trump, and the White House staff was mostly rudderless. Several White House aides felt frustrated and scared when they did not receive clear guidance from Meadows on how to protect themselves inside the West Wing or even on what they should be doing amid the outbreak. They were worried about the president's health, but they also saw the administration falling apart. Trump's reelection chances were slipping. His pompous taunting of the virus had apparently backfired spectacularly.

Shortly before Trump was taken back to the White House in Marine One, it became obvious that he had entered a new phase of the disease, the jubilant survivor phase. He acted as if he had whipped it, as if the virus stood no chance against someone as strong and tough as him. Never mind that he had had access to health care and treatments that few other Americans could receive and that Meadows and the White House apparatus had pulled strings for him in an unprecedented way. "Don't be afraid of Covid. Don't let it dominate your life," he wrote on Twitter. "We have developed, under the Trump Administration, some really great drugs & knowledge. I feel better than I did 20 years ago!"

Other Republican lawmakers followed Trump's lead, tweeting memes and pictures of Trump physically beating the virus. They were sending a dangerous, deeply insensitive, and patently false message: that only the weak succumb to COVID-19; the strong can somehow beat it back.

Just as the country had been watching a few days before, many people tuned in again as Trump took Marine One back to the White House's South Lawn on Monday night. They saw him step out in a navy suit, white shirt, and blue-striped tie, a medical mask on his face. He walked along the grass before climbing the steps to the Truman Balcony, just outside the Yellow Oval Room. That was where, six months earlier, Birx and Fauci had convinced Trump to stay the course and keep restrictions in place.

But Trump didn't go inside. It was a moment of political theater too good to pass up—as triumphant as his trip on Friday had been humbling. He turned from the center of the balcony and looked back toward Marine One and the television cameras. It was clear that he was breathing heavily from the long walk and climbing the flight of stairs. Redfield was watching on television from home. He was praying as Trump went up the steps. Praying that he would reach the top of the Truman Balcony and stress the importance of masks and social distancing. That he would show some humility and remind people that anyone could be susceptible to coronavirus—even the president, the first lady, and their son. But Trump didn't waver. Facing the cameras from the balcony, he used his right hand to unhook the mask loop from his right ear, then raised his left hand to pull the mask off his face. He was heavily made up, his face more orange tinted than in the photos from the hospital. The helicopter's rotors were still spinning. He put the mask into his right pocket, as if he was discarding it once and for all, then raised both hands in a thumbs-up. He was still likely contagious, standing there for all the world to see. He eventually raised his right arm to make a military salute as the helicopter departed the South Lawn, and then he finally turned and entered. He passed White House staffers on his way in, failing to protect them from the virus particles being emitted from his nose and mouth.

Right then, Redfield knew it was over. The "macho man" pose showed that Trump hadn't changed. The pandemic response wasn't going to change, either. It had been the best opportunity for a major course correction. And it had passed.

Now that he had survived COVID-19, Trump wasn't worried about it anymore. Instead, he became even more emboldened, more psychologically indestructible. "Now I'm better and maybe I'm immune," he falsely stated shortly after returning to the White House.

The same day that much of the country was distracted by Trump's discharge, Scott Atlas brought a friend from Stanford University and two others to meet with Azar at HHS. The friend was a doctor and professor of medicine, Jayanta Bhattacharya, who shared Atlas's view that the economic restrictions were doing tremendous economic and psychological damage to millions of Americans. Bhattacharya was one of the doctors Atlas regularly cited in his sparring matches with the task force.

The day before, Bhattacharya and two other doctors had met at a conservative institute in the western Massachusetts town of Great Barrington. There, they had issued a "declaration" that called for a renewed focus on two main ideas. First, the disease was deadly mostly for older people, not younger or even middle-aged ones (thus ignoring the tens of thousands of young and middle-aged people who had succumbed to the disease). Therefore they wanted a greater emphasis on protecting the most vulnerable, such as the elderly. Second, they wanted a greater focus on the consequences of keeping schools and businesses closed. They thought there would be devastating long-term costs associated with the prolonged shutdowns in the United States, something they blamed largely on Fauci and Birx.

They agreed that the primary goal of the response to the pandemic should be to reach herd immunity, as is the goal of the response to every disease. But in every other disease outbreak, herd immunity has been achieved through vaccination. In other words, they did not advocate for relaxing all restrictions and allowing the virus to pick and choose its victims. But by reopening more parts of the economy and allowing people who they felt were at low risk of mortality to circulate more freely, they felt, a greater number of people would build up immunity faster. (That was the approach Birx and most experts felt would slaughter older and other at-risk Americans because they would catch it from younger, stronger people.)

After they signed the Great Barrington Declaration, the three doctors drove to Boston and flew together to Washington. Bhattacharya had spoken with Atlas, and Atlas wanted the doctors to present their conclusions to Azar. Atlas had holed himself up in another HHS conference room after the meeting, and HHS officials walking by could overhear him bragging to reporters about the meeting and how they had put on a show.

When the meeting was set to begin, they marched into the wood-paneled conference room at HHS to make their case. "We are going to have a lost generation of kids," Bhattacharya told Azar. He said there were things the government could do to better protect the elderly, such as helping fund free grocery delivery for older Americans or paying for hotel rooms for older people who lived in multigenerational housing. Schools needed to reopen, they said. More children were dying of the flu in 2020 than of COVID-19 (which did not seem to be true). Keeping them home didn't make any sense. Atlas and the doctors present repeatedly said the goal was to have the US population build up enough immunity to the virus that they could move past this difficult phase.

There was a real animosity toward Fauci and his repeated warnings about reopening too quickly. "I think Fauci is blind that the lockdowns have a real cost," Bhattacharya told Azar.

Azar seemed attentive but also a little distracted. Some in the room wondered how much influence he had within the White House anymore. Still, they felt that he agreed with what they were saying. Unlike the doctors' group, Azar had been pushing a message more in line with Trump's: he advocated "the three Ws"—wash your hands, wear a mask, watch your distance—but also said that schools and businesses should reopen. They thought he appeared generally sympathetic to their ideas, even taking the unusual step of tweeting his support afterward by saying the meeting had been "part of our commitment to ensure we hear broad and diverse scientific perspectives." (Atlas and the other participants wanted to hold a news conference after the meeting, but Azar and his team would agree only to a tweet.)

Azar was one of the only people in the room wearing a mask. After Atlas led his group outside the building, HHS quietly sent a cleaning crew into the conference room to sanitize every square inch of space.

That night, Scott Atlas took the three doctors to dinner at the Trump International Hotel, where he was living during his time in Washington. The dining room was crowded, a common occurrence in the run-up to the election. As dinner concluded, they were each given a chocolate chip cookie, and then Atlas took them upstairs to another room. Atlas had arranged for the three doctors to be interviewed there by Fox News host Laura Ingraham, who was filming from a different location. Atlas wasn't just a neuroradiologist and Trump whisperer; he knew how to book himself and others on conservative cable television networks. He even knew how to arrange private rooms to set everything up.

And just like that, a day that Redfield and others hoped might mark the beginning of a much different approach to battling the virus ended with Atlas and three doctors in a Trump-owned hotel room telling millions of Americans on conservative television that they shouldn't be afraid of the virus, that they should go out and live their lives.

CHAPTER 21

JUDGMENT DAY

October 30, 2020
CONFIRMED US COVID-19 CASES: **9,000,000**
CONFIRMED US COVID-19 DEATHS: **229,293**

In October, the coronavirus began its third, terrifying advance. On the first day of the month, about 46,000 Americans tested positive for the virus. By the end of the month, that daily number had more than doubled, reaching almost 100,000. More than one person was falling ill every second. Someone died every minute and a half. Months beforehand, Donald Trump had promised that the virus would be gone when the air warmed up in the late spring. Then he had promised that the virus would disappear on November 4, the day after the election. But the virus was only strengthening, and the lax attitudes of many Americans enabled it to mount its most deadly assault yet.

The year was becoming one of the worst in US history, one of unending death and illness and tragedy and chaos. The constant turmoil of the Trump administration had exasperated so many aides and government officials that some privately hoped that enough Americans would decide that they couldn't take it anymore. In small, private discussions, certain aides would acknowledge the country couldn't withstand the drama and lack of policy-making process any longer. "Everything got subverted into the political morass," one senior administration official said. "What happens when you mix politics and public health? You get politics."

Since late January, the country had careened from one crisis to the next, with no breaks in between for Americans to catch their breath. Had the virus finally worn them out?

The president had tried to smother news of the virus's resurgence by claiming he had sparked a tremendous economic recovery. But that claim was fading, too. At the end of September, the airline industry announced that it planned to cut thousands of jobs because Congress had failed to pass another economic relief bill. Close to 1 million newly unemployed people each week were filing for unemployment benefits. More and more companies were being pushed to the edge of bankruptcy. Hundreds of thousands of people poured into food banks, wiping out their supplies. One in seven households didn't have enough to eat.

Before 2020, US citizens had voted in fifty-eight presidential elections. One had come during the Great Depression. Several had come during recessions. One had come during the War of 1812, another during the Civil War. There had been elections during World War II, the Korean War, and the Vietnam War.

But there had never been an election like this, during a global pandemic when people were afraid to leave their houses; when standing in line for hours with strangers could be a death sentence; when Americans were sick, scared, confused, exhausted, hungry, and—in many cases—penniless. Millions of Americans knew someone who had died. Millions of families had been ripped apart, deprived of the ability to kiss a loved one goodbye. It seemed like virtually everyone knew someone who had become sick. The virus was such a constant presence in American life that a record number of Americans refused to go to the polls on election day. But they still voted, casting their ballots early or through the mail.

There were several reasons why the virus was surging so aggressively in late October.

First, it feasted on Americans at bars, restaurants, and family gatherings as people headed indoors with the colder weather.

Second, Trump's escape from death in early October had prompted him to drop any pretense of battling the pandemic. He wanted packed, maskless audiences for his rallies and encouraged the masses to believe that they were invincible like he was. Many Americans followed their leader.

Third, the White House Coronavirus Task Force had mostly dissolved, and with it any semblance of a coordinated government response. The officials involved in the US pandemic response were scattered, doing their own thing, all delivering different messages, largely disconnected from one another in that perilous moment.

Olivia Troye, now on the outside, was campaigning vigorously for Biden, opening herself up to fierce attacks from Trump's inner circle and his supporters. They alleged that she had been fired (which she adamantly disputed) because she hadn't been capable of handling the rigors of the task force.

Robert Redfield had recently spent two hours on the phone with a former CDC veteran, who was begging him to resign for the sake of the agency and the country. Redfield was beaten down but refused to do any such thing. Instead, when he was asked to give his opinion on whether Mike Pence could safely participate in a debate given Trump's and other White House officials' diagnoses, he affirmed by letter that Pence did not need to quarantine. Once again, he got dragged into politics, to the dismay of public health experts.

Marc Short, Pence's chief of staff, boarded Air Force Two in the final days of the campaign, seemingly safe with a cadre of aides who had all tested negative for the virus. But one of those results was a false negative. The aide was sick and infected nearly everyone else, including Short, who would vanish from the campaign trail until the election was over, one of the White House's most forceful personalities forced to quarantine.

With Trump and Pence wholly focused on the campaign, there was little leadership coming out of the White House. That meant that some of Trump's aides back in Washington were left to their own devices, free to book themselves on television and do whatever else they saw fit to boost their own images and Trump's reelection effort. October was a mess of contradictions and controversies that no one could seem to keep up with.

FDA commissioner Stephen Hahn faced unrelenting pressure to authorize a coronavirus vaccine before the election, but he held firm and would not dilute the FDA's standards. Trump and his chief of staff, Mark Meadows, were still furious at the guidance the agency had publicized, which they believed had delayed the development of a vaccine. But Hahn didn't blink, even as Alex Azar participated in talks about the FDA commissioner's removal.

Azar did whatever he could to try to help Trump win reelection. Earlier in the month, he had said that 100 million doses of the vaccine would be available by the end of the year, a wildly aspirational figure. He eventually pared it down to 40 million doses, but Operation Warp Speed would fall far short of that goal, too, distributing about 4 million doses by early January.

Scott Atlas was on his own. In mid-October, he seized on a dubious study that questioned the effectiveness of masks in preventing the spread of coronavirus. He texted Jason Miller, Trump's campaign adviser, and asked him to share the paper on Twitter. Miller refused, believing the study to be faulty. Atlas shared it anyway.

"Masks work? NO," Atlas tweeted. Twitter took the unusual step of removing Atlas's tweet from its service, alleging that the neuroradiologist was spreading misinformation about coronavirus. He would later film an interview with RT, a Russian-backed television network that the US government had labeled "Russia's state-run propaganda machine." His appearance on a Russian disinformation network angered numerous White House aides and infuriated Trump. Their relationship would never recover.

Peter Navarro used his position as a senior White House official to launch a series of attacks on the Biden family in the final days before the election, veering far outside his job parameters. In an October 19 appearance with Maria Bartiromo on Fox Business, he said, "One of the things we need to be thinking about in the next fourteen days is the role of China in the world economy and who would stand up to China. We know who's laid down for China and now all this news about Hunter [Biden] and emails and all that stuff. You wonder why the mainstream media won't cover that, but my gosh, if any of that stuff is true it's just unbelievable."

The US Office of Special Counsel found that Navarro "engaged in prohibited political activity" and referred Navarro to Trump for disciplinary action, but the president never pursued it.

Meadows finally said the quiet part out loud on October 25 in a CNN interview: "We are not going to control the pandemic. We are going to control the fact that we get vaccines, therapeutics and other mitigation areas." (Anthony Fauci would later say "I tip my hat" to Meadows for admitting this.)

It was an honest acknowledgment of the White House's strategy in those final months. There was to be no effort to mitigate the spread of the virus. There was to be no promotion of mask wearing or social distancing. The government was going to let the virus run its course so as not to infringe on people's liberties. It was going to let the virus run its course in an effort to win the election.

US hospitals had 47,000 coronavirus patients at the end of October, up from 30,000 at the beginning of the month. States were running out of intensive care beds. With the virus moving like a wildfire, Trump made his last attempts to swat it away. On October 26, he tweeted, "We have made tremendous progress with the China Virus, but the Fake News refuses to talk about it this close to the Election. COVID, COVID, COVID is being used by them, in total coordination, in order to change our great early election numbers. Should be an election law violation!"

Fauci's name was invoked so often on the campaign trail that it was almost as if he were on the ballot. The Trump campaign even produced an advertisement that included a clip of Fauci taken out of context to make it appear that he was praising the president. When an angry Fauci asked for the ad to be taken down, the Trump campaign refused.

What the Trump campaign didn't know, however, was that Fauci was not done trying to stop the virus, even if it meant contradicting them. On October 26, the *Journal of the American Medical Association* printed a "Viewpoint" column by three doctors, one of them Fauci. The article made an aggressive case for the use of face masks in the United States, appealing to the nation's doctors to accept data showing that face coverings were effective in stopping transmission. Ten months after the virus arrived, the doctors said, a big change was still needed if it were finally to be whipped once and for all:

As countries around the world seek to safely reopen businesses, schools, and other facets of society, mask use in the community to prevent the spread of SARS-CoV-2, in conjunction with other low-cost, low-tech, commonsense public health practices, is and will remain critical. Return to normalcy will require the widespread acceptance and adoption of mask wearing and other inexpensive and effective interventions as part of the COVID-19 prevention toolbox.

That, of course, was the complete opposite of the message that Trump was sending in his rallies during the final days of the campaign, where he never appeared with a mask and people were packed together and screaming at the top of their lungs. (At an October 12 rally in Florida, he said he wanted to "kiss everyone in that audience. I'll kiss the guys and the beautiful women. Just give you a big fat kiss.")

Fauci, who was nearing his eightieth birthday, wasn't finished. On October 31, he gave an interview to the *Washington Post* and laid his frustrations bare, predicting that the country was "in for a whole lot of hurt": "All the stars are aligned in the wrong place as you go into the fall and winter season, with people congregating at home indoors. You could not possibly be positioned more poorly."

He then unloaded on the White House. He said that the public health team (himself, Deborah Birx, and others) had been largely ignored in recent weeks and that he wouldn't even set foot in the West Wing anymore because so many people there were infected. Trump hadn't spoken with Fauci since early October, when the president had been recovering at Walter Reed. He also said that the Biden campaign was "taking it seriously from a public health perspective." The Trump campaign, by contrast, was "looking at it from a different perspective." He said that Trump's focus was "the economy and reopening the country."

Fauci was a career civil servant who had studiously avoided injecting himself into politics, but here he was, in the final days before the presidential election, telling it like it was. White House deputy press secretary Judd Deere quickly excoriated him: "It's unacceptable and breaking with all norms for Dr. Fauci, a senior member of the President's Coronavirus Task Force and someone who has praised President Trump's actions throughout this pandemic, to choose three days before an election to play politics."

Trump's advisers were incredulous at Fauci's breach of protocol. "Fire that guy," Jason Miller told Trump and Meadows. "He sucks."

Around midnight the next evening, during a campaign rally in Miami, Trump stood before a large crowd, red MAKE AMERICA GREAT AGAIN hat pulled low over his brow. His speech was relatively low energy until Trump shifted to one of his favorite topics: media coverage of the virus.

"Fire Fauci! Fire Fauci!" the crowd screamed.

"Don't tell anybody but let me wait 'til a little bit after the election," Trump responded, smiling. "I appreciate [the advice]."

The following day, November 2, was election eve. Fauci had made his move. Now it was Birx's turn. Ever since Scott Atlas had arrived in late July, she had found herself sidelined. She thought the looming election was completely tainting the White House's approach to the virus, particularly its communications strategy. Realizing that she wasn't gaining any traction internally, she had leaned harder into her travels and her daily communications bulletins flagging the virus's spread. The tone of those reports became increasingly dire, warning of mass death and catastrophe if the country didn't revise its strategy. The report she circulated on November 2 struck a similar tone. She hoped that once the election results were in and tallied, the White House would pivot back to trying to contain the virus. "We are entering the most concerning and most deadly phase of this pandemic . . . leading to increasing mortality," she wrote in the report circulated throughout the White House that was obtained by the *Washington Post*. "This is not about lockdowns—it hasn't been about lockdowns since March or April. It's about an aggressive balanced approach that is not being implemented."

Her warning was clear: testing was falling in parts of the United States, meaning that it was impossible to know how bad things were becoming. And even though less testing was being done, the number of cases was still rising in 30 percent of US counties.

She wrote that it was "essential" that there be "consistent messaging about uniform use of masks, physical distancing and hand washing with profound limitation on indoor gatherings especially with family and friends." She was trying to convince top White House officials to change course before the deadly winter fully arrived, but they weren't listening. In fact, they were planning a huge indoor gathering for the very next day that would ignore every one of the safeguards that she was urging. The memo was a brutal assessment of the White House's failures in recent months. And it was leaked, out there for everyone to read, just hours before the final votes for president would be cast.

The 2020 election was a referendum on Trump and the virus, full stop. The unending pandemic brought all of his most alienating traits to the forefront, with deadly consequences: his disregard for science and experts; his penchant for governing by gut, impulse, and tweet. The other controversies—his taxes, impeachment, Russia—seemed to fall away. He had desperately tried to make the election about something else: tax cuts or the Supreme Court or law and order. But those topics had never held Americans' attention. One issue was dominating the country: the pandemic. In the final days before the election, both Trump and Joe Biden told Americans that the election came down to a choice of how they wanted to live their lives. And they were right.

Biden said that things were bad and likely to get worse, warning of a dark winter ahead that would require Americans to unify after all the pain and heartache.

Trump wanted Americans to share his insistence that the disease was about to disappear and there would not have to be more sacrifices. But that was what he had been promising all along: in January, then February, then March, then April, and again and again since then. He had always been wrong. Still, he said, the alternative was unthinkable. "Under the Biden lockdown, which he talks about and cherishes, countless Americans will die from suicide, drug overdoses and deferred medical care at a level like you haven't seen before. There will be no school, no graduations, no weddings, no Thanksgiving, no Christmas, no 4th of July, no Easter, no nothing. There will be no future for America's youth," he said at an October 30 rally in Minnesota.

It was the desperate rhetoric of an increasingly desperate president.

———

Even with all the early voting and mail-in voting, millions of Americans poured into the polls on the first Tuesday of November. The virus would not recede. COVID-19 deaths reached a daily record in the state of North Carolina. Pennsylvania reported its highest one-day increase, with 2,875 new cases. Hospitalizations in Indiana, Nebraska, and a number of other states neared capacity.

The mood in the White House was much different: jovial, care-free. That evening, Trump hosted a huge party in the East Room with roughly two hundred guests. Most of the women were dressed in red. The attendees drank wine, mingling face-to-face at tables covered with yellow tablecloths and vases with yellow roses. They huddled shoulder to shoulder beneath the giant crystal chandeliers. Two large television screens broadcast Fox News as the results slowly trickled in. Once again, the scene at the White House was disconnected from what was happening across the country, violating nearly every public health tenet of infection management.

Trump's campaign advisers were there. Trump's adult children were there. Meadows was there. Azar was there, too, the only one within sight wearing a mask, smushed amid throngs of carousing people.

The night was anticlimactic. Because of the huge number of Americans who had voted by mail and the fact that some states did not start counting mail-in votes until election day, it would take several more days to tally all the votes. When Trump addressed the East Room attendees at 2:30 a.m. on the morning after the election, he acted as if he had won. Azar was still among the crowd, standing and applauding enthusiastically. But Trump hadn't won; he had lost. More than 81 million people had voted for Biden, trouncing Trump by 7 million votes. An exit poll conducted by the Associated Press found that four in ten voters said that the pandemic was their top issue. The election produced the highest voter turnout in 120 years, with 66.7 percent of eligible voters casting ballots. People cared about the outcome of the election. To many, it literally felt like the difference between life and death.

Just as Trump had refused to accept the reality of the virus, he would also refuse to accept the outcome of the election. He would deny the results, and millions of people would believe him, as they had believed his false narrative about the deadly pandemic. There was one twist this time, though. His obsession with fighting the election results made him lose interest in one of his final campaign pledges: ousting Anthony Fauci.

The *Washington Post* and other news organizations waited until Saturday, November 7, to call the election for Biden. The former vice president had won Wisconsin, Pennsylvania, and Michigan, the midwestern states Trump had carried in 2016. Biden would end up winning Arizona and Georgia, too. In the end, the election wasn't close. Suburbs all over the country broke in Biden's direction. Trump's support among older Americans—those most at risk from dying from the virus—also slipped, delivering the final blow. Even though he had run his campaign on a promise to return everything to normal, the majority of Americans thought that Biden was best positioned to deliver that. Most people weren't going to be able to return to normal if they didn't feel safe going to the grocery store.

During the final campaign stretch, the rate of infection had picked up with terrifying velocity. More than 59,000 Americans had been hospitalized. There were more than 115,000 new cases each day, and more than 6,600 people died in the six days after the election. It was far worse than anything the country had experienced in the spring, when many people had united to endure a national shutdown.

The Monday after news organizations proclaimed Joe Biden the winner, Biden established his own coronavirus task force, made up of doctors and health experts. In response, Mike Pence called a meeting of his own. Reuniting the Trump task force, though, was like dragging out of retirement an old rock-and-roll band whose members despised one another and had planned never to see one another again. They gathered in the Situation Room, where they had spent so many days and nights in the past ten months.

Tensions were running high, with many pointing fingers over who was to blame for Trump's loss. The same day the election was called for Biden, the FDA received a call. Pfizer's clinical trial was complete, and the results were astonishing. Its vaccine was 95 percent effective in protecting against coronavirus. (The flu vaccine, by comparison, is usually around 40 percent effective. Pfizer's coronavirus vaccine was as efficient as the best childhood vaccines.)

By Sunday, the news had spread to the rest of the administration. Pence's team congratulated top Pfizer officials and joked that their results had arrived a week too late. But Meadows couldn't believe it and immediately suspected a conspiracy between the FDA and Pfizer.

"Look at what they did!" Meadows bellowed on the phone with FDA officials. "They held back these results! If they would have reported these, the president would have won the election."

FDA officials, of course, had no control over when Pfizer reported its results, because the company could report them only after a certain number of people in the trial had contracted coronavirus. No matter; Trump, Meadows, and several other top aides were convinced that the FDA and Pfizer had cost them the election, that the clinical trial results of a vaccine that wasn't being distributed yet would somehow have changed the voters' calculus. Trump also railed to his advisers about the "medical deep state" that had conspired to sabotage his re-election.

So at the task force meeting that Monday, the same day Pfizer publicly reported its results, several people were seething. Pence asked Hahn to explain to the group why there had been a perceived delay in Pfizer's reporting its results. Hahn explained that the FDA did not decide when the company reported its data and recounted the series of events leading up to that day. He also relayed a conversation he'd had with Pfizer's chief executive officer, Albert Bourla.

As Hahn spoke, Azar interjected about how the FDA had delayed the results. He reminded Hahn that the FDA's guidance to companies about needing two months of safety data had been the direct cause of the delay. He thought Hahn was downplaying the situation by saying the guidance had little or nothing to do with the timing of Pfizer's announcement. Hahn said that wasn't true. Hahn also told Pence he thought the FDA could approve the vaccine quickly, potentially within weeks. Azar jumped in again to remind the group that the FDA had taken a month on the application for monoclonal antibodies. The back-and-forth was excruciating for several people in the room to watch, and pieces of it quickly leaked.

Birx gave the final presentation that day. She knew the atmosphere was different now. The messaging had been strained for weeks because of the election. Top White House officials had resisted embracing a more aggressive response because of how it might play with voters. But that was all behind them, and there was no reason to hesitate anymore. They needed to act, once and for all. "Mr. Vice President, we are at a tipping point," she pleaded with Pence, urgency breaking into her voice. "You have to go out and say 'Wear a mask.' And if you don't, many people will die. And I can't say this more strongly." She added, "In Indiana, a lot of people are going to die unless you say it," calling out Pence's home state to resonate with one person she felt had always cared.

"Okay." Pence paused. "I'll talk to the president." It was the type of friendly dismissal that Pence had offered so many times before to members of the task force. He always listened and promised he would take their recommendations to the president. And they'd never hear about it again.

But Birx wasn't going to let it go. She shot back right away, "Those people only listen to you, Mr. Vice President, and the president. They don't listen to me."

The room froze. In two sentences, she had captured the whole year, the whole mess, the whole tragedy.

Those people.

The country had broken in two. There were "these people" and "those people." My people and your people. It had become impossible to coordinate a response to the pandemic because one group of people believed only one group of leaders and the other group believed only Trump. The dynamic had made the task force's job impossible and led to so much suffering.

The meeting ended. Trump had already shifted his focus to denying the election results.

Birx's plea went unanswered, but she was right. The death toll would be tremendous. Between election day and January 20, 2021, Trump's last day in office, COVID-19 killed another 160,000 Americans. Trump said almost nothing about the virus in those ten long weeks. The country would surpass 300,000 new cases and 4,000 deaths in a single day. Americans were dying faster than at any other period in US history. The virus barreled through Thanksgiving gatherings and Christmas dinners, seizing entire families. Still Trump said nothing, changed nothing. Some of the worst moments, Americans' grimmest days, came in that final, leaderless stretch. That was when many members of the Coronavirus Task Force were busy looking for new jobs, plotting their next steps. But 400,000 Americans would never take another step. They were gone.

EPILOGUE

There will be another pandemic. No one, of course, knows when. But there will be one.

And when that time comes, there will be a different government, and the makeup of the United States will probably be a little different, too. Maybe we won't be as divided. Maybe we will be.

The death of nearly 400,000 Americans in 2020, all at the hands of coronavirus, is one of the greatest tragedies in US history. More than 77,000 Americans died of the coronavirus in just December, more than the 58,000 who died over several years during the Vietnam War. Too many to mourn at once. How will we remember them? What did we learn? In some ways, several experts noted, the world got lucky with coronavirus. It was far less devastating in young people and could have had a much more vicious fatality rate. What would have happened with a virus with ten times, or more, the death rate? Like other tragedies that permanently reshaped our country, there are hard lessons as we try to rebuild and make ourselves more resilient.

The virus was always going to be an enormous challenge, no matter who was in charge. There were systemic issues that went underaddressed for decades that were always going to leave the United States underprepared in a pandemic event.

Before the pandemic, the United States did not prioritize investing in public health; these budgets have often been pitifully funded. One of the problems with public health is, if things are going well, no one knows it's there. A well-funded CDC and state health departments can help keep diseases at bay before they spiral out of control. The United States needs to invest in public health not only when disaster strikes, but when things are good, so disaster doesn't have to strike in the first place. This does not mean simply throwing money at states and federal agencies. It means these organizations and their overseers must be making smarter decisions. Questioning the status quo. Modernizing. Adapting.

There is a dearth of public health and biodefense expertise in the government, especially in the White House. The government simply is not well structured to quickly respond to an emerging pathogen. There was plenty of appreciation for the challenge a pandemic event would pose, but few structural or budgetary decisions made to make sure the country was prepared. "It's like mapping your training for a triathlon but not actually doing the training," said Luciana Borio, director for medical and biodefense preparedness on Trump's National Security Council until 2019 and a member of Biden's transition task force. "And then hoping on race day, it somehow comes together. You'll suffer a lot if you take that approach."

Having a national stockpile of expired masks and gowns is unfathomable in a country as wealthy as ours. And despite numerous hearings about reliance on other countries—especially China—for critical supplies and drugs, the United States never took serious action to protect its domestic supply chain. The country simply did not have the capacity to mass-produce personal protective equipment or medicines to slow the virus's spread. Years of off-shoring and globalization moved production of life-saving products and drugs overseas. When the pandemic struck, it was every-country-for-itself, and the US was caught flat footed. Fixing this will require difficult political and economic decisions.

These are issues that will need to be addressed across multiple administrations, with sustained focus. But the crisis, no doubt, was magnified by Trump's leadership and the myriad problems that stemmed from it.

"This would have been hard regardless of who was president," one senior official involved in the response said. "With Donald Trump, it was impossible."

There is no good time to face a public health crisis. But the coronavirus hit in a presidential election year, under a president uniquely ill-suited to lead.

Trump created an environment that preyed on a population with diminished trust. Trust in our institutions, trust in our state and federal leaders, trust in the media, trust in each other. Trump and many of his aides prioritized individual liberties over collective action that could have stemmed the spread of disease. Public health experts lament that masks became a political wedge, something that was exploited by the administration. Many Americans were unwilling to make small concessions and sacrifices for the collective good.

Fierce disagreements are normal and healthy in any administration. Trying to destroy each other or undermining each other is not. Officials tasked with caring for the public good cannot be looking over their shoulder, wondering if stating the truth or throwing out an idea that gets shot down is going to get them fired. If the members of the coronavirus task force did not trust one another, how could the American people trust them?

One of the biggest flaws in the Trump administration's response is that no one was in charge of the response. Was it Birx, the task force coordinator? Was it Pence, head of the task force? Was it Trump, the boss? Was it Kushner, running the shadow task force until he wasn't? Was it Marc Short or Mark Meadows, often at odds, rarely in sync? Ultimately, there was no accountability, and the response was rudderless.

It certainly did not help that the pandemic arrived in a presidential election year, something that colored every aspect of the administration's response. Ironically, however, Trump's singular fixation on securing a second term likely played a key role in his loss. Many of the president's top advisers acknowledged privately that they believe if Trump had been able to show a little bit of empathy and humility, recommended wearing masks, and generally appeared to take the crisis more seriously, he could have won. In an interview on Fox News about a month after Election Day, Trump's former campaign manager Brad Parscale (who was demoted in July 2020) said it out loud. "We lost suburban families," Parscale said. "I think that goes to one thing: the decision on COVID to go for opening the economy versus public empathy." Adding, "I think if he had been publicly empathetic, he would have won."

This obsession with the election also created an environment where the president and many of his aides were dishonest with the American public about the virus's threat, eager to demonstrate they had everything under control. This was a new virus for which there was no vaccine or treatments. Those early months, especially, when we knew little about how transmissible it was or exactly how it spread, were scary. Government and public health officials build trust by leveling with the public; they are supposed to be transparent about what they do and do not know, and reassure people that they are doing everything possible to protect them. There should be no shame for officials in saying there are things we simply do not know yet, especially with a novel pathogen.

But Trump concealed the true risk in order to try to puff up the stock market. And many of his aides were too timid to correct him. Even top health officials were afraid to speak the full truth in public, worried they could lose their jobs if they deviated from the president's message.

"The whole year was a lost opportunity to step up and be the nation we know we could be. Instead, we were divided and looked like a struggling third-world country trying to respond to this threat even though we had intellect, people and resources. We just needed leadership to pull us together," said Richard Carmona, the seventeenth surgeon general of the United States and a distinguished professor of public health at the University of Arizona. "There were blunted press conferences, accusations and using this terrible pandemic as a political device to divide the country further. It was the exact antithesis of what we needed."

Some health experts noted how remarkable it was that so little in the government's response changed from the 1918 flu pandemic. Many of the same issues resurfaced a century later: a public debate on masks, a president unwilling to level with the public, concerns over the effect public health measures would have on the economy, and a generally politicized response. In 1918 and 1919, President Wilson's dishonesty about the scope of the outbreak led to more sickness and more death. Lying about pandemics only kills more people. The truth might be hard to swallow. But it's easier to swallow than unnecessary death.

The coronavirus taught us that everyone has a role to play. The federal government must lead with honesty and integrity and respect for the scientific evidence. It is uniquely suited to break logjams, coordinate across states, and provide much-needed guidance in the face of a new virus. Not every aspect of the response was bad. Dozens of private companies stepped in and went above and beyond to try to help. Many government officials went far outside their remit to try to resolve problems, and stayed even when the environment became unbearable. Operation Warp Speed was evidence that with appropriate focus, leadership, and money, the government could execute on extraordinarily difficult tasks. But that was missing in nearly every other element of the response. Without leadership, states are left to fend for themselves and guess as to what is right.

But beyond state and federal leaders, each of us as individuals bears responsibility in doing what we can to keep others safe. Fighting a virus like this one is equivalent to fighting a war, health experts said. It is a moment to put partisan differences aside and rally together. How will we respond when the next pandemic comes? There will still probably be binge buying of toilet paper and hand sanitizer. But what then? Will we rally together? Will we sacrifice some things in order to get through it faster? Or will we turn on one another?

Storm state capitols? Yell at each other about mask mandates or refuse to cancel family gatherings?

"This was a common threat, but it was invisible," Carmona said. "To have the most senior of officials be able to articulate the most science-based coherent message and what we as Americans can do working together—not dividing us—but joining us to fight a common threat."

This book does not have a happy ending. But dozens of the officials we spoke to were motivated to tell the full, unvarnished truth to ensure this never happens again. To make clear to future generations the mistakes they made and the lessons learned in the hope that next time, we can do better. That the next pandemic has a better ending, one in which the nation rallies together to fight the pathogen, instead of each other.

ACKNOWLEDGMENTS

This book was a sprint. But we didn't run alone. There were so many people who ran alongside us, cheered us, fed us, and even carried us. We owe you so much.

First and foremost, we are forever indebted to our amazing editor, Jonathan Jao. We fell in love with you the first time we met you and believed deeply in the vision you had for this project all those months ago. You were our constant companion, propelling us while keeping us grounded. You pushed us for more and encouraged us to dig deep to tell the most vivid, unflinching story we possibly could. We can't imagine having done this without you. And the rest of the team at HarperCollins, it was such an honor to be your partners on this journey. Thank you for moving heaven and earth to bring this book to life.

To our agent, Keith Urbahn and the team at Javelin. Thank you for believing in us early in 2020, when the tidal wave had not even crested. You helped us see the historic moment we were entering. Your confidence in us gave us confidence in ourselves.

Julie Tate, you are the most eagle-eyed researcher, and we are thankful for the care you brought to this project. You elevated the entire book. You prevented us from veering into hundreds of ditches. You kept *Nightmare Scenario* from becoming, well, a nightmare scenario.

Marty Baron, Tracy Grant, and Cameron Barr blessed us with encouragement and the breathing room to wrestle this project to the ground. They expertly guided the *Washington Post* through this unprecedented crisis, ensuring we could all execute ambitious stories and scoops through less-than-ideal circumstances. We are also indebted to Steven Ginsberg, who played a pivotal role in focusing the *Post*'s coverage of the Trump administration and the pandemic. Thank you also to David Cho, Dan Clarke, Dan Eggen, Carol Eisenberg, Zach Goldfarb, Lori Montgomery, Steve Smith, and Krissah Thompson for their expert guidance through the crisis. We are so thankful.

Bronwen Latimer, you didn't even flinch when Damian breathlessly asked for assistance as the project neared completion. Thank you for helping make the final package sparkle.

Much of this project built on the incredible reporting of our colleagues. We are forever indebted to Josh Dawsey, Ashley Parker, Phil Rucker, Bob Costa, Lena Sun, Laurie McGinley, Carolyn Johnson, and dozens of others across the newsroom who relentlessly covered this story. And we owe a special thanks to Carol Leonnig and Phil Rucker, who were generous in sharing their own experiences in writing a book and guiding us through new terrain.

And finally, to the many sources who spoke to us, often at great personal peril, to help us give readers the most accurate account of what took place. We know this story was a painful one to relive, often several times over months. We know the sleep you lost and the heartache you suffered. Your candor and cooperation made this book possible. Thank you for trusting us.

Abutaleb

To my husband, Ibrahim. You encouraged me to take on this project from the very beginning. I was intimidated by it all, but you pushed me and believed in me and saw this for the incredible opportunity that it was. And through it all, you have been unwavering in your patience, kindness, support, and love. I am so lucky to have you.

To my incredible parents, Hanan Elbakry and Mohammed Abutaleb. You have always been my moral compass, my guiding light. You taught me the value of hard work and how to push myself well outside my comfort zone. More than that, you have been a constant safety net, a soft place to fall, and source of wisdom, advice, encouragement, love, and support. You have given me everything I've ever needed and more, and made this career in journalism possible. I cannot express how grateful I am every single day that I get to be your daughter. I owe everything to you. I love you so much.

To my siblings, Maryam and Ehab Abutaleb. You two have been my lifelong best friends. You have taught me the importance of hard work and passion, but also of letting go and enjoying everything life has to offer. You are always there to make me laugh and pick me up. I hit the sibling lottery with you two.

To Damian Paletta. You have been an absolute dream of a book partner. You inspire me with your passion for storytelling, creativity, and attention to detail. You have been a pillar of support and taught me so much through this crazy, stressful, amazing journey. It has been a privilege to be your coauthor.

To the many, many family and friends who have supported me and encouraged me at every turn. I am blessed beyond measure with more than thirty aunts, uncles, and cousins who have supported me at every step of my career. And to my in-laws, the Alkhalafs, for the kindness and love they've always shown me.

Rachel Roubein and I have been in the reporting trenches together for more than a decade. You have edited cover letters and resumes, listened to far too many complaints, allowed me to bounce ideas off of you, and been by my side for every major life event—including this one. Claire Silverstein and Steve Horn looked at numerous book covers, title pages, and designs and have been unfailingly supportive and encouraging. So have Sara Allen, Lauren Abdill, Yeganeh Torbati, and Eleanor Katz. I have been blessed with an incredible network of friends who long ago became family. There are many others.

To my *Washington Post* editors, Carol Eisenberg, Steve Smith, and Katie Zezima. You enabled us to do our best, most ambitious work and provided emotional support along the way, even as you dealt with your own hardships. Laurie McGinley, Lena Sun, Carolyn

Johnson, and Lenny Bernstein, my incomparable health and science team colleagues, have helped me adapt to the *Post* and were constant companions and confidants, even while we were all at home. And to the rest of my health and science team colleagues and friends: William Wan, Joel Achenbach, Ariana Cha, Amy Goldstein, Frances Stead Sellers, Karin Brulliard, Isaac Stanley-Becker, Fenit Nirappil, Dan Diamond, Akilah Johnson, and Ben Guarino. It is a privilege to work alongside you. Your work explaining this new virus and the government's response has been invaluable.

Josh Dawsey was my reporting partner in crime through all of 2020. You helped me understand how to cover the Trump White House, and I learned so much from your tenacity and drive. To Ashley Parker and Phil Rucker, thank you for your beautiful prose, calm under pressure, and guidance as we sought to make sense of an unrelenting news cycle.

There were many others in the *Post* newsroom who helped pull the best stories out of us and motivate us when we were at our low points.

Finally, there are two people who have had an immeasurable impact on my career. Deb Nelson led me through the first reporting investigation in my career, and remains a cherished friend and mentor to this day. The lessons you taught me guide my reporting today. Michele Gershberg took a chance on me as a college student and was my first editor. She helped give me the best possible training for the first six years of my career. A host of other editors and reporters at Reuters, my first professional home, taught me and elevated me. I am enormously grateful to all of them.

Paletta
To my wife, Colleen. You have always believed in me and encouraged me. I am forever grateful. I could never have crossed this finish line during the most trying year of our lives without your love and support. I am luckier today than the day we married.

To my parents, Blair and Chris. You have always pushed me to understand the difference between right and wrong, whether on the playground or in the White House. I am in your debt.

To Connor and Megan, our amazing kids, 2020 was so difficult and I will spend the rest of my days trying to make it up to you. You lifted me up. Your bravery during this pandemic was an inspiration and gives me hope.

My sisters Rachel and Lauren provided laughter and love (and maple syrup!) when I needed it most. Thank you.

And to Yasmeen, it has been one of my life's greatest honors to work with you on this project. Your passion for journalism and for truth kept me going. I am thrilled to have my name alongside yours in *Nightmare Scenario*. You were my best-case scenario.

I am so thankful for countless family and friends who put wind in my sails. Joe and Judy Doyle with their unconditional love and support. Lenny Scarola for being there when I needed you most. Tony Cremer for being a great companion on those weekend jogs through Old Town. There are too many others to name.

For my children's teachers, I owe you everything. For the complete strangers who tested my family for coronavirus on multiple occasions, putting themselves at risk, I salute you.

I am particularly grateful to my colleagues at the *Washington Post*.

The editors on the financial desk joined together and pushed through during a terrifying year. David Cho, Zach Goldfarb, Christina Passariello, Laura Stevens, Mark Seibel, Suzanne Goldenberg, Renae Merle, Ziva Branstetter, and Robbie DiMesio, I'm so honored to be your teammate. And there is no better partner than Jen Liberto, the *Post*'s deputy economics editor. Your calm hand steered our team through so much.

I am so proud of the *Post*'s economics team. You guys were champions during such a trying year. Erica Werner, Jeff Stein, Heather Long, David Lynch, Rachel Siegel, Tony Romm, Andrew Van Dam,

Eli Rosenberg, and Yeganeh Torbati. We covered this crisis with the relentless excellence it deserved. I will forever be thankful for our daily Zoom calls, when we bucked each other up and rallied for yet another day.

Everyone in the *Post* newsroom has made me better and covered this crisis with brilliance and passion. Thank you especially to Shefali Kulkarni, Lisa Rein, Kenisha Malcolm, Emily Tsao, Seung Min Kim, Anne Gearan, Maggie Penman, and Martine Powers. Dave Jorgenson, you kept us laughing and united during 2020, which—let's be honest—is a heck of a feat.

Also, my heartfelt appreciation to Barbara Vobejda, Scott Vance, and Tim Curran, who helped me see the scale of the crisis in early 2020 and then kept me going even when I didn't think I had anything left in the tank. I learned so much from you.

Finally, to my grandmother Marietta "Mappy" Forlaw and her sister Martha "Martie" Bynum, who grew up during the Great Depression.

You taught me the power of storytelling.

You taught me the importance of listening and troublemaking.

You taught me that life isn't fair, but that doesn't mean we have to sit idly by.

Mappy died peacefully in 2017. She was 97.

Martie also died at the age of 97, passing in November 2020. The cause of death was coronavirus.

NOTES

Chapter 1: The Invisible Enemy

13 *linked to a wet market*: "CHP Closely Monitors Cluster of Pneumonia Cases on Mainland," The Government of the Hong Kong Special Administrative Region, Dec. 31, 2019, https://www.info.gov.hk/gia/general/201912/31/P20 19123100667.htm.

19 *"We have it totally"*: Matthew J. Belvedere, "Trump Says He Trusts China's Xi on Coronavirus and the US Has It 'Totally Under Control," CNBC, Jan. 22, 2020, https://www.cnbc.com/2020/01/22/trump-on-coronavirus-from -china-we-have-it-totally-under-control.html.

Chapter 2: Like Water Through a Net

25 *Pottinger had an extraordinary*: Matt Pottinger, "Outraged Surgeon Forces China to Swallow a Dose of the Truth," *Wall Street Journal*, April 22, 2003, https://www.wsj.com/articles/SB105097464285708600.

29 *carrying 381,000 passengers*: Steve Elder et al., "430,000 People Have Traveled from China to U.S. Since Coronavirus Surfaced," *New York Times*, April 4, 2020, https://www.nytimes.com/2020/04/04/us/coronavirus-china -travel-restrictions.html.

29 *"Trump's demonstrated failures"*: Joe Biden, "Trump Is Worst Possible Leader to Deal with Coronavirus Outbreak," *USA Today*, Jan. 27, 2020, https://www.usatoday.com/story/opinion/2020/01/27/coronavirus-donald -trump-made-us-less-prepared-joe-biden-column/4581710002/.

31 *disregarded or downplayed more than a dozen*: Greg Miller and Ellen Nakashima, "President's Intelligence Briefing Book Repeatedly Cited Virus Threats," *Washington Post*, April 27, 2020, https://www.washingtonpost .com/national-security/presidents-intelligence-briefing-book-repeatedly -cited-virus-threat/2020/04/27/ca66949a-8885-11ea-ac8a-fe9b8088e101 _story.html.

32 *"This will be the largest"*: Michael C. Bender and Gordon Lubold, "On Coronavirus, National Security Threats, O'Brien Picks His Spots," *Wall Street Journal*, April 29, 2020, https://www.wsj.com/articles/on-coronavirus -national-security-threats-obrien-picks-his-spots-11588161602.

42 *"I want to stress"*: Ashley Parker, Josh Dawsey, and Yasmeen Abutaleb, "Ten Days: After an Early Coronavirus Warning, Trump Is Distracted as He Downplays Threat," *Washington Post*, Sept. 16, 2020, https://www.wash ingtonpost.com/politics/trump-woodward-coronavirus-downplay-ten-days /2020/09/16/6529318c-f69e-11ea-a275-1a2c2d36e1f1_story.html.

Chapter 3: Trapped at Sea

46 *called him "Mr. Wu"*: Karen Zhang, "Coronavirus: Hong Kong Resident Denies He Is 'Patient Zero' of *Diamond Princess* Cruise Ship Outbreak," *South China Morning Post*, March 12, 2020, https://www.scmp.com/news/hong -kong/society/article/3074698/coronavirus-hong-kong-resident-denies-he -patient-zero.

46 *"modern-day plague ship"*: Lauren Caruba, "Life Aboard a 'Modern-Day Plague Ship': *Diamond Princess* Passenger Quarantined in San Antonio Writes Book About Ordeal," *San Antonio Express-News*, Nov. 30, 2020, https://www.expressnews.com/news/local/article/Life-aboard-a-modern -day-plague-ship-15763659.php.

47 *And greeting them*: Jayne Orenstein and Monica Rodman, "What It Was Like for *Diamond Princess* Passengers During 28 Days of Quarantine," *Washington Post*, March 6, 2020, https://www.washingtonpost.com/travel /2020/03/06/what-it-was-like-diamond-princess-passengers-during-28-days -quarantine/.

48 *When Chinese researchers released*: Carolyn Y. Johnson, "Scientists Are Unraveling the Chinese Coronavirus with Unprecedented Speed and Openness," *Washington Post*, Jan. 24, 2020, https://www.washingtonpost.com/science /2020/01/24/scientists-are-unraveling-chinese-coronavirus-with-unprece dented-speed-openness/.

60 *forty were still detained there*: "Guantánamo Docket," *New York Times*, https://www.nytimes.com/interactive/projects/guantanamo/detainees/cur rent.

Chapter 4: Testing, Testing

67 *"It is time to reject"*: Mike Stobbe, "Health Official Who Urged Abstinence Says Views Have Changed," Associated Press, June 29, 2018. https://apnews .com/article/31efa34661ff48ffa30e488c013640b7.

68 *In testimony before Congress*: "Preventing Teen Pregnancy: Coordinating Community Efforts," Hearing Before the Subcommittee on Human Resources and Intergovernmental Relations of the Committee on Government Reform and Oversight, House of Representatives, April 30, 1996, 5.

68 *"by mutual agreement"*: Lyn Bixby, "Army's Top AIDS Researcher Transferred amid Controversy," *Hartford Courant*, June 30, 1994, https://www

.courant.com/news/connecticut/hc-xpm-1994-06-30-9406300185-story
.html.

70 *The fight to end*: Lindsey Bever and Lena H. Sun, "The CDC Director's Deeply Personal Reason for Fighting Opioids: His Son Nearly Died of an Overdose," *Washington Post*, July 17, 2018, https://www.washingtonpost.com/news/to-your-health/wp/2018/07/17/the-cdc-directors-deeply-personal-reason-for-fighting-opioids-his-son-nearly-died-of-an-overdose/.

71 *Senator Patty Murray*: Sheila Kaplan, "New CDC Director's $375,000 Salary Draws Scrutiny from Sen. Patty Murray and Others," *Seattle Times*, April 27, 2018, https://www.seattletimes.com/nation-world/nation-politics/new-cdc-directors-375000-salary-draws-scrutiny-from-sen-patty-murray-and-others/.

72 *In the early days of the outbreak*: Chad Terhune et al., "Special Report: How Korea Trounced U.S. in Race to Test People for Coronavirus," Reuters, March 18, 2020, https://www.reuters.com/article/us-health-coronaviruPs-testing-specialrep/special-report-how-korea-trounced-u-s-in-race-to-test-people-for-coronavirus-idUSKBN2153BW.

74 *"Clearly a success"*: "Transcript for CDC Telebriefing: Update on Novel Coronavirus," CDC, Feb. 12, 2020, https://www.cdc.gov/media/releases/2020/t0212-cdc-telebriefing-transcript.html.

Chapter 5: The Panic

88 *"When a country"*: Henry Farrell, "Donald Trump Says Trade Wars Are 'Good, and Easy to Win.' He's Flat-Out Wrong," *Washington Post*, March 2, 2018, https://www.washingtonpost.com/news/monkey-cage/wp/2018/03/02/donald-trump-says-trade-wars-are-good-and-easy-to-win-hes-flat-out-wrong/.

89 *But as the two leaders dined*: Ashley Parker, David Nakamura, and Dan Lamothe, "'Horrible' Pictures of Suffering Moved Trump to Action on Syria," *Washington Post*, April 7, 2017, https://www.washingtonpost.com/politics/horrible-pictures-of-suffering-moved-trump-to-action-on-syria/2017/04/07/9aa9fcc8-1bce-11e7-8003-f55b4c1cfae2_story.html.

90 *"Our door is open"*: Anna Fifield, "China Says the U.S. Is 'Holding a Knife to Our Neck' in Trade War," *Washington Post*, Sept. 25, 2018, https://www.washingtonpost.com/world/china-says-the-us-isholding-a-knife-to-our-neck-in-trade-war/2018/09/25/1d0d4f58-c0a6-11e8-92f2-ac26fda68341_story.html.

91 *On August 1*: David J. Lynch, Heather Long, and Damian Paletta, "Trump Says He Will Impose New Tariffs on $300 Billion of Imports from China Starting Next Month, Ending Brief Cease-Fire in Trade War," *Washington Post*, Aug. 1, 2019, https://www.washingtonpost.com/business/economy/trump-says-he-will-impose-new-tariffs-on-300-billion-in-chinese-imports-starting-next-month-ending-brief-cease-fire-in-trade-war/2019/08/01/d8d42c86-b482-11e9-8949-5f36ff92706e_story.html.

91 *"currency manipulator"*: Damian Paletta and Philip Rucker, "Trump Pressured Mnuchin to Label China 'Currency Manipulator,' a Move He Had Previously Resisted," *Washington Post*, Aug. 15, 2019, https://www.washingtonpost.com/business/economy/trump-pressured-mnuchin-to-label-china-currency-manipulator-a-move-he-had-previously-resisted/2019/08/15/b487bb2e-bf84-11e9-a5c6-1e74f7ec4a93_story.html.

92 *So there he was*: "Peter Navarro on How US Is Fighting the Spread of Coronavirus," *Fox News*, Feb. 23, 2020, https://www.foxnews.com/transcript/peter-navarro-on-how-us-is-fighting-the-spread-of-coronavirus.

93 *"For the American people"*: Evie Fordham, "Coronavirus Crisis Shows Pharmaceuticals Have Offshored Supply Chain, Navarro Says," *Fox Business*, Feb. 23, 2020, https://www.foxbusiness.com/markets/coronavirus-supply-peter-navarro-trump.

95 *"There is an increasing"*: Jonathan Swan and Margaret Talev, "Navarro Memos Warning of Mass Coronavirus Death Circulated in January," Axios, April 7, 2020, https://www.axios.com/exclusive-navarro-deaths-coronavirus-memos-january-da3f08fb-dce1-4f69-89b5-ea048f8382a9.html.

100 *"As more and more"*: "Transcript for the CDC Telebriefing Update on COVID-19," CDC, Feb. 26, 2020, https://www.cdc.gov/media/releases/2020/t0225-cdc-telebriefing-covid-19.html.

102 *"We believe the immediate risk"*: Erica Warner et al., "Coronavirus's Spread in U.S. Is 'Inevitable,' CDC Warns," *Washington Post*, Feb. 28, 2020, https://www.washingtonpost.com/us-policy/2020/02/25/cdc-coronavirus-inevitable/.

105 *Another was a funeral*: Haisten Willis and Vanessa Williams, "A Funeral Is Thought to Have Sparked a Covid-19 Outbreak in Albany, Ga.—and Led to Many More Funerals," *Washington Post*, April 4, 2020, https://www.washingtonpost.com/politics/a-funeral-sparked-a-covid-19-outbreak--and-led-to-many-more-funerals/2020/04/03/546fa0cc-74e6-11ea-87da-77a8136c1a6d_story.html.

106 *New Orleans would soon see*: Katy Reckdahl, Campbell Robertson, and Richard Faussett, "New Orleans Faces a Virus Nightmare, and Mardi Gras May Be Why," *New York Times*, March 26, 2020, https://www.nytimes.com/2020/03/26/us/coronavirus-louisiana-new-orleans.html.

106 *"We sit there"*: Kevin Breuninger, "Media's Coronavirus Stories Trying to Hurt Trump, Mick Mulvaney Says as He Urges Public to Turn Off TV," CNBC, Feb. 28, 2020, https://www.cnbc.com/2020/02/28/trump-chief-of-staff-mulvaney-suggests-people-ignore-coronavirus-news-to-calm-markets.html.

107 *"We are urging Americans"*: "Donald Trump Delivers a Speech at the 2020 CPAC Convention in Maryland—Feb. 29, 2020," Factbase, https://factba.se/transcript/donald-trump-speech-cpac-2020-national-harbor-maryland-february-29-2020.

Chapter 6: The Shutdown

114 *"Anybody that wants a test"*: "President Trump Visits Centers for Disease Control and Prevention," C-SPAN, March 6, 2020, https://www.c-span.org /video/?470138-1/cdc-send-million-coronavirus-testing-kits-week.

115 *"Happy birthday to you!"*: Emily Goodin, "Kimberly Guilfoyle Celebrates Her 51th at Lavish Mar-a-Lago Birthday Bash as Trump Loudly Sings Happy Birthday Before the Former Fox News Presenter Shows Off Her Dance Moves with Beau Don Jr.," *Daily Mail*, March 8, 2020, https://www.dailymail. co.uk/news/article-8088531/Kimberly-Guilfoyle-celebrates-50th-lavish-Mar -Lago-birthday-bash.html.

122 *More than 1.8 million people*: Greg Miller, Josh Dawsey, and Aaron C. Davis, "One Final Viral Infusion: Trump's Move to Block Travel from Europe Triggered Chaos and a Surge of Passengers from the Outbreak's Center," *Washington Post*, May 23, 2020, https://www.washingtonpost.com/world /national-security/one-final-viral-infusion-trumps-move-to-block-travel -from-europe-triggered-chaos-and-a-surge-of-passengers-from-the-out breaks-center/2020/05/23/64836a00-962b-11ea-82b4-c8db161ff6e5_story.html.

125 *"I am confident"*: "Read President Trump's Speech on Coronavirus Pandemic: Full Transcript," *New York Times*, March 11, 2020, https://www.ny times.com/2020/03/11/us/politics/trump-coronavirus-speech.html.

126 *Studies later found*: Carl Zimmer, "Most New York Coronavirus Cases Came from Europe, Genomes Show," *New York Times*, April 8, 2020, https://www .nytimes.com/2020/04/08/science/new-york-coronavirus-cases-europe-ge nomes.html.

129 *"This afternoon, we're announcing"*: "President Trump with Coronavirus Task Force Briefing," C-SPAN, March 16, 2020, https://www.c-span.org /video/?470396-1/president-trump-coronavirus-task-force-issue-guidelines -public.

Chapter 7: Dr. Birx

132 *"WE CANNOT LET"*: Aaron Blake, "Trump Flirts with a Less-Aggressive Coronavirus Response, Echoing Fox News," *Washington Post*, March 23, 2020, https://www.washingtonpost.com/politics/2020/03/23/trump-flirts -with-less-aggressive-coronavirus-response-echoing-fox-news/.

132 *"You are going to lose"*: Annie Kari and Donald G. McNeil, Jr., "Trump Wants U.S. 'Opened Up' by Easter, Despite Health Officials' Warnings," *New York Times*, March 24, 2020, https://www.nytimes.com/2020/03/24/us/pol itics/trump-coronavirus-easter.html.

133 *"Easter is a very special day"*: "Remarks by President Trump, Vice President Pence, and Members of Coronavirus Task Force in Press Briefing," The White House, March 24, 2020, https://trumpwhitehouse.archives.gov/briefings -statements/remarks-president-trump-vice-president-pence-members-corona virus-task-force-press-briefing-10/.

135 *"Third is all right"*: Claudia Vargas and Ellie Rushing, "From Pa. Science Fairs to Coronavirus Response Coordinator: Deborah Birx's Path to the White House," *Philadelphia Inquirer*, March 30, 2020, https://www.inquirer.com/news/nation-world/deborah-birx-white-house-coronavirus-task-force-trump-carlisle-20200330.html.

135 *When she was giving birth*: John Kerry, "Remarks at Swearing-In Ceremony for Ambassador-at-Large and Coordinator of the USG Activities to Combat HIV/AIDS Deborah Birx," U.S. Department of State, April 25, 2014, https://web.archive.org/web/20140720121311/http:/www.state.gov/secretary/remarks/2014/04/225218.htm.

137 *"more freedom to research"*: "Statement of LTC Deborah Birx," Nov. 19, 1992, Jon Cohen AIDS Research Collection, University of Michigan, https://quod.lib.umich.edu/c/cohenaids/5571095.0466.008?rgn=main;view=fulltext.

137 *Birx stood by him*: Ibid.

139 *In an audit of PEPFAR*: "Audit of the Department of State's Coordination and Oversight of the U.S. President's Emergency Plan for AIDS Relief," Office of Inspector General, U.S. Department of State, Feb. 2020, https://www.stateoig.gov/system/files/aud-si-20-17.pdf.

145 *"He's been so attentive"*: Darragh Roche, "Dr. Birx Unbelievably Claims Trump Is 'Attentive to the Scientific Literature and the Details," Politicus-USA, March 27, 2020, https://www.politicususa.com/2020/03/27/dr-birx-claims-trump-is-attentive-to-the-scientific-literature-and-the-details-of-covid-19.html.

145 *"So that's almost 40%"*: Eugene Kiely and Lori Robertson, "Birx Spins 'Extraordinarily Low Numbers' of Coronavirus Cases," Factcheck.org, March 27, 2020, https://www.factcheck.org/2020/03/birx-spins-extraordinarily-low-numbers-of-coronavirus-cases/.

149 *one of Trump's closest friends*: Katharine Q. Seelye, "Stanley Chera, Developer and Friend of Trump, Dies at 77," *New York Times*, April 17, 2020, https://www.nytimes.com/2020/04/17/us/stanley-chera-dead-coronavirus.html.

149 *"I tested positive"*: Donald J. Trump, "Remarks and a Question-and-Answer Session at a Fox News Virtual Town Hall," The American Presidency Project, May 3, 2020, https://www.presidency.ucsb.edu/documents/remarks-and-question-and-answer-session-fox-news-virtual-town-hall.

Chapter 8: Dr. Fauci

153 *They had met just once*: Donald G. McNeil, Jr., "Fauci on What Working for Trump Was Really Like," *New York Times*, Jan. 24, 2021, https://www.nytimes.com/2021/01/24/health/fauci-trump-covid.html.

154 *But social media were swamped*: Davey Alba and Sheera Frenkel, "Medical Expert Who Corrects Trump Is Now a Target of the Far Right," *New York*

Times, March 28, 2020, https://www.nytimes.com/2020/03/28/technology /coronavirus-fauci-trump-conspiracy-target.html.

158 *He ended up curing vasculitis*: Dave Davies, "Long Before COVID-19, Dr. Anthony Fauci 'Changed Medicine in America Forever,'" NPR, April 16, 2020, https://www.npr.org/sections/health-shots/2020/04/16/834873162 /long-before-covid-19-dr-tony-fauci-changed-medicine-in-america-forever.

165 *"I convinced him"*: Annie Maccoby Berglof, "Ebola's Worst Enemy: Disease Control Expert Dr Anthony S Fauci," *Financial Times*, Jan. 30, 2015, https:// www.ft.com/content/fc531c14-a2f6-11e4-9c06-00144feab7de.

166 *"So you're talking"*: Aaron Blake, "Trump's Baffling Coronavirus Vaccine Event," *Washington Post*, March 3, 2020, https://www.washingtonpost.com /politics/2020/03/03/trumps-baffling-coronavirus-vaccine-event/.

167 *But in late March*: Isaac Stanley-Becker, Yasmeen Abutaleb, and Devlin Barrett, "Anthony Fauci's Security Is Stepped Up as Doctor and Face of US Coronavirus Response Receives Threats," *Washington Post*, April 1, 2020, https://www.washingtonpost.com/politics/anthony-faucis-security-is -stepped-up-as-doctor-and-face-of-us-coronavirus-response-receives-threats /2020/04/01/ff861a16-744d-11ea-85cb-8670579b863d_story.html.

169 *"could have saved lives"*: Katie Shepherd, John Wagner, and Felicia Sonmez, "White House Denies Trump Is Considering Firing Fauci Despite His Retweet of a Hashtag Calling for His Ouster," *Washington Post*, April 13, 2020, https://www.washingtonpost.com/nation/2020/04/13/trump-fire-fauci -coronavirus/.

Chapter 9: Of Masks and Men

177 *"If you look"*: Jayne O'Donnell, "Top Disease Official: Risk of Coronavirus in USA Is 'Minuscule'; Skip Mask and Wash Hands," *USA Today*, Feb. 17, 2020, https://www.usatoday.com/story/news/health/2020/02/17/nih-disease -official-anthony-fauci-risk-of-coronavirus-in-u-s-is-minuscule-skip-mask -and-wash-hands/4787209002/.

177 *"Seriously people"*: John Bacon, "'Seriously People—STOP BUYING MASKS!': Surgeon General Says They Won't Protect from Coronavirus," *Florida Times-Union*, March 2, 2020, https://www.jacksonville.com/story /news/healthcare/2020/03/02/seriously-people---stop-buying-masks-sur geon-general-says-they-wont-protect-from-coronavirus/112244966/.

178 *"There's no reason"*: Saranac Hale Spencer, "Outdated Fauci Video on Face Masks Shared Out of Context," FactCheck.org, May 19, 2020, https://www .factcheck.org/2020/05/outdated-fauci-video-on-face-masks-shared-out-of -context/.

179 *In late January*: Camilla Rothe et al., "Transmission of 2019-cCoV Infection from an Asymptomatic Sontact in Germany," *New England Journal of Medi- cine*, Jan. 30, 2020, https://www.nejm.org/doi/full/10.1056/NEJMc2001468.

181 *a person who didn't*: J. Alexander Navarro, "Mask Resistance During a Pan-

demic Isn't New—in 1918 Many Americans Were 'Slackers,'" The Conversation, July 30, 2020, https://theconversation.com/mask-resistance-during-a -pandemic-isnt-new-in-1918-many-americans-were-slackers-141687.

181 *"Three Shot in Struggle"*: "Three Shot in Struggle with Mask Slacker," *San Francisco Chronicle*, Oct. 29, 1918, Influenza Encyclopedia, https://quod.lib .umich.edu/cgi/t/text/idx/f/flu/0030flu.0009.300/1/--three-shot-in-struggle -with-mask-slacker?rgn=full+text;view=image;q1=Place+--+San+Fran cisco%2C+California.

181 *"San Francisco Joyously Discards"*: Grack Hauck, "Celebrating Thanksgiving amid a Pandemic. Here's How We Did It in 1918—and What Happened Next," *Lubbock Avalanche-Journal*, Nov. 25, 2020, https://www.lubbockon line.com/story/news/2020/11/25/celebrating-thanksgiving-amid-pandemic -heres-how-we-did-1918-and-what-happened-next/6401563002/.

182 *And only two years*: Denise Grady, "Deadly Germ Research Is Shut Down at Army Lab over Safety Concerns," *New York Times*, April 5, 2019, https:// www.nytimes.com/2019/08/05/health/germs-fort-detrick-biohazard.html.

192 *"It's not racist at all"*: Quint Forgey, "Trump on 'Chinese Virus' Label: 'It's Not Racist at All,'" *Politico*, March 18, 2020, https://www.politico.com /news/2020/03/18/trump-pandemic-drumbeat-coronavirus-135392.

192 *"We continue our relentless effort"*: Donald J. Trump, "Remarks at a White House Coronovirus Task Force Press Briefing," GovInfo, March 19, 2020, https://www.govinfo.gov/content/pkg/DCPD-202000174/html/DCPD -202000174.htm.

192 *"I'd like to begin"*: "Remarks by President Trump, Vice President Pence, and Members of the Coronavirus Task Force in Press Briefing," The White House, March 20, 2020, https://trumpwhitehouse.archives.gov/briefings-statements /remarks-president-trump-vice-president-pence-members-c-oronavirus-task -force-press-briefing/.

192 *"As we continue"*: "Trump Promises to Roll Out National Guard," Yahoo! News, March 23, 2020, https://news.yahoo.com/trump-promises-roll-na tional-guard-060324604.html.

Chapter 10: "Liberate"

198 *"There's a debate"*: Salvador Rizzo, "Four Pinocchios for Trump's Claim That He Has 'Total Authority" Over the States," *Washington Post*, April 14, 2020, https://www.washingtonpost.com/politics/2020/04/14/four-pinoc chios-trumps-claim-that-he-has-total-authority-over-states/.

198 *Up to that point*: Philip Rucker, Josh Dawsey, and Yasmeen Abutaleb, "As Testing Outcry Mounts, Trump Cedes to States in Announcing Guidelines for Slow Reopening," *Washington Post*, April 16, 2020, https://www.wash ingtonpost.com/politics/as-testing-outcry-mounts-trump-cedes-to-states-in -announcing-guidelines-for-slow-reopening/2020/04/16/202ec300-7ffa-11ea -8013-1b6da0e4a2b7_story.html.

200 *"The media & Govt."*: Paul Egan and Kara Berg, "Thousands Converge on

Lansing to Protest Whitmer's Stay Home Order," *Detroit Free Press*, April 15, 2020, https://www.freep.com/story/news/local/michigan/2020/04/15/lansing -capitol-protest-michigan-stay-home-order/5136842002/.

200 *"They believe we should"*: John P. Wise, "'We Want to Work'—Protesters Disrupt Beshear's Daily Coronavirus Briefing," WAVE3 News, April 15, 2020, https://www.wave3.com/2020/04/15/we-want-work-protesters-disrupt -beshears-daily-coronavirus-briefing/.

203 *"You're going to call"*: Philip Rucker, Josh Dawsey, and Yasmeen Abutaleb, "As Testing Outcry Mounts, Trump Cedes to States in Announcing Guidelines for Slow Reopening," *Washington Post*, April 16, 2020, https://www .washingtonpost.com/politics/as-testing-outcry-mounts-trump-cedes-to -states-in-announcing-guidelines-for-slow-reopening/2020/04/16/202ec300 -7ffa-11ea-8013-1b6da0e4a2b7_story.html.

205 *"Fire Fauci!"*: Alison Medley, "Houston Coronavirus Updates: What You Need to Know About April 18," *Houston Chronicle*, April 19, 2020, https:// www.chron.com/local/article/Houston-coronavirus-updates-What-you -need-to-15209955.php.

207 *"I want him to do"*: Rick Rojas, "Trump Criticizes Georgia Governor for Decision to Reopen State," *New York Times*, April 22, 2020, https://www .nytimes.com/2020/04/22/us/trump-georgia-governor-kemp-coronavirus .html.

212 *"slap Gretchen Whitmer"*: Aaron C. Davis et al., "Alleged Michigan Plotters Attended Multiple Anti-lockdown Protests, Photos and Videos Show," *Washington Post*, Nov. 1, 2020, https://www.washingtonpost.com/investigations /2020/11/01/michigan-kidnapping-plot-coronavirus-lockdown-whitmer /?arc404=true.

213 *"judgment day"*: Abigail Censky, "Heavily Armed Protesters Gather Again at Michigan Capitol to Decry Stay-at-Home Order," NPR, May 14, 2020, https://www.npr.org/2020/05/14/855918852/heavily-armed-protesters -gather-again-at-michigans-capitol-denouncing-home-order.

213 *"The Governor of Michigan"*: "Trump Tweets Whitmer 'Should Give a Little, and Put Out the Fire," WXYZ Detroit, May 1, 2020, https://www.wxyz .com/news/coronavirus/trump-tweets-whitmer-should-give-a-little-and-put -out-the-fire.

Chpter 11: Pharmacist in Chief

217 *"The monster is still loose"*: Victor Garcia, "Gov. Mike DeWine on Reopening Ohio Economy: 'The Monster Is Still Loose and It's Going to Be Out There,'" Fox News, April 7, 2020, https://www.foxnews.com/media/mike -dewine-ohio-economy-reopening.

218 *New York City sets up*: Alan Feuer and Andrea Salcedo, "New York City Deploys 45 Mobile Morgues as Virus Strains Funeral Homes," *New York Times*, April 2, 2020, https://www.nytimes.com/2020/04/02/nyregion/coronavirus -new-york-bodies.html.

218 *Lorna Breen*: Corina Knoll, Ali Watkins, and Michael Rothfeld, "'I Couldn't Do Anything.' The Virus and an ER Doctor's Suicide," *New York Times*, July 11, 2020, https://www.nytimes.com/2020/07/11/nyregion/lorna-breen -suicide-coronavirus.html.

218 *People protest the presence*: Joe M. Murphy and Corky Siemaszko, "Florida Sets Death Toll Record, While Trailer Truck Outside Funeral Home Raises COVID-19 Fears," NBC News, July 28, 2020, https://www.nbcnews.com /news/us-news/florida-sets-grim-death-toll-record-while-trailer-truck-out side-n1235109.

218 *The state of Minnesota purchases*: "Minnesota Buys Former Bix Produce Building in St. Paul to Potentially Store Bodies," Fox9 KMSP, May 19, 2020, https://www.fox9.com/news/minnesota-buys-former-bix-produce-building -in-st-paul-to-potentially-store-bodies.

218 *Many Catholic priests administer*: Daniel Burke, "Coronavirus Preys on What Terrifies Us: Dying Alone," CNN, March 29, 2020, https://www.cnn .com/2020/03/29/world/funerals-dying-alone-coronavirus/index.html.

218 *In order to make room*: Brahm Resnick, "22 Bodies Moved into Rented Coolers as Maricopa County's Climbing Death Rate Puts Stress on Funeral Homes," 12 News, Aug. 5, 2020, https://www.12news.com/article/news /local/valley/22-bodies-moved-into-rented-coolers-as-maricopa-countys -climbing-death-rate-puts-stress-on-funeral-homes/75-cbad55cd-9911-4813 -8235-f120f6a26cd9.

218 *St. Louis officials spend*: "St. Louis County's $2 Million Temporary Morgue for COVID-19 Victims Is Closing," KMOV4, Aug. 24, 2020, https://www .kmov.com/news/st-louis-countys-2-million-temporary-morgue-for-covid-19 -victims-is-closing/article_dd849ef8-e63d-11ea-bafb-73706ed81a2e.html.

218 *Two trucks parked outside*: Alan Feuer, Ashley Southall, and Michael Gold, "Dozens of Decomposing Bodies Found in Trucks at Brooklyn Funeral Home," *New York Times*, April 29, 2020, https://www.nytimes.com/2020 /04/29/nyregion/bodies-brooklyn-funeral-home-coronavirus.html.

219 *On Sunday, April 26*: Jaclyn Reiss, "Sunday's Boston Globe Runs 21 Pages of Death Notices as Coronavirus Continues to Claim Lives," *Boston Globe*, April 26, 2020, https://www.bostonglobe.com/2020/04/26/nation/sundays -boston-globe-runs-21-pages-death-notices-coronavirus-continues-claim -lives/.

219 *Fifty freezer trucks*: Paul Berger, "NYC Dead Stay in Freezer Trucks Set Up During Spring COVID-19 Surge," *Wall Street Journal*, Nov. 22, 2020, https://www.wsj.com/articles/nyc-dead-stay-in-freezer-trucks-set-up-during -spring-covid-19-surge-11606050000.

219 *More than two thousand*: W. J. Hennigan, "Lost in the Pandemic: Inside New York City's Mass Graveyard on Hart Island," *Time*, Nov. 18, 2020, https:// time.com/5913151/hart-island-covid/.

219 *After 58,000 Americans have died*: Mark Maremont, "U.S. Buys 100,000 More Body Bags, Preparing for Coronavirus Worst," *Wall Street Journal*, April 29, 2020, https://www.wsj.com/articles/u-s-buys-more-body-bags-pre paring-for-worst-case-cornavirus-scenario-11588172780.

219 *The state of Maryland uses*: Bruce Leshan, "Ice Rink Converted to Morgue During Pandemic Preparing to Reopen as Skating Rink," WUSA9, Aug. 25, 2020, https://www.wusa9.com/article/news/health/coronavirus/ice-rink-used-as-morgue-during-covid-19-pandemic-prepares-to-reopen-for-skating/65-5091e28b-f5f6-47a5-b87a-122ad6b82587.

219 *The city of Chicago uses*: Omar Jiminez, "Inside Chicago's Refrigerated Warehouse for Bodies," CNN, April 9, 2020, https://www.cnn.com/2020/04/09/us/inside-chicago-refrigerated-warehouse-bodies/index.html.

219 *A seventy-six-year-old California woman*: Susanne Rust and Carolyn Cole, "She Got Coronavirus at a Funeral and Died. Her Family Honored Her with a Drive-Up Service," *Los Angeles Times*, April 8, 2020, https://www.latimes.com/california/story/2020-04-08/coronavirus-drive-by-funeral-woman-previously-infected-at-funeral.

219 *After Washington state bans*: Brendan Kiley, "Honor the Dead, Protect the Living: Coronavirus-Era Funeral Bans Make a Tough Time Even Tougher," *Seattle Times*, March 29, 2020, https://www.seattletimes.com/seattle-news/honor-the-dead-protect-the-living-coronavirus-era-funeral-bans-make-a-tough-time-even-tougher/.

219 *The 15 percent jump*: Mike Stobbe, "US Deaths in 2020 Top 3 Million, by Far Most Ever Counted," Associated Press, Dec. 22, 2020, https://apnews.com/article/us-coronavirus-deaths-top-3-million-e2bc856b6ec45563b84ee2e87ae8d5e7.

221 *Trump again floated*: Yasmeen Abutaleb, Laurie McGinley, and Josh Dawsey, "Oracle to Partner with Trump Administration to Collect Data on Unproven Drugs to Treat Covid-19," *Washington Post*, March 24, 2020, https://www.washingtonpost.com/politics/oracle-to-partner-with-trump-administration-to-collect-data-on-use-of-antimalarial-drugs-to-treat-covid-19/2020/03/24/ecbb8b76-6de2-11ea-b148-e4ce3fbd85b5_story.html.

222 *"Recent guidelines from South Korea"*: James M. Todaro and Gregory J. Rigano, "An Effective Treatment for Coronavirus (COVID-19)," March 13, 2020, https://docs.google.com/document/d/e/2PACX-1vTi-g18ftNZUMRAj2SwRPodtscFio7bJ7GdNgbJAGbdfF67WuRJB3ZsidgpidB2eocFHAVjIL-7deJ7/pub.

223 *"Now, a drug called chloroquine"*: "Remarks by President Trump, Vice President Pence, and Members of the Coronavirus Task Force in Press Briefing," The White House, March 19, 2020, https://trumpwhitehouse.archives.gov/briefings-statements/remarks-president-trump-vice-president-pence-members-coronavirus-task-force-press-briefing-6/.

225 *Bayer's pills, however, came*: Katherine Eban, "Exclusive: FDA May Have Dropped Standards Too Far in Hunt for Chloroquine to Fight Coronavirus—Sources," Reuters, April 16, 2020, https://www.reuters.com/article/us-health-coronavirus-bayer-chloroquine/exclusive-bayers-chloroquine-donation-to-u-s-raises-concern-about-fda-standards-in-pandemic-idUSKBN21Y2LO?fbclid=IwAR3W19V-EH08Whef2-qllB8KoXQw_cV8SWmAKFk$tRut4hCHK6eB-Pw-9Ec.

225 *"This can be a BIG"*: "U.S. Office of Special Counsel Complaint and Dis-

closure Form," https://context-cdn.washingtonpost.com/notes/prod/default
/documents/6bfde4d6-4c3d-4671-8eeb-6b3d39e47c03/note/26f73d7a-d060
-4c25-af4c-a58a167ee2c7., 39.

226 *"there are safety liabilities"*: Ibid., 40.

226 *"drop everything and make"*: Ibid., 41.

226 *"I am not sure"*: Ibid., 43.

227 *"Really want to flood"*: Katherine Eban, "Documents Reveal Team Trump's
Chloroquine Master Plan," *Vanity Fair*, April 23, 2020, https://www.vanity
fair.com/news/2020/04/internal-documents-reveal-team-trumps-chloro
quine-master-plan.

228 *Even the Department of Veterans Affairs*: Jordain Carney, "VA Gave Hydroxychloroquine for COVID-19 to 1,300 Veterans," *The Hill*, May 22, 2020,
https://thehill.com/policy/defense/499166-va-gave-hydroxychloroquine-for
-covid-19-to-1300-veterans.

228 *"NOPE"*: Eban, "Documents Reveal Team Trump's Chloroquine Master
Plan."

228 *STAT, a health and science–focused*: Matthew Herper and Erin Riglin,
"Data Show Panic and Disorganization Dominate the Study of Covid-19
Drugs," STAT, July 6, 2020, https://www.statnews.com/2020/07/06/data
-show-panic-and-disorganization-dominate-the-study-of-covid-19-drugs/.

229 *After winning a full scholarship*: Molly Ball, "Peter Navarro Used to Be a
Democrat. Now He's the Mastermind Behind Trump's Trade War," *Time*,
Aug. 23, 2018, https://time.com/5375727/peter-navarro/.

230 *"The resultant 'cross pollution'"*: Peter Navarro, *The Coming China Wars:
Where They Will Be Fought, How They Can Be Won* (Upper Saddle River,
NJ: FT Press, 2006), 98.

233 *Navarro went ballistic*: Damian Paletta, "Top Trump Trade Officials Still at
Odds After Profane Shouting Match in Beijing," *Washington Post*, May 16,
2018, https://www.washingtonpost.com/news/business/wp/2018/05/16/top
-trump-trade-officials-still-at-odds-after-profane-shouting-match-in-beijing/.

234 *"Canadians, we're polite"*: Damien Paletta and Anne Gearan, "Trump Removes U.S. from G-7 Joint Statement over Escalating Feud with Canada's
Trudeau," *Washington Post*, June 9, 2018, https://www.washingtonpost.com
/business/economy/trump-floats-end-to-all-tariffs-threatens-major-penal
ties-for-countries-that-dont-agree/2018/06/09/a06350be-6bf1-11e8-bea7
-c8eb28bc52b1_story.html.

234 *"There's a special place"*: Gregg Re, "There's a 'Special Place in Hell' for
Trudeau After His G7 'Stunt,' Top WH Trade Adviser Peter Navarro Says,"
Fox News, June 10, 2018, https://www.foxnews.com/politics/theres-a-spe
cial-place-in-hell-for-trudeau-after-his-g7-stunt-top-wh-trade-adviser-peter
-navarro-says.

235 *"That's science, not anecdote," Navarro shot back*: Jonathan Swan, "Scoop:
Inside the Epic White House Fight over Hydroxychloroquine," Axios,
April 5, 2020, https://www.axios.com/coronavirus-hydroxychloroquine
-white-house-01306286-0bbc-4042-9bfe-890413c6220d.html.

236 *"Doctors disagree about things"*: Chandelis Duster, "Peter Navarro on His Qualifications to Disagree with Dr. Anthony Fauci on Coronavirus Treatments: 'I'm a Social Scientist,'" CNN, April 6, 2020, https://www.cnn.com /2020/04/06/politics/peter-navarro-social-scientist-cnntv/index.html.

236 *Ingraham and her "medicine cabinet"*: Philip Rucker et al., "'What Do You Have to Lose?': Inside Trump's Embrace of a Risky Drug Against Coronavirus," *Washington Post*, April 6, 2020, https://www.washingtonpost.com /politics/what-do-you-have-to-lose-inside-trumps-embrace-of-a-risky-drug -against-coronavirus/2020/04/06/0a744d7e-781f-11ea-a130-df573469f094 _story.html.

236 *evidence began to emerge*: Michael M. Grynbaum, "Fox News Stars Trumpeted a Malaria Drug, Until They Didn't," *New York Times*, April 22, 2020, https://www.nytimes.com/2020/04/22/business/media/virus-fox-news-hy droxychloroquine.html.

237 *"I think the only reason"*: Katherine Eban, "'A Tsunami of Randoms': How Trump's COVID Chaos Drowned the FDA in Junk Science," *Vanity Fair*, Jan. 19, 2021, https://www.vanityfair.com/news/2021/01/how-trumps-covid -chaos-drowned-the-fda-in-junk-science.

238 *"The FDA determined"*: "Coronavirus (COVID-19) Update: FDA Revokes Emergency Use Authorization for Chloroquine and Hydroxychloroquine," FDA, June 15, 2020, https://www.fda.gov/news-events/press-announce ments/coronavirus-covid-19-update-fda-revokes-emergency-use-authoriza tion-chloroquine-and.

Chapter 12: Remdesivir

247 *the recovery time*: John H. Beigel et al., "Remdesivir for the Treatment of Covid-19—Final Report," *New England Journal of Medicine*, Oct. 8, 2020, https://www.nejm.org/doi/full/10.1056/NEJMoa2007764.

248 *In the event, the government*: Yasmeen Abutaleb et al., "Administration Initially Dispensed Scarce Covid-19 Drug to Some Hospitals That Didn't Need It," *Washington Post*, May 28, 2020, https://www.washingtonpost.com /health/2020/05/28/remdesivir-coronavirus-trump/.

Chapter 13: Jared's Shadow Task Force

251 *In March, as the government*: Ashley Parker et al., "Infighting, Missteps and a Son-in-Law Hungry for Results: Inside the Trump Administration's Troubled Coronavirus Response," *Washington Post*, March 14, 2020, https:// www.washingtonpost.com/politics/infighting-missteps-and-a-son-in-law -hungry-for-action-inside-the-trump-administrations-troubled-coronavirus -response/2020/03/14/530c28b4-6559-11ea-b3fc-7841686c5c57_story.html.

252 *Boehler had been Kushner's roommate*: Katherine Eban, "How Jared Kush-

ner's Secret Testing Plan 'Went Poof into Thin Air,'" *Vanity Fair*, July 30, 2020, https://www.vanityfair.com/news/2020/07/how-jared-kushners-secret-testing-plan-went-poof-into-thin-air.

254 *"Google is helping"*: "Remarks by President Trump, Vice President Pence, and Members of the Coronavirus Task Force in Press Briefing," The White House, March 13, 2020, https://trumpwhitehouse.archives.gov/briefings-statements/remarks-president-trump-vice-president-pence-members-coronavirus-task-force-press-conference-3/.

255 *The retailers who were supposed*: Parker et al., "Infighting, Missteps and a Son-in-Law Hungry for Results: Inside the Trump Administration's Troubled Coronavirus Response."

262 *"Some have insatiable appetites"*: Philip Rucker and Robert Costa, "Commander of Confusion: Trump Sows Uncertainty and Seeks to Cast Blame in Coronavirus Crisis," *Washington Post*, April 2, 2020, https://www.washingtonpost.com/politics/commander-of-confusion-trump-sows-uncertainty-and-seeks-to-cast-blame-in-coronavirus-crisis/2020/04/02/fc2db084-7431-11ea-85cb-8670579b863d_story.html.

262 *"The notion of the federal stockpile"*: Ben Gittleson, "After Kushner Says 'It's Our Stockpile,' HHS Website Changed to Echo His Comments on Federal Crisis Role," ABC News, April 3, 2020, https://abcnews.go.com/Politics/kushner-stockpile-hhs-website-changed-echo-comments-federal/story?id=69936411.

262 *"The Strategic National Stockpile's role"*: Aaron Blake, "The Trump Administration Just Changed Its Description of the National Stockpile to Jibe with Jared Kushner's Controversial Claim," *Washington Post*, April 3, 2020, https://www.washingtonpost.com/politics/2020/04/03/jared-kushner-stands-trump-proceeds-offer-very-trumpian-claim-about-stockpiles/.

264 *Project Airbridge*: Amy Brittain, Isaac Stanley-Becker, and Nick Miroff, "White House's Pandemic Relief Effort Project Airbridge Is Swathed in Secrecy and Exaggerations," *Washington Post*, May 8, 2020, https://www.washingtonpost.com/investigations/white-house-pandemic-supply-project-swathed-in-secrecy-and-exaggerations/2020/05/08/9c77efb2-8d52-11ea-a9c0-73b93422d691_story.html.

264 *Yet a subsequent investigation*: Chairwoman Carolyn B. Maloney, memorandum, "Information Provided by Medical Distribution Companies on Challenges with White House Supply Chain Task Force and Project Airbridge," House of Representatives, Committee on Oversight and Reform, July 2, 2020, https://oversight.house.gov/sites/democrats.oversight.house.gov/files/documents/Project%20Airbridge%20Memo%2007-02-20.pdf.

265 *The costs of that were evident*: Luis Ferre-Sadurni and Thomas Kaplan, "He Had Never Sold a Ventilator. N.Y. Gave Him an $86 Million Deal," *New York Times*, May 8, 2020, https://www.nytimes.com/2020/05/08/nyregion/ventilators-fema-coronavirus-cuomo.html.

265 *A Washington Post investigation*: Brittain et al., "White House's Pandemic Relief Effort Project Airbridge Is Swathed in Secrecy and Exaggerations."

267 *they had been put together*: Beckie Strum, "Gov. Cuomo Renews Call for Ventilators as Elon Musk Pledges to Provide Hundreds to New York," MarketWatch, March 27, 2020, https://www.marketwatch.com/story/gov -cuomo-renews-call-for-ventilators-as-elon-musk-pledges-to-provide-hun dreds-to-new-york-2020-03-27.

267 *"I don't believe"*: Charles Creitz and Samuel Chamberlain, "Trump Downplays Worst-Case Coronavirus Scenarios: 'I Don't Believe You Need 40,000 or 30,000 Ventilators," *Fox News*, March 26, 2020, https://www.foxnews .com/media/trump-worst-case-coronavirus-scenarios-ventilators.

269 *But the reality was*: Lenny Bernstein, "More Covid-19 Patients Are Surviving Ventilators in the ICU," *Washington Post*, July 3, 2020, https://www.wash ingtonpost.com/health/more-covid-19-patients-are-surviving-ventilators-in -the-icu/2020/07/03/2e3c3534-bbca-11ea-8cf5-9c1b8d7f84c6_story.html.

270 *"I know there is plenty"*: "Kansas Sen. Jerry Moran Concerned over Terminated Ventilator Contracts at Spirit AeroSystems," KSN.com, Sept. 3, 2020, https://www.ksn.com/news/health/coronavirus/coronavirus-in -kansas/kansas-sen-jerry-moran-concerned-over-terminated-ventilator-con tracts-at-spirit-aerosyst.

271 *"Sometimes you have to"*: Dana Kennedy, "Who Is Jack Ma? Where the Alibaba Co-founder Came From and Disappeared To," *New York Post*, Jan. 10, 2021, https://nypost.com/article/who-is-jack-ma-where-alibaba -founder-cam-from-disappeared-to/.

Chapter 14: The Downfall of the Health Agencies

278 *Trump was especially angry*: Eric Lipton et al., "He Could Have Seen What Was Coming: Behind Trump's Failure on the Virus," *New York Times*, April 11, 2020, https://www.nytimes.com/2020/04/11/us/politics/coronavirus -trump-response.html.

279 *he had once advised*: Manuel Roig-Franzia and Rosalind S. Helderman, "Trump Associate Roger Stone Reveals New Contact with Russian National During 2016 Campaign," *Washington Post*, June 17, 2018, https://www.wash ingtonpost.com/politics/trump-associate-roger-stone-reveals-new-contact -with-russian-national-during-2016-campaign/2018/06/17/4a8123c8-6fd0 -11e8-bd50-b80389a4e569_story.html.

279 *The following weekend*: Yasmeen Abutaleb and Josh Dawsey, "Trump Calls Reports He May Fire Alex Azar 'Fake News,'" *Washington Post*, April 26, 2020, https://www.washingtonpost.com/politics/2020/04/26/trump-alexazar -replacement/.

287 *"Transmission was likely facilitated"*: Lea Hamner et al., "High SARS -CoV-2 Attack Rate Following Exposure at a Choir Practice—Skagit County, Washington, March 2020," *Morbidity and Mortality Weekly Report 69*, no. 19 (May 15, 2020): 606–10, https://www.cdc.gov/mmwr/volumes/69/wr /mm6919e6.htm#contribAff.

289 *"Health Official Says"*: Mike Stobbe, "Health Official Says US Missed Some

Chances to Slow Virus," Associated Press, May 1, 2020, https://apnews.com /article/a758f05f337736e93dd0c280deff9b10.

294 *The FDA had encouraged*: Jillian Mock, "The Peculiar 100-Plus-Year History of Convalescent Plasma," *Smithsonian*, Sept. 1, 2020, https://www.smithso nianmag.com/science-nature/peculiar-100-plus-year-history-convalescent -plasma-180975683/.

298 *"The deep state"*: Matthew Herper and Nicholas Florko, "Drug Makers Rebut Trump Tweet That FDA 'Deep State' Is Delaying Covid-19 Vaccines and Drugs," STAT, Aug. 22, 2020, https://www.statnews.com/2020/08/22/drug -makers-rebut-trump-tweet-that-fda-deep-state-delaying-covid19-vaccines -drugs/.

299 *"We saw about"*: Laurie McGinley, Yasmeen Abutaleb, and Lenny Bernstein, "Some Trump Admiistration Claims on Effectiveness of Convalescent Plasma Are Wrong or Dubious, Scientists Say," *Washington Post*, Aug. 24, 2020, https://www.washingtonpost.com/health/2020/08/24/some-administration -claims-effectiveness-convalescent-plasma-are-wrong-or-dubious-scientists -say/.

Chapter 15: From Bad to Worse

305 *In Boston, 20 percent*: Bianca Vázquez Toness, "One in Five Boston Public School Children May Be Virtual Dropouts," *Boston Globe*, May 23, 2020, https://www.bostonglobe.com/2020/05/23/metro/more-than-one-five-bos ton-public-school-children-may-be-virtual-dropouts/.

307 *At one point, 80 percent*: Rachel Weiner, "More than 80 Percent of Hospitalized Covid-19 Patients in Georgia Were African American, Study Finds," *Washington Post*, April 29, 2020, https://www.washingtonpost.com /health/more-than-80-percent-of-hospitalized-covid-patients-in-georgia -were-african-american-study-finds/2020/04/29/a71496ea-8993-11ea-8ac1 -bfb250876b7a_story.html.

307 *early weeks of the pandemic*: Akilah Johnson and Talia Buford, "Early Data Shows African Americans Have Contracted and Died of Coronavirus at an Alarming Rate," ProPublica, April 3, 2020, https://www.propublica.org/article /early-data-shows-african-americans-have-contracted-and-died-of-corona virus-at-an-alarming-rate.

307 *make up just 33 percent of the local population*: Elliott Ramos and Maria Ines Zamudio, "In Chicago, 70% of COVID-19 Deaths are Black," WBEZ -Chicago, April 6, 2020, https://www.wbez.org/stories/in-chicago-70-of -covid-19-deaths-are-black/dd3f295f-445e-4e38-b37f-a1503782b507.

307 *make up just 31 percent of the local population*: Eboni G. Price-Haywood, M.D., M.P.H., Jeffrey Burton, Daniel Fort, and Leonardo Seoane, "Hospitalization and Mortality among Black Patients and White Patients with Covid-19," *New England Journal of Medicine*, June 25, 2020, https://www .nejm.org/doi/full/10.1056/NEJMsa2011686.

308 *"Avoid alcohol, tobacco"*: Zeeshen Aleem, "The Problem with the Surgeon General's Controversial Coronavirus Advice to Americans of Color," Vox, April 11, 2020, https://www.vox.com/2020/4/11/21217428/surgeon-general -jerome-adams-big-mama-coronavirus.

308 *Adams has a brother*: Manuel Roig-Franzia, "Surgeon General Jerome Adams May Be the Nicest Guy in the Trump Administration. But Is That What America Needs Right Now?," *Washington Post*, July 12, 2020, https:// www.washingtonpost.com/lifestyle/style/surgeon-general-jerome-adams -may-be-the-nicest-guy-in-the-trump-administration-but-is-that-what-amer ica-needs-right-now/2020/07/11/39529cec-a1c1-11ea-9590-1858a893bd59 _story.html.

308 *"Jerome, you did it beautifully"*: Joe Concha, "Fauci Defends Jerome Adams's Remarks on African American Alcohol, Tobacco Usage amid Pandemic," *The Hill*, April 10, 2020, https://thehill.com/homenews/media/492266-fauci-de fends-jerome-adamss-remarks-on-African-American-alcohol-tobacco-usage -amid-pandemic.

309 *The White House mostly*: Dan Diamond, "Surgeon General Gets Pushed to Sidelines, Sparking Questions," *Politico*, April 20, 2020, https://www.politico .com/news/2020/04/20/surgeon-general-coronavirus-197508.

309 *It was rarely meeting*: Robert Costa et al., "Trump's May Days: A Month of Distractions and Grievances as Nation Marks Bleak Coronavirus Mile-stone," *Washington Post*, May 31, 2020, https://www.washingtonpost.com /politics/trumps-may-days-a-month-of-distractions-and-grievances-as-na tion-marks-bleak-coronavirus-milestone/2020/05/31/123e7e6a-a120-11ea -81bb-c2f70f01034b_story.html.

310 *A clerk at Cup Foods*: "Read the 911 Transcript for George Floyd Call in Minneapolis," *Star Tribune*, May 28, 2020, https://www.startribune.com /read-the-911-transcript-for-george-floyd-call-in-minneapolis/570852181/.

314 *The next day he hatched*: Peter Baker et al., "How Trump's Idea for a Photo Op Led to Havoc in a Park," *New York Times*, June 2, 2020, https://www .nytimes.com/2020/06/02/us/politics/trump-walk-lafayette-square.html.

314 *"These are not acts"*: Donald J. Trump, "Remarks on the Nationwide Demonstrations and Civil Unrest Following the Death of George Floyd in Minneapolis, Minnesota," GovInfo, June 1, 2020, https://www.govinfo.gov /content/pkg/DCPD-202000421/pdf/DCPD-202000421.pdf.

314 *As the words were leaving*: Ashley Parker, Josh Dawsey, and Rebecca Tan, "Inside the Push to Tear-Gas Protesters Ahead of a Trump Photo Op," *Washington Post*, June 1, 2020, https://www.washingtonpost.com/politics/inside -the-push-to-tear-gas-protesters-ahead-of-a-trump-photo-op/2020/06/01 /4b0f7b50-a46c-11ea-bb20-ebf0921f3bbd_story.html.

315 *"It's coming back strong"*: Karl Gelles, Veronica Bravo, and George Petras, "How Police Pushed Aside Protestors Ahead of Trump's Controversial Church Photo," *USA Today*, June 5, 2020, https://www.usatoday.com/in -depth/graphics/2020/06/05/george-floyd-protests-trump-church-photo -curfew-park/3127684001/.

315 *The tear gas drifted*: Egan Millard, "Outraged Episcopal Leaders Condemn Tear-Gassing Clergy, Protesters for Trump Photo Op at Washington Church," Episcopal News Service, June 2, 2020, https://www.episcopalnewsservice .org/2020/06/02/episcopal-leaders-express-outrage-condemn-tear-gassing -protesters-for-trump-photo-op-at-washington-church/.

315 *"The slide of the United States"*: John R. Allen, "A Moment of National Shame and Peril—and Hope," *Foreign Policy*, June 3, 2020, https://foreign policy.com/2020/06/03/trump-military-george-floyd-protests/.

Chapter 16: The Second Wave

320 *A new poll*: Tamara Lush, "Poll: Americans Are the Unhappiest They've Been in 50 Years," Associated Press, June 16, 2020, https://apnews.com/article /0f6b9be04fa0d3194401821a72665a50.

320 *"That's probably the downside"*: "Donald Trump June 15 Roundtable Transcript 'Fighting for America's Seniors,' " Rev, June 15, 2020, https://www.rev .com/blog/transcripts/donald-trump-june-15-roundtable-transcript-fighting -for-americas-seniors.

322 *"There Isn't a Coronavirus 'Second Wave'"*: Mike Pence, "There Isn't a Coronavirus 'Second Wave,' " *Wall Street Journal*, June 16, 2020, https:// www.wsj.com/articles/there-isnt-a-coronavirus-second-wave-11592327890.

322 *In fact, Project Airbridge*: Rebecca Ballhaus, "Pence Overstates Coronavirus Supplies Delivered by Administration's 'Airbridge' Program," *Wall Street Journal*, June 19, 2020, https://www.wsj.com/articles/pence-over states-coronavirus-supplies-delivered-by-administrations-airbridge-program -11592584447.

323 *"Since I don't have"*: Benjamin Swasey, "Pence: 'I Should Have Worn a Mask' When Visiting the Mayo Clinic," NPR, May 3, 2020, https://www.npr.org /sections/coronavirus-live-updates/2020/05/03/849856919/pence-i-should -have-worn-a-mask-when-visiting-the-mayo-clinic.

325 *Then, on Friday, May 7*: Colby Itkowitz, "A Top Aide to Vice President Pence Tests Positive for Coronavirus," *Washington Post*, May 8, 2020, https://www .washingtonpost.com/politics/a-top-aide-to-vice-president-pence-tests-pos itive-for-coronavirus/2020/05/08/7d80520c-914e-11ea-a0bc-4e9ad4866d21 _story.html.

326 *"No. I'm in"*: Erin Banco and Olivia Messer, "Fauci: No Need for a Second Lockdown for COVID-19," Daily Beast, June 17, 2020, https://www.thedaily beast.com/dr-fauci-no-need-for-a-second-covid-lockdown?ref=scroll.

326 *Around 6,200 people ultimately attended*: Felicia Sonmez, Josh Dawsey, and Taylor Telford, "Trump Campaign, Democrats Joust Over Tulsa Rally Turnout," *Washington Post*, June 21, 2020, https://www.washingtonpost .com/politics/trump-campaign-democrats-joust-over-tulsa-rally-turnout /2020/06/21/06ecb95e-b3c8-11ea-a510-55bf26485c93_story.html.

327 *"When you do testing"*: Derek Hawkins et al., "Trump Tells Oklahoma Rally He Directed Officials to Slow Virus Testing to Find Fewer Cases," *Washing-*

ton Post, June 20, 2020, https://www.washingtonpost.com/nation/2020/06/20/coronavirus-live-updates-us/.

327 *"It's a disease, without question"*: J. Edward Moreno, "Trump Refers to Coronavirus as 'Kung Flu' During Tulsa Rally," *The Hill*, June 20, 2020, https://thehill.com/homenews/campaign/503756-trump-refers-to-coronavirus-as-kung-flu-during-tulsa-rally.

330 *Eighty people who had visited*: Carol Thompson, "Saturday Update: 85 Coronavirus Cases Linked to Harper's in East Lansing," *Lansing State Journal*, June 27, 2020, https://www.lansingstatejournal.com/story/news/2020/06/27/85-coronavirus-cases-now-linked-harpers-east-lansing/3270972001/.

330 *United Airlines announced*: David Roeder, "United Might Trim Nearly Half of U.S. Employees," *Chicago Sun-Times*, July 8, 2020, https://chicago.sunstimes.com/business/2020/7/8/21317402/united-airlines-layoffs-furloughs-half-us-workforce-coronavirus-travel.

Chapter 17: Opening Day

340 *"We haven't done"*: Jesse Dougherty, "Sean Doolittle Sees Sports as a Reward America Hasn't Earned Yet," *Washington Post*, July 5, 2020, https://www.washingtonpost.com/sports/2020/07/05/sean-doolittle-nationals-testing/.

341 *In early July*: Yasmeen Abutaleb, Josh Dawsey, and Laurie McGinley, "Fauci Is Sidelined by the White House as He Steps Up Blunt Talk on Pandemic," *Washington Post*, July 11, 2020, https://www.washingtonpost.com/politics/2020/07/11/fauci-trump-coronavirus/.

343 *"But the following day"*: Peter Navarro, "Anthony Fauci Has Been Wrong About Everything I Have Interacted with Him On," *USA Today*, July 14, 2020, https://www.usatoday.com/story/opinion/todaysdebate/2020/07/14/anthony-fauci-wrong-with-me-peter-navarro-editorials-debates/5439374002/.

Chapter 18: Atlas, Shrug

350 *"They are dying, that's true"*: Rebecca Shabad, "'It Is What It Is': Trump in Interview on COVID-19 Death Toll in the U.S.," NBC News, Aug. 4, 2020, https://www.nbcnews.com/politics/donald-trump/it-what-it-trump-interview-covid-19-death-toll-u-n1235734.

352 *"extraordinarily widespread"*: Veronica Stracqualursi and Alison Main, "Birx Defends Herself as Pelosi Accuses Trump Administration of Spreading Disinformation on Covid-19," CNN, Aug. 2, 2020, https://www.cnn.com/2020/08/02/politics/birx-pelosi-confidence-disinformation-coronavirus-cnntv/index.html.

354 *He proudly considered himself*: Yasmeen Abutaleb and Josh Dawsey, "New Trump Pandemic Adviser Pushes Controversial 'Herd Immunity' Strategy, Worrying Public Health Officials," *Washington Post*, Aug. 31, 2020, https://

www.washingtonpost.com/politics/trump-coronavirus-scott-atlas-herd-im munity/2020/08/30/925e68fe-e93b-11ea-970a-64c73a1c2392_story.html.

354 *"contaminated public policy and science"*: Freddie Sayers, "Scott Atlas: I'm Disgusted and Dismayed," video interview with UnHerd, YouTube, Oct. 20, 2020, https://www.youtube.com /watch?v=vpn3JxXqnp4.

362 *That year, he supported*: Jennifer Haberkorn, "Some Advisers Dislike Mitt Health Law," *Politico*, April 9, 2012, https://www.politico.com/story/2012 /04/some-romney-advisers-dont-like-his-health-law-074956.

364 *"My background is"*: "Scott Atlas: I'm Disgusted and Dismayed."

365 *On September 11, YouTube removed*: Lateshia Beachum and Kim Bellware, "YouTube Removed Trump Adviser's Video for Misinformation. He Com- pared It to 'Third World' Censorship," *Washington Post*, Sept. 17, 2020, https://www.washingtonpost.com/nation/2020/09/17/scott-atlas-youtube/.

Chapter 19: A Shot in the Dark

371 *"We're going to have"*: Jordyn Phelps, "Trump Makes Rosy Vaccine Timing Front and Center in Campaign, Predicting It's Possible Before Election Day," ABC News, Sept. 3, 2020, https://abcnews.go.com/Politics/trump-makes -rosy-vaccine-timing-front-center-campaign/story?id=72877119.

383 *"Maintaining the American public's trust"*: Patricia Cavazzoni et al., "Senior FDA Career Executives: We're Following the Science to Protect Public Health in Pandemic," *USA Today*, Sept. 10, 2020, https://www.usatoday.com/story /opinion/2020/09/10/sound-science-to-meet-covid-challenges-fda-career-of ficials-column/5756948002/.

383 *"The circumstances of your statements"*: Eric Topol, "Dear Commissioner Hahn: Tell the Truth or Resign," Medscape, Aug. 31, 2020, https://www .medscape.com/viewarticle/936611.

386 *By September, the number*: Alec Tyson, Courtney Johnson, and Cary Funk, "U.S. Public Now Divided over Whether to Get COVID-19 Vaccine," Pew Research Center, Sept. 17, 2020, https://www.pewresearch.org/science/2020 /09/17/u-s-public-now-divided-over-whether-to-get-covid-19-vaccine/.

388 *"If the public health professionals"*: "Quotes from Policy-Heavy Debate Between Kamala Harris, Mike Pence," Reuters, Oct. 7, 2020, https://www .reuters.com/article/usa-election-debate-quotes-factbox/quotes-from-pol icy-heavy-debate-between-kamala-harris-mike-pence-idUSKBN26T052.

Chapter 20: Long Live the King

392 *"I don't wear face masks"*: Ashley Collman, "2 Days Before His Coronavirus Diagnosis, Trump Mocked Biden for Wearing a Face Mask," Business Insider, Oct. 2, 2020, https://www.businessinsider.com/trump-coronavirus-mocked -biden-face-mask-presidential-debate-2020-10.

393 *"If you're going to cough"*: Devan Cole, "Trump Chastises Mulvaney for

Coughing During TV Interview," CNN, June 17, 2019, https://www.cnn
.com/2019/06/17/politics/mick-mulvaney-donald-trump-coughing-oval-of
fice/index.html.

397 *The doctors gave Trump*: Kevin Breuninger, "White House Reveals Trump's
Coronavirus Treatment, Says He Is 'Fatigued but in Good Spirits,'" CNBC,
Oct. 2, 2020, https://www.cnbc.com/2020/10/02/white-house-reveals
-trumps-coronavirus-treatment-says-he-is-fatigued-but-in-good-spirits.html.

399 *Trump didn't want to go*: Philip Rucker et al., "Invincibility Punctured by Infection: How the Coronavirus Spread in Trump's White House," *Washington
Post*, Oct. 2, 2020, https://www.washingtonpost.com/politics/trump-virus
-spread-white-house/2020/10/02/38c5b354-04cc-11eb-b7ed-141dd88560ea
_story.html.

400 *The drug was believed*: Meryl Kornfield, "Trump Was Treated with Dexamethasone. Here's What We Know About Its Risks and Side Effects," *Washington Post*, Oct. 6, 2020, https://www.washingtonpost.com/health/2020/10
/06/trump-dexamethasone/.

401 *"Trump supporters set up camp"*: Darcy Spencer and NBC Washington
Staff, "Trump Supporters Outside Walter Reed Call for Prayers, Well Wishes
as President Is Treated," NBC4 Washington, Oct. 4, 2020, https://www
.nbcwashington.com/news/local/walter-reed-hospital-president-trump-sup
porters-protests/2434798/.

401 *On April 3, 1919*: Steve Coll, "Woodrow Wilson's Case of the Flu, and How
Pandemics Change History," *New Yorker*, April 17, 2020, https://www
.newyorker.com/news/daily-comment/woodrow-wilsons-case-of-the-flu
-and-how-pandemics-change-history.

402 *Conley held a press conference*: Seung Min Kim, Josh Dawsey, and Colby
Itkowitz, "White House Gives Confusing and Incomplete Answers About
Trump's Health as President Says He Is 'Feeling Well,'" *Washington Post*,
Oct. 3, 2020, https://www.washingtonpost.com/politics/trump-walter-reed
-doctors/2020/10/03/332a7914-05a5-11eb-897d-3a6201d6643f_story.html.

402 *He would later say*: Betsy Klein, Sam Fossum, and Tami Luhby, "White House
Physician Sows Confusion with Briefings," CNN, Oct. 4, 2020, https://www
.cnn.com/2020/10/04/politics/white-house-physician-sean-conley-trump/in
dex.html.

402 *"The president's vitals"*: Seung Min Kim, Josh Dawsey, and Colby Itkowitz,
"White House Gives Confusing and Incomplete Answers About Trump's
Health as President Says He Is 'Feeling Well,'" Washington Post, Oct. 3,
2020, https://www.washingtonpost.com/politics/trump-walter-reed-doctors
/2020/10/03/332a7914-05a5-11eb-897d-3a6201d6643f_story.html

404 *"We're going to beat"*: Peter Wade, "Trump Rambles Endlessly During New
Video from Walter Reed," *Rolling Stone*, Oct. 4, 2020, https://www.roll
ingstone.com/politics/politics-news/trump-rambles-during-new-video-from
-walter-reed-1070702/.

Chapter 21: Judgment Day

415 *"We are not going to control"*: Devan Cole, "White House Chief of Staff: 'We Are Not Going to Control the Pandemic,'" CNN, Oct. 25, 2020, https://www.cnn.com/2020/10/25/politics/mark-meadows-controlling-coronavirus-pandemic-cnntv/index.html.

416 *The Trump campaign even produced*: Sheryl Gay Stolberg, "Battered by Trump, the C.D.C.'s Director Faces Pressure to Speak Out," *New York Times*, Oct. 10, 2020, https://www.nytimes.com/2020/10/10/us/politics/trump-cdc-coronavirus.html.

416 *"As countries around the world"*: Andrea M. Lerner, Gregory K. Folkers, and Anthony S. Fauci, "Preventing the Spread of SARS-CoV-2 with Masks and Other 'Low-Tech' Interventions," *Journal of the American Medical Association*, Oct. 26, 2020, https://jamanetwork.com/journals/jama/fullarticle/2772459?guestAccessKey=256417c3-dbfd-4a6e-b10b-25068ca46a31&utm_source=twitter&utm_medium=social_jama&utm_term=&utm_campaign=article_alert&linkId=102908151.

417 *"kiss everyone in that audience"*: Annie Karni and Maggie Haberman, "Votes and Vitality in Mind, Trump Addresses Rally in Florida," *New York Times*, Oct. 12, 2020, https://www.nytimes.com/2020/10/12/us/politics/trump-rally-florida.html.

417 *"in for a whole lot of hurt"*: Josh Dawsey and Yasmeen Abutaleb, "'A Whole Lot of Hurt': Fauci Warns of Covid-19 Surge, Offers Blunt Assessment of Trump's Response," *Washington Post*, Oct. 31, 2020, https://www.washingtonpost.com/politics/fauci-covid-winter-forecast/2020/10/31/e3970eb0-1b8b-11eb-bb35-2dcfdab0a345_story.html.

417 *"It's unacceptable and breaking"*: Ibid.

418 *"Don't tell anybody"*: Rebecca Shabad, "Trump Suggests He Might Fire Fauci After the Election," NBC News, Nov. 2, 2020, https://www.nbcnews.com/politics/2020-election/trump-suggests-he-might-fire-fauci-after-election-n1245735.

418 *"We are entering"*: Lena H. Sun and Josh Dawsey, "Top Trump Adviser Bluntly Contradicts President on Covid-19 Threat, Urging All-Out Response," *Washington Post*, Nov. 2, 2020, https://www.washingtonpost.com/health/2020/11/02/deborah-birx-covid-trump/.

419 *"Under the Biden lockdown"*: "Donald Trump Rally Speech Transcript, Rochester, MN October 30," Rev, Oct. 30, 2020, https://www.rev.com/blog/transcripts/donald-trump-rally-speech-transcript-rochester-mn-october-30.

420 *Pennsylvania reported its highest*: "Pa. Reports Highest Daily Increase in COVID-19 Cases," *Pittsburgh Post-Gazette*, Nov. 3, 2020, https://www.post-gazette.com/news/health/2020/11/03/COVID-19-Allegheny-County-pittsburgh-pennsylvania-data-deaths-cases-2/stories/202011030102.

421 *Biden established his own*: Yasmeen Abutaleb and Laurie McGinley, "President-elect Biden Announces Coronavirus Task Force Made Up of Physicians and

Health Experts," *Washington Post*, Nov. 9, 2020, https://www.washington-post.com/health/2020/11/09/biden-coronavirus-task-force/.

422 *Trump also railed*: Laurie McGinley et al., "Trump Rails Against 'Medical Deep State' After Pfizer Vaccine News Comes after Election Day," *Washington Post*, Nov. 11, 2020, https://www.washingtonpost.com/politics/2020/11/11/trump-angry-about-pfizer-vaccine/.

INDEX

ABOUT THE AUTHORS

YASMEEN ABUTALEB covers health policy for the *Washington Post*. She chronicled the Trump administration's coronavirus response and White House task force in 2020. She previously reported for Reuters.

DAMIAN PALETTA is the economics editor at the *Washington Post* and previously covered the White House for the *Post* and the *Wall Street Journal*.